LOST
CITIES,
ANCIENT
TOMBS

previous page: This lidded tripod vessel dating from A.D. 425—typical of ceramics made in Teotihuacan—was found in the tomb of K'inich Yax K'uk' Mo', a Maya king of Copán.

The steep-sided pyramids that mark royal Nubian tombs at Meroë, Sudan, are enduring testaments to one of Africa's great ancient civilizations.

LOST CITIES, ANCIENT TOMBS

100 Discoveries That Changed the World

ANN R. WILLIAMS, *General Editor*

Introduction by DOUGLAS PRESTON

Afterword by FREDRIK HIEBERT

NATIONAL GEOGRAPHIC

Washington, D.C.

Published by National Geographic Partners, LLC
1145 17th Street NW, Washington, DC 20036

Library of Congress Cataloging-in-Publication Data

Names: Williams, A. R. (Ann R.), editor. | Preston, Douglas J., writer of
    introduction.
Title: Lost cities, ancient tombs : 100 discoveries that changed the world
    / general editor, Ann R. Williams ; introduction by Douglas Preston.
Other titles: One hundred discoveries that changed the world
Description: Washington, D.C. : National Geographic, [2021] | Includes index. | Summary: "The story of human civilization, as told through 100 key discoveries spanning six continents, including firsthand reports from explorers, scientists, and antiquarians"--Provided by publisher.
Identifiers: LCCN 2021014585 (print) | LCCN 2021014586 (ebook) | ISBN
    9781426221989 (hardcover) | ISBN 9781426221996 (ebook)
Subjects: LCSH: Archaeology. | Civilization, Ancient. | Extinct cities. | Tombs.
Classification: LCC CC165 .L628 2021 (print) | LCC CC165 (ebook) | DDC
    930.1--dc23
LC record available at https://lccn.loc.gov/2021014585
LC ebook record available at https://lccn.loc.gov/2021014586

Since 1888, the National Geographic Society has funded more than 14,000 research, conservation, education, and storytelling projects around the world. National Geographic Partners distributes a portion of the funds it receives from your purchase to National Geographic Society to support programs including the conservation of animals and their habitats.

Get closer to National Geographic Explorers and photographers, and connect with our global community. Join us today at national geographic.com/join

For rights or permissions inquiries, please contact National
Geographic Books Subsidiary Rights: bookrights@natgeo.com

Interior design: Nicole Miller

Printed in Italy

21/EV/1

CONTENTS

———◆———

INTRODUCTION

The Moment of Discovery

By Douglas Preston

———◆———

Most great archaeological discoveries involve a transcendent moment of revelation. That moment came for Howard Carter when he first peered into the dimness of King Tut's tomb and exclaimed, "Everywhere the glint of gold." It arrived when Donald Johanson and Tom Gray spied a small fragment of arm bone sticking out of a slope, revealing the remains of the celebrated Lucy. And for Robert Ballard, it came on September 1, 1985, at 1:05 in the morning, when video cameras on a remotely operated vehicle (ROV) illuminated the gigantic boilers of a large wreck on the seafloor, and he knew he had found the *Titanic*.

But these thrilling moments give a misleading impression of how key discoveries are made. The vast majority take years to develop and are often the culmination of tedious research, false starts, failures, political opposition, professional doubt and even disparagement, permitting vexations, bureaucratic nightmares, and dreary fundraising. The discovery of a pre-Columbian city in Honduras, which I participated in (see page 392), followed that pattern, taking 20 long and frustrating years. In 1996, I happened to be visiting NASA's Jet Propulsion Laboratory in Pasadena, researching a story for *National Geographic* magazine on the mapping of Angkor temples from space. One of the scientists, Ron Blom,

Former soldier Andrew Wood hacks through foliage in Honduras to clear the way for scientists to investigate an archaeological site identified by lidar.

mentioned in passing a confidential project he was working on for an amateur archaeologist and filmmaker named Steve Elkins. Blom was searching satellite imagery for a legendary lost city in Honduras called Ciudad Blanca, the White City, or the Lost City of the Monkey God, and his analysis had identified possible "unnatural rectilinear and curvilinear" features in an unnamed valley surrounded by steep, densely forested mountains, with only one point of access. It was one of the last scientifically unexplored places in Central America, truly a lost world.

I began following Elkins's struggles to investigate the mysterious valley. His efforts were stymied again and again by various fiascoes, including lack of money, unreliable partners, failed attempts, Honduran military coups, political turmoil, and a deadly hurricane. Fifteen years went by, and it seemed the project was about as dead as it could get. And then, quite suddenly, it came together. By adopting a technology called lidar—light detection and ranging—Elkins realized he could map the 20 square miles of the valley from the air in less than a week. There was no need to go in on the ground, a daunting and dangerous prospect. Elkins and his team raised close to a million dollars and engaged the expertise of the National Center for Airborne Laser Mapping (NCALM) at the University of Houston. In 2012, I accompanied the team and a plane carrying a lidar machine to Honduras. To be frank, I was deeply skeptical. It seemed crazy that a lost city could still be found somewhere on the surface of the earth in the 21st century.

For three days in May, the lidar plane flew in a lawn-mower pattern over the target area, firing billions of harmless laser pulses into the canopy, a tiny fraction of which reached the ground and bounced back, thus allowing the terrain underneath to be scanned. The data was collected and uploaded to Houston, processed, and downloaded back to our base of operations. We saw the first scans on Sunday, May 5.

That was, to be sure, an astonishing moment of discovery. When the images popped up on the lidar engineer's laptop, you didn't have to be an archaeologist to see the plazas, terracing, and the monumental structures of a major, prehistoric site. Along with everyone else, I was stunned.

And yet, curiously enough, that wasn't for me, personally, *the* moment of discovery. There was a city there, to be sure, but it was still abstract, a collection of geometric patterns on a black-and-white lidar plot. The real moment didn't come until 2015, when, in a joint Honduran-American expedition, we were able to explore the ruins on the ground. After three years of anticipation, the actual experience of entering the lost city was a disappointment. The jungle was so thick that, even standing in the central plaza facing the main earthen pyramid, we could see nothing but tree trunks, leaves, and vines. The second day exploring the city was particularly miserable. Incessant rain sounded a dull roar in the treetops and streamed down everywhere. Thoroughly drenched, I had shed my useless raincoat, and we were filthy from wallowing through waist-deep muck holes and scrambling up muddy slopes. I could feel countless tiny chiggers burrowing into my flesh around my waist and ankles.

After many hours macheting our way through several plazas and earthworks of the ancient city, still unable to see much, we decided to call it a day and return to camp. As we were walking back along the base of the pyramid, a team member shouted, "Hey, there are some weird stones over here." We all converged to where he was pointing, an area we had walked past many times.

The first thing I saw was the stone head of a jaguar rising from the ground, its teeth bared. As my eyes adjusted to the dimness of the jungle floor, all kinds of unusual shapes became visible, poking above the earth—large stone jars decorated with vultures, snakes, and monkeys; stone seats carved with geometric designs; and other mysterious things. In a tiny area of perhaps 200 square feet, the tops of more than 50 stone sculptures emerged from the earth.

We forgot everything our archaeologists had told us. We crowded into the area, bumping into one another, exclaiming loudly, tramping about, kneeling, and pulling back vines and leaves to see more—until the expedition's chief archaeologist, Chris Fisher, interrupted with a yell. "Whoa, whoa, *whoa!*" he cried furiously, holding up his hands. "Everybody *stop,* back *off,* don't touch *anything!*" He quickly roped off the area with crime-scene tape and gave us all a stern lecture.

We had stumbled upon a cache of sculptures. Excavations would reveal more than 500 of them, apparently left when the city was abandoned 500 years ago. The people of this city had deposited their sacred objects here, ritually broke them to release their spirits, and walked away, never to return. These sculptures had rested undisturbed in the gloom of the rainforest for half a millennium, until our arrival.

Up to then, the vanished civilization that had built this city had been vague and theoretical. But now, in gazing at this snarling jaguar so furiously thrusting upward as if struggling to free itself from the earth, this long-vanished culture became real. I was overwhelmed by a sense of its richness and power. The people who created this sculpture had been confident, sophisticated, and bold. They knew who they were. They had strong beliefs and rituals, and they had thrived in one of the most challenging environments on Earth.

In the book you hold in your hands, there are many such moments. They represent more than the thrill of discovery; they are about that ineffable feeling of touching our human past in a profound way. In the end, a discovery isn't about things and artifacts, no matter how beautiful or rare. It's about the human beings who made them and understanding how they once lived, thought, and felt.

The discovery of the lost city was remarkable in a different way. It was the first time the advanced technology of lidar had been used in archaeology as a tool of pure discovery, in a speculative search for an unknown site—as opposed to mapping a known site. In this way it exemplified a watershed moment in archaeology, in which innovative fields of science and technology are revolutionizing the way we make discoveries about our human past.

It's commonly said that there's not much more to find on the surface of the earth, that the great discoveries have already been made, the tombs found, the temples explored, the rivers mapped, the deserts crossed, and the fossil treasures uncovered. Nothing could be farther from the truth. The 20th century was possibly the greatest one hundred years of archaeological revelation, as attested to in these pages. The discoveries of the 21st century will be different, but no less remarkable, from those of the 20th.

In the past 20 years, the cutting edge of archaeological research has started to shift to other fields, including remote sensing, artificial intelligence, nuclear chemistry, paleopathology, and medicine. The change has not been without controversy and pushback, as traditional archaeologists and anthropologists see engineers, mathematicians, chemists, and geneticists intruding into their domain.

Archaeologists are facing a choice of either incorporating the new technologies and disciplines into their work or finding themselves left behind. This is happening at a time when traditional dirt archaeology—digging up sites—has fallen out of favor, because no matter how carefully a site is excavated, it is irrevocably disturbed. Far better to map an ancient city from the air using lidar, or explore a shipwreck with an underwater ROV, or peer into a tomb with ground-penetrating radar.

The rich tombs of the Scythians (see page 212) provide a telling example of how brand-new science can be applied to age-old problems. The Scythians are famous for their burial mounds, called kurgans, that dot the steppes from the Ukraine across Russia and into Mongolia. The Scythians were fearsome nomads, expert riders and archers, and masters of mounted warfare who terrorized their neighbors, particularly the ancient Greeks.

The kurgan burials of the Scythians have been the subject of archaeological fascination and intensive looting since at least the 18th century. Some of the richest tombs outside of Egypt have been found in the steppes, packed with gold, weapons, horse equipment, pottery, and sometimes entire chariots along with horses. One Scythian kurgan contained a single necklace fashioned out of four pounds of gold.

Most of the obvious kurgans have been found and either excavated (or, more commonly, looted). As many as an estimated 90 percent of kurgans have been robbed.

With the arrival of satellite imagery via Google Earth, it became possible to spot possibly undisturbed kurgans from space in remote areas, as well as identifying others that might not be visible to observers on the ground. Gino Caspari, a research archaeologist with the Swiss National Science Foundation, began using Google Earth to identify and locate kurgans. But he found that examining thousands of Google images of the barren steppes was a process of mind-numbing tedium. "It's essentially a stupid task," Caspari said.

Computers are ideal at performing tasks that are both stupid and tedious. Caspari teamed up with an expert in artificial intelligence, Pablo Crespo. The two collaborated to create a powerful new archaeological tool, using what is known as a convolutional neural network (CNN). A CNN is a kind of artificial intelligence program patterned after the way neurons in the brain process visual imagery; it is capable of "learning" and can be trained to recognize images, even the most subtle.

Today, Crespo and Caspari are teaching their CNN program to recognize burial mounds on Google Earth. The program is now 98 percent proficient in distinguishing kurgans from other sorts of mounds and circular features on the landscape. Caspari is in the process of identifying kurgans across thousands of square miles, some of which may prove to be untouched, ushering in a new era of discovery.

Convolutional neural network computer programs are also being applied to other archaeological fields, including identifying shipwrecks on the seafloor, sorting and cataloging thousands of potsherds, and searching the internet for images related to illegal

Some 5,000 years ago in the northern Caucasus, a Maikop chieftain was buried in a kurgan with four bull figures—two gold (including this one) and two silver.

trade in such things as ivory and human bones. Some have speculated a CNN survey might be useful in searching for quasi-legendary sites, such as Genghis Khan's long-lost tomb.

And another innovative science is also throwing light on the Scythians. Despite centuries of archaeological attention, one of the most enduring mysteries is where they originated. One school holds they were a people who migrated from Central Asia to the steppes, while another group claims they were descended from a local tribe who lived on the shores of the Black Sea.

The new science of ancient DNA sequencing, scarcely 10 years old, recently resolved this century-old debate. Geneticists extracted DNA from Scythian bones and confirmed the local-origin hypothesis. They also showed the Scythians were descended from a much older but strikingly similar culture, the Yamnaya, also called the Yamna.

The Yamnaya tribe occupied the steppes north of the Caspian and Black Seas around 5,000 years ago. By adopting the wheel and horse—two recent innovations—they were able to abandon settled village life and embark on an extraordinary expansion across Europe and western Asia, reaching as far as Spain, the British Isles, the Middle East, and India. They carried with them a proto-Indo-European language that is the ancestor of most of the languages of Europe. Although few have heard of the Yamnaya, DNA sequencing has revealed that almost all people of western European ancestry carry a large percentage of Yamnaya genes.

The Yamnaya and their descendant cultures swept into Europe around 4,500 years ago. Their arrival triggered profound changes in technology, pottery, weapons, metallurgy, and burial customs.

Because there isn't clear archaeological evidence of a surge of violence during this time, many archaeologists thought these changes were the result of a relatively peaceful cultural diffusion.

Ancient DNA genomics upended that idea. By sequencing European DNA from that time period, geneticists saw what one called a "genetic scar that speaks volumes." In parts of Europe, the local male Y chromosome types vanished, replaced by the Y chromosome type of the invading Yamnaya. The Y chromosome is only carried by males and passed from father to son, which means that the newcomers somehow prevented the local males from fathering children. Although genetics cannot say for sure what happened, the most likely scenario is that the invaders engaged in the mass killing of men, boys, and possibly even infants, and took the local women for themselves—a process that, if more recent history is any guide, likely also involved sexual coercion and mass rape.

What makes the Scythians so interesting is that, among the thousands of descendant cultures of the Yamnaya, they retained the nomadic, horse-riding, warrior culture of their distant forebears. And, like the Yamnaya, the Scythians buried their dead in kurgans, with arrays of grave goods.

There is one striking difference, however: in their treatment of women. The kurgan burials of the Yamnaya suggest they were a male-dominated, hierarchical society in which a small number of elite men accumulated most of the power and wealth, while women were subservient. The Scythians, on the other hand, appear to have accepted women into the warrior elite and gave them rich burials similar to the men, often with weapons and gold.

Solving the Scythian origin debate is just one way the study of ancient DNA is coming sideways into archaeology to change or even overturn established ideas. For example, the discoveries in Shanidar cave (see page 54) fascinated archaeologists because they provided more evidence that Neanderthals were not brutish and crude, as previous supposed. Ten years ago, the sequencing of the Neanderthal genome took that farther, by proving that most of us *are* a little Neanderthal, caused by our ancestors interbreeding with them.

At the same time, geneticists sequenced the DNA from an ancient pinkie bone from a Siberian cave and revealed the surprise existence of another extinct hominin group like the Neanderthals—the Denisovans. That research showed that the Denisovans, too, had interbred with modern humans; the Australian Aborigines, among others, carry a significant portion of Denisovan DNA (see page 60). Because we have found almost no Denisovan bones, almost all we know of them comes from DNA analysis.

Tremendous discoveries lie ahead in the field of ancient DNA. The leading laboratory doing this work in the United States, the Reich Lab in the Department of Genetics at Harvard Medical School, is halfway into a five-year project to create an atlas of human migration and admixing. It has so far sequenced the DNA from more than 10,000 ancient people from all over the world, producing major surprises about our human past.

As you'll see, this illuminating book tells of the great findings in archaeology and paleoanthropology made using mostly traditional methods. The future will be equally rich in discoveries—not by digging in the ground and slashing through jungles with machetes, but through powerful novel technologies that can see, find, and explore the world in extraordinary new ways.

3.6 MYA–50,000 B.C.

— Bones of Our Ancestors —

Decades of discoveries have revealed that the human family tree is much more complex than first believed. Anthropologists have charted millions of years of evolution by scrutinizing such fossils as bipedal, chimplike "Lucy" and a crafty toolmaker, known as *H. habilis,* that paleoanthropologist Louis Leakey found in Tanzania's Olduvai Gorge. The greatest discoveries in this field require luck, a good eye, and leading-edge science: A fluke of geology preserved a haunting trail of footprints for over 3.6 million years until Leakey's wife, Mary, spotted them, and the mere chip of a pinkie bone in Siberia served up enough DNA to identify a new kind of hominin once widespread throughout Asia. As for Neanderthals, whose name has become synonymous with dumb brutes, the remains from a cave in Iraq prompt us to reconsider their reputation.

The remains of one of our most mysterious extinct human relatives—tiny *Homo floresiensis*—came to light in this limestone cave in Indonesia.

1

THE FIRST STEPS OF HUMANKIND

3.66 million years ago ◆ Laetoli, Tanzania ◆ *Australopithecus afarensis*

Some 70 footprints, preserved in volcanic ash
for millions of years, proved that our
earliest ancestors walked much like we do today.

———◆———

It happened some 3.66 million years ago, at the onset of a rainy season on an East African savanna pocked with wind-sculpted acacia trees. A volcano to the east, now called Sadiman, heaved restlessly, spewing ash over the flat expanse. Over a period of days the churning volcano blanketed the plain with thin layers of ash, which were interspersed with light rains. At Laetoli, in what is now Tanzania, a group of bipedal, apelike creatures continued on their way unfazed, leaving their tracks behind in the dampened ash. The conditions were perfect for preservation: Without the gentle rains, the bone-dry footprints would have disappeared in a gust of wind, while a harder shower would have obliterated them. As the dampened ash hardened, more debris settled on top, protecting the footprints in exquisite detail. Through the millennia, sediments buried them deeper, then faulting and erosion brought them near the surface again. Finally, in the late 1970s, a combination of luck

Mary Leakey examines fossilized footprints her team found at Laetoli, Tanzania, in 1978. The site proves that hominins walked upright about 3.66 million years ago.

and perseverance would lead to their discovery by a team led by Mary Leakey. They remain by far the oldest footprints of hominins—members of the human family—ever uncovered.

At a time when few women worked in paleoanthropology, Mary Leakey was in a league of her own. She first explored Tanzania's Laetoli Beds in 1935 with her husband, Louis Leakey, but her passion for the past started long before that. The daughter of a painter, Mary had spent her childhood traveling through southern France with her father. "The area is full of prehistoric caves," she said. "Both my parents were interested in them, and I scraped around the caves while father painted . . . After that, I don't think I ever really wanted to do anything else." Mary prepared for her future life with courses in geology and prehistory at University College London. Her career took off at the age of 17 with a post as an illustrator at a dig in Devon, England. She had a gift for creating incredibly detailed sketches of archaeological artifacts and the process of their extraction. That talent brought her to the attention of her future husband, who requested that she illustrate one of his books.

Beginning in the early 1930s, the pair focused their work in Africa at Tanzania's Olduvai Gorge, some 20 miles northeast of Laetoli, even though most Western experts at the time thought humans evolved first in Asia. They kept returning to Olduvai Gorge over the years, and in the late 1950s and '60s, they made momentous finds that confirmed their belief that East Africa was the cradle of humankind. But Mary had never forgotten Laetoli. "I could not help feeling," she said, "that, somehow, the mystique of Laetoli had eluded us."

Then in 1974, an associate found a hominin tooth at Laetoli that proved to be at least 2.4 million years old, kicking off a resurgence of interest in the site. Though her husband had passed away, Mary Leakey was drawn back to where they had begun their African adventures. In 1975, with support from the National Geographic Society, she mounted an extensive survey of the Laetoli Beds.

The team was into their second field season when fortune arrived, courtesy of an impromptu elephant dung fight. "Dr. Andrew Hill of the National Museums of Kenya and several colleagues were larking about on the beds," Mary later wrote, "pelting each other with dry elephant dung. As Andrew ducked low to avoid one such missile, he noticed a series of punctures in the volcanic tuff." They turned out to be animal prints, perfectly preserved in the ground beneath them. Slowly, painstakingly, the surveyors uncovered the tracks, hoping to find ancient hominin footprints among them.

After two years of searching, the effort paid off. In 1978, Paul Abell, who had joined Leakey's team that year, came upon the first hominin imprint. It turned out to be part of an 88-foot-long,

70-footprint trail left behind by three individuals: two walking side by side, and a third following behind. Based on fossil teeth and jaws Leakey and her team also found at Laetoli, the tracks had been left by members of the earliest known human ancestor: *Australopithecus afarensis,* best known from the famous "Lucy" skeleton, found in Ethiopia a few years earlier, and dated to around 3.1 million years ago. The footprints pushed back the evolution of upright walking another half a million years.

The implications were astounding. The prints suggest that even at the beginning of our evolution, our ancestors' feet were similar to ours in form and function. Besides being clearly evolved for bipedalism, with big toes in line with the rest of the foot instead of splayed out for an apelike grip when climbing, they show that early humans walked with a "heel-strike" motion, with the heel of the foot hitting first and the toes pushing off last. "This unique ability freed the hands for myriad possibilities," Mary wrote later. "Carrying, toolmaking, intricate manipulation. From this single development, in fact, stems all modern technology."

The compact stride of the prints suggested that *A. afarensis* individuals had much shorter legs than modern humans, but the record of their passage still felt eerily familiar. While studying one set, presumed to be a female's, Mary mused: "At one point . . . she stops, pauses, turns to the left to glance at some possible threat or irregularity, and then continues to the north. This motion, so intensely human, transcends time."

"At one point . . . she stops, pauses, turns to the left to glance at some possible threat or irregularity, and then continues to the north. This motion, so intensely human, transcends time."

—*Mary Leakey,*
paleoanthropologist

In 2015, 14 more footprints were added to the collection by two Tanzanian archaeologists, who were there to evaluate whether the site could safely hold a museum. The tracks of two individuals are in the same ash layer and orientation as the ones found in 1978, intimating that they may have been made by members of the same group traveling across the landscape. One set of tracks showing larger strides was likely made by an individual over 5.5 feet tall— among the largest known members of the species. The researchers see this as a clue to the social structure of *A. afarensis*. If males and females of the species had substantially different body sizes, a trait called sexual dimorphism, the footprints can be read as one adult male—the large individual—along with two or three adult females and as many juveniles. This social organization would resemble that of modern-day gorillas, where one male shares multiple females. Some other researchers aren't convinced, pointing out that it's impossible to know the age of the individuals based on their footprints, or whether the new tracks belong to members of the same group as the original ones. Future scientists will no doubt have more to say—and discover.

2

WALKING
WITH LUCY

3.2 million years ◆ Hadar, Ethiopia ◆ *Australopithecus afarensis*

*An iconic skeleton from the desert transforms
the understanding of our origins.*

───◆───

I t was a blistering morning in November 1974, and paleoanthropologist Donald C. Johanson and his colleague Tom Gray had all
but given up looking for fossils in the badlands of Hadar in Ethiopia's Afar Triangle. Johanson had been to Hadar before: in 1972
on a reconnaissance trip, and again in 1973, when he had discovered
the knee joint of an ancient hominin—a member of the human
family. With the temperature at 110 degrees Fahrenheit, they were
heading back to their Land Rover when Johanson noticed something protruding out of the ground halfway up the slope: a fragment
of a little arm bone. Johanson knew right away it was hominin.
Then they noticed other pieces of bone scattered about—a piece of
a skull, a bit of thighbone, some vertebrae, ribs, part of a pelvis.
Incredibly, they had come upon the skeleton of a single individual
over three million years old. "Tom let out a yell," Johanson later
recalled, "and then I heard myself yelling too, and we were hugging
each other and dancing up and down in the heat."

That night they celebrated back at camp, a Beatles cassette tape
playing on repeat. Johanson already suspected their specimen was
female, so when "Lucy in the Sky With Diamonds" came on, the

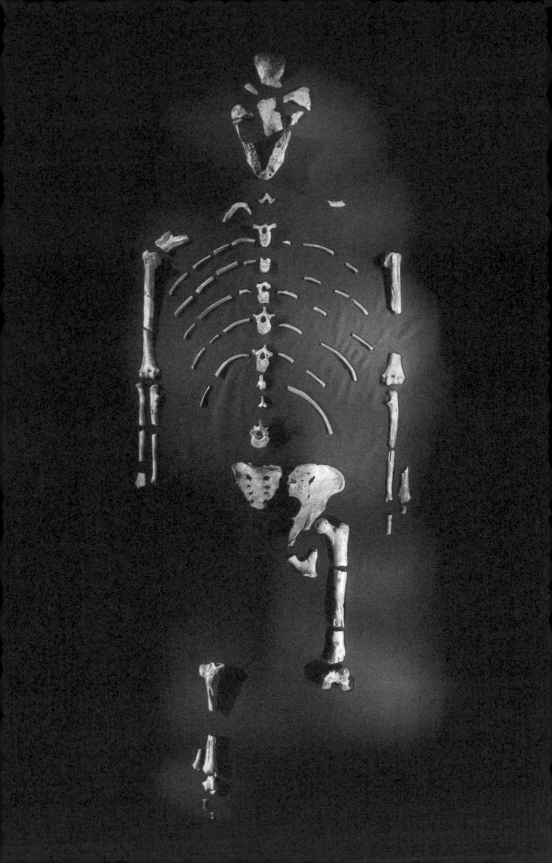

nickname seemed to suit her. She would also get an Ethiopian name, Dinknesh—the Amharic term for "You are marvelous." And marvelous she was: both the oldest known hominin ever found, and with 40 percent of her skeleton preserved, among the most complete.

> "Tom let out a yell, and then I heard myself yelling too, and we were hugging each other and dancing up and down in the heat."
>
> —*Donald C. Johanson, paleoanthropologist*

She prompted as many questions as she had answers. What species did she belong to? Could she be our direct ancestor? What was her habitat like? How did she live, and how did she die? Johanson could confirm from the form of the pelvis that she was female. "She was small of stature," he wrote. "The short leg bones suggested a height of three and a half to four feet." Her erupted wisdom teeth and the growth state of certain bones indicated she was a young adult when she died.

Lucy's most telling feature was that she clearly walked on two legs. Though her brain wasn't much larger than a chimp's, her pelvis, femur, foot, and knee bones were all evolved to allow her to move upright with minimal muscle fatigue. Her pelvis, for instance, was flared out to carry muscles for stability, and the angle of her femur brought her legs under her body—clear signs of bipedal ability. The discovery of Lucy thus strengthened the idea that upright walking was the earliest selective trait driving human evolution, appearing at least a million years before there was evidence for a bigger brain or toolmaking.

In addition to her small brain, Lucy had a mix of other primitive features. Her long, dangling arms, curved finger bones, and shoulder joints all indicated that in spite of its upright manner of walking, her species still climbed trees, probably in search of food or safety. "If Lucy saw an attractive fruiting tree, she would have climbed it,"

Discovered in Ethiopia, the fossilized skeleton nicknamed "Lucy" is the most complete example of the human ancestor species *Australopithecus afarensis*.

wrote Johanson. "Most of the time, however, she walked on two legs like us."

Lucy was not the only fossil Johanson would find. The following year, his team uncovered something even more amazing: a trove of almost two hundred hominin fossils from another Hadar site, including jaws, teeth, leg bones, foot and hand bones, cranial fragments, and even a piece of an infant skull. Together with Lucy and some jaws from the site of Laetoli in Tanzania, these additional specimens allowed Johanson and his colleague Tim White to name a new species they called *Australopithecus afarensis* ("southern ape from Afar"). It wasn't the first *Australopithecus* found—that was *Australopithecus africanus,* discovered in South Africa in 1924, and other australopithecines with huge jaws and teeth were later found in both East and South Africa. But Johanson and White argued that *A. afarensis* alone was the direct ancestor of our own genus *Homo.* On their family tree, the other australopiths occupied a side branch in evolution that went extinct some 1.5 million years ago. Later discoveries suggested that *A. afarensis* was also the longest-lived hominin species ever, surviving more than 900,000 years—some three times as long as *Homo sapiens* have been on the planet so far.

For 20 years, Lucy remained our oldest known human ancestor. But later finds, notably *Ardipithecus ramidus,* another species found in the Afar, pushed the human lineage's split from the ones leading to chimps back at least to 4.4 million years ago. Analyses of the evolution of genes suggest the split may be even more ancient. Yet Lucy remains the most iconic hominin skeleton, both for her profound antiquity and her relative completeness. "As I walked to my tent," Johanson wrote at the end of one Hadar field season, "it comforted me to realize that Hadar would wait for us, the forces of nature slowly uncovering more fossils from the layers of time. And there would always be more to learn in the quest for understanding of mankind's origins." Lucy changed our understanding of human history, and she and her homeland may yet have more secrets to share.

3

THE TOOLMAKER OF OLDUVAI GORGE

2.4 to 1.4 million years ago • Olduvai Gorge, Tanzania • *Homo habilis*

The Leakey family's finds in Tanzania helped convince the world that East Africa was the cradle of our ancestors.

———◆———

Passionate and strong-willed, focused and devoted: Louis and Mary Leakey and their son Richard came to be known as the first family of paleoanthropology in the mid-20th century. The Leakeys played a pivotal role in convincing the scientific community that Africa held the key to understanding our origins, but it was a long road, and one paved with potholes.

Born in colonial Kenya to Anglican missionaries, Louis grew up among the local Kikuyu, who taught him to throw a spear, love wildlife, and carefully observe his surroundings. At Cambridge, where Louis picked up degrees in anthropology and archaeology, he was in every way a contrarian, and one who wasn't afraid to ruffle feathers. When he proclaimed that he planned to search for early human remains in East Africa, his professors scoffed. But as a boy in Kenya he had discovered stone arrowheads and tools in the dirt, and ". . . from my reading I knew that they had to be prehistoric tools. Yet most prehistorians dismissed East Africa as a potential site of human fossils." At the time, most thought the key to our ancestry lay in Asia, but Louis wasn't convinced. He and a fellow student raised funds and took a steamship back to East Africa in 1926. On one of his many trips there over the years, he found hand axes where experts told him there would be none. Nothing would deter him from proving his theory right.

Bold and gregarious, Louis was known to make grandiose pronouncements about his findings—some of which turned out to be wrong, which damaged his standing in the scientific community. Yet he made promising discoveries. In 1948 in Kenya, he reported finding a 20-million-year-old skull he named *Proconsul africanus,* the first fossilized ape skull ever found. But the real breakthroughs lay in wait at Tanzania's Olduvai Gorge, which he would later call "a fossil-hunter's dream."

Louis was accompanied on his African expeditions by his wife, Mary, who made critical archaeological discoveries of her own at Olduvai. It was a wild, remote place, reachable only with an arduous journey. The anthropologists and a team of local staff lived in a camp of canvas tents, sharing the gorge with lions, rhinos, leopards, hyenas, and other Serengeti wildlife. Their days in the field, Louis explained, consisted of "crawling up and down the slopes of the gorge with eyes barely inches from the ground, stopping at the slightest fragment of a fossil bone or stone implement and delicately investigating the clue with a fine brush or dental pick. All this in heat that sometimes reaches 110°F." He noted that he and Mary spent more time on their hands and knees than on their feet. As children, their sons would come to work at the site while the family's loyal Dalmatians frolicked among the fossil beds.

In the 1930s Louis and Mary began finding primitive stone tools, which they named Oldowan after Olduvai Gorge. The tools were clearly very old, but it wasn't until the 1950s that a new technique called potassium-argon dating determined that they were around a million and a half years old—by far the most ancient tools found up to that time. Oldowan tools were not the hammers, spears, or harpoon points later crafted in the Middle and Late Stone Ages; they were much cruder implements made by chipping a few flakes off a stone with another stone to form a sharpened edge. Nevertheless, to the Leakeys, this ability to fashion crude tools is what truly separated humans from apes.

Now the hunt was on to find the elusive toolmaker who had crafted these artifacts. It was Mary who was struck by "Leakey's luck." One day in 1959, she sped into camp in her truck, yelling "I've got him! The one we've been looking for. Come quick. I've found his teeth." The find was a skull, including the upper jaw and teeth, which Mary painstakingly reconstructed from 400 small fragments. Louis concluded that the hominin must have made the Oldowan tools. He named it *Zinjanthropus boisei,* claiming that it was the "connecting link between the South African near-men . . . and true man as we know him." It was later determined to be close enough in form to australopiths to be reclassified as *Australopithecus boisei,* then later reclassified as *Paranthropus boisei.* The hominin came to be nicknamed "Nutcracker Man" because of its big, flat molar teeth and powerful jaw. Mary and Louis called it Zinj, or more affectionately "dear boy."

The discovery was momentous. Similar fossils had been found in South Africa, but there was no easy way to determine the age of fossils found in South Africa's limestone caves. In contrast, Olduvai Gorge's fossils were found in deposits sandwiched between layers of volcanic ash, which could be precisely dated using the new potassium-argon method. Dating the ash layer above where Zinj was found revealed that the skull was 1.75 million years old—far older than the Neanderthals of Europe or any other hominin outside Africa. More than the fossils themselves, this precise yardstick for dating them trained the search spotlight for early humans squarely on East Africa.

With a grant from National Geographic, Louis, Mary, and their three sons went back to Olduvai in 1960 and worked with a vengeance, putting in more hours in 13 months than they had in the previous 30 years combined. They made a few fragmentary finds. Then their 19-year-old son, Jonathan, discovered a jawbone that made all the toil well worth it. As additional pieces of the skull were unearthed, it was clear they had found something much more humanlike than *Zinjanthropus*, with a bigger brain, smaller face, and no gorilla-like crest on the top of the skull. All in all, it was a much better candidate for the maker of the primitive Oldowan tools previously found in the Olduvai Gorge.

The fossil, nicknamed "Jonny's Child," had been pulled from sediments presumed to be even older than *Zinjanthropus*. Louis and his team were convinced it was an ancient species of *Homo*. They called their find *Homo habilis*, or "handy man," because they suspected it to be the true first toolmaker. Its somewhat larger brain

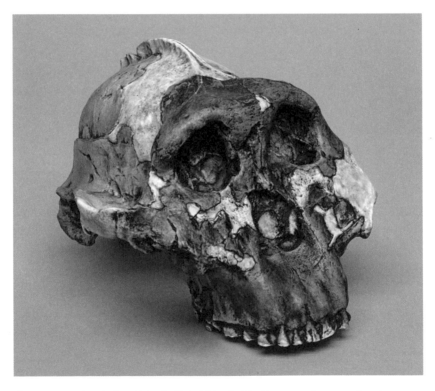

One group of early hominins in East Africa led to *Homo sapiens*, modern humans. Others—including *Paranthropus boisei*, represented by this skull—died out.

and the thousands of stone tools they had found at Olduvai made that seem like a perfectly plausible notion.

"Theories on prehistory and early man constantly change as new evidence comes to light," Leakey wrote in 1965. "A single find such as *Homo habilis* can upset long-held—and reluctantly discarded—concepts."

Upset people, it certainly did. When Louis Leakey and his team published a paper in *Nature* in 1964 called "A New Species of the Genus Homo from Olduvai Gorge," maintaining that the find was the first member of the human genus and the first true toolmaker, it generated heated debate. Letters flew to newspapers and journals from Louis's colleagues, arguing that *H. habilis* was just an *australopithecine,* not an early species of *Homo.* At the time, there was a loose agreement that to be called *Homo,* a fossil must cross "the cerebral Rubicon" and have a minimum brain capacity of 750 cubic centimeters. The brain volume of Jonny's Child fell well short. In naming the new *Homo* species, Louis was tinkering with the definition of the genus *Homo.*

Controversies aside, Louis's insights and indefatigable energy contributed hugely to the field. Later, his son Richard would make sensational discoveries of his own at the site of Koobi Fora on Kenya's Lake Turkana, including another magnificent skull often described as *H. habilis* and a stunning skeleton of a juvenile member of a later species called *Homo erectus.* Many scientists view *H. habilis* as the direct ancestor of *H. erectus,* which in turn was the direct ancestor of *Homo sapiens.* But such a simple linear relationship has been called into question as more evidence has accumulated. Finds made in 2000 of a 1.44-million-year-old *Homo habilis* and a 1.55-million-year-old *Homo erectus,* both from northern Kenya, suggest that rather than one having descended from the other, the two species may have coexisted in East Africa for hundreds of thousands of years. Further discoveries will be needed to resolve this question. But whatever the future holds, our understanding of our origins will be forever indebted to the Leakeys' efforts in the past.

4

THE CURIOUS CASE OF DMANISI

1.8 to 1.7 million years ago ◆ Dmanisi, Georgia ◆ *Homo erectus*

*A trove of fossils found in the Caucasus represents
the earliest known ancestors outside Africa.*

———◆———

In the shadow of a medieval castle, paleoanthropologist David Lordkipanidze and his team "hit the jackpot," as he described it. The spotlight for human origins research had long been trained on East Africa—home to famous fossils like Lucy and the rich lode of evidence from Tanzania's Olduvai Gorge. Lordkipanidze's lucky strike was thousands of miles away, in his home country of Georgia, where Europe ends and Asia begins.

The small town of Dmanisi in the Caucasus has long been a crossroads for travelers along the fabled Silk Road. In 1991, Lordkipanidze and his team began discovering remains of far older wayfarers: the earliest hominins yet known to leave Africa and venture into the rest of the world.

Almost two million years ago, before hominins inhabited Dmanisi, a series of volcanic eruptions flooded the site with lava, which hardened into basalt. Later, more eruptions dumped tons of ash on top of the rock. In between those catastrophic rains of ash, life crept back onto the plateau, including hominins. Buried by later ashfalls, their remains lay entombed until the 1990s, when archaeologists began finding very old bones beneath the crumbling cellars of medieval ruins.

Funded by a National Geographic grant, Lordkipanidze and his colleagues made an initial find of a jawbone—merely a taste of what was to come. In the decade that followed, the team unearthed several crania and mandibles. All appeared to be early members of the species *Homo erectus.* This wasn't surprising in itself: Specimens of *H. erectus,* including the famous early finds of "Java Man" and "Peking Man," had turned up in both Africa and Eurasia. What was surprising about the find at Dmanisi was that the sediments were between 1.8 and 1.7 million years old—at least 200,000 years older than any other *H. erectus* in Eurasia and nearly as old as the oldest in Africa. It had long been thought that what enabled *H. erectus* to leave Africa for the harsher environments of Eurasia was the invention of a new stone tool kit, including distinctive two-sided hand axes. But the only tools found at Dmanisi were cruder implements similar to ones associated with more primitive hominins in East Africa. So it seemed our ancestors started exploring the world much earlier than we thought—and for reasons that remain a mystery.

In 2000, while visiting another dig in western Georgia, Lordkipanidze got a call from Dmanisi: Another skull was coming out of the earth. He rushed back, and the skull he saw half-buried in the dirt astonished him. Usually fossil skulls are crushed almost beyond recognition, but this one looked almost as complete as one you'd find at a modern crime scene. Most of the fragile bones of its face were intact. The jawbones had many of their teeth, including prominent canines. The braincase was tiny—less than two-thirds the size of an average *Homo erectus,* again challenging the notion that greater intelligence played a role in the first migration out of Africa. Lordkipanidze also considered the face of the new skull to be more similar to *Homo habilis,* the more primitive hominin believed to be the maker of those cruder stone tools in East Africa.

Paleoanthropologist David Lordkipanidze shows off a 1.7-million-year-old fossilized *Homo georgicus* skull that he found at the Eurasian site of Dmanisi, Georgia.

The implications of the find were profound. Scientists had long thought that the more sophisticated hand axes typically associated with *H. erectus* allowed them to effectively butcher and process meat, enabling them to take in more energy-rich fat, which in turn could supply nourishment for bigger brains and taller bodies. But the simple scrapers and choppers found at Dmanisi were more suited to a scavenging lifestyle. The average height for a male of this species was only some four feet. Tooth-wear patterns suggested an omnivorous diet, and the sites where the teeth were found show no evidence of cooking fires, as had been found in some later *H. erectus* sites. In spite of these apparent disadvantages, the Dmanisi people were able to survive in a climate offering challenges not found in Africa, including potentially severe winters and dangerous predators like hyenas the size of lions. How?

One possible clue in the finds was the inclusion of an older, toothless individual, suggesting that a man had survived into old age because others helped him—perhaps a very early sign of compassion in one of our ancestors, though such thinking is difficult to confirm. "What we are doing is like reconstructing a crime scene," Lordkipanidze said. "The crime was long ago, and you can't find witnesses."

As if to prove himself wrong, in 2005 Lordkipanidze found another spectacular Dmanisi witness. "It was discovered on August 5," he said. "In fact, on my birthday." Skull 5, as it's called, is what paleoanthropologists often refer to as a "mosaic," or mixture of features seen in earlier and later humans. The skull's face, large teeth, and small brain size resemble those of earlier fossil hominins, but the detailed anatomy of its braincase is similar to *Homo erectus.*

> **"It was discovered on August 5, 2005—in fact, on my birthday."**
>
> —*David Lordkipanidze, paleoanthropologist, on finding Skull 5*

This combination of features, along with the primitive traits of the fossils found previously, has fueled a long-running discussion over whether the Dmanisi humans really are *H. erectus* at all. Some researchers prefer to call them a new species, *Homo georgicus*. With the discovery of Skull 5, Lordkipanidze himself maintained that all the various early *Homo* species, including *habilis,* are members of *H. erectus*. "We think that many African fossils can be lumped in this category and aligned with the single-lineage hypothesis," he said.

This theory remains very controversial—most scientists believe that the amount of variation seen in fossils spanning hundreds of thousands of years and great geographical distance is too much for one species name to embrace. But whatever one calls them, the Dmanisi humans and the many contradictions they embody are a puzzle to be reckoned with.

5

HOMO NALEDI DEFIES DEFINITION

335,000–236,000 years ago ◆ Rising Star cave, South Africa ◆ *Homo naledi*

An accidental find deep in a South African cave yields remarkably complete skeletons with a baffling mix of primitive and modern features.

———◆———

A stunning trove of hominin remains—the single richest fossil site of its kind ever uncovered in Africa—was found by happenstance, deep in a cave. It was arguably the greatest fossil discovery in South Africa in the past half century and adds a bewildering new twist to our understanding of human evolution.

In 2013, a pair of recreational cavers entered a cave called Rising Star, some 30 miles northwest of Johannesburg. Rising Star is a popular draw for cavers, and its filigree of channels and caverns is well mapped. Steven Tucker and Rick Hunter were hoping to find some less trodden passages. But in the back of their minds was another mission. In the first half of the 20th century, this region of South Africa produced so many fossils of our early ancestors that it later became known as the Cradle of Humankind. Though the heyday of fossil hunting there was long past, the cavers knew that a scientist in Johannesburg was looking for bones.

Lee Berger, the American paleoanthropologist who had asked cavers to keep an eye out for fossils, had taken a position at South Africa's University of the Witwatersrand in the 1990s. In the first half of the 20th century, major finds had emerged from nearby limestone caves, including in 1924 the "Taung Child," the first *Australopithecus* species ever discovered. By the time Berger arrived, however, the spotlight in human evolution had long been shifted to the Great Rift Valley of East Africa. Most researchers regarded South Africa as an interesting sidebar to the story of human evolution, but not the main plot.

What Berger most wanted to find were fossils that could shed light on the most perplexing mystery in human evolution: the origin of our own genus, *Homo*. On the far side of that event are the apelike australopiths, epitomized by *Australopithecus afarensis* and its most famous representative, Lucy, a skeleton discovered in Ethiopia in 1974. On the near side is *Homo erectus*, a tool-wielding, fire-making, globe-trotting species with a big brain and body proportions much like ours. Within a murky million-year gap, a bipedal animal was transformed into a nascent human being. How did that evolution happen?

In 2008, while searching in a place later called Malapa, some 10 miles from Rising Star cave, Berger and his son, Matthew, found some hominin fossils poking out of hunks of dolomite. Over the next year, his team painstakingly chipped two nearly complete skeletons out of the rock. Dated to about two million years ago, they were the first major finds from South Africa published in decades. Berger decided the skeletons were a new species of australopith, which he named *Australopithecus sediba*. He believed its features suggested it was a candidate for the ancestor of the first species of our genus. Though the doyens of paleoanthropology credited him with a "jaw-dropping" find, most dismissed Berger's interpretation of it as ancestral to *Homo*. But a *Homo* jaw more than half a million years older had already been found in Ethiopia. *A. sediba* was too young, too weird, and not in the right place. It wasn't one of us.

Berger shook off the rejection and got back to work. Then one night Pedro Boshoff, a caver and geologist Berger had hired to look for fossils, knocked on his door. With him was Steven Tucker. Tucker explained how he and Rick Hunter had found a narrow, vertical chute in the Rising Star cave, in some places less than eight inches wide. A passageway led into a larger cavity, its walls and ceiling covered with gnarls of calcite and jutting flowstone fingers. But what was on the floor drew the two men's attention. There were bones everywhere. They weren't stone heavy, like most fossils, nor were they encased in stone—they were just lying there, as if someone had tossed them in. They noticed a piece of a lower jaw, with teeth intact. Even to their inexpert eyes, it looked human.

Berger could see from the photos that the bones were indeed human. But they did not belong to a modern human being. Certain features, especially those of the jawbone and teeth, were far too primitive. But what *was* it? How old were the bones? And how did they get into that cave?

Tucker and Hunter lacked the skills needed to excavate the fossils, and no scientist Berger knew—certainly not himself—had the physique to squeeze through that narrow chute. He put the word out on Facebook: Skinny individuals wanted, with scientific credentials and caving experience; must be "willing to work in cramped quarters." Within a week and a half, he'd heard from nearly 60 applicants. He chose the six most qualified; all were young women. Berger called the crew "the underground astronauts."

With funding from the National Geographic Society, he gathered some 60 scientists and set up an aboveground command center, a science tent, and a small village of sleeping and support tents. Local cavers helped thread two miles of communication and power cables down into the fossil chamber. Marina Elliott, then a graduate student at Simon Fraser University in British Columbia, was the first scientist down the chute.

"Looking down into it, I wasn't sure I'd be OK," Elliott said later. "It was like looking into a shark's mouth. There were fingers and tongues and teeth of rock."

Working in two-hour shifts with a three-woman crew, Elliott's team plotted and bagged more than 400 fossils on the surface, then started carefully removing soil around a half-buried skull. Over the next several days, the other scientists huddled around the video feed in the command center above in a state of near-constant excitement.

During November 2013 and March 2014, they found some 1,550 specimens, representing at least 15 individuals: the largest collection of a single hominin species ever found in Africa. Skulls. Jaws. Ribs. Dozens of teeth. A nearly complete foot. A hand, virtually

This re-creation of a *Homo naledi* face was crafted from skull remains found in two chambers of the Rising Star cave system near Johannesburg, South Africa.

every bone intact, arranged as in life. A second chamber had been located with additional bones. "We've found a most remarkable creature," Berger said.

Parts of the skeletons looked astonishingly modern, but other parts were just as remarkably primitive. The hand looked fully modern except for its wackily curved fingers, fit for a creature climbing trees. The shoulders were apish too, and the widely flaring blades of the pelvis were as primitive as Lucy's. The lower half of the pelvis, however, looked like a modern human's. The leg bones started out shaped like an australopith's but seemed to gather modernity as they descended toward the ground. The feet were virtually indistinguishable from our own.

Berger and his team named the species *Homo naledi,* after the Sesotho word for "star." It was a curious anomaly that posed a lot of questions—most important, how old was it? Dating finds in South Africa's limestone caves has always been a challenge, and *H. naledi* was no different. It took two more years to complete analyses of the age of the rock surrounding the fossils. The fossils turned out to be between 335,000 and 236,000 years old, far younger than anyone had expected, given their primitive features. That age implied that while our own species *Homo sapiens* was evolving from other, large-brained ancestors, a little-brained shadow lineage was lingering on from a much earlier period.

How can one explain how two kinds of human, alike in some ways, very different in others, could coexist for so long a period? The conventional metaphor for an evolutionary lineage is a tree branching from a single root. Berger himself thinks that a better metaphor is a braided stream: a river that divides into channels, only to merge again downstream. Similarly, the various hominin types that inhabited the landscapes of Africa, including *H. naledi,* must at some point have diverged from a common ancestor. But then farther down the river of time, they may have coalesced again, so that we, at the river's mouth, carry in us today a bit of East Africa, a bit of South Africa, and a whole lot of prehistory we have yet to discover.

6

THE ANCESTOR IN A TEST TUBE

200,000–50,000 years ago ◆ Altai Mountains, Siberia ◆ Denisovans

A cave in Russia added a mysterious member to the human family—the first fossil hominin identified as a new species based on its DNA alone.

———◆———

There is a cave, nestled under a rock face in the Altai Mountains of southern Siberia, that has long been a draw to wayfaring humans. Neolithic hunters camped there, and later Turkic pastoralists found welcome shelter, gathering their herds around them to ride out the Siberian winters. It is said that a hermit, Denis, made the cave his home in the 18th century, and so it came to be called Denisova. But beneath the years of accumulated sheep dung lie paleontological treasures that are much, much older.

In the back of the cave, in a small side chamber, a young Russian archaeologist named Alexander Tsybankov was digging one day in July 2008, in deposits believed to be 30,000 to 50,000 years old. He came upon a tiny piece of bone. It was hardly promising: a rough nubbin about the size and shape of a pebble you might shake out of your shoe. Later, the paleoanthropologist charged with identifying the bone called it "the most unspectacular fossil I've ever seen. It's practically depressing." Still, it preserved just enough anatomy for him to recognize it as a chip from a primate fingertip, specifically the part that faces the last joint in the pinkie. Because

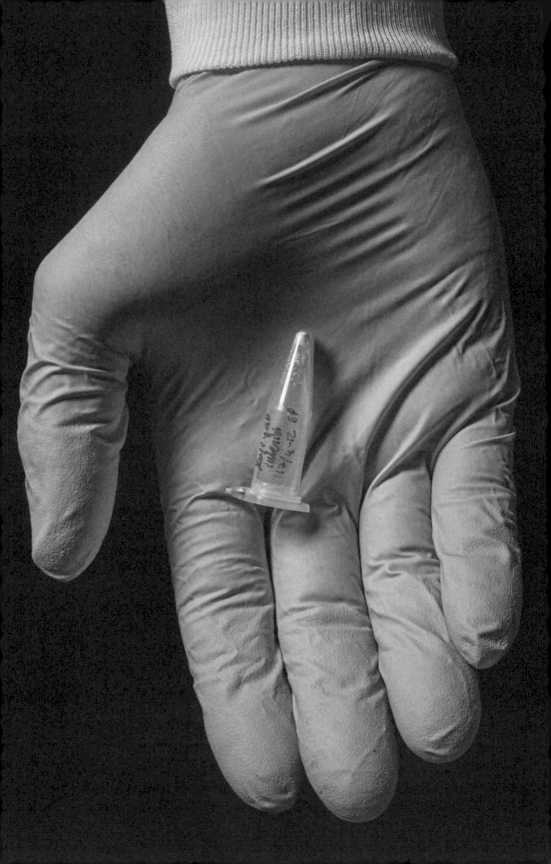

there is no evidence for primates other than humans—no apes or monkeys—in Siberia 30,000 to 50,000 years ago, the fossil was presumably from some kind of human.

Anatoly Derevianko, leader of the Altai excavations and director of the Institute of Archaeology and Ethnography in Novosibirsk, had an idea. Bones from a nearby site had yielded enough trace of genetic material to identify them as Neanderthals. Was this also from a Neanderthal? Or could it be a modern human? Artifacts from Denisova, including a gorgeous bracelet of green stone, had clearly been made by humans like us. Derevianko sent the bone chip to Svante Pääbo, an evolutionary geneticist at the Max Planck Institute for Evolutionary Anthropology in Germany, and arguably the world's leading expert in ancient DNA. There, the case of the Denisovan pinkie bone took a startling turn.

Johannes Krause, at the time a senior member of Pääbo's team, and his student extracted the finger bone's mitochondrial DNA (mtDNA), a small bit of the genome that exists in hundreds of copies in living cells and is therefore easier to find in ancient bone. They compared the DNA sequence with those of living humans and with Neanderthals. Then they repeated the analysis, because they couldn't believe the results they'd gotten the first time around. Then Krause called his boss.

"Johannes asked me if I was sitting down," Pääbo remembered of their phone call. "I said I wasn't, and he replied that I had better find a chair."

The tiny chip of a finger bone was not from a Neanderthal. Nor was it from a modern human. Based on its DNA, it belonged to a whole new kind of human being, never before seen.

> "Johannes asked me if I was sitting down. I said I wasn't, and he replied that I had better find a chair."
>
> —*Svante Pääbo, evolutionary geneticist*

Using a sample from a right-hand little finger bone found in a Siberian cave, scientists sequenced the genome of a Denisovan, a close Neanderthal relative.

The evidence was strong. DNA degrades over time, so usually very little remains in a bone tens of thousands of years old. Moreover, the DNA from the bone itself—called endogenous DNA—is typically just a tiny fraction of the total DNA in a specimen, most of which comes from soil bacteria and other contaminants. None of the Neanderthal fossils that Pääbo and his colleagues had ever tested contained even 5 percent endogenous DNA, and most had less than one percent. To their amazement, the DNA in the finger bone (which they identified as belonging to a young girl) was some 70 percent endogenous. Not Neanderthal, not modern human, but a new population the team called the Denisovans. It was the first fossil hominin identified through its DNA alone.

In the years to come, a human toe bone emerged at Denisova, as well as some enormous teeth. The DNA from the teeth showed they too were Denisovan, but to everyone's shock, the toe bone turned out to be Neanderthal. Along with the stone bracelet and other modern human artifacts, this meant that three kinds of humans had occupied that one magical cave—perhaps overlapping in time.

By 2010 scientists had sequenced the full Denisovan genome. It showed that though they were more closely related to the Neanderthals, they had also left their mark on living humans—but the geographic pattern of that legacy was odd. When the researchers compared the Denisovan genome with those of various modern human populations, they found no trace of it in Russia or nearby China. Surprisingly, Denisovan DNA turned up in the genomes of New Guineans, other people from islands in Melanesia, and Australian Aborigines.

Putting all the data together, Pääbo and his colleagues proposed a scenario to explain what might have occurred. In Africa sometime before 500,000 years ago, the ancestors of modern humans split off from the lineage that would give rise to Neanderthals and Denisovans. While our ancestors stayed in Africa, the common ancestor of Neanderthals and Denisovans migrated out.

Those two lineages later diverged, with the Neanderthals initially moving west into Europe and the Denisovans spreading east, perhaps eventually populating large parts of the Asian continent. Later still, when modern humans ventured out of Africa themselves, they encountered Neanderthals in the Middle East and Central Asia, and to a limited extent interbred with them. Modern humans venturing farther into Asia bred with Denisovans as well—accounting for the traces of their DNA in living Southeast Asian people.

Later discoveries have added new twists to the story. In 2018, Viviane Slon and Pääbo did a genome analysis on a 90,000-year-old hominin bone fragment from Denisova Cave and found that it had a Neanderthal mother and Denisovan father, providing the first proof of an ancient-human hybrid, which added to the mounting evidence that ancient species cohabited at Denisova. In 2019, Chinese researchers announced the discovery of a Denisovan jawbone found on the Tibetan Plateau—the first of its kind found outside the Siberian cave. The discovery confirmed that the Denisovans were more widespread. That same year, DNA from a large sampling of living Southeast Asians suggested that the Denisovans may not have been a single population, but three distinct ones. One group may have outlasted even the Neanderthals, who disappeared some 40,000 years ago. According to the study, these Denisovans coexisted and mixed with modern humans in New Guinea until at least 30,000 years ago, and perhaps as recently as 15,000 years ago. If confirmed, that date would mean the Denisovans were the last known humans other than ourselves to walk the Earth.

7

THE TINY PEOPLE TIME FORGOT

100,000–50,000 years ago ◆ Flores, Indonesia ◆ *Homo floresiensis*

Miniature beings sprang from an ancient line of human ancestors in a remote island location, where no one expected them to be.

———◆———

Open ocean has long separated the islands of Indonesia from mainland Asia. Scientists had assumed that none of our ancient relatives could have reached the islands without the ability to build boats. But life finds a way.

In 2003, when a joint Indonesia-New Zealand team led by archaeologist Mike Morwood unearthed a little skeleton in a spacious cave on the Indonesian island of Flores, they thought at first it was a child, perhaps three years old. But a closer look showed that the tiny, fragile bones belonged to a fully grown adult, just over three feet tall. Was it a modern human, stunted by disease or malnutrition? Apparently not. The bones looked too primitive, and the remains of at least four similarly sized individuals from Liang Bua, which means "cool cave" in the local Manggarai language, confirmed that the skeleton was not a unique deformed individual. Instead, it was typical of a whole population of tiny beings who once lived on this remote island. Morwood's team had discovered a new, remarkable kind of human, long isolated by time and space.

The full dimensions of what they had discovered began to emerge upon analysis. Incredibly, this tiny human relative, which they nicknamed the "hobbit," could have been around as recently as 18,000 years ago, at least according to original dating of the fossil. This was long after modern humans had begun their march around the globe. Yet in some ways, the hobbit looked like a diminutive version of human ancestors from Africa a hundred times older. The team appeared to have stumbled upon pygmy survivors from an earlier era, hanging on far from the main currents of human prehistory. Who were they? How did they reach—and survive on—a remote Indonesian island that was never connected by a land bridge to either Asia or Australia? What could this lost relative have to tell us about our evolutionary past?

The first far-flung human species, *Homo erectus*, crossed land bridges from Asia to Indonesia. But their trail seemed to end at Java, the site of *Homo erectus* bones some 1.5 million years old. No one believed these early humans could cross the ocean barrier, called the Wallace Line. Scientists thought it wasn't until 50,000 years ago that people—modern *Homo sapiens*—made that leap. In the 1950s and '60s, priest and part-time archaeologist Theodor Verhoeven had found ancient stone tools in the Soa Basin of Flores—perhaps a sign that *Homo erectus* crossed the Wallace Line much earlier than previously thought. But no one took this amateur archaeologist's claims very seriously. It wasn't until the 1990s that other researchers used advanced techniques to confirm that Soa Basin's tools were indeed 840,000 years old. Still, no actual remains of Flores's earlier inhabitants had shown up.

The skeleton's pelvic structure told scientists that the hobbit—given the species name *Homo floresiensis*—was a female, and her tooth wear confirmed that she was an adult. Her sloping forehead and prominently arched brow ridges resembled the anatomy of *Homo erectus*. But she was only half as tall as a modern human, with an estimated weight of about 55 pounds. Then there was her star-tlingly small brain. Peter Brown, the paleoanthropologist in Austra-lia who first examined the hobbit, calculated its volume at less than a third of a modern human's. Her brain was among the smallest of any member of the genus *Homo*. That, along with her startlingly young age and other strange, primitive traits, sparked debates about where she fit within the human family tree.

Most experts now think she probably evolved from an earlier *Homo erectus* population, perhaps the makers of the tools Verhoeven found. Her ancestors may have stood several feet taller at first, but over hundreds of thousands of years of isolation on Flores, they dwindled in size. Biogeographer Mark Lomolino, who studies the phenomenon called island dwarfism, said such a reduction in size is fairly common. "We know that when evolutionary pressures change, some species respond by shrinking." It's a common fate among large mammals marooned on islands, because having fewer predators makes size and strength less important adaptations.

The discovery underscored a puzzle going back to Theodor Ver-hoeven: How could ancient hominins ever have reached Flores? Was *Homo erectus* a better mariner than anyone suspected, able to build rafts and plan voyages? "How they managed to get there," said Mor-wood at the time, "is still a real mystery."

And it raised a new and haunting question. Modern humans col-onized Australia from mainland Asia about 50,000 years ago, popu-lating Indonesia on their way. Did they and the hobbits ever meet? In 2016, a new study called into question the original date range for *Homo floresiensis*. Their analysis of the sediments at Liang Bua revealed that these humans had lived between 100,000 and 60,000 years ago (tools found in the same deposits were dated from 190,000 to 50,000 years). Another study that year found stone tools on the neighboring island of Sulawesi that also predate the arrival of modern humans. They were likely made by *Homo erectus,* but it's also possible that the tool-makers are yet undiscovered relatives of *Homo floresiensis,* or mem-bers of that group who had migrated to a more hospitable place.

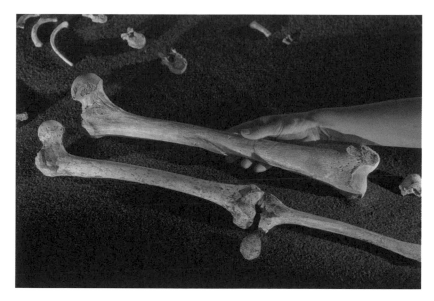

A side-by-side comparison of two femurs—one from a modern human and the other from a *Homo floresiensis*—shows how small the extinct species from Indonesia was.

What happened to the hobbits? Did they ever encounter modern humans? In 2019, a study of rat bones found in Liang Bua added new clues to *H. floresiensis*'s fate. Measuring more than 12,000 rat bones and grouping them by size, they discovered that medium-size rats that prefer more open habitats dominated the site until about 60,000 years ago, when the bones gave way to smaller, more forest-adapted rats, suggesting a marked environmental change. Previously, scientists hypothesized that all the large fauna on Flores went extinct. "The signal from the rats, however, suggests *H. floresiensis*'s departure from Liang Bua may simply be because they—along with other large animals—left in search of more open environments," said study leader Elizabeth Veatch. The results could mean that the hobbit species lingered on into the more recent past—and may have even come into contact with our most immediate ancient ancestors. Resolving such puzzles will require additional discoveries.

8

NEW LIGHT ON NEANDERTHALS

45,000–35,000 years ago ✦ Iraqi Kurdistan ✦ *Homo neanderthalensis*

Remains in Shanidar cave in Iraq show us that Neanderthal life was hard, but they helped one another through it.

———◆———

Neanderthals have captured our imaginations since the first traces of their existence tumbled out of a lime quarry in Germany in 1856. Early investigators regarded their behavior as more apish than human, and their lives, to echo Thomas Hobbes, as "nasty, brutish, and short." But a discovery in Iraq some 100 years later proved that, in some critical ways, the Neanderthals were much more like us than their low foreheads and glowering browridges would suggest.

In the 1950s, Smithsonian anthropologist Ralph Solecki, together with Kurdish workers and a team from Columbia University, unearthed the fossilized bones of eight adult and two infant Neanderthal skeletons at a site called Shanidar cave, in the Kurdistan area of northern Iraq. Many other Neanderthal remains had been found before in Europe, but this was one of the largest samples, and it changed our perception of the species more than any previous discovery.

Paleontologist Erik Trinkaus spent the late 1970s studying the remains. What he found suggested that life for these ancients was far from easy. The practice of hunting big animals in their prime is rarely seen among hominins before the Neanderthals, and the Shanidar remains made it clear that big-game meat came at a price. One male, called Shanidar 1, had suffered crushing wounds to his right leg, ankle, and foot; a blow to his skull that probably blinded him in one eye and left him deaf; and a shattered right arm, which was severed above the elbow. The rib of another individual was notched, possibly by a stab wound. Painful arthritis, visible on the anklebones, plagued several other Shanidar cave dwellers.

So many Neanderthal bones across their range showed traumatic breaks that one of Trinkaus's graduate students, Tomy Berger, decided to investigate their patterns. He analyzed the bones of 17 Neanderthals who had suffered a total of 27 traumatic injuries. "I noticed that they were mostly injuries to the head and upper body—almost no lower limb injuries," Berger said. He compared the injuries to those suffered by a variety of active modern humans, such as firefighters. The closest match? Rodeo riders. "Neanderthal life was clearly very hard and very dangerous," said Trinkaus. "They were tough survivors."

And, he said, their bodies were built for just such a bruising lifestyle. "These guys would have made Schwarzenegger look like a wimp," Trinkaus said. "If I had muscles like that, all I'd have to do is flex my pecs and I'd break my ribs. Their bones tell us they had a lot of strength and endurance. That must be what their lives demanded of them."

Their battered bones told stories of woe, but also of compassion. Four out of the six adult Neanderthal skeletons found in the Shanidar cave were deformed by disease and injuries, but all the injuries show signs of healing. Another specimen, called Shanidar 3—one of the only specimens that lived into his 40s—seemed as if something had punched between his ribs and stayed there. "He probably died eventually of infection following a punctured lung," Trinkaus said. "But he lived for a while. Someone must have taken care of him."

The fact that the battered Shanidar individuals survived past the average age of 30 and with partially healed injuries showed they were not left to die, and suggests others in the community fed, protected, and helped them—a sign of empathy and cooperation not seen in earlier hominin species.

The placement of their bodies intimated another sign of care, and a milestone in prehistory: ritual burying of the dead. Flower pollen was found with one of the skeletons. It seemed unlikely that flowers would have grown at that site, or that animals or the wind had carried in the pollen. So how did it get there? Solecki and his wife, anthropologist Rose L. Solecki, theorized that the Shanidar cave doubled as a cemetery plot, where the dead were laid to rest

Burials in the Shanidar cave in Kurdistan, Iraq, have revealed signs of Neanderthal empathy and cooperation, including care of the gravely wounded.

with an arrangement of flowers. "Some person or persons once ranged the mountainside collecting these flowers one by one," he wrote in *Science* magazine in 1975. The idea was strengthened, he thought, by the types of flower pollen found with the bones: daisy and yarrow, both long considered healing herbs, perhaps placed there for their therapeutic properties.

It was a romantic idea that captured the public imagination, but not everyone agrees about the flower burials. Some scientists think the pollen may indeed have been brought in by animals. In February 2020, however, researchers found a new skeleton at Shanidar, the first articulated Neanderthal skeleton to come out of the ground in more than 20 years. It was found quite near the flower burial site, and there's strong evidence that the discovery, called Shanidar Z, was also deliberately buried. Perhaps there is truth in the romance.

50,000–3000 B.C.

The Dawn of Culture

Some 44,000 years ago, artists began to record the world as they saw it and the makeup of the cosmos as they imagined it. Long before they mastered written language, ancient storytellers expressed themselves through paintings, architecture, and craftsmanship with unbounded creativity. In the painted caves of France, lions, mammoths, and bison caper across the stone walls just as rocky outcroppings in the Sahara show a lost landscape of antelope, crocodiles, and giraffes. Religion was a common pillar of emerging cultures around the globe, producing such remarkable sites as the ziggurats of Uruk, the world's oldest temple at Göbekli Tepe, and the monoliths at Stonehenge. Rock art in Australia shows that Aboriginal beliefs practiced by communities today have persisted for tens of thousands of years.

Weathered and broken, Stonehenge's otherworldly monoliths have been studied extensively but still guard secrets after more than 4,500 years.

9

ROCK ART OF ABORIGINAL DREAMTIME

At least 30,000 B.C. ◆ Australia ◆ Aboriginal

More than 100,000 paintings and engravings across Australia represent the world's longest continuing art forms.

———◆———

Aboriginal people have lived in Australia for at least 60,000 years, and for the overwhelming majority of that time they had the continent to themselves. There were once about 250 distinct Aboriginal languages, hundreds more dialects, and many more clans and subgroups. But there is deep spiritual and cultural overlap among them. These people lived for a couple thousand generations in small, nomadic bands, as befits a hunter-gatherer existence, moving in their own rhythms about the vast expanse of Australia. Then, on April 29, 1770, British explorer James Cook landed his ship, the *Endeavour,* on the southeastern shore. The next two centuries saw the horror of cultural obliteration—massacres, disease, alcoholism, forced integration, surrender. Aboriginals now make up less than 4 percent of the Australian population. Many anthropologists credit them with possessing the world's longest enduring religion as well as the longest continuing art forms—the cross-hatched and dot-patterned painting styles once inscribed in the caves and shelters that make up Australia's 100,000 rock art sites.

According to Aboriginal cosmology, all of Earth's surface was once a featureless expanse of mud or clay. Then Ancestral Beings emerged from beneath the surface or from the sky, assumed the form of an animal or plant or human, and journeyed across the land, performing great deeds of creation, shaping the mud into rivers, hills, islands, and caves, and making the animals and people. This took place in an age known as the Dreamtime. And the path each of these beings took, the countryside they molded before burrowing back into the ground, is called a songline. They bestowed language, law, ritual, and faith. These stories form the basis of Aboriginal life, and through ritual and art, this community continues to interact with the beings from that period of creation.

Owl-men, serpent-headed women, spiny anteaters, fish, and spiders are among the figures painted on the walls of caves and cliffs in Australia's rugged Top End, where some of the continent's most spectacular images are found. Where tribespeople once met in solemn ritual during the wet seasons, tourists now gather at Burrungkuy (Nourlangie) in Kakadu National Park. Busloads of visitors from Darwin regularly reach the stone outcropping to view one of the most beautiful collections of rock art yet documented. One complex cliffside mural of spirits features Namarrgon, a creation ancestor who holds a lightning bolt in his hands. Backbones and hatching designs of the x-ray art style decorate the bodies. In the part of northwestern Australia known as the Kimberley, natural rock art galleries are decorated with ghostly forms that have humanlike heads but no mouths, representing a particular type of Ancestral Being known as Wandjina.

Some Aboriginal groups have resisted the Western framing of these rock art sites as static monuments that should remain untouched for all time. The rock paintings are not merely representations of spiritual beings but living beings themselves that are

still in conversation with the people. A controversy ensued in 1987 when a group of Ngarinyin people from the western Kimberley repainted some rock art images. But as Ngarinyin leader and artist David Mowaljarlai explained in 1988, "Those images were put down for us by our Creator, Wandjina, so that we would know how to stay alive, make everything grow and continue what he gave to us in the first place." He added that young people are meant to learn to read these images so that they will take on their responsibilities to the land in adulthood. Those obligations to the land include maintaining and repainting images.

> "Those images were put down for us by our Creator, Wandjina, so that we would know how to stay alive, make everything grow and continue what he gave to us in the first place."
>
> —*David Mowaljarlai, Ngarinyin leader, 1988*

It was always known that the artwork was old. But just how old? Despite centuries of research by both outsiders and Aboriginal-led teams, rock art sites in Australia have been notoriously difficult to date with scientific methods. It's often hard to get an accurate age for mineral paints because they lack datable carbon. One set of reliably dated engravings, up to 15,000 years old, has been found in northern Queensland's Laura Basin. In 2012, archaeologists obtained a sample from art made with charcoal at the Nawarla Gabarnmang cave in the Arnhem Land of the Northern Territory and found that those images were around 28,000 years old, making the rock art site the oldest directly dated in Australia. But archaeologists have reason to believe many other sites are much older; at some, they've found pieces of red ocher crayons that date back over 50,000 years, which would make them older than the Paleolithic paintings found in European cave sites like Lascaux and Chauvet. Some creative new dating techniques could help scientists get

Some 28,000 years ago, Aboriginal Australians started painting a cathedral-like cave called Nawarla Gabarnmang, or "cleft in the rock" in the local language.

better answers. In 2020, researchers reported that they were able to determine when the slender, headdress-wearing Gwion figures of the Kimberley were created. Dating a fossilized wasp nest built directly over the art put the date of the figures' creation at about 12,000 years ago.

Australia's rock art faces severe threats. Tribes have been displaced from their traditional lands, and development continues to endanger sites. About 1,700 engraved boulders became damaged after they were removed to make way for a gas plant on Western Australia's Burrup Peninsula in the early 1980s. Residents of Western Australia were outraged when reports in 2014 revealed that many Gwion rock paintings had been harmed as a result of the local government's scheduled fire-prevention burning strategy. In May 2020, the Rio Tinto company destroyed the 46,000-year-old Juukan Gorge rock shelters in the Pilbara region of Western Australia while expanding an iron ore mine. Some rock art experts complained that Australia has lacked a coordinated approach to document these sites. Others have urged that measures be taken to prevent their deterioration and that Indigenous artists be encouraged to perpetuate their traditional skills. With adequate protection and periodic restoration, the immortality of such cliffside masterpieces could be assured.

10

ICE AGE ARTISTS

38,000 B.C. ✦ France ✦ Paleolithic

*Representing an explosion in human creativity,
the lifelike cave paintings at Lascaux and Chauvet
attest to a world that no longer exists.*

———✦———

On a September afternoon in 1940, four teens—Marcel Ravidat, Georges Agniel, Simon Coencas, and Jacques Marsal—made their way through the woods on a hill overlooking Montignac in southwest France. They had come to explore a dark, deep hole one boy had found when his dog Robot fell between the roots of a dead tree. The boys had a knife, a few bits of rope, a homemade oil lamp. They believed the hole could be a rumored secret underground passage to the nearby manor of Lascaux.

They tossed a few stones down the hole to judge its depth. The stones fell and rolled a long time. After clearing rocks and vegetation from the entrance, they squeezed through one by one, sliding, tumbling, and beginning to explore. They soon saw lines and spots in red and black. Holding the lamp to examine the walls more closely, they discovered—to their surprise—paintings of bulls and deer. The boys told a schoolmaster, who was so impressed upon visiting the galleries that he sent a telegram about the discovery to Abbé Henri Breuil, the "pope of prehistory." The site quickly attracted researchers who wanted to excavate and members of the public who wanted to catch a glimpse of the running horses, swimming deer, wounded bison, and other beings depicted in these wonderfully lifelike paintings, which may be up to 20,000 years old.

The collection of paintings in Lascaux, remarkable for their rich detail, are among some 147 prehistoric sites dating from the Paleolithic era, including two dozen decorated caves that have been documented in France's Vézère Valley to date. This corner of southwestern Europe seems to have been a hot spot for figurative art. The biggest discovery since Lascaux occurred in southern France in December 1994, when three spelunkers named Eliette Brunel, Christian Hillaire, and Jean-Marie Chauvet scrambled through a narrow crevice in a cliff and dropped into the dark entry. They laid eyes on artworks that had not been seen since a rock slide 22,000 years ago closed off entry to the cavern.

Here, by flickering firelight, prehistoric artists began to draw on this cave's bare walls: profiles of cave lions, herds of rhinos and mammoths, magnificent bison, and a chimeric creature—part bison, part woman—conjured from an enormous cone of overhanging rock. Other chambers harbor horses, ibex, and aurochs; an owl traced out of mud by a single finger on a rock wall; an immense bison formed from ocher-soaked handprints; and cave bears walking casually, as if in search of a spot for a long winter's nap. The works are often drawn with nothing more than a single and perfect continuous line. In all, the artists depicted 442 animals over perhaps thousands of years, using nearly 400,000 square feet of cave surface as their canvas. Some animals are solitary, even hidden, but most congregate in great mosaics in the deepest part of the cave.

The site, now known as Chauvet cave, is sometimes considered the "Sistine Chapel of Prehistory." The first photographs of the place captivated specialists and the public alike. For decades, scholars had theorized that art had advanced in slow stages from primitive scratchings to lively, naturalistic renderings. Surely the subtle shading, ingenious use of perspective, and elegant lines of Chau-

France's Minister of Culture called the masterfully painted Chauvet cave "an extraordinary testimony to man's first steps in the adventure of art."

vet's masterworks placed them at the pinnacle of that progression. Then carbon dates came in, and prehistorians reeled. At about 36,000 years old, approximately twice as old as those in the more famous caves like Lascaux, Chauvet's images represented not the culmination of prehistoric art but its earliest known beginnings. A few thousand years after anatomically modern humans appeared in Europe, cave painting was as sophisticated as it would ever be.

Since its discovery, Chauvet has been ferociously protected by the French Ministry of Culture, which rarely allows visits. (Lascaux was closed to the public in 1963, after heritage officials recognized that the presence of visitors, expelling carbon dioxide and moisture, was damaging the artwork.) For a 2015 *National Geographic* report, journalist Chip Walter was allowed a peek at the artwork in Chauvet and captured the feeling of being inside:

> The ceiling closes in, and in some places the heavy cave walls crowd close enough to touch my shoulders . . . [then] we enter

the belly of an expansive chamber. This is where the cave lions are. And the woolly rhinos, mammoths, and bison, a menagerie of ancient creatures, stampeding, battling, stalking in total silence. Outside the cave, where the real world is, they are all gone now . . . The age of these drawings makes youngsters of Egypt's storied pyramids, yet every charcoal stroke, every splash of ocher looks as fresh as yesterday. Their beauty whipsaws your sense of time. One moment you are anchored in the present, observing coolly. The next you are seeing the paintings as if all other art—all civilization—has yet to exist.

The search for the world's *oldest* cave paintings continues. Rock art discovered in the rest of the world has disrupted the belief that visual storytelling emerged first in Europe. On the Indonesian island of Sulawesi, for example, scientists found a chamber of figurative paintings of part-human, part-animal beings that are estimated to be 44,000 years old, older than any sites located in Europe. Archaeologists look to rock art for clues as to when humans developed self-awareness and modern cognition. Stone tools reveal ancient humans' strategies of survival, but paintings and sculptures, with no discernible utilitarian function, attest to their ability to grasp more abstract intellectual concepts. Artworks like the ones that decorate Chauvet and Lascaux create such a strong impression on viewers for that reason, even if we cannot reconstruct the cosmology that colored the worldview of these ancient artists. Scholars don't know if art was invented independently many times over, in disparate geographic locations, or if it was a skill developed early in our evolution. Nor have researchers confirmed if it was an ability unique to *Homo sapiens* or if Neanderthals were also painters. What we do know is that creativity and the needs for artistic expression run deep into our ancestry.

11

THE MOST ANCIENT AMERICANS

18,000 B.C. ◆ Monte Verde, Chile ◆ Early peoples of the Americas

Experts once believed that people first came to the Americas 13,000 years ago. Recent discoveries have pushed that date much further back.

———◆———

New archaeological finds, novel hypotheses, and a trove of genetic data have shed fresh light on who the first Americans were and when they might have come to the Western Hemisphere. But for all that forward motion, what's clearest is that the story of the ancient people who settled a new land is still very much a mystery.

For most of the 20th century, the mystery had been assumed more or less solved. In 1908, a cowboy in Folsom, New Mexico, found the remains of an extinct subspecies of giant bison that had roamed the area more than 10,000 years ago. Later, museum researchers discovered spearpoints among the bones—clear evidence that people had been present in North America much earlier than previously believed. Not long after, spearpoints dating to 13,000 years ago were found near Clovis, New Mexico; what became known as Clovis points were subsequently found at dozens of sites across North America where ancient hunters had killed game.

Given that Asia and North America were connected during the last ice age by a broad landmass called Beringia, and that the first Americans appeared to be mobile big-game hunters, it was easy to conclude that they'd followed mammoths and other prey out of Asia, across Beringia, and then south through an open corridor between two massive Canadian ice sheets. And given that there was no convincing evidence for human occupation predating Clovis hunters, a new orthodoxy developed: They had been the first Americans. Case closed.

That all changed in 1997, when a team of high-profile archaeologists visited a small settlement site in southern Chile called Monte Verde. There, U.S. archaeologist Tom Dillehay claimed to have discovered evidence of human occupation dating to more than 14,000 years ago—a thousand years before Clovis hunters appeared in North America.

Similarly early dates had been emerging from other sites as well—Meadowcroft Rockshelter in Pennsylvania, for instance, and

Archaeologists Tom Dillehay (standing) and Mario Pino found evidence at Monte Verde, Chile, that humans came to the New World far earlier than once thought.

Pedra Furada in Brazil—but the evidence was controversial. The question of whether humans had arrived in the Americas before the Clovis people was so hotly debated, in fact, that it split New World archaeologists into two deeply entrenched camps. Dillehay was even accused of planting artifacts and fabricating data. But after reviewing the evidence, the expert team concluded it was solid, and the story of the peopling of the Americas was thrown wide open.

The site of Monte Verde came to light in 1976, when local lumbermen, cutting back the banks of Chinchihuapi Creek to widen a trail for their oxcarts, unearthed mastodon bones and pieces of wood in the wet peat. The next year Dillehay, then at the Anthropology Department at Southern University of Chile, in Valdivia, began nearly a decade of excavation with Chilean colleagues.

What they uncovered were the traces of a settlement along a creek once lined with evergreens. The inhabitants had hunted mastodons; gathered a bounty of foods, including wild potatoes, bamboos, mushrooms, and juncus seeds; and were able to treat the sick and injured with seaweed, at least 22 varieties of medicinal plants, and analgesic tree leaves imported from the far north.

In 2013, Dillehay returned to Monte Verde and gathered evidence that would introduce a new possible time frame for the site. Radiocarbon dating of fire-charred plants and bones suggests that people had built cooking fires and made stone tools there some 18,500 years ago—or even earlier.

Fortunately, many of those perishable remains were preserved because Monte Verde died a sudden death. For unknown reasons— perhaps increased rainfall— the water table rose abruptly. Water pooled at the camp, forcing the residents to leave. Soon a peat bog smothered the campsite, protecting it from bacterial attack and destructive changes in humidity. The peat also preserved one human footprint, about five inches long, probably left in the sandy mud as the Monte Verdeans were moving on. "That footprint made Monte Verde human for me," recalled Rick Gore, the writer *National Geographic* sent to report on the investigation. "I saw a child, rain soaked and crying, running after its mother as she abandoned the settlement. The steps of that child insisted that someone like us had indeed reached the forests of Chile surprisingly long ago."

In the years since the initial Monte Verde bombshell, no one has been able to know for sure how people came to the southern reaches of South America at such an early date. But the original question—Was Clovis first?—has been answered repeatedly. Some sites providing evidence have been known and studied for years and have gained fresh credibility in the wake of Monte Verde's acceptance.

> "That footprint made Monte Verde human for me. I saw a child, rain soaked and crying, running after its mother as she abandoned the settlement. The steps of that child insisted that someone like us had indeed reached the forests of Chile surprisingly long ago."
> —*Rick Gore, journalist*

But there have been new finds as well. One site, in the Texas Hill Country north of Austin, is located along a tiny stream called Buttermilk Creek. Archaeologists uncovered more than 16,000 pre-Clovis artifacts—including stone blades, spearpoints, and chips—suggesting that people settled there as early as 15,500 years ago. Another site, in Mexico's Yucatán Peninsula, lies inside an immense submerged cavern nicknamed Hoyo Negro, or "black hole." There, a team of Mexican divers found a bed of prehistoric bones, including at least one nearly complete human skeleton, that of a teenage girl who fell into the hole and died some 12,000 to 13,000 years ago.

The newest archaeological data comport with an increasingly important line of evidence in our understanding of the peopling of the Americas. In recent years geneticists have compared the DNA of modern Native Americans with that of other populations around the world; based on mutation rates in human DNA, they concluded that the ancestors of Native Americans were Asians who separated from other Asian populations and remained isolated for about 10,000 years. During that time, they developed unique genetic signatures that only Native Americans currently possess. Those same genetic markers were found in the DNA recovered from two ancient sources: the Yucatán cave skeleton and the remains of a child buried 12,600 years ago in western Montana at a place now called the Anzick site.

And then there are fossilized human feces—surely the most indelicate evidence of pre-Clovis occupation in North America. In 2008, Dennis Jenkins of the University of Oregon reported that he'd found human coprolites, or ancient excrement, dating between 14,000 and 15,000 years ago in a series of shallow caves overlooking an ancient lake bed near the town of Paisley. Jenkins speculates that the people who left them might have made their way inland from the Pacific by way of the Columbia or Klamath Rivers.

As at Monte Verde and the Buttermilk Creek site, people living by the lake seem to have settled in, comfortable with their environment and adept at exploiting it. All this suggests that long before the Clovis culture began spreading across North America, the land hosted diverse communities of humans—people who may have arrived in any number of migrations by any number of routes. Some may even have come in such small numbers that traces of their existence will never be found.

"There's a whole lot of stuff that we don't know and may never know," says David Meltzer, an archaeologist at Southern Methodist University. "But we're finding new ways to find things and new ways to find things out."

12

THE WORLD'S OLDEST TEMPLE

ca 9600 B.C. ◆ Anatolia, Turkey ◆ Prehistoric

Discoveries at the site of Göbekli Tepe, a religious sanctuary built by hunter-gatherers, suggest the urge to worship sparked civilization.

———◆———

Most of the world's great religious centers, past and present, have been destinations for pilgrimages. Think of the Vatican, Mecca, Jerusalem, and other monuments for spiritual travelers who often come from great distances. The prehistoric site of Göbekli Tepe ("belly hill" in Turkish) may be the first of them all. Its early date, in fact, suggests that the human sense of the sacred—and love of a good spectacle—may have given rise to civilization itself.

What archaeologists have uncovered stands atop a mound that rises 50 feet above the countryside. With stone pillars arranged into a set of rings, it is vaguely reminiscent of Stonehenge, except that this was built much earlier, with limestone pillars bearing bas-reliefs of animals—a cavalcade of gazelles, snakes, foxes, scorpions, and ferocious wild boars. The assemblage was created some 11,600 years ago. So far as we know, the pillars represent the first structure human beings put together that was bigger and more complicated than a hut.

At that time, much of the human race lived in small nomadic bands that survived by foraging for plants and hunting wild animals; construction of the site would have required more people coming together in one place than had likely occurred before. Amazingly, the temple's builders were able to cut, shape, and transport 16-ton stones hundreds of feet despite having no wheels or beasts of burden.

Discovering that hunter-gatherers had constructed Göbekli Tepe was like finding someone had built a 747 in a basement with

The discovery of an ancient temple's pillars at Göbekli Tepe, Turkey, has changed the way archaeologists think about the origins of civilization.

an X-Acto knife. "I, my colleagues, we all thought, What? How?" said archaeologist Klaus Schmidt, the first director of excavations there.

In the 1960s, archaeologists from the University of Chicago surveyed the region and concluded that Göbekli Tepe was of little interest. Disturbance was evident at the top of the hill, but they attributed it to the activities of a Byzantine-era military outpost. Here and there were broken pieces of limestone they thought were gravestones.

In 1994, Schmidt came across the Chicago researchers' brief description of the hilltop and decided to check it out. Within minutes of arriving, he realized that he was looking at a place where scores or even hundreds of people had worked in millennia past. The limestone slabs were not Byzantine graves, but something much older. He began digging the very next year.

Inches below the surface, shovels struck an elaborately fashioned stone. Then another, and another: a ring of standing pillars. As the months and years went by, Schmidt's team—a shifting crew of German and Turkish graduate students and 50 or more local villagers—found a second circle of stones, then a third, and then more. Geomagnetic surveys in 2003 revealed at least 20 rings piled together, higgledy-piggledy, under the earth.

The circles follow a common design. All are made from limestone pillars shaped like giant spikes or capital T's. Bladelike, the pillars are easily five times as wide as they are deep. The tallest are 18 feet in height and weigh 16 tons.

They stand an arm span or more apart, interconnected by low stone walls. In the middle of each ring are two taller pillars, their thin ends mounted in shallow grooves cut into the floor.

Puzzle piled upon puzzle as the excavation continued. For reasons yet unknown, the rings at Göbekli Tepe seem to have regularly lost their power. Every few decades people buried the pillars and put up new stones—a second, smaller ring, inside the first. Sometimes, later, they installed a third. Then the whole assemblage would be filled in with debris, and an entirely new circle was created nearby. The site may have been built, filled in, and built again for centuries.

Archaeologists are still excavating the site—and debating its meaning. What they know is that the place is the most significant in a volley of unexpected findings that have overturned earlier ideas about our species' deep past. Scholars long thought that when hunter-gatherers settled down and started growing crops, the resulting food surplus made it possible for people to organize complex societies.

Göbekli Tepe calls that into question. Before he died in 2014, Schmidt argued that it might have worked the other way around: The labor force needed to build the enclosures pushed people to develop agriculture as a way to feed workers. Indeed, scientists now believe that one center of agriculture arose in southern Turkey—well within trekking distance of Göbekli Tepe—at exactly the time the temple was at its height.

Some archaeologists believe Göbekli Tepe was a regional gathering place. "Back then people would have to meet regularly to keep the gene pool fresh and exchange information," said Jens Notroff, an archaeologist who has worked at the site. One imagines chanting and drumming, the animals on the great pillars seeming to move in flickering torchlight. Surely there were feasts; Schmidt's team uncovered stone basins that could have been used for beer. The temple was a spiritual locus, but it may also have been the Neolithic version of Disneyland.

Today, about a tenth of the 22-acre site is open to the sky. As archaeologists continue to work, new discoveries may well change the current understanding of the site's importance. Still, after years of digging, Schmidt believed he understood why hunter-gatherers settled down in the first communities. "I think what we are learning," he said, "is that civilization is a product of the human mind."

> "I think what we are learning is that civilization is a product of the human mind."
>
> —*Klaus Schmidt, archaeologist*

13

THE FIRST
TRUE CITY

ca 4500 B.C. ◆ Iraq ◆ Sumerian

*From the earliest known writing to pioneering
urban planning, Uruk is the city of firsts.*

———◆———

The first mass-produced product. The first stone architecture. The first ziggurat. The first written words. For the ancient Sumerians in Mesopotamia, Uruk was the urban center of their world. For archaeologists and historians, it's one of history's most important archaeological finds—not just for its significance as the first true city in the world, but also for the first-of-its-kind evidence of some of the building blocks of modern civilization. The city's innovations were emulated in surrounding settlements, but for proof of its ongoing influence you need only look at the structure of any modern city, the production floor of a factory, the letters in our alphabet, and our file cabinets of contracts.

Located a few hours' drive southeast of Baghdad in modern-day Iraq, where it is known as Warka, the city was the work of ancient Sumer people. Uruk was built in the fifth millennium B.C. and shows signs of continuous habitation for 5,000 years before being abandoned in the first century A.D.

In 1849, British explorer William Kennett Loftus began initial excavations there. "I know of nothing more exciting or impressive than the first sight of one of these Chaldaean piles, looming in solitary grandeur from the surrounding plains and marshes," he wrote of the city's ziggurats, which are visible for miles. "Of all the desolate sites I ever beheld, that of Warka incomparably surpasses all."

Nonetheless, Loftus soon abandoned the project. In 1912, a group of archaeologists financed by an association of German explorers began an excavation staffed by Bedouin laborers. As the dig progressed, they uncovered a long series of Uruks, each built atop the remains of the last for nearly a thousand years. At the beginning of the third millennium B.C., a great wall of perhaps 306 million bricks was built around the city.

Some legends say the wall was built by Gilgamesh, the protagonist of the first surviving work of epic literature. The prologue includes a tour of the city: "[T]he outer wall where the cornice runs, it shines with the brilliance of copper; and the inner wall, it has no equal. Touch the threshold, it is ancient . . . Climb upon the wall of Uruk; walk along it, I say; regard the foundation terrace and examine the masonry: is it not burnt brick and good?" Construction was certainly an undertaking of epic proportions; historians calculate that a force of 1,000 laborers working six months a year would have needed 13.5 years to complete the wall.

The city consisted of two sections, the Anu District and the Eanna District, each dedicated to Sumerian gods. The structures weren't built at random: Evidence points to an advanced planning and construction process. Uruk's infrastructure included irrigation works, food warehouses, homes, and businesses. Researchers believe canals full of water from a branch of the Euphrates River once crisscrossed the city, creating a kind of "Amsterdam on the sand." Uruk also contained temples, which are thought to have functioned both as places of worship and of government.

Many artifacts unearthed at Uruk show skilled craftsmanship and artistic expression, but archaeologists have also found evidence of mass production there: cheap, similar-size bevel-rimmed bowls, thought to have been used as vessels for daily rations of grain, then discarded in waste pits. The consistency in size and design means

A clay tablet about two inches tall bears a text about barley administration, likely created in the city of Uruk as cuneiform writing was first taking shape.

the vessels were manufactured from the same mold or model, which could quickly be replicated to distribute to a large population.

Archaeologists have unearthed nearly 5,000 clay tablets, most from apparent waste piles, that recorded financial transactions with pictographs and signs thought to be the world's first numerals. Sumerian accountants also used clay tokens to represent things like jars of oil or kinds of livestock. The cache is an ancient example of bureaucracy still with us today: accounting and contracts. One clay tablet records the world's oldest known mathematical problem, dated to the fourth millennium B.C. Researchers say it shows a numeral system based on the number 60; it documents calculations related to length and area.

Perhaps the most fascinating innovation at Uruk was the written language called cuneiform. The inhabitants began writing inscriptions in pictographs, small pictures or icons that could be strung together to create a narrative. Over centuries pictographs gradually abstracted into the simpler markings of cuneiform, signs representing syllables that can be pieced together to write words and sentences. Writing enabled dissemination of knowledge far beyond Uruk's walls and was adopted by the Akkadians, Babylonians, Sumerians, and Assyrians to write their own languages. Scribes wrote in cuneiform for more than three millennia, offering a precious window into the poetry, laws, medical recipes, scientific observations, and bookkeeping of the world's first cities.

14

THE FATE OF ÖTZI THE ICEMAN

ca 3300 B.C. ◆ Ötztal Alps, Italy ◆ Neolithic

Frozen in time under a glacier in the Alps,
this Neolithic hunter felled by a foe's arrow is the
oldest intact human ever discovered.

———◆———

When German couple Helmut and Erika Simon set off for a hike in the Ötztal Alps on Italy's border with Austria on September 19, 1991, they likely expected to see some stunning scenery. But as they roamed slightly off the trail, Erika instead spotted something that would stun the world.

Sticking unexpectedly out of the ice in a rocky hollow was a small head atop a pair of shoulders. Was it a victim of a hiking accident? Over the following four days, a well-intentioned small crowd—including hikers, police officers, and a forensics team—overran the discovery site at 10,530 feet. They used implements ranging from ice picks to ski poles to a jackhammer to extricate the body and several of the deceased's belongings, including an unusual ax, from the icy tomb. The incredibly well-preserved body had been naturally mummified—a clue that this was not a recent traveler through this Alpine area.

The body and belongings were transported to the University of Innsbruck's Institute for Prehistory and Early History. There, archaeologist Konrad Spindler took one look at the salvaged ax and knew this "iceman" was a time traveler from the Copper Age. Indeed, further investigation revealed that 5,300-year-old Ötzi the Iceman—named for the Ötztal Valley near his death site—is the oldest intact human ever found. "Not since Howard Carter unlocked the tomb of King Tutankhamun in the early 1920s had an ancient human so seized the world's imagination," wrote mountaineer David Roberts.

Over the ensuing three decades, scientists have used an array of high-tech tools, including 3D endoscopy and DNA analysis, to

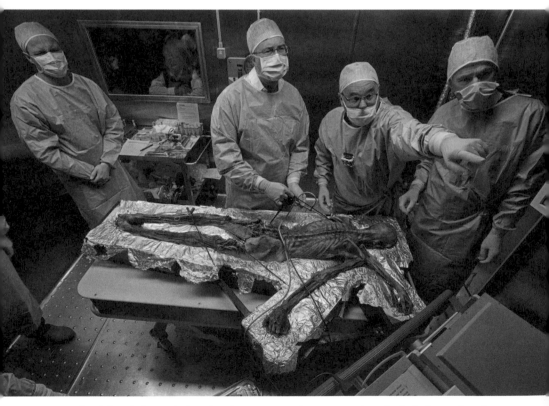

In a lab in Bolzano, Italy, scientists use an endoscope to view the lethal arrowhead that remains lodged in the shoulder of Ötzi, the prehistoric iceman.

examine the Iceman exhaustively, removing him only when necessary from the refrigerated chamber in the South Tyrol Museum of Archaeology in Bolzano, Italy, where he has resided since 1998. They have refined his biography in exquisite detail. What at first appeared to be a tale of a solitary Neolithic hunter overtaken by the elements has morphed into a riveting murder mystery in which a foe, rather than the weather, caught up with the Iceman.

Nature did play a starring role, however, in performing one of the best embalming jobs in the history of human remains. The frigid glacial environment of the Ötztal Alps tucked the Iceman in like a cold, wet blanket, immobilizing and preserving his body in snow, ice, and glacial meltwater. The little hollow protected his lifeless form from the bone-grinding action of the Niederjoch Glacier, which passed just a few feet overhead for the next 5,300 years.

In March 1991, a dust storm in the Sahara blew particles as far north as the Alps. As they soaked in the sun's rays, they triggered an unprecedented melting of the glaciers, including the portion covering the Iceman's final resting place. The Simons happened upon him at just the right time, for three days later another snowfall would have buried him anew.

Thorough examinations of the Iceman showed that he was missing only his hair, toenails, all but one fingernail, and an outer layer of skin. His small, sinewy frame was covered in more than 50 tattoos, made by rubbing charcoal into fine cuts in the skin. The dark lines and crosses were mostly located on the joints and along the back, parts of the body prone to injury or pain. This has led some researchers to believe that the tattoos marked acupuncture points.

If so, the Iceman must have needed a lot of treatment, which isn't so surprising given what scientists have learned about his age and ailments. He was in his mid-40s, a rather elderly man for his times. He had worn joints, hardened arteries, and gallstones. His right hand and wrist bore cuts of the kind made by a hatchet, inflicted just days before he died.

Furthermore, the Iceman's gut contained the eggs of parasitic worms. He seems to have been the earliest known human infected by the bug that causes Lyme disease. He had alarming levels of arsenic in his system (probably due to working with metal ores). He also had advanced gum disease and tooth decay.

Although these health factors would have made the Iceman's life uncomfortable, they did not kill him. In 2001, an Italian radiologist x-rayed the Iceman's chest and detected an object his earlier colleagues had missed: a stone arrowhead, smaller than a quarter, lodged beneath the Iceman's left shoulder blade. "This 'casual discovery'. . . instantly turned an inexplicable death more than 5,000 years ago into archaeology's most fascinating cold case," journalist Stephen Hall reported for *National Geographic*.

> "This 'casual discovery' . . . instantly turned an inexplicable death more than 5,000 years ago into archaeology's most fascinating cold case."
>
> —*Stephen Hall, journalist*

The forensic evidence became even more intriguing in 2005, when new CT scan technology revealed that the sharpened arrowhead, probably flint, had made a half-inch gash in the Iceman's left subclavian artery. Such a serious tear in the main vessel carrying oxygenated blood from the heart to the left arm would have caused uncontrollable bleeding that would almost immediately have been fatal.

Since that astonishing breakthrough, scientists have pieced together the Iceman's last days. Based on isotopes found in his teeth and bones and microscopic chips of mica in his intestines, researchers think he likely started his journey from the lower Val Venosta. He ascended a forested path into the mountains in the late spring or early summer, when pollen from blooming hop hornbeam flowers dusted the water and food he consumed. He wore three layers of garments and sturdy shoes with bearskin soles. He was well equipped with a flint-tipped dagger, a fire-starting kit, and a birch-bark container holding embers wrapped in maple leaves. He also carried the precious copper-bladed ax, which indicated he was likely a person of considerable social significance.

Yet he also headed into a harsh wilderness curiously under-armed. Only two of the 14 arrows in his deerskin quiver were completed. The six-foot longbow he carried was yet to be notched and strung with a cord in his quiver (now considered the oldest known bowstring in the world).

It appears he hiked in and out of pine forests at higher altitudes. When he reached a mountain pass now known as Tisenjoch, he likely paused to rest after completing a vertical climb of 6,500 feet from the valley below and to enjoy a meal. He did not know that the greasy, filling repast of ibex and grain would be his last.

An attacker, positioned behind and below his target, fired the arrow that struck the Iceman's left shoulder blade. Within minutes, the Iceman collapsed, lost consciousness, and bled out. Scientists suspect his assailant may have struck the back of his head as a final coup de grâce. The shaft of the arrow is broken, suggesting Ötzi struggled to extract it, or the killer removed it from the scene.

For all the answers that scientists have found about the Iceman, many questions still remain. Did the cuts on his hand and wrist result from an assault by younger rivals? What drove him up into the Alps so lightly armed? Who killed this elder, and why? Although not a single grunt or cry has passed through the Iceman's mummified lips in more than 5,000 years, the ongoing investigation continues to reveal new and startling things about life—and death—in the Stone Age.

15

IF STONES
COULD SPEAK

ca 3000 B.C. ◆ Wiltshire, England ◆ Neolithic

*Archaeologists have identified the homes and the quarries of
the builders of Stonehenge, completely changing the interpretation of England's most famous prehistoric monument.*

———◆———

When archaeologist Michael Parker Pearson launched the
multiyear Stonehenge Riverside Project in 2003 at
Durrington Walls in England, he and his team hoped
that the Neolithic site on the Salisbury Plain would have an avenue
connecting it to the River Avon just like Stonehenge, its famous
neighbor less than two miles away. After all, scientists had known
since the early 1800s that Durrington Walls was also a henge, a
circular earthen ditch-and-bank monument. It was later discovered
to be the largest known henge in Britain. Subsequent excavations
revealed that two timber circles once stood within the circle; they
might have served as monuments or ceremonial centers. Perhaps
the archaeologists would uncover other similarities and connections between Durrington Walls and Stonehenge.

To their great satisfaction, the team did uncover a broad roadway
90 feet wide and 560 feet long that led from the eastern entrance of
the Durrington Walls henge to the river. As they excavated along the
road, they made an even greater discovery: a cluster of seven small
Neolithic houses. The tiny wattle-and-daub dwellings, measuring

roughly 16 by 16 feet, had central hearths and clay floors, some with indentations of heels and, maybe, buttocks. Five of the houses showed evidence of furniture, including slot marks for the edges of wooden beds. Remains of a cooking area lay to one side, and food waste was found inside and outside the houses. Parker Pearson and the team realized the tremendous importance of the artifacts: They represented the village of the builders of Stonehenge.

More than a million people each year visit Stonehenge, the most famous relic of prehistory in Europe and one of the best known, most contemplated monuments in the world. Legends and theories abound about this mysterious 4,500-year-old site: That the wizard Merlin created it with the help of a giant, that aliens gave humans the technical know-how to build it, and so on. Over the decades, scientists have made great strides in their understanding of the extraordinary feat of prehistoric engineering. What was once viewed as standing in glorious isolation is now believed to be at the heart of a larger, elaborately sculpted, and historically rich landscape. "This is really all one monument complex," said Michael Parker Pearson. "Durrington Walls and Stonehenge are not two separate cultures and society. This is the same community."

> "This is really all one monument complex. Durrington Walls and Stonehenge are not two separate cultures and society. This is the same community."
>
> —*Michael Parker Pearson, archaeologist*

The iconic outer Sarsen Circle at Stonehenge took shape in about 2500 B.C. as the tall sandstone slabs were erected and the crosspieces were set in place, affixed by mortise-and-tenon joints taken straight from carpentry. On the summer solstice, the sun rises just to the left of the Heel Stone along the avenue to the entrance, and on the winter solstice, the sun would have set between the uprights of the tallest trilithon—which has since partially collapsed—and into the rock known as the Altar Stone.

But there is much more to Stonehenge, it turns out. Some 500 years earlier, a circular earthen ditch-and-bank monument 375 feet across was cut into the chalky ground together with a ring of pits now called the Aubrey holes. Parker Pearson and his team excavated one of those pits and discovered hints that it may have served as a hole for a bluestone, one of the megaliths that were moved inside the circle of sarsens during a later remodeling.

Also, Parker Pearson was able to track down the quarries where the bluestones were extracted, following up on the work of an early 20th-century geologist that identified the source of the bluestones as the Preseli Hills in western Wales. But that source was 180 miles away. Why hadn't the builders of Stonehenge used local stone?

Part of the mystery was solved in the team's 2021 publication of evidence suggesting that the bluestones may once have formed a henge in Wales. The site of Waun Mawn has toppled bluestones as well as empty sockets forming a circle that uniquely matches the earthen ditch enclosing Stonehenge. No other henge in Britain has those dimensions. Also, the entrance at Waun Mawn aligns with sunrise on the summer solstice, as it does at Stonehenge. The Welsh monument stood for 400 years until some of the local population migrated to Durrington Walls and transported the stones to Stonehenge. What prompted the move is unknown, but it would have been an arduous undertaking, given that each stone weighs some three tons.

At Durrington Walls, surveys have shown that the village had as many as 300 houses, making it the largest such Neolithic site found in Britain. The isotope analysis of bones found there revealed that grown animals were brought to the site from places across western and northern Britain and Wales.

Parker Pearson thinks that large groups came together from across the land to share in the enormous undertaking of constructing Stonehenge as well as its timber counterpart at Durrington Walls. The monoliths from Waun Mawn likely account for only a small portion of the 80 or more bluestones at Stonehenge, and he

Stonehenge worshippers once lived at Durrington Walls, a seasonally occupied village of wattle-and-daub houses with hearth-warmed plaster floors.

believes that the sandstones, too, were likely transported from earlier sites.

According to Parker Pearson's theory, Durrington Walls was the domain of the living, while Stonehenge was dedicated to the dead, and the two were linked by seasonal processions along a route formed by the carefully aligned avenues and the river. Stonehenge is, in fact, the largest cemetery in Britain from its time. Archaeologists have discovered the cremated remains of as many as 150 individuals, mostly men but also women and children. They date between 2600 and 2500 B.C., the era when Durrington Walls was inhabited. Parker Pearson believes that Stonehenge's relocated bluestones may have been a link to Welsh ancestors, the memory of a world before the migration.

The discoveries that continue to be made on the Salisbury Plain—and beyond—underscore how much may yet be revealed by archaeologists uncovering clues long hidden in the ancient landscape.

16

MASTERPIECES OF THE SAHARA

12,000–7000 B.C. ◆ Sahara, northern Africa ◆ Neolithic

*Stunning paintings and engravings on rock walls of the
Sahara recall a time when this desert was teeming with life.*

———◆———

One could hardly imagine a more desolate place than
Tassili-n-Ajjer, a devil's garden of grotesquely shaped
rock, heat, wind, and sand. Night brings biting cold to an
eerie moonscape. Yet this remote massif in Algeria is enlivened by
some 15,000 paintings and many more engravings. "I consider it
the world's greatest collection of prehistoric art," stated French
explorer Henri Lhote.

The very name Tassili-n-Ajjer, "plateau of the rivers," evokes a
time when the Sahara blossomed with life. As the last ice age waned
12,000 years ago, a shift in weather patterns brought a moist climate
to North Africa, making it a far more hospitable place than it is
today. The region was once home to Neolithic people who collected
grains, hunted buffalo with bows and arrows, and drove cattle over
grasslands where giraffes browsed and hippos wallowed in lakes.
That abundance and vitality of this lost landscape is preserved in
the region's art.

The local Algerian population had always known of the artwork
in their midst, but Europeans didn't learn of it until the mid-19th
century. The ethnic Tuareg who worked as guides described the

location of some known paintings, which were soon recorded and surveyed in German, French, and Swiss reports. In the 1930s, Lhote was among the early Western researchers to see the paintings. Since that first visit, he knew these artworks should be documented and publicized, but two decades passed before he could mount an expedition to study the mysterious scenes.

Traveling from the Algerian oasis village of Djanet with a 30-camel caravan, Lhote led a team of artists on an arduous two-week trek to Tassili. As they washed the dust-covered rocks—a damaging practice now forbidden—they were stunned by the vivid colors. The Tassili painters favored shades of yellow, red, and brown, made by mixing ocher with a liquid, which they applied with feathers or animal-hair brushes. To make reproductions, the team fought the wind to tape transparent paper over the paintings for tracing. From those, they made watercolor copies of 800 major works. Though some of Lhote's ideas and methods are considered controversial today, his publications about the Tassili artwork and a 1950s exhibition of reproductions at the Louvre helped introduce African rock images to the rest of the world and helped raise their reputation to the level of fine art.

Indeed David Coulson, founder of the Nairobi-based Trust for African Rock Art, wrote that when he first saw a Tassili engraving known as "The Crying Cows," he was "stunned by its almost Picassoan sophistication." In a 1999 report for *National Geographic,* he continued: "The cattle seem to emerge, horns first, from the rock face on which they were carved some 7,500 years ago. The artist chose his canvas carefully, looking for a surface that would catch the sun's rays and create depth and the illusion of motion through shadow. At the right time of year, as the light plays across this engraving, you can almost see the cattle move."

> **"At the right time of year, as the light plays across this engraving, you can almost see the cattle move."**
>
> —*David Coulson, archaeologist*

Tassili, covering an area of more than 27,000 square miles, is now a UNESCO World Heritage site, but across the wider Sahara region there are likely thousands more rock art sites. It has been difficult to date these artworks with scientific methods, but researchers have established a basic chronology based on the content, archaeological context, and superimposition of the paintings and engravings. A 4,000-year period starting 12,000 years ago, known as the Bubalus period, was dominated by engravings of large game animals. Then about 9,000 years ago, overlapping with the end of the Bubalus period, representations of people ushered in what experts called the Round Head period. By about 7,000 years

About 10,000 years ago, prehistoric artists engraved male and female giraffes more than 18 feet tall onto weathered sandstone in Niger's Ténéré Desert.

ago, domesticated livestock entered the scene—a momentous change immortalized in art of the Pastoral period.

Coulson has led various efforts to preserve rock art in the Sahara, including an operation to make a silicone impression of stunning rock giraffes in Niger that are between 9,000 and 7,000 years old. Their mold revealed small details, such as a line leading from the muzzle of each giraffe to a tiny human figure. The sheer size of the Sahara— 3.5 million square miles—and thousands of years of migration to and from the region make it difficult to track down the rock artists' descendants. Fortunately, some of the customs they chronicled, such as body painting, are easier to trace. Coulson noted striking similarities between the traditional clay-and-water body-paint patterns that the Surma of southern Ethiopia use to intimidate an opponent during ritual battles and the patterns in the massive engravings he saw in the Ennedi Massif in Chad with human figures as tall as nine feet.

Some Algerian Tuareg now act as custodians of Tassili-n-Ajjer or serve as tourism guides. Unlike Lhote, today's archaeologists are more likely to seek a collaborative partnership with the local population to advocate for the urgent preservation of these unique sites scattered across ethnic lines and national borders, and vast areas vulnerable to looters and weathering. "Africa's rock art is the common heritage of all Africans, but it is more than that," said Nelson Mandela in 2005. "It is the common heritage of humanity."

3000-1500 B.C.

── The Foundations of Society ──

What makes a civilization is often difficult to define, but most experts agree that the first examples developed in Mesopotamia. As nomads settled into urban areas, they developed stratified social classes, a division of labor, and a shared style of art and architecture; common laws and forms of communication, including written language, soon followed. The dawn of settled agriculture also meant surplus food, which allowed for pursuits beyond hunting, herding, and farming. The pioneering societies of this age left behind iconic testimonials to their significant achievements, from the Pyramids at Giza and the painted palaces of Knossos to the well-planned expanse of Harappa. For archaeologists who study them, bringing the stories of these early communities to light is a reward greater than gold.

Crowning the Giza Plateau, the pyramid tombs of Egypt's 4th-dynasty kings stand as enduring testaments to what human ingenuity can create.

17

THE DAWN OF ANCIENT EGYPT

2900 B.C. ◆ Abydos, Egypt ◆ Egyptian

A royal burial ground reveals startling clues about funerary practices during a formative period for civilization along the Nile.

———◆———

King Aha, "the fighter," was not killed while unifying the Nile's two warring kingdoms, nor while building the capital of Memphis. The details of his demise are hazy, but one history of Egypt written many centuries later suggests that the first ruler of a united Egypt was killed in a hunting accident after a reign of 62 years, unceremoniously trampled to death by a rampaging hippopotamus. News of his demise surely brought a separate, special terror to his staff. For many, the honor of serving the king in life would lead to the more dubious distinction of serving the king in death.

On the day of Aha's burial, experts believe, a solemn procession made its way through the sacred precinct of Abydos, the royal necropolis of Egypt's first kings. Led by priests in flowing white gowns, the funeral retinue included the royal family, vizier, treasurer, administrators, trade and tax officers, and Aha's successor, Djer. Just beyond the town's gates, the procession stopped at a monumental structure with imposing brick walls surrounding an open plaza. Inside the walls the priests waded through a cloud of incense to a small chapel, where they performed cryptic rites to seal Aha's immortality.

Outside, situated around the enclosure's walls, were six open graves. In a final act of devotion, or coercion, six people were poisoned and buried along with wine and food to take into the afterlife. One was a child of just four or five who was expensively furnished with ivory bracelets and tiny lapis beads.

The procession then headed westward into the setting sun, crossing sand dunes and moving up a dry riverbed to a remote cemetery at the base of a high desert plateau. Here, Aha's three-chambered tomb was stockpiled with provisions for a lavish life in eternity. There were large cuts of ox meat, freshly killed waterbirds, loaves of bread, cheese, dried figs, jars of beer, and dozens of wine vessels each bearing Aha's official seal. Beside his tomb, more than 30 graves were laid out in three neat rows. As Aha's body was lowered into a brick-lined chamber, a select group of loyal courtiers and servants took poison and joined their king in the next world.

Is this how an Egyptian king's funeral in 2900 B.C. actually unfolded? It's a plausible scenario, experts say. For more than a century, archaeologists have been drilling through the dry sands of the immense royal burial center at Abydos, 260 miles up the Nile from Cairo. Now they have found compelling evidence that ancient Egyptians indeed engaged in human sacrifice, shedding new light on one of the most celebrated ancient civilizations of all.

Work on the graves and ceremonial funerary enclosures from Egypt's 1st dynasty has uncovered evidence from a pivotal period when Aha and other kings laid down the roots of religion, government, and architecture that would last for the next 3,000 years. All of the 1st-dynasty tombs and most of the enclosures excavated so far are accompanied by subsidiary graves—hundreds in some cases—containing the remains of elite officials and courtiers. Egyptologists have long speculated that these graves might hold victims of sacrifice, but also acknowledged that they could simply be graves

Arranged like a fleet moored at a wharf, 5,000-year-old wooden boats were buried at Abydos with one of Egypt's earliest kings for his use in the next world.

reserved for the king's staff, ready to use as each person died naturally.

When British archaeologist W. M. Flinders Petrie excavated heavily looted 1st-dynasty tombs in the early 1900s, he found 35 subsidiary graves beside Aha's tomb. Although he didn't dwell on it in his published papers, he hinted at human sacrifice. Modern experts also believe the evidence strongly suggests this scenario, because it's unlikely that 41 people—the six at Aha's enclosure plus 35 at his tomb—would have died of natural causes at the same time, and the skeletons showed no signs of trauma. "The method of their demise is still a mystery," explained associate dig director Matthew Adams. "My guess is that they were drugged."

Enthusiasm for this grim practice seems to have waned quickly, though. By the 2nd dynasty, it had simply stopped. Instead, funerary statuettes began to appear. In time, grave goods began to include legions of *shabtis*—small figurines that were meant to magically come alive in the afterlife to serve the deceased.

This period at Abydos also suggests that boats were thought to be crucial elements of the afterlife. In 1991 dig director David O'Connor found an eerie fleet of 14 wooden vessels, each buried in an enormous brick-lined grave. "Huge wooden boats, brought to this desert location, make quite a statement of royal power and privilege," said O'Connor's colleague Matthew Adams. Measuring up to 75 feet long, the boats were expertly crafted and had been fully functional when buried; later studies revealed that they were likely made of local tamarisk wood for an early ruler, perhaps even Aha. They proved to be the world's oldest surviving boats built of planks (as opposed to those made of reeds or hollowed-out logs).

> **"Huge wooden boats, brought to this desert location, make quite a statement of royal power and privilege."**
> —*Matthew Adams, archaeologist*

"The boats are like the servants who were buried at Abydos," said O'Connor. "The king intended to use them in the afterlife in the same manner that he used them before his death."

In life, the boats enabled the kings to travel rapidly up and down the Nile in a powerful display of wealth and military might. Because the Egyptian kings also expected to be kings in the afterlife, the boats would be useful tools. It was a concept that would endure as a key element of religious imagery for the rest of the pharaonic era—a sign of hope that in the wake of death comes eternal life.

18

UNTOLD RICHES IN UR'S ROYAL TOMBS

2600–2300 B.C. ◆ Iraq ◆ Sumerian

The historic excavation unearthed a royal cemetery bursting with treasure and hints of mass human sacrifice.

━━◆━━

I t started with two trenches, dug without much ceremony by hundreds of workmen hired in 1922 by Leonard Woolley, a British archaeologist tasked with turning a dust-swept floodplain into the largest archaeological dig in Iraq's history. From those two trenches would emerge the ancient city of Ur—and a network of royal tombs bursting with some of antiquity's most stunning treasures.

Shifting sands had swallowed the city itself, but at least the towering peak of the ziggurat stayed visible. The first extensive excavation was a joint mission mounted by the British Museum and the University of Pennsylvania Museum. They commissioned Woolley to lead the project based on his experience excavating in Crete, Turkey, and Egypt, and the daring he'd shown as an intelligence officer for British forces during World War I. But the intrepid archaeologist's strongest qualification was his exacting approach to archaeology. Yes, he longed to pull a cache of riches from the sand, but he wouldn't allow the excavation to devolve into a mere treasure hunt. Only by preceding methodically would his team be able to peel back the layers of time all the way to the city's founders.

The ancient city of Ur played an important role in Sumerian society. Located about 140 miles southeast of Babylon in what is now Iraq, it was once a bustling urban center due to its strategic positioning near the juncture of the Tigris and Euphrates Rivers in fertile Mesopotamia. It is also mentioned in the Bible as the hometown of the biblical patriarch Abraham. One of the first cities in the world, Ur was dominated by its distinctive ziggurat, a stepped pyramid built of mud brick. Ur's patron deity, Nanna, would choose a woman to serve as high priestess by sending an omen to the royal family. Usually the king's daughter, the priestess would live on the temple platform, perform ceremonial duties, and serve as the god's human wife.

Beginning in the third millennium B.C., Ur became a bureaucratic and cultural hub of 20 to 30 competing city-states. Under three different dynasties, it witnessed the technological, cultural, and urban flourishing of a people credited with inventing the hallmarks of civilization as we know it, including law, urban planning, and writing.

In one of Woolley's trenches, the team found ruins; in the other, gold artifacts. They were excited to pursue what they called the "gold trench," but Woolley put off digging for what he suspected was a complex of tombs. Not only were his men too inexperienced to tackle a complicated burial excavation, Woolley was convinced they had stolen some of the gold and precious stones that had already been uncovered. Instead, he had the team focus on the ziggurat and the public buildings they unearthed around it.

At last, during his fifth season at the site, Woolley gave the green light to work on the gold trench. In just three months, they uncovered over 600 tombs; within eight years, they would uncover almost 2,000 burials. Assisted by a young British archaeologist named Max Mallowan, Woolley meticulously oversaw the slow, careful excavation.

Among the most impressive tombs in the cemetery complex was the tomb of a woman identified as Queen Pu-abi. Her entire body was strewn with precious beads, and her fingers were adorned with 10 rings. She wore an elaborate headdress sparkling with golden leaves and strings of lapis lazuli and carnelian beads, which field assistant Katharine Keeling painstakingly reconstructed from the surviving fragments. Possessions like makeup and a chariot also spoke to her wealth and position. The bodies of servants and soldiers surrounded her.

In another chamber, which Woolley called the Great Death Pit, were the bodies of six men and 68 elaborately dressed women arranged in careful order. "As we cleared the shaft . . . it appeared almost as if we were treading on a carpet of gold, such was the wealth of jewelry," Mallowan later wrote. Woolley had a less glamorous take on the excavation. "I'm sick to death of getting out gold headdresses," he wrote.

The number of bodies, the relative lack of men, and the arrangement of the corpses fascinated the archaeologists, who surmised that the deceased had taken some kind of poison before the burial. Later analysis has shown that at least some of the people buried in the tombs had suffered blunt-force head trauma, supporting a hypothesis that the dead were killed and taken into the tomb and arranged before rigor mortis set in. It remains unclear if the bodies represent willing victims or coerced sacrifices.

For Mallowan, the site also yielded another kind of treasure: He met his future wife, detective novelist Agatha Christie, on the dig. Christie, who was fascinated by archaeology, would later set *Murder in Mesopotamia* on an archaeological dig in Iraq, and dedicated her novel *Murder on the Orient Express* to Mallowan. They were not the only match made at the excavation site: Katharine Keeling took on the role as second in command of the dig and later married Woolley, though hers was a marriage of convenience, as British society wouldn't tolerate a single woman working as an archaeologist.

All in all, the expedition yielded tens of thousands of artifacts, now housed in the British Museum, the University of Pennsylvania's museum, and Iraq's state museum. The treasure's undeniable allure draws crowds to this day, but Woolley's greater wish came true: The Sumerians are recognized for their pioneering contributions to human civilization.

The most richly adorned woman in the Great Death Pit—one of the mass burials uncovered at the Sumerian site of Ur in Iraq—wore this stunning array of jewelry.

19

PEACEFUL CITIES OF THE INDUS VALLEY

2500–1900 B.C. ◆ Indus Valley, Pakistan ◆ Indus

Ruined cities Mohenjo Daro and Harappa reveal
advanced urban planning and sophisticated writing.
Was this achieved without a ruler or an army?

———◆———

In the 1850s, British railroad builders in the Indus Valley needed ballast for a new track. They sent laborers into Punjab Province, where the latter found piles of old bricks to cart away. When archaeological surveyor Rakhaldas Banerji began excavating in the area some seven decades later, it became clear those railway workers had unwittingly scattered rare evidence of the ancient Indus culture's surprisingly urban sophistication.

One of the most rewarding sites proved to be Harappa. Nearly 400 acres in size and with 20,000 or more inhabitants, Harappa was among the largest cities of a civilization that flourished from roughly 2500 to 1900 B.C. along the Indus and other rivers in Pakistan and India. Harappa was spread over five large mounds that expanded over the centuries as people continually raised houses and laid down streets over the constructions of their ancestors.

Harappa was probably one of many urban centers linked by trade and kinship that made up what is usually known today as the Indus civilization. The Indus territory was a Texas-size quarter million square miles, reaching from the Arabian Sea north to the Himalayan foothills and east to New Delhi. The Indus people employed the wheel for transport as well as to turn pottery, and they were the first to make large-scale use of fire-hardened bricks in construction.

The people of Harappa left behind more than piles of bricks, however. Archaeologists have uncovered thousands of examples of script, leading them to believe that the people of Harappa developed the earliest form of writing known in the Indian subcontinent. Seals the size of a postage stamp, usually of stone, bear writing as well as carved figures that may be deities. But despite the efforts of many scholars, the symbols have yet to yield a credible sentence—a major reason that the Indus culture, surely one of the greatest of the ancient world, has remained vexingly obscure. "To try to solve all the riddles is like picking up pebbles on a seashore," confessed Indian archaeologist Ravindra Singh Bisht.

> "To try to solve all the riddles is like picking up pebbles on a seashore."
> —*Ravindra Singh Bisht, archaeologist*

Maybe even more significant are the things *not* found: no remains of great temples such as Mesopotamia's or sumptuous tombs such as those that ushered Egypt's pharaohs to the next world. In other words, no evidence of a kingship or theocracy. "Rather, what we see in Harappa is an elaborate middle-class society," says archaeologist Richard Meadow, whose years of work with his colleague J. Mark Kenoyer has broadened and deepened our knowledge of the Indus culture. The archaeologists wonder if Harappa even had an army. Although a few weapons have been unearthed, no carved pieces depict war scenes like those in the sculpture and texts of Egypt and Mesopotamia.

Almost 40 feet long, and sealed with gypsum plaster and bitumen, the
Great Bath at Mohenjo Daro likely served in rituals of purification and renewal.

Other finds indicate that Harappa was a city of craftsmen and
traders. Its merchants probably sent goods to other Indus urban
centers and also to Oman and the Persian Gulf region. Working several kinds of stone, gold, and silver, artisans turned out exquisite
jewelry. More than 60 sites have yielded seals and tokens. Traders
supplied Harappan artisans with raw materials such as lapis lazuli
from what is now Afghanistan. From the Arabian Sea, 500 miles to
the south, came conch shells to be sawed into bangles.

From artifacts like these, it seems clear that as many as 53 centuries ago, the Harappan people were linked to a vast trade network.
Much of that trade likely traveled on the Ravi River, eventually
reaching the Indus. And some of it surely went by that river to
Mohenjo Daro, Harappa's sister city some 400 miles to the south.

A well-planned street grid and an elaborate drainage system hint
that the city's occupants were skilled urban planners with a reverence
for the control of water. Sitting on elevated ground, Mohenjo Daro
spread out over about 250 acres on a series of mounds, like Harappa.
According to Kenoyer, the mounds grew organically over the centuries as people kept building platforms and walls for their houses.

Also like Harappa, Mohenjo Daro lacks ostentatious palaces, temples, or monuments despite the evidence of its wealth and stature. With no obvious central seat of government or evidence of a king or queen, it was likely governed as a city-state, perhaps staffed by elected officials or elites from each of the mounds. Modesty, order, and cleanliness were apparently important. Pottery and tools of copper and stone were standardized. Seals and weights suggest a system of tightly controlled trade. A watertight pool called the Great Bath, perched on top of a mound of dirt and held in place with walls of baked brick, is the closest structure Mohenjo Daro has to a temple.

After a thousand years of resilience, the Indus civilization faded from history. Paleoclimatologists point to a 200-year drought that began around 2000 B.C. and suspended monsoon rains in the Indus Valley at the same time as a drought threatened civilizations across Bronze Age civilizations in Egypt, Greece, and Mesopotamia. Archaeologists puzzle over the few clues that may indicate the reason for the Indus cities' decline. Kenoyer suggests that the Indus River changed course, which would have hampered the local agricultural economy and Mohenjo Daro's importance as a center of trade. But no evidence exists that flooding destroyed the city, and the city wasn't totally abandoned, Kenoyer says.

Enough of the structures remained to evoke a sense of awe among the first archaeologists who arrived to survey the site in 1922. The survey's director, Englishman John Marshall, wrote that the Indus people possessed an "advanced and singularly uniform civilization . . . in some respects even superior to that of contemporary Mesopotamia and Egypt." Although he was an appointee of the empire of Great Britain, Marshall promoted Indian scholarship and advocated for the artifacts to stay on the subcontinent rather than be shipped back to Britain. His dedication to conservation alongside discovery helped preserve this priceless World Heritage site. Now future generations of archaeologists have a chance to decipher the mysteries of the Indus Valley.

20

EGYPT'S PYRAMID BUILDERS

2550–2470 B.C. ◆ Giza, Egypt ◆ Egyptian

*Excavations have revealed the lives of the laborers
and overseers who raised the monumental wonders
at Giza more than 4,000 years ago.*

———◆———

Mention ancient Egypt to most people and they will likely think of the Sphinx and the three great Pyramids at Giza, which today make up the most famous site from the Old Kingdom. That familiarity makes it easy to forget that basic questions about that early time have remained unanswered. Only within the past few decades have Egyptologists begun to fill in the gaps, sifting through the sands for clues about enduring monuments and the people who built them.

Archaeologist Mark Lehner has been working on Giza's desert plateau for more than 40 years. "We've focused too much on *how* the pyramids were built," he says. "I'm less interested in how the Egyptians built the pyramids than in how the pyramids built Egypt." His excavations have gradually uncovered evidence of the lives of the pyramid workers, and of the impact that the immense construction projects had on the country as a whole.

> "I'm less interested in how the Egyptians built the pyramids than in how the pyramids built Egypt."
>
> —*Mark Lehner, archaeologist*

"Imagine yourself as a 15-year-old kid in some rural village of about 200 people in the 27th century B.C.," said Lehner. "One day the pharaoh's men come. They say, 'You, and you, and you.' You get on a boat and sail down the Nile. You don't know where you're going, or why. Eventually you come around a bend and you see this huge geometric structure, like nothing you've ever known. There are hundreds of people working on it. They put you to work. And someone keeps track of you: your name, your hours, your rations. All this was a profoundly socializing experience. You might go back to your village, but you would never again be the same."

In the early 1990s, Lehner and Zahi Hawass, then director general of the Giza Pyramids and Saqqara, began to excavate two sites near the pyramids in their search for signs of the pyramid builders. Within months they hit pay dirt. Lehner found a pair of adjacent mud-brick rooms that were Egypt's oldest known bakery. Its ovens once turned out golden loaves of bread, a staple food of the workers, along with beef, fish, and hearty beer. Next door, Lehner would uncover a large building, likely a commissary for the workers. South of the Sphinx lay the remains of a community where as many as 20,000 people may have lived, and barracks where 2,000 people could have slept at one time.

Hawass, meanwhile, unearthed a cemetery of some 600 tombs nearby: the graves of workers. He discovered evidence of toil in their skeletons, their vertebrae compressed and damaged by years of carrying heavy loads. Some were missing fingers and even limbs. A few of the tombs were adorned with mini-pyramids several feet high, made of mud brick. Nothing like them had been found before.

In the past, experts believed that the pyramid-shaped tomb was invented for royalty. But Hawass argued the pyramid form may have arisen among the common people. He believed that the mini-pyramids evolved from sacred mounds found in tombs long before the Old Kingdom—the first era of royal dynasties after independent regions had been united into one country. The pyramids built for the kings may have been, as Hawass put it, "just more enduring examples of traditional folk architecture."

In the work of these archaeologists and others may lie the origins of a whole new way of seeing the Old Kingdom: not just as a brilliant civilization of the elite trickling down to the masses, but also as a culture built from the bottom up, standing on the daily toil of workers and the very beliefs and values of ordinary men and women.

From excavation, and from scenes carved on the walls of tombs, researchers have begun to fill in the details of everyday life at Giza. A pyramid—the mystical gateway for a king's leap to the afterlife—drew resources from all of Egypt. From a population of as many as a million and a half souls, farmworkers were conscripted into national service in a rotating roster, while provincial shipments of crops and domesticated animals fed workers and managers during construction. "It was a coming together of people from throughout the land," said Lehner. "By coming and working in this place, it socialized information and bound all these disparate areas, these provinces, into a whole. It was really the beginnings of Egyptian unity."

The labor was certainly hard. For one pyramid, workers hauled an estimated 23 million limestone and granite blocks, most weighing 2.5 tons, and possibly set a block in place every two and a half minutes. Although Herodotus, the ancient Greek historian, declared that 100,000 men were needed to build one of the Giza Pyramids, Lehner calculated that as few as 10,000 could have pulled off the job. As he put it, "A pyramid turns out to be a very doable thing."

The entire Egyptian society was built around a preoccupation with these preparations for the king's immortal life. But why? "What held the Old Kingdom together was not so much a belief in the divine nature of the king as a belief that through the king was expressed the divine nature of society itself," explained German

Archaeologist Anna Wodzińska examines pottery uncovered at the pyramid builders' settlement at Giza, including various bowls, bread molds, and a beer jar.

archaeologist Rainer Stadelmann. "Much later, after the fall of the Old Kingdom, Egypt would become something like a police state. But in the Old Kingdom, the people really believed in the importance of building a pyramid. It's like a small town that builds a huge cathedral in the Middle Ages. Faith is the spur."

21

THE "PRINCESS" OF KHOK PHANOM DI

2000–1500 B.C. ◆ Thailand ◆ Neolithic

A mysterious woman buried with over 120,000 shimmering, handmade beads is recovered from a bountiful burial plot in Thailand that spans 20 generations.

———◆———

Environmental changes can make it hard—or impossible—to recover the archaeological remains of past societies, particularly in oceanbound communities. But in Thailand, a multigenerational cemetery survived thousands of years of rising and falling sea levels, bearing witness to those climate cycles and preserving information on how the area's inhabitants adapted over time. That alone would have made Khok Phanom Di worth excavating. Then archaeologists uncovered a stunning grave: Thailand's "Princess Di," a mysterious woman who brought exquisite wealth with her into the afterlife and whose careful preservation shed light on the funeral rituals and daily lives of her people.

In 1984, archaeologist Charles Higham was working on another dig in Thailand when his colleagues told him about Khok Phanom Di, a large burial mound on the floodplain of the Bang Pakong River near the Gulf of Thailand. Higham and his colleagues dug through

30 feet of deposits and uncovered layer after layer of graves. The bones covered 17 to 20 generations—154 graves in all.

Only a few months into the dig, Higham unearthed a pyramid of clay cylinders. "Things were getting exciting," he later recalled. "Down we went, over a metre, until suddenly the grave-fill turned blood red. It was red ochre, and some of it covered a human skull." Inside the grave lay a woman's skeleton, a variety of pottery vessels, and equipment thought to be used to create pottery. Her entire skeleton was covered in beads.

The woman had been buried near two children: One of them, an 18-month-old baby, was also covered in ocher and buried with thousands of shell beads and a miniature potter's anvil.

"Ultimately, we counted over 120,000 disc beads that had been stitched onto at least two, possibly three, garments of a woman who died probably in her 30s," Higham later wrote. "She would literally have dazzled in reflected sunlight when she walked across Khok Phanom Di 3,600 years ago." Because of her glittering finery and her seemingly high status within her community, Higham and his colleague, Rachanie Thosarat, dubbed her "the princess."

Based on the quality of the pottery and the strength of the woman's wrist muscles, the archaeologists concluded she was likely a master potter. A man of similar age buried nearby was decorated with 56,000 beads, a turtle shell carapace, and a pottery vessel. More sinister, a shallow grave to her right contained a headless male.

The woman's status may also have been reflected in the details of her grave; though her grave faced eastward, like others at the site, it was larger and deeper than most others in the burial area.

The bodies within the burial mound reflect the ability of hunter-gatherer societies to adapt to environmental changes. The first settlement was on the bank of a mangrove-lined estuary that offered a rich diet of marine animals. When the sea level fell, men in the community stopped paddling canoes as evidenced by the abrupt decrease in upper-body strength in the bodies from that era. When there was more plentiful freshwater, the residents made

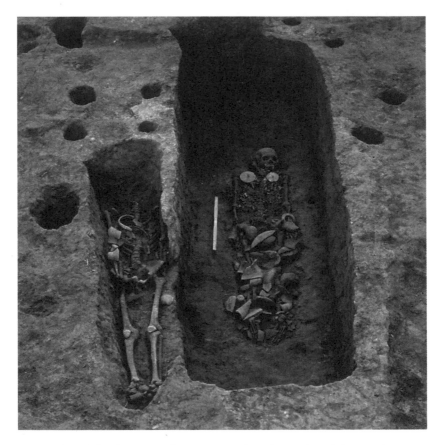

In burials by the Bang Pakong River, archaeologists found the remains
of a woman who was likely a master potter, with a headless man at her side.

agricultural tools for growing crops. Archaeologists offer differing
views on whether the family group descended from coastal hunter-
gatherers or immigrant rice farmers of inland groups. It is unclear
what role the "princess" actually played within her community, and
some experts dislike the moniker because it does not seem that the
group had any kind of royal tradition.

Nevertheless, the generations of burials show meaningful rituals. The dig at Khok Phanom Di preserved evidence of a family
that clearly clung to tradition—and buried its dead with items that
had mattered during their lives.

22

KNOSSOS' CRYPTIC TABLETS

1750–1490 B.C. ◆ Crete ◆ Minoan, Mycenaean

*In a labyrinthine palace, Arthur Evans discovered
tablets scrawled with Europe's oldest written language,
which would stump scholars for decades.*

———◆———

After Mycenae was excavated in mainland Greece in the late 19th century, the trail of discovery for the heroic Bronze Age led southward across the Aegean to the island of Crete, the legendary home of King Minos. Unmistakable clues that something very ancient was to be found there—in the form of huge *pithoi,* or storage jars for grain or olive oil or wine—had come to light on a hill called Kephala, just south of Heraklion, thanks to a short-lived excavation by a Greek amateur archaeologist, Minos Kalokairinos. German businessman turned archaeologist Heinrich Schliemann, the excavator of Troy and Mycenae, attempted to buy the site, as others had before him, but the price was exorbitant, and Crete was governed by a Turkish administration not disposed to approve the excavation. After Schliemann withdrew, Kephala was bought by a British man named Arthur Evans, who was wealthy, well educated, and filled with a lively curiosity about an unknown script he had seen on some Cretan sealstones in Athens. Like other scholars, Evans had been surprised that Schliemann found no evidence of writing among the ruins of Mycenae's advanced civilization. "Was it possible that such master-pieces . . . were the work of 'Man before Writing'?" Evans wrote. "Such a conclusion I could not bring myself to accept." He hoped he might be able to resolve this conundrum in Crete.

> **"Was it possible that such masterpieces . . . were the work of 'Man before Writing'? Such a conclusion I could not bring myself to accept."**
>
> —*Arthur Evans, archaeologist*

In 1900, after Crete gained political autonomy, Evans started to open ground at Kephala and discovered the totally unsuspected splendors of Knossos. An entire previously unknown civilization of vast material accomplishment and artistic achievement was now revealed. A labyrinth indeed, the complex Evans uncovered, which he called "Palace of Minos," had hundreds of rooms and was bigger than Buckingham Palace. Few would have been surprised had Evans announced that in the midst of the maze he had found the bones of the Minotaur.

The Minoans flourished between 2000 and 1500 B.C. Ships of this first maritime empire dominated the commerce of the Eastern Mediterranean and the Aegean Sea, where copper and tin were traded for the all-important production of bronze. Later archaeological excavations revealed that Crete was highly urbanized by this time, with Knossos perhaps the most dominant center.

Evans's vast labors at Knossos extended over 25 years. Not content with unearthing the palace, he reconstructed it in parts, a procedure the more meticulous archaeologists would later scorn, yet one that has helped make Knossos an international tourist attraction for those who want to experience the Minoan world. "What an alluring world it was," wrote Joseph Judge, a *National Geographic* editor who visited Crete for a 1978 article, with "its bull-leaping spectacles, its lithesome men and handsome, bare-breasted women, its great goddess with her snakes and doves and dances in the sacred groves . . . And its essential peace; we know of not a single fortified Minoan site." The lack of defensive infrastructure or military garrisons led scholars to believe that the Minoan age marked a peaceful era on the Aegean Sea. More recent excavations have uncovered Minoan fortifications. Regardless, any stretches of peace and prosperity the Minoans enjoyed came to an abrupt halt.

At the zenith of its power and brilliance in the 15th century B.C., the Minoan civilization collapsed in flames. The end was so sudden and emphatic that some scholars initially attributed it to the volcanic eruption at Santorini, some 70 miles north of Crete, though newer scientific evidence suggests that this natural disaster happened a century or more earlier. Others cite the all too familiar pattern of aggression and plunder by invaders bent on conquest— perhaps the Mycenaeans from mainland Greece, who we know later took over Knossos before its final destruction.

A sprawling, multistory complex, the Knossos palace had spaces for religious ceremonies, stunning frescoes, and a plumbing system, but little fortification.

Fragments of a fresco discovered at the palace of Knossos inspired this re-creation of what the original may have shown—a trio of finely dressed women.

Perhaps far greater than Evans's discovery of an alabaster throne, expressive wall paintings, and wooden columns at Knossos was his discovery of clay tablets scrawled with a hieroglyph-type script and filed away in boxes like bureaucratic records. Evans later wrote that finding this writing at Knossos was "the dramatic fulfillment of my most sanguine expectations." Some of the tablets were written in what Evans called Linear A, a still undeciphered form of writing. Most of the tablets were marked with a script Evans labeled Linear B and dated to the later Mycenaean occupation of the site. This early written form of Greek would remain undecipherable for decades, despite the persistent work of scholars and amateur codebreakers, and Evans would die (in 1941) before getting the chance to read the enigmatic tablets. The Yale instructor and military cryptanalyst Emmett L. Bennett, Jr., made great strides by cataloging the Linear B signs into a definitive list of about 80 syllables, and an American classics professor Alice Kober came extremely close to cracking the code before her death in 1950. A passionate amateur, English architect Michael Ventris, finally deciphered Linear B in 1952.

Inscriptions in this ancient language have been found beyond Knossos, at Mycenae, Thebes, Pylos, and other centers of the Mycenaean world. Ventris thought the translated script would be Etruscan or an indigenous Cretan language but was surprised to find that theory was incorrect. He described his breakthrough to BBC Radio: "During the last two weeks I've suddenly come to the conclusion that the Knossos and Pylos tablets must after all be written in Greek. A difficult and archaic Greek, seeing that it's written 500 years older than Homer, and written in a rather abbreviated form, but Greek none the less. Once I made this assumption most of the peculiarities of the language and spelling which had puzzled me seemed to find a logical explanation. And, although many of the tablets remain as incomprehensible as before, many others are suddenly beginning to make sense." The translation revealed no great works of literature—the Knossos tablets held mostly mundane administrative records such as lists of livestock, commodities, and land leases—but cracking the riddle of the labyrinth opened the door to many more possibilities.

The tablets document a pivotal moment just before the destruction of palatial centers across the Mediterranean like Knossos, known as the Late Bronze Age collapse. Archaeologists cannot fully explain this phenomenon, but it ushered in a dark age in the Aegean for several centuries before ancient Greek culture would reach another apex in the classical age. These writings at Knossos are witness to the everyday interactions of Mycenaeans just before the world as they knew it went to ruin. We are still awaiting the answer to what language the Linear A tablets bear, however. Perhaps their eventual decipherment will help solve the mystery of the origins of the Minoan civilization.

23

THE LAW CODE
OF HAMMURABI

ca 1792–1750 B.C. ✦ Susa, Iran ✦ Babylonian

*Etched onto a stone monument
is one of history's most famous sets of laws.*

———✦———

A towering monument to a Babylonian king's sense of justice, the Code of Hammurabi is one of history's oldest, and most influential, bodies of law. Inscribed on an imposing, 7.4-foot-tall basalt stela, Hammurabi's laws offer a tantalizing view into everyday life in the Mesopotamian civilization of the First Babylonian Empire.

The black basalt artifact was discovered in 1901 by Swiss archaeologist Gustave Jéquier, a member of a French delegation excavating in the ancient city of Susa, located at the crossroads of several great civilizations dating to prehistory. The archaeologists found a treasure trove of artifacts and managed to snag exclusive rights to display them under a convention with the shah, who only charged them for the gold and silver artifacts.

Covered in cuneiform script, the stela is now held by the Louvre, where the expedition leader, Jacques de Morgan, brought it. Its text was decoded and first translated from Akkadian to French by Jean-Vincent Scheil, a Dominican priest and noted Assyriologist, in 1902.

It is thought to be one of several similar stelae erected in cities ruled by Hammurabi, a member of the nomadic Amorite tribes and the Babylonian Empire's first major king, who ruled from about 1792 to 1750 B.C. Regardless of where it first stood, the stela was brought to Susa as plunder by Shutruk-Nahhunte, a rival Elamite king, in the 12th century B.C. By the time it was recovered in modern times, it had been broken into three pieces.

Though the original location of the stela is unknown, Hammurabi's profound legacy is not. During his reign, the king expanded the city-state of Babylon into an empire by conquering neighboring cities. Along the way, he developed an ongoing interest in his people's legal disputes and recognized the law as a tool to consolidate power. His lengthy codex covered everything from standard wages to domestic disputes and violent crimes. Its purpose, he declared poetically, was to cause justice "to rise like the sun over the people, and to light up the land."

The magnificence of the stela and its public display were carefully calculated to reinforce the eminence and divinity of the king and to ensure his memory was preserved. Such imposing stones were erected in temples, but the codes were also copied onto stone tablets and circulated throughout the empire. The carving at the top of the example in the Louvre shows the sun deity, Shamash, seated on a throne as he gifts Hammurabi the symbols of sovereignty and justice. The inscription urges people with legal disputes to meet beneath the image of the king standing before Shamash, hear the words of his code, and pray to him. "Let him read the inscription, and understand my precious words," the stela reads. "Let him see his judgement, let his heart become soothed."

> **"Let him see his judgement, let his heart become soothed."**
>
> *—Hammurabi, Babylonian ruler*

Hammurabi's laws weren't the first in the ancient world, but their age and the impressive number—282 total—made the discovery at Susa exceptionally valuable. The infamous concept of "an eye for an eye, a tooth for a tooth" is brutish by today's standards, but it mirrors the style of justice by retribution common at the time.

Babylonian values and customs are evident in these civil laws. Corn, oil, and cattle come up repeatedly as important commodities that were used as wages and currency. In an interesting preview of labor economics, standard wages fluctuated based on effort and productivity. For instance, day laborers received a marginal bump in pay during long, hot summer days. Laws dictate the rights of concubines, apprentices, and enslaved people—all common positions in ancient Mesopotamia. Men who couldn't pay their loans could gain a temporary reprieve by washing their "debt-tablet" in water—evidence of both loan forgiveness and a written system for keeping records.

The code was not intended as a democratic equalizer; it reflects the status-driven hierarchy of Babylonian society. It favored people of wealth and rank, who were required only to pay a fine if they injured or killed an individual of a lower class. If a physician healed a man's broken bone, the patient owed his doctor five shekels. But if the healer accidentally killed a patient of high status during an operation, his hands would be cut off. The code also favored men over women. For instance, adultery by a husband might go unpunished, but an unfaithful wife would be executed.

Despite such inequities, the laws promulgated by Hammurabi offered certain protections to women, commoners, and enslaved people, and promised that his law ensured that the "strong may not oppress the weak." Wives could sue an adulterous husband for divorce, and a man divorcing his wife had to pay her a settlement or return the marriage dowry. If a man had a child with an enslaved woman, he was not required to leave the child an inheritance, but both mother and child were entitled to freedom. All defendants were somewhat shielded from false testimony by a law prescribing the death penalty for witnesses who committed perjury.

A basalt stela more than seven feet tall bears 282 laws enacted by Babylonian king Hammurabi, the most complete list of legal codes surviving from antiquity.

Hammurabi's dynasty lasted only a few generations before it toppled, but his code of laws set a vital and enduring precedent. Putting laws in writing discouraged judges from ruling arbitrarily and promoted the idea of justice as universal. As the king conquered new lands, people with different customs and conceptions of justice were united under one code—common laws that discouraged them from taking the law into their own hands. Future emperors, from Augustus Caesar to Napoleon Bonaparte, would replicate this strategy. Today, Hammurabi imperiously oversees justice served from a marble frieze in the U.S. Supreme Court.

At the bottom of the stela, Hammurabi condemns all future kings who ignore his rules: "[M]ay their destinies be cursed, their kingdoms overthrown, their people scattered, and their very existence forgotten." The effects of the curse remain to be seen, but one thing is certain: Thanks to this stone monument for justice, Hammurabi will never be forgotten.

24

THE MINOAN "POMPEII"

ca 1600 B.C. ◆ Santorini, Greece ◆ Minoan

*Buried beneath volcanic debris, Akrotiri provides
vivid glimpses into everyday life during
the Bronze Age's glittering zenith.*

———◆———

In the piercing Aegean sunlight, the Greek island of Santorini—
also called Thera—can seem a dream of stillness and peace.

It is not. The island and its satellites are the shattered shell
of a mighty and still active volcano. In past epochs Thera has
erupted, subsided, and erupted again, visiting death and devasta-
tion upon a wide area. The sea has flooded through the blasted
crater walls that now form Thera's bay. So deep is this old crater,
or caldera—1,300 feet in places—that ships cannot anchor in it.

More than 3,500 years ago, Thera blew its top in one of the biggest eruptions humans witnessed in the past 10,000 years. The
mammoth upheaval darkened the sky, created a tidal wave, and
cloaked the island with layers of pumice and ash as thick as 200 feet.

Buried under the volcanic debris near the south coast of Thera
is the ancient site of Akrotiri. The Minoan town was destroyed in
the disaster and possibly inspired the legend of the lost city of
Atlantis. It's also one of the best preserved prehistoric settlements
in Europe, with private homes, workshops, and spectacular artworks fixed in time like an Aegean Pompeii.

The seafaring, copper-trading Minoan civilization that dominated the Eastern Mediterranean in the Bronze Age—long before the Greek or Roman Empires—was born just 70 miles to the south, on Crete. For generations, archaeologists have attempted to find the cause for its mysterious demise.

In the 1930s, Greek archaeologist Spyridon Marinatos theorized that an eruption on Thera was to blame for the Minoan cradle's demise, since a tsunami triggered by the blast could have flooded and destroyed much of it. World War II and the Greek Civil War delayed Marinatos's search for direct proof on the "strange, sinister" island of Thera. In 1967, he finally began a systematic excavation in a ravine near Akrotiri, then a poor and remote village without electricity or a road connecting it to the other towns on the island. Santorini, now synonymous with glamorous vacations, was still years away from its major tourist boom.

In the 19th century, a French company mining pumice unearthed prehistoric buildings and pottery at Akrotiri, and archaeologists found scattered artifacts in the area, but Marinatos's discoveries offered an unprecedented glimpse into everyday life for a wealthy outpost of Minoan Crete. Within the first few hours of digging on a hot summer day, Marinatos and his crew discovered loose stones with fragments of imported Cretan pottery he thought had been made sometime around 1520 to 1500 B.C. Soon those loose stones became recognizable as the crumbled walls of the upper story of a building. In the rubble they found a stone lamp with traces of soot; clearly it had been burning just before the catastrophe.

As excavations expanded over the years, a veritable city was revealed. Ancient Akrotiri had public squares, homes that reached up to three stories, and sophisticated infrastructure like paved streets and a sewer system with clay pipes that linked private water installations, including toilets. The walls of many buildings stand just as they did when their inhabitants fled more than 3,500 years ago.

"[O]urs is the privilege not of excavating the usual decayed ruin, but of exploring a town abandoned and obliterated in the space of a few weeks," Marinatos observed.

In their homes, people left behind wooden furniture, ceramic storage jars, and food—sea urchins, beans, onions, sesame seeds, snails, ground barley, olive oil—that now offer clues about the ancient diet. Fine pottery and other imports prove that people at Akrotiri had contacts not just with Crete, but also with the Greek mainland, Cyprus, Syria, and Egypt. Inscriptions in Linear A, one of the earliest writing systems found in Europe, show that at least some people were literate.

Metal weapons, tools, utensils, and jewelry are rare discoveries at Akrotiri, as are human skeletons, a sign that people living here had time to save not only themselves but also some of their valuables before the city was destroyed. Crumbled walls buried beneath layers of volcanic debris suggest that earthquakes in the weeks leading up to the most devastating phases of the eruption tipped off residents to their city's impending doom.

The individual artifacts pale against Akrotiri's most stunning finds, though: murals that survived remarkably intact and still brightly colored beneath ash. The most famous scenes include lilies and swallows in a lively springtime landscape, boys wearing boxing gloves as they fight, and seafarers setting out on long, narrow ships. The wall paintings are valued not only for their artistic merit but also for their wealth of information about the natural world. For example, depictions of antelope and scenes of blue monkeys ambling up Thera's hills suggest that these animals, now found only in East Africa, once roamed this island and those nearby.

Contrary to Marinatos's theory, there's no evidence that Thera's eruption brought a swift end to Crete's glory. But the cataclysm may have had rippling negative effects on the Minoan economy, and Crete went into decline by the late 15th century B.C.

After Marinatos died suddenly in an accident at Akrotiri in 1974, archaeologist Christos Doumas took over and became the longtime director of excavations at the site. Most of the city is still buried under hardened layers of ash, and as more of it is uncovered, a mystery endures: When did the eruption occur?

The disaster could be an important anchor in time for archaeologists to establish chronologies across the ancient Mediterranean. But pinpointing a date has been a notoriously difficult task. Archaeological evidence, radiocarbon analysis, and tree-ring and ice-core data have all offered various possibilities between 1700 B.C. and 1500 B.C. The exact date remains as elusive as the cause for the Minoan civilization's demise.

The primates that caper across a fresco at Akrotiri may be a species of monkey from India, indicating that the city had far-reaching trade connections.

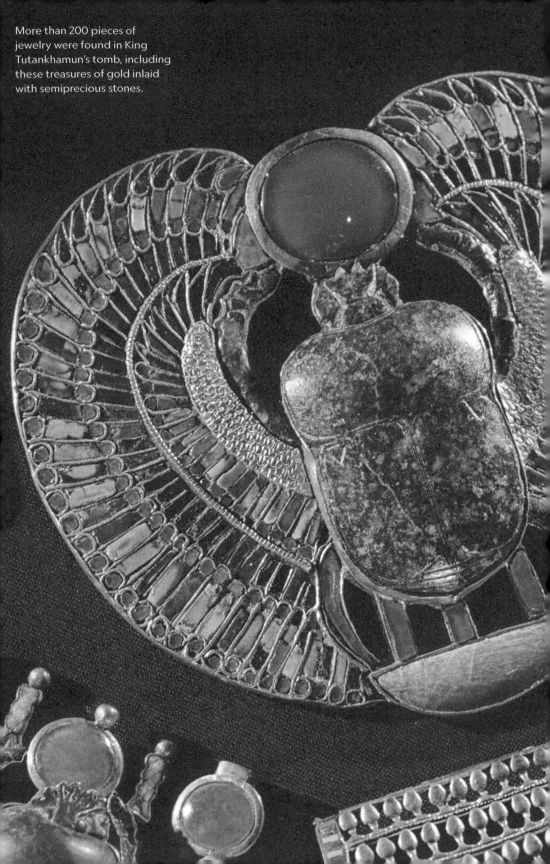

More than 200 pieces of jewelry were found in King Tutankhamun's tomb, including these treasures of gold inlaid with semiprecious stones.

1500–1000 B.C.

Converging Worlds

The Late Bronze Age in the Eastern Mediterranean was a time of trade and conflict, legendary conquerors, and fabled cities. At the same time, Europe and China also shone as beacons of culture. Civilizations had developed into superpowers by this time, connected by wide-ranging commerce akin to globalization. Clay tablets from the ruins of Hittite and Egyptian capitals detail some of the connections in trade and politics, along with the clashes that arose. The cargo of a ship that went down off the coast of Turkey is a prime example of the varied goods being exchanged: ingots of copper and tin (the raw materials used to make bronze) as well as glass beads, a scarab from Egypt, fine pottery from Cyprus, and ebony and ivory from sub-Saharan Africa. Explorers bent on uncovering treasures from this age of wealth discovered King Tut's gold-laden burial and the ruins of the storied city of Troy.

25

HATTUSHA'S WRITTEN RECORDS

ca 1650–1200 B.C. ✦ Anatolia, Turkey ✦ Hittite

Texts inscribed on clay tablets tell the story of
the Hittites—one of the most quarrelsome empires
in the ancient Middle East.

———◆———

Famous for their epic battle against the Egyptians in about 1275 B.C., the Hittites dominated eastern Anatolia and beyond for more than four centuries. Their entry onto the world's stage was mysterious, as was their exit. In between, they were frequently beset by foreign enemies and confounded by dynastic conflicts.

Their capital, Hattusha, was the center of the Hittites' political and religious life. Its ruins lie about a hundred miles east of modern Ankara, Turkey's capital, and are often referred to by the old name of a nearby community, Boğazköy (Turkish meaning "gorge village").

French archaeologist Charles Texier came upon the site in 1834 while searching for the lost Roman city of Tavium. Large-scale excavations began in 1906, and the ongoing work has revealed traces of a palace, administrative buildings, granaries, water reservoirs, one-story houses of mud brick, and some 30 temples. All were

This inscribed clay tablet is one of nearly 30,000 documents recovered from the archives at Hattusha that record the varied concerns of the Hittite capital.

surrounded by a massive wall of mud brick more than four miles long, with monumental stone lions, sphinxes, and gods guarding the gates. The real treasure, though, was some 30,000 clay tablets (whole and fragmentary) with texts in eight different languages. They include diplomatic letters, trade contracts, ritual instructions, prophecies, prayers, and literature. Much of what we know about the Hittites—in sporadic episodes—is contained in this archive.

Local people known as the Hatti first settled the site of Hattusha in about 2500 B.C. The city eventually became so important that Assyrian traders from what is now northern Iraq established their own neighborhood there. Donkey caravans conveyed precious raw materials such as gold, silver, and copper from Anatolia eastward, and returned laden with goods such as tin and textiles. The clay tablets that recorded transactions included the name of the city: Hattush.

Hittites probably infiltrated the area from southern Russia and Ukraine. In about 1700 B.C., a king named Anitta launched an attack on Hattush, burned down the city, and recorded this curse in the Indo-European Hittite language: "At night I took the city by force; I have sown weeds in its place. Should any king after me attempt to resettle Hattush, may the Stormgod of Heaven strike him down."

Power struggles occupied the Hittite elite until finally, in about 1650 B.C., King Hattushili I was able to unify the feuding factions.

Defying the historic curse, he rebuilt Hattush, which became Hattusha with an "a" at the end in Hittite, and expanded his empire's territory into Syria. His son and successor, Murshili I, pushed eastward, sacking the city of Babylon some 750 miles away. But when Murshili returned home, he was murdered. In the ensuing chaos, the Hittites lost much of the territory they had just conquered.

> "At night I took the city by force; I have sown weeds in its place. Should any king after me attempt to resettle Hattush, may the Stormgod of Heaven strike him down."
>
> —*King Anitta, Hittite king ca 1700 B.C.*

In the late 15th century B.C., the Hittites faced a number of foreign threats—raiders known as the Kaska set Hattusha ablaze; the Ahhiyawa, likely Greeks, attacked the Hittite territory of Cyprus; and the Egyptians, under Pharaoh Amenhotep III, undermined the Hittites by forging a connection with the Arzawa of western Anatolia.

A new line of kings in the 14th century B.C. managed to repel these enemies, shore up the empire, and rebuild Hattusha. In a testament to his empire's newly restored fortunes, King Shuppiluliuma I received a desperate letter from an Egyptian queen, perhaps the widow of teenage Pharaoh Tutankhamun. "He who was my husband is dead and I have no son," she wrote. "Should I then perhaps take one of my servants and make of him my husband? I have written to no other country, I have written to you. They say that you have many sons. Give me one of your sons and he will be my husband and lord of the land of Egypt." In response, Prince Zannanza was sent off to Egypt but was murdered en route.

The Hittites and Egyptians came to blows in the next century at the Battle of Kadesh, in modern Syria, as Ramses II sought to block the Hittites' southern expansion. Although Ramses declared victory, and later took a Hittite princess as one of his many wives, neither side won decisively. A copy of their peace treaty was uncovered in the ruins of Hattusha, and a reproduction now hangs in the United Nations' headquarters in New York as one of the earliest examples of such a document.

In a new burst of power in the late 13th century B.C., King Tudhaliya IV more than doubled the size of Hattusha and built a massive new wall. He successfully countered a cousin's challenge to his legitimacy, but his concern is clear in the text of an address he delivered to palace officials. "Regarding the kingship, you must acknowledge no other person (but me, Tudhaliya)," he said. ". . . you must protect only His Majesty and the descendants of His Majesty. You must approach no other person!"

Tudhaliya's son Shuppiluliuma II was the last Hittite ruler of Hattusha. His time there ended when the city went up in flames, again. Who were the attackers? No one knows for sure, but the Kaskans are likely suspects. Archaeologists believe the city was mostly empty by then. The royal family and their court probably fled as the enemy approached, and the ordinary folk followed. Some Hittites seem to have taken refuge in Syria, but the empire was finished.

As a succession of other peoples occupied the site of Hattusha, the identity of the Hittite inhabitants faded—until their records were dug out of the city's ruins and the history of their once great empire was resurrected.

26

THE ULUBURUN
SHIPWRECK

ca 1320 B.C. ◆ Kaš, Turkey ◆ Mediterranean

*A 3,300-year-old shipwreck with undreamed-of
treasures offered a rare glimpse at how raw materials
moved across the Mediterranean.*

———◆———

The first hint of a shipwreck came in the summer of 1982, when
a young sponge diver named Mehmet Çakir told his captain
that he had seen strange "metal biscuits with ears" on the
seabed while working at a depth of 150 feet near the sheer promontory called Uluburun on Turkey's southern coast. The captain
recognized the description. Wreck-hunting archaeologists from the
Institute of Nautical Archaeology (INA) of Texas A&M University
had been circulating a drawing of a Bronze Age copper ingot among
modern seafarers. "Long experience has taught us that the best
sources of information about ancient shipwrecks are the divers on
Turkey's sponge boats," explained INA founder George Bass.

When divers from INA and Turkey's Museum of Underwater
Archaeology in the town of Bodrum visited the site, they confirmed
the existence of a wreck. They estimated that it sank during the Late
Bronze Age—an era marked by the reign of King Tut and the fall of
Troy. At the time of its discovery, the wreck at Uluburun was the
oldest known sunken ship in the world, and a preliminary survey
proved that an astonishing amount of the cargo remained intact.

Beginning at a depth of 140 feet and stretching another 30 feet down a steep slope lay a 50-foot ship with neat rows of cargo arranged just as it had been stowed 33 centuries ago. Scattered among six enormous storage jars were dozens of terra-cotta amphorae and several small two-handled jars known today as pilgrim flasks, because their shape made them convenient to carry on long journeys. Examining all the sketches and photographs, then INA president Don Frey told his colleagues, "We're looking at an archaeologists' dream."

"We're looking at an archaeologists' dream."

— Don Frey, 1987

In the end, that proved an understatement; Uluburun held undreamed-of treasures. The next summer the team mounted a full-scale expedition led by Bass and supported by the National Geographic Society to map and excavate the site. Because of the dangerous depth, they limited the initial time on the wreck to only five minutes a dive, and gradually increased to 20 minutes twice a day, though that required long periods of subsequent decompression on pure oxygen.

Thousands of objects were recovered over the course of 11 seasons between 1984 and 1994, in which the team logged 22,000 dives. The ship had been transporting ebony logs, ostrich eggshells, both elephant and hippopotamus ivory, bronze daggers, and amphorae full of glass beads, pigment, resin, and pomegranates. As divers began to raise one of the huge storage jars, known as *pithoi,* they were amazed when Cypriot pottery poured from its mouth. They found a "book"—the first from the Bronze Age—made up of two ivory-hinged wooden leaves recessed to hold beeswax that could be inscribed with a stylus. (Alas, the message from antiquity that might have been was not to be, for no wax survived.) There were hundreds of 60-pound copper ingots as well as ingots of pure tin—the very substance that spurred on the Bronze Age, but that is seldom found from that period in raw form. The team discovered deliberately damaged jewelry that likely belonged to a hoard of precious scrap metal to be used as payments. They found silver bracelets, gold pendants, and a well-worn gold scarab bearing the title of Nefertiti, queen of Pharaoh Akhenaten. When one archaeologist climbed aboard the research vessel with news that he discovered a gold chalice in the first season of excavation, he joked, "The insurers took a pounding when this ship sank, I'll tell you that!"

Why this unlucky ship sank around 1320 B.C. remains a mystery. Perhaps unfavorable winds drove the vessel against the rocky promontory after it left a port in Turkey. The artifacts found at the wreck came from at least nine different cultures. Most of the cargo

Re-created for modern divers to visit, a cargo ship that sank off Turkey's southwestern coast carried thousands of objects, including 10 tons of copper ingots.

had Eastern Mediterranean origins, suggesting the vessel left from a port in Cyprus or the Levant and was traveling westward, perhaps destined for the Aegean, when catastrophe struck. Personal items like weapons and galley wares indicate a Canaanite crew may have operated the vessel, but other Aegean artifacts suggest some Mycenaean passengers may have been on board.

At the time the Uluburun wreck was discovered, many scholars insisted that the Mycenaeans held a virtual monopoly on seaborne commerce during the Bronze Age, pointing to the widespread distribution of Mycenaean pottery throughout the Mediterranean. But that pottery told only half the story. It wasn't given away; something had to have been traded in return. Bass long believed that the missing commodity was raw materials such as copper, tin, ivory, glass, and other substances that were quickly converted on arrival into tools, weapons, ornaments, and household goods. Egyptian tomb paintings depict such raw materials in the hands of Canaanite merchants delivering them to the pharaohs, but the commodities themselves are seldom if ever found. Only a disaster such as a shipwreck would preserve them in their original form.

It was a staggering loss when this vessel, laden with precious goods and vital raw materials from around the Mediterranean and beyond, came to rest on the seabed. But the value only grew over the 3,300 years of disappearance—making the Uluburun wreck one of the most important windfalls in the history of underwater archaeology.

27

LETTERS TO THE PHARAOHS

1360–1336 B.C. ◆ Amarna, Egypt ◆ Egyptian

*A collection of foreign correspondence,
inscribed on clay tablets, offers rare insights into Egypt's
diplomacy and power during the 18th dynasty.*

———◆———

Tell el-Amarna, some 200 miles south of Cairo, has been called the Pompeii of Egypt. Its monuments and houses are gone, but the foundations are largely intact. No one built over its ruins, as in most ancient cities, so the site is the only place today where people can walk the streets of an ancient Egyptian city. In this dusty, long-abandoned place, around 1887, locals uncovered one of the most significant caches of ancient texts yet found: diplomatic correspondence and other documents, now called the Amarna letters, that reveal Egypt's wide-ranging contacts abroad during a time of turmoil at home.

The details of the discovery have been lost, but one widely circulated story says a local woman found strange, inscribed clay tablets when she was digging up buried mud bricks to use as fertilizer. The tablets were of no use to her, and she destroyed many before selling the rest to a neighbor, who then peddled them on the antiquities market. Examples of the tablets are now scattered in museums around the world—from Istanbul to Oxford, Moscow to New York—and in private collections as well.

At first, many experts failed to appreciate the importance of the tablets, and at least one eminent scholar believed they were fakes. But E. A. Wallis Budge, assistant curator at the British Museum, was able to read some of the wedge-shaped cuneiform signs that they bore. "I felt certain that the tablets were both genuine and of very great historical importance," he said, after reading a passage mentioning the "king of the land of Egypt."

> **"I felt certain that the tablets were both genuine and of very great historical importance."**
> —E. A. Wallis Budge, Egyptologist

Archaeologists were later able to uncover parts of a few letters and school texts from the building where the original cache was said to have been found. Other letters came to light in nearby structures, in what was likely an administrative complex near the royal palace. Today, 382 tablets are known, most written in Akkadian, a common diplomatic language in the 14th century B.C.

The survival of these fragile artifacts is due to one of the most bizarre chapters in ancient Egypt's history. Amenhotep III, a powerful pharaoh, ruled for 37 years during a golden age of empire. His connections stretched north along the coast of the Mediterranean Sea and south into Nubia, and he tapped the wealth of that great expanse to build an unprecedented series of monuments. These included elaborate constructions in the capital of Thebes (now Karnak and Luxor), the religious center of the god Amun, who soon merged with the ancient sun god Re to become Amun-Re.

Amenhotep III's son, who came to the throne as Amenhotep IV, rejected Amun-Re and adopted a deity called Aten, represented by the disk of the sun, as Egypt's one and only god. Whether by faith or force, Amenhotep IV turned Thebes upside down in the first four years of his reign, building four new temples to Aten around Amun's temple at Karnak. "For a short time the Egyptians believed the sun god had come back to earth in the form of the royal family," says Ray Johnson, a University of Chicago Egyptologist. "The whole country was in jubilee."

Then the pharaoh did two things that shook his world to the core. He changed his name from Amenhotep, meaning "Amun is content," to Akhenaten, "glory of the sun disk." And he built a new capital called Akhetaten, "horizon of the Aten"—the archaeological site Tell el-Amarna, named for a modern village. "It must have been a horrific time," says Johnson. "The family that had ruled for centuries was coming to an end, and then Akhenaten went a little wacky."

Akhenaten's revolution didn't last. The pharaoh was barely cold in his grave when the royal court moved back to Thebes. In time, the empty former capital crumbled, burying archives of Amenhotep III and Akhenaten in the debris.

The remarkable collection of rescued letters from Amarna offers a rich and varied snapshot of international connections in the Middle East, in which Egypt was a major player. Some of these, exchanged between Egypt and its vassal states, dealt with local

In its heyday, this palace at Akhetaten included a well, storerooms, a sunken garden, and a room painted with scenes of the marshes along the Nile.

squabbles—a litany of accusations, complaints, conspiracies, defenses, justifications, and requests that Egypt step in to help settle a variety of issues.

Other letters were sent from independent rulers to the Egyptian royals. In one, Tushratta, the king of the Mitanni, wrote to Amenhotep III's wife Tiye to say, "I had asked your husband for statues of solid cast gold.... But now ... your son has [sent me] plated statues of wood. With gold being dirt in your son's country, why have they been a source of such distress to your son that he has not given them to me?" In another exchange, Akhenaten and the king of Alasiya (now modern Cyprus) heatedly discussed the pirates who were disrupting trade and security. Akhenaten accused the foreign king of abetting sea raiders from Lukka (in Anatolia); the king replied, indignantly, that the Lukkans were raiding his own coast, and he had taken measures to punish anyone involved in the attacks.

These views of the wider world, saved by a shift in politics, are important to understanding Egypt at one of the peaks of its power. Their unique insight into its international status, commerce, and diplomatic connections as well as the desirability of raw materials such as gold is invaluable; without them, the historical narrative would have lost a vital external counterpoint to the country's debilitating internal chaos.

28

MYCENAE, MORE THAN MYTH

ca 1600 B.C. ◆ Peloponnese, Greece ◆ Mycenaean

When gold treasures emerged from its tombs,
Mycenae, the legendary seat of power for
King Agamemnon, proved to be more than lore.

———◆———

D uring the second century A.D., the geographer Pausanias
traveled far and wide over Greece, describing its temples,
tombs, and settlements, many of which were by then ancient
and in ruins. In the northeastern Peloponnese, he made a stop at
Mycenae, the abandoned hilltop capital of the Mycenaean civilization that dominated much of Greece from about 1600 to 1100 B.C.
As the legendary home of Agamemnon, the king of Homer's epics
who launched a long campaign against Troy, Mycenae was a central
location in Greece's mythological past. Its grand architecture and
imposing fortifications certainly made a fitting backdrop for stories
about macho warriors. Pausanias described the architectural features he saw, writing that "parts of the wall are still preserved as
well as the gate over which lions stand. These also they say are the
work of the Cyclopes who built the wall for Proteus at Tiryns,"
another powerful Mycenaean city to the northeast. Constructed

Archaeologist Heinrich Schliemann (right) poses above Mycenae's Lion Gate
along with colleague Wilhelm Dörpfeld (left) and visitors below in about 1885.

with massive and rough limestone blocks, such walls indeed
seemed to be the work of mythical one-eyed giants. (The walls at
Tiryns are up to 26 feet thick and 43 feet high.)

Despite the size and importance of Mycenae, the city would
disappear in the written record and in the landscape for many centuries after Pausanias's visit. It wasn't until 1841 that Greek archaeologist Kyriakos Pittakis uncovered and restored the Lion Gate, an
entrance in the thick defensive wall built from monolithic stones

and topped by an iconic carved stone weighing nearly two tons. Then, in 1876, Heinrich Schliemann, in his characteristically showy style, began an excavation of the city with blockbuster results.

Schliemann had a burning faith in the historical veracity of Homer at a time when many scholars thought the epics were based on pure fantasy. Many of his contemporary Victorian scholars believed Greek society prior to the eighth century was in the Dark Ages with minimal signs of civilization. In the early 1870s, Schliemann became world-famous for excavating a mound in Turkey that seemed to correspond to the ancient city of Troy. He then received an excavation permit from the Greek government to begin digging at Mycenae in 1874, and within a few years he gave substance to Homer's description of Mycenae as "rich in gold." Schliemann opened the now famous Shaft Graves, revealing an incredible treasure of gold objects, that weighed some 44 pounds. There were death masks of unforgettable visage, the most elaborate of which reportedly moved Schliemann to cable King George I of the Hellenes: "I have gazed on the face of Agamemnon." That statement is forever associated with the dramatic archaeological discovery, even though the graves dug dated to several hundred years before the era in which the Trojan War was said to have taken place.

Considering his other finds at Troy, Schliemann may be the luckiest archaeologist to have ever lived. The discovery of Mycenae was a genuine huge archaeological achievement that opened up a whole new world for exploration of the Greek Bronze Age. Mycenae and nearby Tiryns became UNESCO World Heritage sites in 1999.

After Schliemann, archaeologists continued to study Mycenaean sites, but it would be more than a century before they would find similarly spectacular tombs. In 2015, archaeologists Jack Davis and Sharon Stocker launched an excavation at the end of the Peloponnese Peninsula at Pylos, a place Homer mentioned in *The Odyssey* as the site of King Nestor's palace with its "lofty halls." Excavations before and after World War II had revealed remnants of a large Mycenaean palace dating to about 1300 B.C., as well as hundreds of clay tablets written in the Linear B script developed on Crete, an island about 100 miles offshore. Those texts led Michael Ventris to the translation of Linear B and confirmed the identity of Pylos.

But little is known about the earlier period around 1500 B.C., when Mycenaean society was taking shape. Archaeologists have long debated the influence of Minoan civilization, which began to flourish in Crete around 2500 B.C., on the rise of Mycenaean society a thousand years later. Linear B tablets, bull horn symbols, and goddess figurines found at Mycenaean sites like Pylos attest to the impact of Minoan culture. Based on archaeological evidence of destruction, many scholars believe that the Mycenaeans invaded and conquered Crete around 1450 B.C.

On the first day of the dig, workers clearing a field spotted a rectangle of stones that proved to be the top of a four-foot-by-eight-foot shaft. Three feet down, the excavators spotted the first bronze artifacts. Based on their style, Davis and Stocker are confident that the remains date to about 1500 B.C. Once in the grave, the team revealed a well-preserved skeleton of the "Griffin Warrior," a man in his early 30s, alongside more than 1,400 objects arrayed on and around the body, including gold rings, silver cups, and an elaborate bronze sword with an ivory hilt. He was buried with a plaque depicting a creature called a griffin, with the head and wings of an eagle and the body of a lion. Also found at Pylos, a limestone-encrusted gemstone the size of a thumb was cleaned and revealed to have an intricate scene of combat. The level of detail in this 3,500-year-old carving that wouldn't be seen in Greece for another millennium inspired the same awe that Schliemann felt for his mask. "It's so moving to actually look at," said Stocker of the gemstone. "Almost always the reaction is to cry."

29

TOMB OF A TEENAGE PHARAOH

1322 B.C. ◆ Valley of the Kings, Egypt ◆ Egyptian

*As fabulous artifacts began to emerge from
his underground burial chambers, King Tut took the
world by storm to become an enduring global celebrity.*

———◆———

The world had never seen anything like it: a royal burial, untouched for 3,300 years, filled with treasures from one of history's most intriguing civilizations. The occupant, Tutankhamun Nebkheperure—King Tut for short—became an instant sensation. His tomb would intrigue experts and amateurs alike, rewriting the end of the 18th dynasty and inspiring endless speculation about how he died and the particulars of the place where he was laid to rest.

In the late 19th century, wealthy Europeans began to explore the various royal burial grounds near the New Kingdom capital of Thebes (modern-day Karnak and Luxor), searching for stunning artifacts to fill their homes and museums. One of these was Lord Carnarvon, whose home, Highclere Castle, became famous as the setting for the television show *Downton Abbey*.

Beginning in 1907, Carnarvon employed a fellow Brit, Howard Carter, to supervise the excavations he was funding. They had some success, finding upper-class tombs and previously looted royal burials. But by the winter of 1921–22, they had yet to make the big score they had hoped for. Carnarvon was ready to pull the plug, but Carter convinced him to hang in for one more season of digging. It was one of the best calls in the history of archaeology.

In November 1922, Carter's workmen began clearing debris from a previously neglected triangle of ground in the Valley of the Kings, the cemetery for rulers and their relatives during the 18th

Treasures in King Tut's tomb—including two sentinels at the sealed doorway to the burial chamber—appear in a photo from December 1922, recently colorized.

One of the most famous artifacts from antiquity, a gold mask inlaid with semi-precious stones and glass fit over the head and shoulders of King Tut's mummy.

and 19th dynasties. After just a few days, they hit the stone staircase that would lead them to Tut's underground grave.

By the end of the month, they had come to a doorway sealed in plaster with Tutankhamun's name stamped all over it. Carter broke a small hole through the plaster, held up a candle, and looked in. What he saw would make newspaper headlines around the world: "At first, I could see nothing," he wrote later, "the hot air escaping from the chamber causing the candle to flicker. But presently, as my eyes became accustomed to the light, details of the room within emerged slowly from the mist, strange animals, statues, gold—everywhere the glint of gold."

It would take Carter the next 10 years to catalog all of Tut's treasures. The young king had been provided with more than 5,000 things he might need in the next life—everything from a solid gold coffin and face mask to beds and thrones, chariots and archery bows, food and wine, sandals and fresh linen underwear.

> "... as my eyes became accustomed to the light, details of the room within emerged slowly from the mist, strange animals, statues, gold—everywhere the glint of gold."
>
> —*Howard Carter, archaeologist*

Although looters had broken into the tomb at least twice in antiquity, it remains the most spectacular burial ever discovered in Egypt—and this was for a teenager with a relatively short reign. (The mind boggles at the thought of the wealth that must have been buried with one of the big names—for example, the celebrated 18th dynasty Queen Nefertiti.)

The young pharaoh ruled at a time when Egypt had become fabulously rich and powerful. The country had prospered for more than a thousand years, keeping traditions that had arisen even before the now famous Pyramids at Giza were built. By Tut's time, Egypt had gained access to the legendary gold mines of Nubia to the south, and had conquered territory along the Mediterranean coast to the northeast.

But the country was in turmoil when Tut took the throne. A pharaoh named Akhenaten, possibly Tut's father or half brother, had turned traditions upside down by ordering everyone to worship the sun god Aten, smashing statues of other gods, and moving the capital to a new location.

It's unclear who became pharaoh right after Akhenaten died, but Tutankhamun soon rose to the throne. He was only nine years old, which must have set his subjects to worrying all over again. A boy king? How could he rule a whole country? And how could he ever hope to protect Egypt from its enemies?

His top officials, though, offered him wise advice and worked diligently to set Egypt right. For starters, that meant moving the capital back to Thebes. During his decade-long reign, Tut became a symbol of this restoration, a return to *ma'at,* the proper order of things.

And then, stunningly, the teenage ruler died. The cause is uncertain. Maybe a lethal infection set in after he broke his leg in an accident. Or perhaps malaria did him in. Or he had a fatal genetic weakness that arose from the royals' habit of marrying their siblings. However it came about, Tut's passing created an immediate practical problem: There was no finished tomb to put him in. No one could have imagined that someone so young would drop dead; Egypt's officials must have thought they had plenty of time to prepare his place of eternal rest. And then, suddenly, time ran out.

Many experts think Tut was buried in a tomb that had already been prepared for someone else: a quick and easy solution. In time, as other tombs were carved into the valley's cliffs, rocky debris covered the entrance to Tut's chambers, and the location was forgotten. Also, the record of Tut himself all but disappeared. Because he was so closely associated with the horrors of the Akhenaten era, his name—along with others—was stricken from the official list of kings. With the discovery of his final resting place, his life's story has been revived, and his tomb has become famous as KV62—the 62nd discovery in the Valley of the Kings.

But what if KV62 was already occupied, and Tut was buried in a few small rooms near the entrance? Maybe the first occupant is lying in larger rooms beyond Tut's modest suite. And if it's Nefertiti, or a royal of the same stature, the rooms might be filled with great treasures, all untouched by looters. A series of investigations in recent years, using technology such as ground-penetrating radar, has sought to discover whether any adjacent chambers exist.

Results have been tantalizingly inconclusive—maybe yes, maybe no—and the intrigue continues, along with the hope that something amazing is awaiting discovery.

Meanwhile, Egypt has constructed the billion-dollar Grand Egyptian Museum, known as the GEM, where King Tut's funerary artifacts are now exhibited as never before. For decades, the teen's possessions were housed in the Egyptian Museum in downtown Cairo near historic Tahrir Square. But that building, which opened in 1902, had space to present only the most stunning pieces: chariots, nested funerary shrines, fabulous jewelry. The new facility, overlooking the grandeur of the Giza Pyramids, was designed to display together for the first time all the goods meant for Tut's use in the next world. Two large galleries showcase the pharaoh's personal effects in a way that evokes the treasure-packed chambers of his tomb.

The names of all but a few ancient Egyptians are long forgotten. Although each hoped for eternal life after death, the memory of them as individuals here on Earth has mostly faded away. King Tut is the fantastic exception. Not only does his name live on, but his fame—in all its overblown, rock-star dimensions—has taken on a life of its own, resurging with every new exhibit and every rumor of another long-forgotten tomb in the Valley of the Kings.

30

THE LEGEND
OF TROY

1180 B.C. ◆ Hisarlik, Turkey ◆ Anatolian, Greek

In the early days of archaeology, an eccentric German businessman proved the besieged city of Homer's Iliad *was indeed a real place.*

———◆———

Heinrich Schliemann was a German businessman who amassed a huge fortune as a merchant in the 19th century. In the grand tradition of millionaires who sink their money into ambitious, if quixotic, quests, Schliemann began chasing a dream he later claimed to have had since boyhood. He wanted to find and excavate Troy, the lost ancient city whose walls defied a decade-long siege by a Greek army led by Agamemnon, only to fall by a cunning false-retreat strategy and to open their gates for a wooden horse concealing Greek warriors.

Thanks to Greek myth and Homer's eighth-century B.C. epic poems, history preserved the tale of the beautiful Queen Helen of Sparta whose abduction by Paris instigated the war, meddlesome gods who chose sides, and the dramatic duals that immortalized Ajax, Hector, Ulysses, and Achilles. But looking for Troy's material remains in Schliemann's day may have been like looking for Atlantis today. Scholars weren't sure if a real city like the one described in *The Iliad* had existed, or if a conflict like the Trojan War had really taken place. Nevertheless, Schliemann fashioned himself into an amateur archaeologist and launched his search. In 1870, he began an excavation at Hisarlik, a 100-foot-high artificial mound in the plains of northwestern Turkey overlooking the Aegean coast and not far from the entrance to the Dardanelles strait.

British diplomat Frank Calvert had already made some promising trial excavations of the mound in the 1860s. But Schliemann's energetic digging unearthed a veritable city—in fact, he unearthed many cities. Troy had fallen into ruins and had been rebuilt and renovated many times during its 4,000 years of history, and there were at least nine distinct layers of occupation beginning around 2700 B.C. Schliemann was working at a time when archaeology was in its infancy, and much to the annoyance of modern practitioners, he dug straight through many of these layers with hardly the level of care and documentation required today.

According to one version of the events, digging was progressing on a May morning in 1873, in one of the lowest levels of the city, known as Troy II. Schliemann dismissed his workmen for an early break when he saw a glint of gold behind a large copper object emerging next to one of the walls of a building believed to be the palace of Priam, legendary king of Troy. Schliemann continued digging himself and later recounted: "I cut out the treasure with a large knife. It was impossible to do this without the most strenuous exertions and the most fearful risk to my life, for the large fortification-wall, which I had to undermine, threatened at every moment to fall down on me. But the sight of so many objects, each one of which is of inestimable value for science, made me foolhardy and I had no thought of danger." He claimed his wife, Sophia, who often dug alongside him, stood by ready to carry away in her shawl the objects he

> "The sight of so many objects, each one of which is of inestimable value for science, made me foolhardy and I had no thought of danger."
>
> —*Heinrich Schliemann, explorer*

cut out. Schliemann imagined he was looking at a hoard of valuables hastily packed by a member of Priam's family while their palace was under attack.

"Priam's treasure" contained battle-axes and daggers; vases, cups, and dishes made of precious metals, including a gold sauceboat; and an astonishing haul of jewelry, including two gold diadems, 60 earrings, and thousands of beads, buttons, and other ornaments. Schliemann smuggled the objects out of Turkey into his residence in Athens. There, Sophia was photographed wearing the exquisite jewelry. The iconic portrait helped make the discovery famous (and helped kick off a legal battle with the Turkish authorities).

Even in his day, Schliemann was a controversial figure, ridiculed for his self-promotion, exaggeration, and eagerness to associate his finds with figures from myth. Noting various inconsistencies in his accounts of the discovery, many scholars now question whether all the items of the treasure were found together at all; they suspect Schliemann may have arranged a composite hoard with older finds or even purchases to maximize publicity. Sophia wasn't even present at the dig during the supposed discovery. And in any case, archaeologists now know that these objects and the adjacent building were far older than the Homeric era. Troy II actually dates from 2500 to 2300 B.C. Schliemann and his workmen dug past the destroyed city that archaeologists later believed better corresponded to the period of the legendary Trojan War—Troy VI, dating from 1700 to 1250 B.C. They threw stones of a palatial building and probably related artifacts from that era into a spoil heap.

Despite Schliemann's mixed legacy, the importance of Hisarlik as an archaeological site is undeniable. After Schliemann died in 1890, his assistant Wilhelm Dörpfeld took over excavations and better documented the features of Troy VI, including its massive walls. In the 1930s, archaeologist Carl Blegen proposed that Troy

A gold diadem, earrings, and necklaces unearthed at the site of Troy adorn Sophia Schliemann, wife of the explorer who found the long-lost city.

VI was not destroyed by the blaze of warfare, but by an earthquake, and that wartime destruction was more apparent in Troy VII. After a lapse of 50 years, new work began at Troy in the late 1980s, under archaeologist Manfred Korfmann, of Germany's University of Tübingen.

Some doubted there would be much left to find at the site in the wake of Schliemann. One lingering argument against Hisarlik as Troy was that the city seemed too small to be worth a decade-long battle. But Korfmann and his colleagues found an impressive U-shaped ditch that surrounded the city in the Late Bronze Age. Inside, the archaeologists discovered an entire lower portion of the city that hadn't been detected before. Troy was actually 15 times bigger than previously thought. Counteracting the biases of previous excavators like Schliemann who were based in Greece, the new crop of researchers also showed that Troy actually had more connections to Anatolia than the Aegean. The city was part of the kingdom of Wilusa, also mentioned in Hittite and Egyptian sources.

Korfmann's research pinpointed Troy's violent attack to 1180 B.C. By Homer's day, the city was in ruins, but Greeks were reoccupying the city and called it "Ilion." Over the next several centuries, visitors would come from all over the Mediterranean and beyond to see the fabled city for themselves. Alexander the Great and the Persian ruler Xerxes supposedly made appearances. But did the legendary war that drew them to the western shores of Turkey really occur? Korfmann thought it was likely that several armed conflicts occurred in and around Troy at the end of the Late Bronze Age. Maybe it would be impossible to ever know whether one of these fights could be attributed to the Trojan War of myth or if Homer distilled them into one conflict.

One thing Homer understood with certainty is human nature: the lengths people will take to immortalize their name and leave a legacy, whether by waging war across the sea or searching for the stones of a lost city. He asks in *The Iliad,* "Who in future story will speak well of you?"

31

REDISCOVERING THE SHANG

1600–1045 B.C. ◆ Anyang, Henan Province, China ◆ Shang dynasty

Thousands of so-called "oracle bones" proved conclusively that the Shang dynasty wasn't a fable, but a Bronze Age civilization with a rich cultural tradition.

———◆———

The fabled Shang dynasty, known for its cultural and scientific advances, ruled China from 1600 to circa 1045 B.C. Some scholars had dismissed it as mythical until traces of the Shang began to reappear in the Yellow River plain after more than 3,000 years.

The rediscovery began in 1899 in the city of Anyang, located in Henan Province, when a man named Wang Yirong came down with a case of malaria. The story goes that he went to a pharmacist for help and was given "dragon bones," an important ingredient in traditional Chinese medicine (which were actually turtle shells). Before the shells could be ground up, a family member noticed that they were inscribed with strange characters. To average citizens, they were at first glance unintelligible. But Wang, the chancellor of the Imperial Academy and an expert on ancient Chinese texts, believed them to be an early form of Chinese script.

The malaria tale is likely apocryphal, but Wang did become the first major collector of what scholars came to call "oracle bones": the turtle shells and cattle scapulae the Shang once used for divination. The collection soon came into the possession of Liu E, who published the first catalog of the inscriptions in 1903. The shells and bones had been cleaned and treated, then thinned by drilling notches into the back. The diviner would inscribe them with yes or no questions so when a hot object was applied to the surface until it cracked, the cryptic fissures could be read like a palm reader reads hands. Occasionally, an inscription would include a prediction (for example, "Lady Hao's childbearing will be good"), and courtiers would later record whether the prediction held true. (One memorable epilogue reads, "After 31 days [Lady Hao] gave birth; it was not good; it was a girl.")

But their secrets weren't revealed until after the Qing dynasty fell in 1911, when intellectuals began calling for the country to embrace Western science and philosophy. Realizing that archaeology could provide a fresh perspective on the past, the newly established Academia Sinica—China's national research institute—sent an excavation team led by Li Chi to Xiaotun in 1928. The earliest digs, which followed in the tracks of looters and dealers, focused on retrieving oracle bones. Over 15 seasons in the 1920s and early 1930s, as more than 100,000 were discovered, the Shang dynasty officially became a historical reality. These deceptively simple objects not only possessed the power to authenticate the past, but they also constituted the first archaeological evidence of an ancient Indigenous civilization.

The bones' inscriptions bear testament to the development of one of the world's oldest systems of writing, as well as a sophisticated belief and social system. They reveal much about the Shang, from wars and harvests to births and deaths; there are even comments on the toothaches of kings. They are heavy with descriptions of sacrifices, both human and animal. Foreign tribes can be allies or enemies. Statements are brief and to the point. And yet some inscriptions ring across the centuries with haunting beauty and mystery: "In the afternoon a rainbow also came out of the north and drank in the Yellow River."

The bones also reference figures who appear in traditional historical texts, demonstrating that the ancient tales were more than myth. Wu Ding, the 21st Shang king who presided over the dynasty at its zenith, is mentioned frequently, as is his queen consort, Fu Hao. All told, the oracle bones found at Xiaotun document more than 150 years at the end of the Shang era, from around 1200 to 1045 B.C.

In 1937, as the Japanese invasion of China pressed inland, the Academia Sinica was forced to abandon its Xiaotun excavations. With the advent of the Cultural Revolution in 1966, the search for the Shang all but ended. By 1975, national propaganda campaigns were demanding that local villages flatten hilly terrain to improve farming. "We didn't want the ancient sites to get plowed over," said Zheng Zhenxiang, an archaeologist at Anyang who resisted the government's petitions to enact this plan at Xiaotun. "So we did test excavations first." Under one hill they made a massive discovery: the tomb of queen consort and military general Fu Hao, and the first

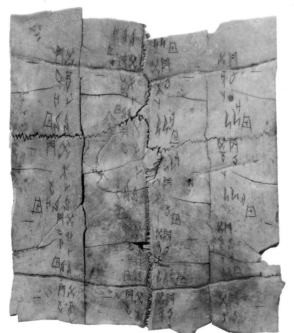

unlooted Shang burial chamber ever found by archaeologists.

Unfortunately, Zheng and his team were hamstrung by limited resources and political turmoil. "We should have used pumps and wells to drain the site," he said, "but we couldn't afford it." So in 1976, locals dove into freezing mud to

An example of China's ancient "oracle bones," this tortoise shell is inscribed with a divinatory text from the Shang dynasty, 14th to 13th century B.C.

The tomb of queen consort and military leader Fu Hao held some 2,000 items, including weapons, jades, bone hairpins, and bronzes such as this wine vessel.

pull out relics from the tomb site at Xiaotun. "They drank shots of grain alcohol beforehand because it was so cold," Zheng observed. Their discomfort paid off; Zheng's team found treasures made of jade, ivory, and bone, as well 195 bronze vessels, which outside of oracle bones are the most distinctive relics of Shang culture.

With each Shang relic uncovered, researchers paint an ever clearer picture of this once mysterious dynasty. "Just as the Shang were divining the will of their ancestors . . . we're doing the same thing," says the University of California's David N. Keightley, an expert on oracle bones. "We're engaged in a kind of academic divination."

> "Just as the Shang were divining the will of their ancestors . . . we're doing the same thing. We're engaged in a kind of academic divination."
>
> —David N. Keightley, professor of Chinese history

32

ARMIES CLASH AT THE CAUSEWAY

ca 1250 B.C. ◆ Tollense Valley, Germany ◆ Bronze Age

The remains of hundreds of warriors, killed in battle along Germany's Tollense River, dispel the notion of a peaceful Bronze Age in northern Europe.

———◆———

The meandering Tollense River flows gently through the rolling landscape of the North German Plain near the Baltic Sea. The idyllic image of this tranquil river valley near the town of Weltzin was forever shattered in 1996, when a single upper arm bone was discovered sticking out of the riverbank—with a flint arrowhead embedded in the shoulder. A wooden club lay nearby.

As archaeologists excavated along and beneath the river, they uncovered thousands of bones, many closely packed together, that dated to the Late Bronze Age, around 1250 B.C. Had this been a cemetery that flooded? As they examined the bones more closely, they found gruesome evidence of combat: skulls pierced by arrowheads, stab marks on rib cages. The sheer scale and violence of the scene made it clear: The Tollense valley was Europe's oldest battlefield.

Scholars throughout the 20th century had thought that the Bronze Age in northern Europe was a relatively peaceful and uneventful time period. The region seemed a stark contrast to the more advanced civilizations in Greece and the Near East, which at the time were engaged in the Trojan War and campaigns by such warrior kings as Ramses II. There were scant historical accounts of conflict in northern Europe. Bronze weapons unearthed from the time period were found in ceremonial burials. The excavations at Tollense turned those notions upside down, for such an immense battle required far more organization and wrought far greater violence than had ever been imagined in the region at the time.

In the 25 years since the initial discovery at Tollense, scientists have used metal detectors and scuba diving equipment in addition to their usual excavation techniques to uncover nearly 12,000 pieces of human bone and other intriguing artifacts along a 1.5-mile-long stretch of the river. They've identified more than 140 individuals, mostly men between the ages of 20 and 40, and estimate 2,000 to 4,000 combatants likely participated in the battle.

What might have provoked such a large-scale engagement? Geomagnetic scans revealed that an approximately 400-foot-long stone-flanked wooden causeway had traversed the valley from east to west. Radiocarbon dating pegged parts of the structure to more than 500 years before the battle, with other parts updated in the centuries that followed. Scientists suspect that the causeway might have long served as an important crossroads along a trade route and was likely a recognized—and highly prized—landmark.

Researchers theorize that the conflict started at the causeway. The armies advanced along both sides of the river, fighting hand-to-hand with clubs, spears, swords, and knives. Archers fired diamond-shaped bronze arrowheads, leaving telltale scars on their victims. Some higher-ranking warriors rode on horseback; the bones of five small horses have been discovered on site.

Combatants were killed as they moved downriver, leaving their bones and belongings behind. None of the bodies showed healed wounds, which means the battle was brief, perhaps a few days at most.

In the sediment of the river scientists found several gold rings, which most likely were worn in the hair of a powerful person present at the battle. A cache of artifacts near the causeway included several tools, a round star-ornamented belt box, and fragments of copper that might have been used as a form of currency. Bronze cylinders may have been fittings for bags or boxes designed to hold personal gear—objects that until now have only been discovered hundreds of miles away.

These artifacts lend credence to the theory that this massive battle wasn't just a local conflict, but drew combatants from long distances. They reinforce an earlier chemical analysis of teeth found on the battlefield that concluded there were two groups of fighters: one group of northern German locals and another more diverse group from somewhere in central Europe.

"It was a surprise to find a battlefield site," archaeologist Thomas Terberger told *Smithsonian* magazine. "It was a second surprise to see a battlefield site of this dimension with so many warriors involved, and now it's a big surprise that we are dealing with a conflict of a European scale."

Historians hope further excavations will reveal the motivation that led these men so far from home. What caused the conflict at the causeway that sparked their final battle?

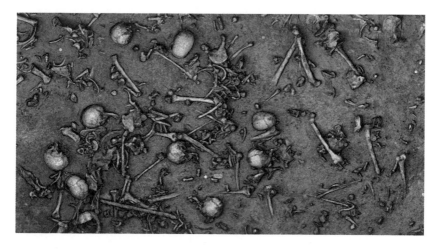

As two armies fought along the Tollense River, their spears, arrows, swords, and knives pierced flesh and bone, leaving hundreds dead on the battlefield.

33

A SETTLEMENT LEFT IN HASTE

ca 1000–800 B.C. ◆ Cambridgeshire, U.K. ◆ Prehistoric

The remains of Must Farm, abandoned after a catastrophic fire, offer an extraordinary snapshot of daily life 3,000 years ago.

———◆———

I n the Late Bronze Age, fire swept through a small settlement perched at the edge of a now vanished tributary of the River Nene. Roof beams collapsed, blazing thatch and walls of wattle fell, and wicker floors crashed onto the marshy ground, along with the charred household items that had sat on them. Silt quickly covered the ruins, preserving everything just as it had landed. The evidence of that single event, uncovered at a site called Must Farm, has offered an unprecedented look at ordinary life in the ancient fens of Cambridgeshire. "So much has been preserved, we can actually see everyday life during the Bronze Age in the round. It's prehistoric archaeology in 3D," archaeologist David Gibson told the BBC.

In modern times, until about 140 years ago, this part of eastern England mainly produced crops and

> "So much has been preserved, we can actually see everyday life during the Bronze Age in the round. It's prehistoric archaeology in 3D."
>
> —*David Gibson, archaeologist*

cattle. But when Victorian-era building generated a demand for bricks, a quarry opened to mine a deposit of exceptionally fine clay. The quarrying continues to this day. In the summer of 1999, an archaeologist spotted timbers uncovered at the edge of an extraction pit. Initial investigations revealed promising clues—potsherds, worked flint, textiles—which led to 10 months of excavation beginning in August 2015.

Digging through muck in all kinds of weather, archaeologists slowly exposed the remains of the most complete, best preserved Bronze Age settlement ever discovered in Britain. At least five buildings—four round and one trapezoidal—were connected by a raised walkway inside a wooden palisade. Each building measured about 25 feet in diameter and stood on stilts above a broad, slow-flowing river. Judging from the quantity and quality of artifacts recovered, this was a prosperous, well-connected settlement, perhaps located on the waterway to control trade, and drawing resources from cultivated areas on dry land nearby. It was probably less than a year old when disaster struck—the oak house beams and ash palisade posts were still green, and thousands of wood chips and other construction debris littered the ground.

According to the University of Cambridge, whose archaeologists conducted the excavation, "The site has revealed the largest collections in Britain of Bronze Age textiles, beads, domestic wooden artefacts (including buckets, platters, troughs, shafts and handles) and domestic metalwork (axes, sickles, hammers, spears, gouges, razors, knives and awls). It has also yielded a wide range of household items; among them are several complete 'sets' of storage jars, cups and bowls."

Charring from the fire, and the wet environment that the houses and their contents fell into, preserved organic items stunningly well. Archaeologists even found the remains of meals in pots and bowls, one of which held a wooden spoon—maybe left midmeal as the fire closed in. The diet included stews of vegetables, emmer wheat, and barley. "Think porridge and add a few extra

An oak wheel at Must Farm survived the fire that destroyed nearby buildings. About three feet wide, it is the oldest complete wheel ever found in the U.K.

herby things—and if you were lucky you might have had honey to dollop in the middle," said University of Oxford archaeologist Chris Gosden. "It isn't a great meal, and if someone put a bowl in front of you, you wouldn't light up." Meats were also on the menu—wild game such as deer and boar, domesticated lambs and calves, and the occasional freshwater fish such as pike and carp.

The people who lived here were not only excellent carpenters but skilled in textile arts as well. Plant fibers included cultivated flax and wild nettle. Threads wound into balls or around sticks have survived, along with finely woven fabrics, some with strands as thin as human hairs.

In the silt of the ancient river channel near the largest round-house, archaeologists uncovered yet another surprise: a wooden wheel three feet in diameter—the largest and earliest complete example ever found in Britain. Its wood was scorched in a way that suggests it was close to, but not in, the big fire. Experts believe the wheel was part of a cart that could have held two people. Its discovery "demonstrates the inhabitants of this watery landscape's links to the dry land beyond the river," said archaeologist David Gibson. The skeleton of a horse—a rare animal during this period—was found close by, perhaps the remains of the very creature that once pulled the cart.

The wealth of evidence uncovered at Must Farm reveals both intimate moments close to home and connections farther afield. Footprints trod into wet silt include those of sheep and cow hooves, as well as a size 10 human foot, left as the owner went about his daily chores. But this riverside community was no backwater. A wide-reaching trade network brought in, for example, a necklace of blue glass, amber, and jet beads that had been created in the Balkans and the Middle East.

What caused the fire that destroyed this place and prompted residents to leave? It could have been a ritual destruction, which was not uncommon during this period. One expert believes the fire started outside; in that case, jealous neighbors may have set houses alight in an attack. Or sparks may have accidently scattered onto a roof's dry thatch. But we may never know for sure.

As artifacts continued to emerge from the mud, the time allotted for the excavation was extended twice. Eventually, though, the quarry reclaimed the site, the excavation area was reburied, and a road was built on top. Although plans move ahead to display pieces at a museum in neighboring Peterborough, the collection is currently in the hands of researchers and conservators. Work will surely continue for years to come, building the most detailed picture of life in Bronze Age Britain that has ever been possible.

1000–500 B.C.

Ancient Tribes & Dynasties

Retaining power was a high-wire act during the first millennium B.C. as leaders conquered new territory while keeping a wary eye on local rivals and foreign threats. Whether they ruled a loose affiliation of people or a great empire, leaders took big risks and reaped equal rewards. In Mexico, the Olmec appear to have honored these larger-than-life figures by carving colossal stone heads to represent them. In Germany, the Celts laid a great chieftain to rest adorned in the eternal glimmer of gold. In western Asia, kings expressed their considerable power by constructing great cities and palaces. In Nubia, they built steep-sided pyramids. And what of the immortal King David? Clues about his rule in the land of Israel are scant, but archaeologists continue to search—and debate what they have found.

Standing in the shadow of the Zagros Mountains, the ruins of Persepolis offer a glimpse of how beautiful the Achaemenid capital must have been.

34

BEYOND THE BLUE HORIZON

950–660 B.C. ◆ Éfaté, Vanuatu ◆ Lapita

An island cemetery has revealed new clues about pioneering voyagers who used simple canoes to reach remote outposts in the Pacific Ocean.

———◆———

On a sun-drenched knoll on the island of Éfaté, about half an hour's drive east of Port Vila, the old colonial capital of Vanuatu, Matthew Spriggs sat on an upturned bucket, gently brushing away dirt from a richly decorated piece of pottery unearthed only a few minutes earlier. "I've never seen anything like this," he said. "Nobody has. This is unique."

That description fit much of what was coming out of the ground. "What we have is a first- or second-generation site containing the graves of some of the Pacific's first explorers," said Spriggs, an archaeologist from the Australian National University and co-leader of an international team that excavated the site between 2004 and 2010.

It came to light only by luck. A backhoe operator, digging up a derelict coconut plantation to prepare a shrimp farm, scraped open a grave in a burial ground some 3,000 years old. It was the oldest cemetery ever found in the Pacific islands, and harbored the bones of an ancient people archaeologists call Lapita, a label that derives

Decorated by pressing a carved stamp into clay, distinctive Lapita pottery offers evidence of migration from the western Pacific to the islands of Vanuatu.

from New Caledonia, where a landmark cache of their pottery was found in the 1950s.

The Lapita were daring adventurers who roved the sea not just as explorers but also as pioneers, bringing along everything they would need to build new lives—their families and livestock, taro seedlings and stone tools. "The really fascinating part of this story isn't the methods they used, but their motives," said archaeologist Geoff Irwin. "The Lapita . . . didn't need to pick up and go; there was nothing forcing them, no overcrowded homeland. They went because they wanted to go and see what was over the horizon." Within the span of a few centuries, they stretched the boundaries

> "The really fascinating part of this story isn't the methods they used, but their motives. The Lapita . . . didn't need to pick up and go; there was nothing forcing them, no overcrowded homeland. They went because they wanted to go and see what was over the horizon."
>
> —*Geoff Irwin,*
> *archaeologist*

of their world from jungle-clad Papua New Guinea to the loneliest coral outliers of Tonga, at least 2,000 miles eastward in the Pacific. Along the way they explored millions of square miles of unknown sea, discovering and colonizing scores of tropical islands never before seen by human eyes: Vanuatu, New Caledonia, Fiji, Samoa.

Their descendants, centuries later, became the great Polynesian navigators: the Tahitians and Hawaiians, the New Zealand Maori, and the people who erected the statues of Easter Island. But the Lapita laid the foundation—bequeathing to the islands the language, customs, and cultures that their more famous descendants carried around the Pacific.

Although the Lapita left a glorious legacy, they also left few clues about themselves. What little is known or surmised about them has been pieced together from fragments of pottery, animal bones, obsidian flakes, and such oblique sources as comparative linguistics and geochemistry. Although their voyages can be traced back to Papua New Guinea, their language—variants of which are still spoken across the Pacific—came from Taiwan. And their pottery decoration, created by pressing a carved stamp into clay, probably had roots in the Philippines.

With the discovery of the Éfaté cemetery, the volume of data available to researchers expanded dramatically. Among the finds were some 68 graves holding the bones of individuals who included old men, young women, and even babies.

Archaeologists were also thrilled to uncover six complete Lapita pots; before this, only four had ever been found. Other artifacts included a burial urn with modeled birds arranged on the rim as though peering down at the human bones sealed inside. The discovery conclusively identified the remains. "It would be hard for anyone to argue that these aren't Lapita when you have human bones enshrined inside what is unmistakably a Lapita urn," Spriggs said.

Several lines of evidence bolster Sprigg's conclusion that this was a community of pioneers making their first voyages into the remote reaches of Oceania. For one thing, the radiocarbon dating of bones and charcoal places them early in the Lapita expansion. For another, the chemical makeup of the obsidian flakes littering the site indicates that the rock wasn't local; it was imported from a large island in Papua New Guinea's Bismarck Archipelago, the springboard for the Lapita's Pacific voyages. This beautiful volcanic glass was fashioned into cutting and scraping tools—exactly the type of survival gear explorers would have packed into their canoes.

A particularly intriguing clue comes from chemical tests on the teeth of several skeletons. The elements absorbed from foods

Three thousand years ago, adventurous sailors from the western Pacific found safe harbor on the island of Éfaté and began to settle its 353 square miles.

indicated that several of the Lapita buried on Éfaté didn't spend their childhoods there, but came from somewhere else. At some point in their lives, these people left the villages of their birth and made a voyage by seagoing canoe, never to return.

There is one stubborn question for which archaeology has yet to provide any answers: How did the Lapita accomplish the ancient equivalent of a moon landing, many times over? No one has found a canoe, or any rigging to reveal how canoes were sailed. Nor do the oral histories and traditions of later Polynesians offer any insights, for they segue into myth long before they reach as far back in time as the Lapita.

"All we can say for certain is that the Lapita had canoes that were capable of ocean voyages, and they had the ability to sail them," said Geoff Irwin, an emeritus archaeologist at the University of Auckland and an avid yachtsman. Those sailing skills were developed and passed down over thousands of years by earlier mariners who worked their way through the archipelagoes of the western Pacific, making short crossings to islands within sight of each other. The real adventure didn't begin until their descendants neared the end of the Solomon chain—for this was the edge of the known world. The nearest landfall, the Santa Cruz Islands, is almost 230 miles away, and for at least 150 of those miles, the Lapita sailors would have been out of sight of land.

However they achieved it, the Lapita spread themselves a third of the way across the Pacific, then called it quits for reasons known only to them. Perhaps they were too thinly stretched to venture farther. They probably never numbered more than a few thousand in total, and in their rapid migration eastward they encountered hundreds of islands—more than 300 in Fiji alone. Supplied with such an embarrassment of riches, they could settle down and enjoy what for a time were Earth's last Edens.

35

HOMES OF THE HIGH AND MIGHTY

912–609 B.C. ✦ Northern Iraq ✦ Neo-Assyrian

*Some of the most powerful kings who ever lived
filled their palaces with strange, protective statues
and fine reliefs that were meant to inspire awe.*

———◆———

I n the spring of 1929, archaeologists from the University of Chicago's Oriental Institute were excavating at Khorsabad in northern Iraq when they found pieces of a massive sculpture. In the eighth century B.C., that colossus—a human-headed, winged bull called a lamassu—guarded the entry to the throne room in the palace of Neo-Assyrian King Sargon II. Carved from a single stone, the figure stood more than 16 feet tall and weighed some 40 tons. Edward Chiera, who headed the dig, cabled the news to James Henry Breasted, director of the institute: "FOUND WINGED BULL FIVE METERS BY FIVE FACE TURNING SIDEWAYS GOOD CONDITION STOP SHIPPING POSSIBLE MONTH MAY ONLY STOP COST TRANSPORTATION ABOUT TEN THOUSAND DOLLARS STOP."

Shipping the beast home would be costly and difficult. Even the smallest of its dozen fragments weighed five tons. Also, the move would have to be done immediately. The Tigris River, about 12 miles away, could serve as transportation, but the river was only

A mysterious, colossal figure called a genie once stood in Sargon's palace at Dur-Sharrukin, one of the sites ISIS militants reportedly attacked in 2015.

navigable during the flooding season, which would end just a few weeks later. And then there was the question of how Iraq would divide up the finds—some to stay in Iraq, some to be given to the Oriental Institute as the sponsor of the excavation.

"DIVISION APRIL TWENTY SIXTH STOP SHALL WE ASK FOR BULL," Chiera queried in his message. Breasted said yes. So did the Iraqis. And thus began the task of getting heavy, intricately carved, crated stones to Chicago—15 days moving them to the Tigris, three days loading them onto the boat, travel down the river, an ocean voyage, and a complicated railroad journey across the eastern United States.

Finally, three years after the discovery, the reassembled statue was put on display. Today, it's the centerpiece of the Oriental Institute's re-creation of a palace courtyard where carved stone reliefs of the king receiving tribute once lined the base of the plaster-coated, mud-brick walls.

Though reviled in the Bible as cruel and despotic rulers, Neo-Assyrian kings created the first truly international empire where trade, religion, and artistic ideas flowed freely. Their cities, meant to awe, were showcases of grand palaces, temples, and monumental works of sculpted stone. Since the mid-1800s, archaeologists have probed the ruins to gain an understanding of an ancient culture that preceded the Persian, Greek, and Roman Empires—and to fill museums with their finds.

An earlier Assyrian culture, based in the city of Ashur, flourished between the 14th and 12th centuries B.C. The new empire—what modern scholars call Neo-Assyrian—arose in the same place in the 10th century B.C. Relying on a professional army of infantry, mounted cavalry, and charioteers, powerful rulers reconquered lands that their forebears had lost, and launched campaigns to gain new territory. Their realm, at its height, stretched south to Babylon, west into what is now Turkey, and southwest into Egypt.

King Ashurnasirpal II, who reigned between 883 and 859 B.C., moved the capital from Ashur to the ancient city of Kalhu—Calah in the Bible—today known as the archaeological site of Nimrud. "That city I built anew," he declared in an inscription displayed at his residence. "A palace of cedar, cypress, juniper, boxwood, mulberry, pistachio-wood, and tamarisk, for my royal dwelling and for my lordly pleasure for all time I founded therein." Under that palace, in 1989, Iraqi archaeologists uncovered the burials of several queens. The royal jewelry included crowns, earrings, and bracelets, and ranks among the finest ancient gold ever found.

After Sargon II rose to power in 721, he began work on a new capital, Dur-Sharrukin—"Fortress of Sargon"—today the site of modern-day Khorsabad. His laborers apparently had as much trouble moving the winged bull statues as the Oriental Institute did more than 2,600 years later. "Good health to the king, my Lord!" wrote an official named Ashur-bani. "Ashur-sumi-ke'in called me to help and loaded the bull colossi on the boats, but the boats could not carry the load and sank. Now, although it cost me a great trouble, I have now hauled them up again."

In 706 B.C., Sargon II moved to the purpose-built city. It wasn't finished, but at least the palace was decorated. The reliefs, carved in typical boldly delineated detail, depict military triumphs, courtiers, men bearing tribute, banqueting, and hunting. Sargon hardly had time to enjoy it, though. He died in battle the very next year.

The new king, Sennacherib, abandoned Dur-Sharrukin in short order and moved to Nineveh, where he began to build a new royal residence. He called it the "Palace without Rival" in his inscriptions. It, too, was decorated with elaborate reliefs, including scenes of quarry workers and the transportation of the ever unwieldy lamassus. Sennacherib's grandson Ashurbanipal built his own palace, set amid orchards and gardens and designed to proclaim his wealth and power, with a splendor to outshine what his predecessors had created. Among the exquisite reliefs that survive is a series showing the details of a lion hunt—bows being prepared, dogs straining at their leashes, the king's chariot in full chase, and the mortally wounded prey.

That era of grand architecture came to an end around 609 B.C., after a coalition of enemies sacked the Neo-Assyrians' cities and brought down their empire. Islamic militants, who took over northern and western Iraq in 2014, destroyed much of what was still standing and proceeded to smash lamassus, pulverize reliefs, and bulldoze ruins into oblivion. As Iraq's future remains uncertain, so does the future of archaeology and the traces of antiquity that still lie, undiscovered, beneath the ground.

36

THE SEARCH
FOR KING
DAVID

ca 900 B.C. ◆ Tel Dan, Israel ◆ Judaean

*Was the biblical king fact or fiction? An inscription
fueled hopes and controversy about the figure.*

———◆———

To Muslims he is Daoud, the venerated emperor and servant
of Allah. To Christians, he is the natural and spiritual ancestor of Jesus, who thereby inherits his messianic mantle. To
the Jews, he is the unifier of Israel—the shepherd king anointed by
God—and they in turn are his descendants and God's Chosen People. Michelangelo's rendering of David in a battle-ready stance of
alluring grace transformed marble into a masterpiece. The young
warrior's duel with the giant Goliath has made him one of history's
greatest underdogs and birthed an enduring metaphor. That he
might be something lesser, or a myth altogether, is to many unthinkable. But was David a real historical figure?

That question has intrigued archaeologists and historians
for centuries. "Almost everyone agrees that the Bible is an ancient
text relating to the history of this country during the Iron Age,"
explains Israeli archaeologist Amihai Mazar. But despite the

biblical importance of a King David who ushered in the golden age of the kingdom of Israel and Judah and had an approximate ruling date of 1000 B.C. derived from the Bible, scholars were stumped by the lack of physical evidence of his life and reign.

In the 1980s, the scholarly movement known as "biblical minimalism," asserted that David and his son Solomon were simply fictitious characters. No one had found evidence beyond the Bible, whether textual or physical, that pointed to David's supposed reign. That changed in 1993, when Gila Cook, the surveyor on an expedition to the ancient city of Dan—the site known as Tel Dan—in northern Israel, noticed a fragment of a basalt stone tablet in what was left of a wall near the entrance to the city. The tablet was covered with early Aramaic writing, and one line contained the words "House of David." The extraordinary find made headlines around the world.

Other parts of the stela were located the following year. Though not complete, the monumental inscription recounts the defeat of a king of the house of David by a king of Aram-Damascus in the ninth century B.C. That corroborates a biblical story in 1 Kings.

The Tel Dan stela attracted intense interest not just from archaeologists, but also from biblical scholars in search of evidence of the holy book's historical reliability. Because the books of the Old Testament outlining the story of David and Solomon consist of scriptures probably written at least 300 years after their supposed rule, by not-so-objective authors, scholars had long struggled to find a firm historical footing for two of the Bible's most charismatic characters. Without contemporaneous texts to validate biblical claims about David, his origin story had long been shrouded in mystery.

The stela's discovery didn't dispel all doubts. When Avraham Biran, the dig's director, translated the text, he claimed that the word "DWD" stood for "David." Aramaic does not have written vowels, though, so alternative interpretations may apply. Today, few argue that it may not refer to the biblical king, but there's still the problem of the tablet's silence on David himself: "House of

An Aramaic inscription from the site of Tel Dan contains the earliest historic reference to the House of David, highlighted on the basalt fragment at right.

David" is another way of referring to the nation of Judah, and because the stela was inscribed more than a century after David's supposed reign, some scholars argue it cannot be seen as evidence that David was really a historical figure.

Archaeologist Eilat Mazar announced in 2005 that she believed she had unearthed the palace of King David based on its location and pottery, but the date of construction and her methods are contested. On the heels of Mazar's claim, other archaeologists unveiled remarkable finds. Thirty miles south of the Dead Sea in Jordan, a University of California, San Diego professor named Thomas Levy has excavated a vast copper-smelting operation that would have had the capacity to produce the bronze objects from the biblical description of Solomon's Temple. Meanwhile, 20 miles southwest of Jerusalem in the Elah Valley—the very spot where the Bible says the young shepherd David slew Goliath—Yosef Garfinkel, a professor at the Hebrew University of Jerusalem, claims to have unearthed the corner of a large Judaean city. "Maybe Goliath never existed," he says. "The story is that Goliath came from a giant city, and in the telling of it over centuries, he became a giant himself. It's a metaphor. Modern scholars want the Bible to be like the Oxford Encyclopedia. People didn't write history 13,000 years ago like this. In the evening by the fire, this is where the stories like David and Goliath started." Both Levy and Garfinkel support their contentions with scientific data, including pottery remnants and

"In the evening by the fire, this is where the stories like David and Goliath started."

—*Yosef Garfinkel,*
professor of archaeology

radiocarbon dating of olive and date pits found at the sites.

Since 1993, David's name has been spotted on other stelae and monuments, adding to evidence outside the Bible. But due to damage and interpretive challenges, it's still unclear whether the word refers to a nation or an actual historical figure. The ongoing research has uncovered much valuable knowledge about the ancient people who built cities, farmed, fought, and prayed in this sliver of the ancient world, but archaeologists have yet to find the hard evidence that David existed among them—and so the search for the first king of Israel goes on.

37

MEXICO'S COLOSSAL STONE HEADS

1200–400 B.C. ◆ Southeastern Mexico ◆ Olmec

Monumental carvings in basalt—likely portraits of rulers—
have become the hallmarks of one of Mexico's earliest and
most mysterious cultures.

———◆———

I n 1858, a local workman was clearing a virgin patch of rainforest in the Mexican state of Veracruz when he found, embedded in the heavy black soil, what he thought was the bottom of an enormous inverted kettle.

Excitedly, he reported his discovery to the owner of the nearby hacienda of Hueyapa. With visions of buried treasure, the owner brought in a crew of men to excavate the "kettle."

As the digging progressed, the object was revealed to be the upper part of an enormous head, skillfully carved from a great block of basalt. Disappointed in the search for fabulous wealth, the investigators continued no further.

Nature and the process of erosion soon reburied much of the giant piece of sculpture. But the tradition of what came to be known as the colossal head of Hueyapa lingered in the region, and on at least three subsequent occasions attracted the attention of

scientifically minded travelers in the vicinity. In spite of its spectacular nature, though, the find never came to general public notice and was all but forgotten.

Until 1938, that is, when Matthew W. Stirling, head of the Smithsonian Institution's Bureau of American Ethnology, was traveling on vacation in that part of the world. He had read about the head, seen pictures, and wanted to examine it himself. After an eighthour horseback ride and a trek on foot, he found the sculpture, covered to its forehead, near the village of Tres Zapotes.

Returning home to Washington, D.C., Stirling mounted a joint Smithsonian-National Geographic expedition to explore the area and its intriguing traces of the past. His 1939 field season would be the first of eight that took him to Veracruz and the nearby states of Tabasco, Campeche, and Chiapas to conduct the first systematic study of the culture now known as Olmec.

Traveling by boat from the flat, alluvial coast of the Gulf of Mexico, Stirling headed for the base of the Sierra de los Tuxtlas, passing through a maze of mangrove swamps, hyacinth-choked streams, and dense tropical forests where parrots flew noisily overhead and iguanas sunned themselves on walls of vines. Finally, a team of mules hauled the crew and their gear to camp. "We began immediately the work of excavating the colossal head, which lay not more than 100 yards from our camp," Stirling wrote in a report for *National Geographic* magazine. The monument, they discovered, was approximately six feet tall and 18 feet in circumference, with an estimated weight of more than 10 tons. "Despite its great size the workmanship is delicate and sure, the proportions perfect . . . Fully exposed to view for the first time in modern times, it still remains as great a mystery as ever, for it fits into no known aboriginal American cultural picture . . . Could his great mouth but speak, one of the most important chapters of American history would doubtless be revealed to us."

At the site of Tres Zapotes, explorer Matthew Stirling measures a colossal pre-Columbian Olmec head sculpted from a basalt boulder, which he discovered.

> "Could his great mouth but speak, one of the most important chapters of American history would doubtless be revealed to us."
>
> —*Matthew W. Stirling, ethnographer*

The expedition would last almost four months, December to April, revealing carved stone slabs known as stelae, fragments of an ornately decorated basin, stone yokes in the shape of a stylized frog and the mouth of a jaguar, and eerily lifelike clay masks. The team included Stirling's wife, Marion. Like other women married to high-profile male colleagues throughout the history of scientific investigation, she played a crucial role in discoveries and research but never got the same level of recognition. Matthew described her as his "co-explorer, co-author and general co-ordinator," but she merely said that she "cleaned the pottery, packed, kept notes, dug the spring, kept up with the correspondence, supervised the camp." Nevertheless, her name is worth remembering for the role she played in rewriting Mesoamerican history. In 1939, she calculated that a calendar carved into a monument found at Tres Zapotes referred to the year 31 B.C., making it, at that time, the oldest known date recorded in the New World.

The Stirlings and the rest of the team devoted part of each day to exploration, and it soon became apparent that their site marked the location of a once great ceremonial center. By their count, more than 50 mounds dotted an archaeological zone that stretched for more than two miles.

Stirling at first described what he found as it related to the Maya, the best known frame of reference for pre-Hispanic cultures in the region. But after his second season, in 1940, he was able to offer more detail. "The mysterious producers of this art have been called the 'Olmecs,' whose origin and fate are unknown," he wrote. "Present archaeological evidence indicates that their culture, which in many respects reached a high level, is very early and may well be the basic civilization out of which developed such high art centers as those of the Maya, Zapotecs, Toltecs, and Totonacs."

Subsequent explorations by Stirling and others would uncover additional colossal heads at sites such as La Venta and San Lorenzo, bringing the total to 17. These unique monuments have come to symbolize a culture that is still not well understood and whose impact is still debated.

For years, many scholars believed that the Olmec were Mexico's mother culture, which gave rise to such innovations as writing, a sophisticated calendar, and the brutal ritual ball game, most widely known from the Maya, that sometimes ended in human sacrifice. Their theory held that the Maya derived their entire society— including architecture and social structure—directly from the Olmec. When the Olmec were busy building their civilization along the Veracruz coast, according to this scenario, the people who would become the Maya were living in loosely associated nomadic groups in jungles to the south and east.

Evidence has been slowly emerging, however, of a more complex, nuanced history. At the pre-Classic Maya site of Ceibal, for example, University of Arizona anthropologist Takeshi Inomata has found signs of ritual architecture that are some 200 years older than structures at La Venta, which flourished from about 800 to 400 B.C.

"This does not mean that the Maya developed independently," Inomata says. Instead, he believes, the influence flowed both ways. La Venta and Ceibal appear to have developed in tandem in a great cultural shift throughout the region. "It seems more likely that there was a broad history of interactions across these regions, and through these interactions, a new form of society developed."

What made the Olmec civilization fade into the mists of time and the Maya go on to develop their own iconic language and culture? Answering that will require further evidence from future excavations, as is the case with so many of archaeology's puzzles.

38

PYRAMIDS OF THE BLACK PHARAOHS

715 B.C.–A.D. 325 ◆ Sudan ◆ Kushite

In a long-ignored chapter of history, African kings conquered Egypt, then kept the country's ancient burial traditions alive for centuries to come.

———◆———

Sudan's many pyramids—more than double the 90 or so known in Egypt—are haunting spectacles in the Nubian Desert. They speak to a little-known time whose traces have been hiding in plain sight for more than two millennia, overshadowed by the world-famous sites to the north. "The first time I came to Sudan, people said: 'You're mad! There's no history there! It's all in Egypt!'" explained Swiss Egyptologist Charles Bonnet. But he and other modern archaeologists are now revealing the rich history of a long-ignored culture.

In the year 730 B.C., a man named Piye decided the only way to save Egypt from itself was to invade it. The magnificent civilization that had built the Great Pyramids had lost its way, torn apart by petty warlords. For two decades Piye had ruled over his own kingdom in Nubia, a swath of Africa located mostly in present-day

Marking the burials of Kushite kings and queens, more than 20 ancient pyramids sprawl across 170 acres of Sudanese desert at the ancient cemetery of Nuri.

Sudan. But he considered himself the rightful heir to the traditions practiced by the great pharaohs.

He and his soldiers sailed north on the Nile River. At Thebes, the capital of Upper Egypt, they disembarked. Believing there was a proper way to wage holy wars, Piye instructed his soldiers to purify themselves before combat by bathing in the Nile; they dressed themselves in fine linen and sprinkled their bodies with water from the temple at Karnak, a site sacred to the ram-headed sun god Amun, whom Piye identified as his own personal deity. Piye himself feasted and offered sacrifices to Amun. Thus sanctified, the commander and his men commenced to do battle.

By the end of a yearlong campaign, every leader in Egypt had capitulated. In exchange for their lives, the vanquished urged Piye to worship at their temples, pocket their finest jewels, and claim their best horses. He obliged them, and became the anointed Lord of the Two Lands.

When Piye died at the end of his 35-year reign in 715 B.C., his subjects honored his wishes by burying him in an Egyptian-style pyramid at a site known today as El Kurru. He was the first pharaoh to receive such entombment in more than 500 years.

Piye was the first of the so-called Black pharaohs, the five Nubian rulers of Egypt's 25th dynasty. Over the course of 75 years, those kings reunified a tattered Egypt and created an empire that stretched from the southern border at present-day Khartoum all the way north to the Mediterranean Sea.

Until recently, theirs was a chapter of history that largely went untold. In the past several decades, though, archaeologists have recognized that the Black pharaohs didn't appear out of nowhere. They sprang from a robust African civilization called Kush that had flourished on the southern banks of the Nile going back at least as far as the first Egyptian dynasty.

The Egyptians didn't like having such a powerful neighbor to the south, especially because they depended on Nubia's gold mines to bankroll their dominance of western Asia. So the pharaohs of the 18th dynasty (1539–1292 B.C.) sent armies to

About two inches tall, a pendant of rock crystal topped with a golden head of the Egyptian goddess Hathor was discovered in a Kushite queen's tomb at El Kurru.

conquer Nubia and built garrisons along the Nile. Subjugated, the elite Nubians began to embrace Egypt's cultural and spiritual customs—venerating Egyptian gods, using the Egyptian language, and adopting Egyptian burial styles.

The Nubians were arguably the first people to be struck by "Egyptomania." Without setting foot inside Egypt, they preserved Egyptian traditions and revived the pyramid—a burial monument forsaken by the Egyptians centuries earlier—for their royal tombs. As archaeologist Timothy Kendall put it, the Nubians "had become more Catholic than the pope."

In the seventh century B.C., Assyrians invaded Egypt from the north. Although the Nubians retreated permanently to their homeland, they continued to mark their royal tombs with pyramids, dotting sites such as El Kurru, Nuri, and Meroë with the steep-sided profiles that characterize their interpretation of the ancient Egyptian monuments. Like their mentors, Kushite kings filled their burial chambers with treasure—much of it later plundered—and decorated them with images that would assure a rich afterlife. Unlike the Egyptians, however, they placed their tombs under the pyramids, rather than within.

Little was known of these shadowy kings until experts such as Harvard Egyptologist George Reisner arrived in Sudan in the early 20th century. Reisner located the tombs of the five Nubian pharaohs of Egypt and many of their successors, who continued to rule the kingdom of Kush until the fourth century A.D. These discoveries, and subsequent investigations by Bonnet, National Geographic grantee Pearce-Paul Creasman, and others that continue to this day, have resurrected from obscurity the first high civilization in sub-Saharan Africa.

39

CITIES OF THE DEAD

900–100 B.C. ◆ Italy ◆ Etruscan

Sensuously decorated tombs in the Etruscan necropolises of Tarquinia and Cerveteri offer an intimate glimpse into the lives of the people who dominated central Italy right before the Romans.

————◆————

The Etruscans have long been the magical mystery people of antiquity. They rose from the mist of Italian prehistory around 900 B.C. and for some 500 years dominated most of the country from Rome to the Po Valley. With their loose confederation of 12 city-states, they forged Italy's first urban civilization. They cultivated grapes and olives and exploited the rich mineral resources of central Italy, spawning a wealthy merchant class that competed mightily with the Greeks for trade throughout the Mediterranean. They gave us the toga and used a precursor of the Latin alphabet that we use today. Yet, unlike the Greeks and Romans, the Etruscans left behind a sparse written record—no heroic poems, no histories, no literature, only short official or religious inscriptions with a glut of words that have yet to be deciphered.

For centuries, much of the information on these people came via the partisan reports of ancient Greek and Roman histories. Even those writers debated who the Etruscans were and where they came from. The Etruscan language was alien to their neighbors. Their customs were spiritual and sensual. Etruscan women enjoyed uncommonly high status for the ancient, male-dominated Mediterranean world. The Greeks and Romans considered the Etruscans hedonistic. They were indeed a different people. Although Greek historian Herodotus claimed they were Lydians who had migrated to Italy from Asia Minor, many modern scholars believe the Etruscans evolved from an Indigenous group of Iron Age farmers.

Thousands of their burial chambers are scattered around their sparsely preserved cities. Much of what is known about the Etruscans comes from these sepulchres—how they lived, their religion and art, the music, dancing, and athletic games they enjoyed. The two most important necropolises were discovered at Tarquinia and Cerveteri, both northwest of Rome, though "discovered" is perhaps the wrong word to describe cemeteries that looters from antiquity to the present and, only more recently, archaeologists dug into again and again.

At Cerveteri's Banditaccia necropolis, the earliest simple tombs were dug in the ninth century B.C., but in later periods the cemetery transformed into a replica of an Etruscan town. Through excavations in the early 20th century, archaeologist Raniero Mengarelli discovered that some tombs at Cerveteri were carved in the shape of huts or houses and were organized along streets with small squares and neighborhoods. (The Romans became expert roadbuilders by learning from the engineering skills of the Etruscans.) Because many of the cities where the Etruscans lived were built over by centuries of Italian history, the details inside these chambers offer a rare peek at what an Etruscan home may have looked like, particularly because the dead were provided with many worldly goods to use in the afterlife. The carved sarcophagi are surrounded by weapons, armor, shields, mirrors, jewelry, silver boxes of cosmetics, urns, and other treasures.

Although very few of the Banditaccia tombs had wall paintings and carvings, Tarquinia's Monterozzi necropolis is famous for its wealth of underground artwork. Tarquinia was the cultural capital of the Etruscans 2,700 years ago. From a plateau it looked in splendor toward the Tyrrhenian Sea. Once 20,000 people inhabited the site. Today, only the scant remains of an excavated temple mark the site of the ancient city center, but its cemetery has at least 6,000 graves cut in the rock. More than 200 painted tombs, the oldest of which date to the seventh century B.C., have been identified there. Scholars in the 18th and 19th centuries already knew many of the most famous artworks. Those early discoveries prompted a wave of "Etruscomania" among European art lovers drawn to the frescoed walls depicting an afterlife where garlanded Etruscans recline on couches, fine-robed and sipping wine served by enslaved people. In the lush murals, dancers tap their sandaled feet to the tune of flutes and lyres, lovers touch hands, spotted leopards pace between trees, and dolphins leap from the sea.

In the 1920s, English author D. H. Lawrence toured the network of underground art at Tarquinia and described the dizzying experience of entering the decaying chambers: "So we go on, seeing tomb after tomb, dimness after dimness, divided between the pleasure of finding so much, and the disappointment that so little remains . . . Fragments of people at banquets, limbs that dance without dancers, birds that fly in nowhere, lions whose devouring heads are devoured away!" Traversing the winding tumulus passages to the tombs deep within felt like "burrowing inside some ancient pyramid."

> "So we go on, seeing tomb after tomb, dimness after dimness, divided between the pleasure of finding so much, and the disappointment that so little remains."
>
> —*D. H. Lawrence,*
> *author*

These paintings could indeed quickly degrade once exposed to air and humidity. To find and conserve the ancient tombs, researchers had to turn to less-invasive prospecting technologies introduced to archaeology in the mid-20th century. In the 1950s engineer

A painted tomb at Tarquinia includes a scene of a drinking party, with Etruscan aristocrats reclining on couches. Another wall shows dancers and musicians.

Carlo Lerici used aerial photos and electrical sounding methods to pinpoint the location of tombs at Cerveteri and Tarquinia. The researchers devised a periscope camera to take photographs of what remained inside as an easier alternative to digging. As their work progressed, they were amazed to find the extent to which clandestine diggers in both ancient and more recent times had opened and rifled Etruscan tombs. Of more than 500 tombs they located and investigated in Cerveteri, nearly all had been opened at one time or another, some many times, by looters who made off with vases, jewelry, and other riches.

After a couple months of prospecting at Tarquinia, Lerici's team finally captured images of underground paintings. There were scenes of athletes running and hurling the discus. Others showed horses galloping in a spirited chariot race. The paintings were still vividly colored and seemed in fair condition. "I can scarcely convey the tremendous emotion these tiny photographs of a buried room gave me," Lerici wrote in 1959. The team organized an excavation and named the chamber the Tomb of the Olympiad.

A similar method was used to probe a tomb beneath a road where officials in Tarquinia wanted to put a new water main in 1985. Archaeologists at that time revealed scenes of feasting and celebration but also black- and blue-skinned demons ushering the deceased to the underworld in a Greek-inspired nightmare. Those scenes were painted in the late fifth century B.C. Soon after, the Etruscans began their slow decline, squeezed by pressure from the Gauls and the Greeks, and eventually overtaken by the Romans. Their way of life eventually vanished, but their playfulness lives on in the art they left behind. Perhaps D. H. Lawrence perceived their secret best: "There seems to have been in the Etruscan instinct a real desire to preserve the natural humour of life. And that is a task surely more worthy, and even much more difficult in the long run, than conquering the world or sacrificing the self or saving the immortal soul."

40

BABYLON'S CROWNING GLORY

*Built by a fabled king, the Ishtar Gate served as
the portal for a parade of gods during the celebration
of the new year at the spring equinox.*

———◆———

When architect Robert Koldewey traveled to Mesopotamia in 1897 to scout out potential excavation sites for the German Oriental Society, he found traces of a stunning gateway to one of the most famous cities in the ancient world: the structure now known as the Ishtar Gate of Babylon.

On his tour, Koldewey visited Ashur, Larsa, Nineveh, Uruk, and other important historical places in the cradle of Middle Eastern civilization. But it was the remains of the gate that sealed the deal. "I saw a number of fragments of enameled brick reliefs, of which I took several with me to Berlin," he wrote later. Those artifacts backed up his arguments in favor of digging at Babylon and secured funding, some of which came from Kaiser Wilhelm II himself.

Work began on March 26, 1899. Over the next 15 years, Koldewey and his team would reveal the remains of streets and temples, the king's palace, and a ziggurat that some believe is the Tower of Babel.

They would also recover tens of thousands of pieces of the gate, which became the raw material for a spectacular reconstruction.

Babylon was a minor village when Sumerians made their breakthrough to civilization in the mid-fourth millennium B.C. It rose from obscurity under the monarch Hammurabi, who began his reign around 1792 B.C. Hammurabi took advantage of the chaotic situation in Mesopotamia that had existed since Sumer fell to invaders around 2000 B.C. and consolidated the warring states into what historians call the Old Babylonian Empire.

A direct heir to the culture of ancient Sumer, Babylon remained the great metropolis and cultural hub of western Asia, unrivaled in prestige for two thousand years. Biblical tradition associated Babylon with decadence and vice, but the city was, in fact, a center of

The main entrance to King Nebuchadnezzar's Babylon, now reconstructed in a museum, was a gate of tiled mud brick displaying protective dragons and bulls.

learning and religion. Under Hammurabi, Babylon developed a centralized administration, a bureaucracy, and a professional merchant class. Hammurabi also promulgated a now famous legal code—282 laws, inscribed in stone—including the principle of an "eye for eye, tooth for tooth" that is set forth in the Old Testament.

Through the subsequent invasions of Hittites, Kassites, and Assyrians, the tradition-bound city of Babylon retained its cultural importance. In time, a tribe from southern Mesopotamia called the Chaldeans established a dynasty in Babylon. In 612 B.C. the Chaldeans and their allies struck the mighty Assyrian Empire a death-blow, and Nebuchadnezzar II, monarch of Babylon, began to bring a new grandeur to the ancient city.

The Old Testament remembers Nebuchadnezzar as the ruthless conqueror who destroyed Jerusalem in 586 B.C. Babylonian history, however, celebrates him primarily as the conscientious administrator and tireless builder who made his capital the greatest metropolis in the world at that time. Lavish buildings and the famed Hanging Gardens with their multiple terraces—one of the seven wonders of the ancient world—date from this Neo-Babylonian period.

Among the many attractions was the main entrance through the city's formidable inner and outer walls, the Ishtar Gate. "I placed wild bulls and ferocious dragons in the gateways and thus adorned them with luxurious splendor so that people might gaze on them in wonder," boasted King Nebuchadnezzar. Flanking a spacious vaulted passageway, the gate's four towers were faced with mud bricks glazed in a brilliant cobalt blue. Rows of dragons symbolizing Marduk, the chief Babylonian god, and bulls symbolizing Adad, the weather god, were embossed on the bricks. Striding lions symbolizing Ishtar, the goddess

> "I placed wild bulls and ferocious dragons in the gateways and thus adorned them with luxurious splendor so that people might gaze on them in wonder."
>
> —*Nebuchadnezzar II, Babylonian king*

of love and war, lined the walls of the passage that led to the gate. The overall effect of the grand structure was to inspire awe in everyone who entered the city, and to remind them of the divine protections that the city enjoyed.

The avenue that passed through the gate was called Aibur-shabu in Babylonian—meaning "the enemy shall never pass." Today it's known as the Processional Way, named for the annual parade of gods during the New Year's festival. Assembled from all the provinces of the kingdom, the statues of the principal deities were first moved with solemn ceremony, and in a rigidly observed order of precedence, through the Ishtar Gate to the northern outskirts of the city. There they were taken up the Euphrates River to the Garden Temple, where the most dramatic part of the ritual took place: the consummation of the sacred marriage of the principal god and goddess, on which depended the fertility and prosperity of the whole land.

Koldewey's meticulous excavation removed tons of earth to reveal the city's grid, which covered more than three square miles, and the location of many of its monumental buildings. The archaeologists also filled 900 boxes with glazed fragments of the Ishtar Gate. But the outbreak of World War I in 1914 shut down the dig, and in the ensuing chaos the gate's pieces ended up in Portugal. After Koldewey died in 1925, a colleague, Walter Andrae, retrieved the boxes and launched a project to reassemble the gate.

Spreading out the fragments on long benches, experts sorted them by color and theme to try to solve the colossal architectural puzzle. Over the course of two years, they were able to put together 30 lions, 26 bulls, and 17 dragons, some of which now appear in a reconstruction of the gate's two front towers that was inaugurated in Berlin's Pergamon Museum in 1930.

The two back towers were much taller and more difficult to display, though. They remain in storage—hidden testaments to the grandeur that greeted all who entered one of history's most extraordinary cities.

41

THE CELTIC KING TUT

ca 550 B.C. ◆ Hochdorf, Germany ◆ Celtic

*Bedecked in gold, a chieftain was buried in resplendent style
and venerated like a pharaoh.*

———◆———

Jorg Biel, staff archaeologist with the State Service of Antiquities, had a good feeling as he embarked on the 30-minute drive from his office in Stuttgart, Germany, to the small village of Hochdorf one day in 1978. Renate Leibfried, a local teacher and archaeologist with a solid record for uncovering ancient sites, had summoned Biel to Hochdorf to investigate some suspicious mounds.

The surrounding state of Baden-Württemberg had a tradition of significant and splendid finds. One grave chamber found in the region yielded gold ornaments and two painted cups made in Athens around 450 B.C. Biel's own boss had discovered a burial mound with a nearly life-size statue of an early Celtic warrior. Perhaps, Biel thought, Leibfried's mysterious mounds would yield similar treasures.

However, Biel's anticipation quickly turned to disappointment. The mounds proved to be of no importance. As perhaps an afterthought or consolation, Leibfried mentioned that farmers had repeatedly struck large stones with their plows on an unusual rise in a different field northeast of the village. Because Biel was already in town, there was no harm in him checking out this other site.

In an instant, Biel realized that this field, rather than the first, was definitely fertile ground for treasure, for he'd seen such formations before. Yet this one was so worn by centuries of erosion and cultivation that no one had recognized it—until now.

After getting permission from the landowner and the mayor, Biel and his team sank a trench in the one-acre site to confirm his suspicions. He hoped to hit a stone wall, which he knew from other similar sites should be there. The first turns of their spades were rewarded with stones, stones, and more stones—big ones. Then bronze objects started to emerge: a bronze disk, some pendants. Encouraged, the team ran more trenches through the core of the hill. They penetrated layers of yellow clay, then gray soil patterned with grass, straw, and wood splinters. To Biel's relief, the layers were undisturbed, with no signs of looters.

Digging even deeper, they came upon a large rectangular chamber, its ceiling collapsed under the weight of the stones. Nestled within was what Biel had been hoping to find: a smaller burial chamber. A man's skeleton lay on a nearly 10-foot-long bronze funeral bed. A gold-handled dagger was fastened to the man's wide leather belt, itself adorned with a delicate band of gold. His fine richly patterned garments had been fastened with intricately twisted gold brooches. Fine latticed strips of gold trimmed the disintegrated remains of the man's burial shoes.

> "As we came upon one precious relic after another, what surprises and what racing heartbeats attended our discoveries!"
>
> —Jorg Biel,
> archaeologist

Around the man's neck was a crucial clue to his identity: He wore a large necklace in the form of a gold ring, known as a torc. This was an important status symbol of a Celtic chieftain during the Hallstatt period of the Iron Age, from roughly 800 B.C. to 450 B.C. "As we came upon one precious relic after another, what surprises and what racing heartbeats attended our discoveries!" Biel recalled.

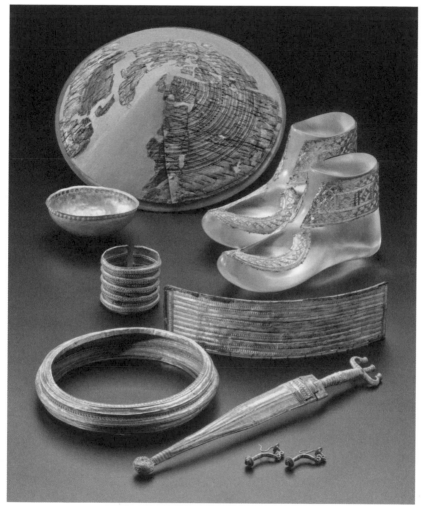

A Celtic chieftain's burial included gold shoe ornaments, belt cover, scabbard, pins to fasten clothing, neck ring, bracelet, bowl, and birch-bark hat.

Biel had unearthed the find of a lifetime, now known as the "Hochdorf treasure." Such large, elaborate burial mounds, often grouped around fortified hilltop settlements, were constructed for Celtic chieftains throughout southwest Germany, central Switzerland, and eastern France during the sixth and fifth centuries B.C. However, in the ensuing centuries, most of the region's other princely tombs from the Hallstatt period had been looted. This treasure chamber, dating to around 550 B.C. (older than the Parthenon in Athens), was remarkably intact. The discovery is one of the richest troves found in Germany, one that archaeologists now consider the "Celtic King Tut." The Celts' prosperity was nowhere near the wealth of the Egyptian kingdom ruled by Tut, but the two rulers were treated with similar veneration in death. Most strikingly, both cultures clearly believed in an afterlife where those who passed on would retain their status and would need their worldly belongings.

The chieftain's grave goods reflect the robust trade ties that local Celtic merchants had with markets in areas as distant as the Baltic and Mediterranean Seas. Patterned woolen and linen textiles and embroidered draperies hung on the chamber's walls and ceiling. A Greek-made bronze cauldron, topped by a ring of lions, was probably presented as a gift to the chieftain during his reign. Wealth from trade and rich natural resources fueled the creation of a stratified society, over which the chieftain reigned.

As befitting the chieftain's status, the burial chamber was prepared for a royal feast. A four-wheeled bronze wagon was set with nine plates and three bronze platters, along with the requisite carving tools. Nine drinking horns hung on the wall, including an ornate gold-trimmed one for the host. A huge round bronze cauldron would have held more than 100 gallons of mead, a fermented honey beverage.

Scientists determined that the chieftain died at around 40 years of age, a full decade later than the average life span of his time. His ornate funeral bier is unlike any other ever recovered. The bed, designed like a high-backed bench, was held up by eight cast-metal statues of women a foot tall. These figures balance, almost like circus acrobats, on wheels of bronze and iron, enabling the bed to be rolled like a couch on casters. Across the back of the bench, embossed figures perform a funeral dance. Two horses pull a four-wheeled cart, possibly representing the Celtic chieftain's final journey into the afterlife.

42

PERSEPOLIS, PRIDE OF PERSIA

518 B.C. ◆ Iran ◆ Persian

Darius the Great immortalized his powerful reign
with multilingual inscriptions on the side of mountains
and a vast palatial complex at Persepolis.

———◆———

M
ost rulers aim to control the narrative of their own reign, but few have done it with the flair of Darius the Great. The Persian king carved his story directly into the side of a mountain, pronouncing, "If thou shalt conceal this record and not tell it to the people, may Ahura Mazda be a smiter unto thee and may there not be unto thee a family." With a high brow and a straight nose, Darius still stands today in the stone-cut relief 340 feet above the springs that bubble up at the base of the mountain, in a place known as Behistun, in western Iran. Before Darius floats the winged figure of the god Ahura Mazda. Beneath the god stand eight rival contenders for power, their necks roped together, hands tied behind their backs; a ninth, the usurper Gaumata, lies prostrate under the king's left foot. (A 10th enemy, a Scythian named Skunkha, was added later as per the emperor's orders.) The images alone were inadequate for Darius. He commanded that his autobiography be recorded in the three languages of the empire: Old Persian, language of the king and court; Babylonian, an adopted administrative language; and Elamite, the language spoken at the great urban

center of Susa. The gigantic cliffside boast became, like Egypt's famed Rosetta stone, a major key to understanding these long-forgotten languages and the cuneiform scripts, with wedge-shaped characters, in which they were written. Beginning in the 19th century, scholars made perilous journeys to try to copy and interpret the famed Behistun Inscription.

Darius the Great undoubtedly had big shoes to fill since his father, Cyrus the Great, founded the Persian Empire, arguably the world's first great superpower. The concepts of freedom and human rights may not have originated with the classical Greeks but in Iran, in as early as the sixth century B.C. under Cyrus. Reputedly a brave and humble leader, Cyrus established what has been called the world's first religiously and culturally tolerant empire. Among

Persian king Darius the Great commissioned a relief 49 feet tall on the side of Mount Behistun, portraying his triumph over rebellious contenders for power.

other things, he freed the enslaved Jews of Babylon in 539 B.C., sending them back to Jerusalem to rebuild their temple with money he gave them. His realm would become the largest, most powerful kingdom on Earth. Ultimately, it comprised more than 23 different peoples who coexisted peacefully under a central government, originally based in Pasargadae.

Darius I, born around 550 B.C., came to power at age 28, and quickly proved himself a great military leader and an even greater administrator. His ascension to king of the Persian Empire was cloaked in intrigue. It's thought he may have staged a coup to claim the throne. Some Persians viewed Darius as a usurper, and many subjects in distant lands saw the succession crisis as an opportunity to rebel. As a result, Darius spent his first three years quelling uprisings. With his elite imperial guard, known as the Ten Thousand Immortals, he commandingly restored order to the realm and expanded its scope. He advanced its eastern frontier to the Indus River and its western boundary beyond the Bosporus, the strait separating Asia from Europe.

More significant than his conquests, though, were the measures he took to consolidate his vast dominion. Darius demonstrated an organizational genius rivaled by few ancient or modern rulers. He divided the empire into some 20 provinces (called satrapies) and issued coins to facilitate taxation and trade, a practice he adopted from Lydian and Greek rulers. He improved on an irrigation system that was in place during Cyrus's reign, leading to a significant expansion of agriculture and settlement throughout the empire's parched landscape. Irrigation tunnels called qanats moved water from underground sources at high elevations, and bridges resembling the Roman aqueducts that would follow centuries later carried the water to distant villages. Traders, troops, and imperial spies moved smoothly on roads built by Darius (and maintained by his successors). The greatest of those was the Royal Road, which stretched more than 1,500 miles, from Ephesus on the Aegean Sea to Susa in western Iran, the empire's administrative center. Under

Darius's rule, Zoroastrianism became the state religion, providing a cohesive sense of identity across his far-flung empire. Yet Darius did not impose the belief system on those of other faiths. His subjects in conquered lands could continue to worship their own gods and keep their own cultural traditions. All these measures helped Darius promote trade and productivity. Accordingly, the standard of living in Persia rose, and Persian dominance in the Near East became entrenched.

More so than Behistun, the archaeological ruins most closely associated with Darius are found at Persepolis, the ceremonial capital he established in 518 B.C. but that the conquering army of Alexander the Great would burn down two centuries later. Foreign travelers and explorers knew of the ancient city since at least the 17th century. Standing in the dry, sunbaked valley of Marvdasht, 38 miles northeast of Shiraz, this ruined city of tombs, colossal statuary, harems, and palaces was first excavated in the 1930s by a team led by archaeologist Ernst Herzfeld from the Oriental Institute of the University of Chicago.

Charles Breasted, a *National Geographic* writer who visited the expedition in its early days, saw the ancient city in 1933 as it was being unveiled. Breasted wrote:

> When we flew over Persepolis last spring, our impression of the site was awe-inspiring. Where once had dwelt pomp and circumstance, with all the bickering and intrigue, the ambitions and the loves and hates surrounding one of the foremost capitals of all time, there was now only brooding desolation and silence, broken only by the noise of workmen singing, by the shouting of orders, and the general hubbub of an archeological expedition hard at work.

The excavators found evidence of Alexander's destruction, in the form of layers of ashes and charcoal between the palace walls. The conquerors had burned the library but, fortunately, thousands of clay tablets inscribed with cuneiform characters, including the archives of the Persian kings, survived the blaze. As the debris of time was slowly swept away from the artificial terrace upon which the city was built, Herzfeld was able to make an authentic ground plan of the complex for the first time. He found a discrete group of buildings formed by the winter palaces of Darius and his son Xerxes, who famously invaded Greece during the Persian Wars, as well as a harem and a palace of a later emperor, Artaxerxes.

The entrance to this royal palace area was between two massive audience halls known as apadanas. The roof of one of these halls had been supported by a forest of 100 lofty stone columns, all superbly carved and fluted. The debris resulting from the destruction and disintegration of such enormous structures formed a layer of rubbish as deep as 26 feet in places for archaeologists to clear. The excavators found two superb sets of double stairways leading to the audience hall of Xerxes and the gate to the palace area. In just a few days' time, Herzfeld laid bare a series of wall reliefs and sculptures along these hallways that almost doubled the volume of ancient Persian art known up to that time.

What's so striking about the ruins of Persepolis today is the absence of violent imagery on what's left of its stone walls. The carvings depict soldiers, but they're not fighting; there are weapons, but they're not drawn. Mainly one sees emblems, suggesting that something humane went on here instead—people of different nations gathering peacefully, bearing gifts, draping their hands amiably on one another's shoulders. In an era noted for its barbarity, Persepolis, it seems, was a relatively cosmopolitan place—and to many Iranians today its ruins are a breathtaking reminder of who their Persian ancestors were and what they accomplished.

One of the finest known examples of ancient goldsmithing, a Thracian vessel bearing mythological scenes was found at Panagyurishte, Bulgaria.

500–200 B.C.

An Age of Artisans

In the workshops of ancient Greece, artists transformed marble and metal into gods and heroes to adorn temples, sanctuaries, and public buildings, creating a hallowed atmosphere of refined beauty. Although much has been lost, known masterpieces include the Elgin Marbles, famously stolen from the Athenian acropolis, and the brawny Riace bronzes rescued from a shipwreck. The Greeks wrote disdainfully about their Thracian neighbors and the wild Scythian nomads of the Eurasian steppes, but the brilliance of the metal-working from both those cultures tells a different story. Works in terra-cotta are compelling in their own right: In Nigeria, sculptures of that material have changed our understanding of African history, and in China, terra-cotta soldiers buried en masse attest to the concerns of a powerful emperor as he entered the great beyond.

43

RIDING WITH THE AMAZONS

900–200 B.C. ✦ Eurasian Steppe, Ukraine, and Russia ✦ Scythian

*Fine artifacts from Scythian graves continue to
deepen our understanding of this tough,
horse-riding tribe of master goldsmiths.*

———————

Ruthless warriors who used their victims' skulls as drinking cups—that's how the Greek historian Herodotus described the Scythians, the horse-riding, seminomadic collection of tribes that flourished on the Eurasian Steppe 2,500 years ago. Traces of these shadowy tribes span more than a thousand years, from perhaps the ninth century B.C. to the third century A.D.

Few ancient scholars spent time among the Scythians—and as a result, few eyewitness accounts exist. Moreover, most of what was written was far from flattering. Portrayed by the Greeks as "barbarians," the Scythians were often described as bloodthirsty and brutish; their women were said to be the inspiration for the fabled Amazons of Greek myth. "Lured on by pastures," Roman geographer Pomponius Mela wrote around 44 B.C., they "live in camps and carry all their possessions and wealth with them. Archery, horseback riding, and hunting are a girl's pursuits."

Although these nomads left no cities or written records to know them by, their history is not lost. It has instead come down to us through burial mounds, called kurgans, from which archaeologists have unearthed a cultural treasure trove. So far, more than 1,000 of these sacred time capsules have been discovered in Russia, Ukraine, and Siberia. Some were looted by grave robbers, stripped long ago of their gold and jewels; others held objects the pillagers had missed. All contained valuable artifacts—startlingly well-preserved human remains, piles of weapons, stunning artwork, remains of food and other objects of everyday life—that proved the so-called Scythians were far more than the simple barbarians Herodotus described.

Archaeologists began excavating these kurgans as early as the 18th century. Since then, the tombs' treasures have continued to complete our understanding of this ancient people: They were craftsmen and artisans as well as fighters, with a sophisticated culture focused on more than war.

In 2001, a team set to dig at a kurgan dubbed Arzhan 2, in the Siberian Republic of Tuva, embarked on their project with low expectations. At the center—the place kings were usually buried, and where looters always looked first—the excavators indeed found nothing. But 45 feet from the center, they hit the jackpot: an undisturbed wooden vault with two skeletons and a whopping 44 pounds of gold. The 5,700 pieces found there dated to the seventh century B.C.; most were small animal figures, revealing a unique artistic style. "These people were excellent craftsmen," said Anatoli Nagler, one of the expedition directors. "[This find] rejects the stereotype that Scythians were just wild horsemen and warriors, migrating and destroying other people. They had a high level of cultural development."

The site yielded 13 graves, providing tantalizing glimpses into its culture. "This may be the most informative of all the Scythian kurgans ever excavated," Nagler said. The mound also contained the remains of 14 sacrificed horses. A measure of wealth and highly revered by the culture, horses are a frequent find in such burials.

The Scythians' sophisticated artwork often adorned the bodies of its people. A kurgan on Russia's Ural Steppes, excavated by Leonid

Yablonsky in 2013, held tattooing equipment—pigments and spoons for mixing them, along with gilded iron needles and other tools—that shed light on how body art was used as a form of personal expression. In 1993, a Scythian tattoo was famously discovered on the body of the so-called "Ice Maiden," or Ukok Princess, found in eastern Russia's Altai Mountains. Her body, wrapped in fur and lying on its side, had been surrounded by ice for thousands of years, perfectly preserved. "We had intercepted a suspended moment," said Natalia Polosmak, chief archaeologist at the site. "Time traveled to an ancient tableau so perfectly intact that we could literally smell her last symbolic meal of mutton, unfinished on a low wooden table by her side."

> "We had intercepted a suspended moment, time traveled to an ancient tableau so perfectly intact that we could literally smell her last symbolic meal of mutton, unfinished on a low wooden table by her side."
>
> —*Natalia Polosmak, archaeologist*

Remarkably, the tattoos on the Ice Maiden's body could still be seen: a blue rendering of a mythical creature on her shoulder, artfully twisted and elongated, and a deer on her wrist. Archaeologists found grave goods, too: silk and wool clothes, a headdress, a hand mirror. "We wouldn't be as happy if we had found solid gold," Polosmak said. "These are everyday things. Through them, we see life as it was."

Those everyday objects have taught us much about the Scythians. In 2013, archaeologist Andrei Belinski began excavating a kurgan in Russia's Caucasus Mountains, called Sengileevskoe-2, while clearing the way for a power-line project. At first, Belinski wasn't optimistic, as there were telltale signs that the kurgan had been plundered. But a few weeks into the excavation, his team came across a thick layer of clay. Digging underneath, they discovered a rectangular chamber lined with broad, flat stones. Inside was something looters had missed: golden treasures placed there 2,400 years ago. The chamber contained some seven pounds of gold—two bucket-shaped gold vessels, three gold cups, a heavy gold finger ring, two neck rings, and a gold bracelet.

These well-preserved artifacts spoke not only to Scythian artistry, but also to the tribe's way of life. Many of the scenes carved into the gold vessels were surprisingly intricate. "I've never seen such a detailed representation of the clothing and weaponry of the Scythians," Belinski said. "It's so detailed you can see how the clothing was sewn."

In 2013, criminologists analyzed black residue they found inside the golden vessels. The test results came back positive for opium and cannabis, proving Herodotus's theory of the tribe's drug use; the historian wrote that the Scythians threw herbs onto the fires they lit inside felt tents, where they would gather and "howl with joy, awed and elated by their vapor-bath."

New findings also reveal that ancient Greek tales of the Amazon warrior women weren't entirely flights of fancy. At first, archaeologists assumed that anyone buried with weapons in kurgans must be male, while those buried with household goods must be female. But DNA testing and other bioarchaeological scientific analysis has

An elaborate Scythian diadem some 2,300 years old shows that the notorious horsemen of the ancient steppe had a surprising flair for graceful works of gold.

demonstrated that about a third of all Scythian warrior graves belong to women who were buried with weapons and armored war belts: fighters in life who were honored as such in death. In 2017, a team led by archaeologist Valerii Guliaev unearthed the remains of four female warriors, ranging in age from roughly 12 or 13 to 45 or 50. They were buried with a cache of arrowheads, spears, and horse-riding equipment in a tomb in western Russia; the oldest wore a lavish golden headdress and clearly died from a battle wound.

Such discoveries add to mounting evidence that Scythian women were afforded the same burial rites as men. Jewelry, spindles, mirrors, and cooking items in the kurgans of both sexes reveal an egalitarian society where women and men worked and fought side by side. Their remains, which show signs of badly healed breaks and chronic diseases, prove that their lives were far from easy.

Of course, not every kurgan yields startling revelations. But each find allows the Scythians to step beyond the ancient Greek tales and finally speak for themselves.

44

THE NEBRA SKY DISK

Unknown date ✦ Germany ✦ Unknown culture

Looters hinder the interpretation of a star-ornamented bronze disk, setting archaeologists at odds.

———◆———

The smuggler slowly pulled an object enfolded in a towel from beneath his shirt. He then unwrapped a bronze disk the size of a large dinner plate, studded with a gold moon or sun and a field of glimmering gold stars. He knew it was valuable, but he didn't realize its true significance. This artifact was first and last seen in Berlin, Germany, three years earlier, in 1999. Black market profiteers had tried to sell it to the Museum of Prehistory and Early History in that city for half a million dollars. But the find was illegal. By law, it belonged to the German state of Saxony-Anhalt, where looters had purportedly discovered it.

Since then, the bronze disk had been handed off among smugglers on the black market. Its newest owner, though, got greedy. In January 2002, he persuaded a German news magazine to run a story on his treasure, hoping the media frenzy would drive up its value. Instead, it prompted the police to launch a sting operation.

Archaeologist Harald Meller played the Indiana Jones role, pretending to represent a large bank buying the disk for his museum. He persuaded the smuggler and an accomplice to meet him in a basement café in Switzerland, assuring them that Switzerland's neutral status would afford a safe haven for their rendezvous.

The smuggler first offered a sword. Meller knew it dated to 1600 B.C., but he claimed it was a worthless forgery. For if the smugglers knew its true origin, they would never part with the real prize: the bronze disk from the same haul. If authentic, the disk would be one of the most important finds of the early 21st century, and its value would far surpass that of the sword.

When the smuggler unwrapped the disk, Meller stifled a gasp. "At this moment, with my heart racing, I know how Howard Carter must have felt when he first glimpsed King Tut's tomb," he said. Meller agreed to pay $400,000 for the disk and the other items found with it: two swords, two axes, two spiral armbands, and a chisel—all forged from bronze. Meller then alerted the Swiss police, who swarmed the café and arrested the smugglers. The disk and other items were entrusted to Meller's museum, the State Museum of Prehistory in Halle in Saxony-Anhalt, the state where they were first discovered.

> "At this moment, with my heart racing, I know how Howard Carter must have felt when he first glimpsed King Tut's tomb."
>
> —*Harald Meller, archaeologist*

After the arrests, the police traced the disk to one of its previous owners. He took Meller to the site where looters had found the disk with a metal detector, explaining that they extricated it with an improvised firefighter's pickax. The disk had been lodged in a stone mound buried close to the summit of Mittelberg hill, near the town of Nebra. It has since been known as the Nebra sky disk.

Inhabited by humans for at least 440,000 years, the Unstrut Valley surrounding Nebra had long been considered an area of archaeological significance. After the East German government fell in 1989, and the Berlin Wall became an artifact of history, looters poured into this newly opened landscape and scoured it for artifacts.

About a foot in diameter, the controversial bronze Nebra sky disk, inlaid with symbols of gold, may represent astronomical observations.

Pinpointing the Nebra disk's very location and date is the key to deciphering whether the arrangement of stars and a possible sun or moon is merely decorative or if the disk served as a celestial chart. If this was, indeed, the oldest map of the night sky ever discovered, the Bronze Age stargazers who used it would predate Greek astronomy by 1,000 years. The ends of the disk's two gold bands along its outer edges could mark the points on the horizon where the sun rises and sets on the summer and winter solstice—the longest and shortest days of the year. Although heavily forested now, Mittelberg hill circa 1600 B.C. had a clear view of distant landmarks. Viewed from there, on the summer solstice, the sun descends on the Brocken, the highest peak in the Harz massif. If the northern end of the Nebra sky disk's western band is oriented with the Brocken, the opposite end of the band aligns with sunset on the winter solstice. An astronomer could have followed the sun's path along the bands to establish a rudimentary calendar, providing information critical for planting and harvesting. The bronze disk's vivid malachite-hued patina— the result of corrosion—serves as the backdrop for 32 gold stars, seven of which are arranged in a circular group, suggesting they represent the Pleiades star cluster in the western sky. In early March, the disappearance of Pleiades from the sky in central Germany signals the beginning of planting season.

Scientists have tested the disk's radioactivity, corrosion, and alloy composition to confirm its authenticity as an ancient artifact rather than a modern piece faked to appear corroded by age. Those results proved crucial in defeating a 2004 court case that claimed the disk was a forgery. The celebrated disk was later added to UNESCO's Memory of the World Register in 2013. However, determining an exact date was not so simple. The swords and axes in the Nebra hoard were dated to the Bronze Age so one might conclude that a disk from the same hoard, made of the same copper, should be the same age. This interpretation relies on one questionable premise: that the looters are telling the truth. If the artifacts were not found together, then the disk could be much younger.

In 2020, a new study evaluated the age of the Nebra sky disk as 1,000 years younger than previously believed, manufactured perhaps at the end of the first millennium B.C. The authors, German archaeologists Rüdiger Krause and Rupert Gebhard, posit that the disk was not found with the swords and other artifacts and should not be considered part of a single hoard. They believe the piece is more likely from the Late Iron Age, when motifs of stars and the crescent moon were common in Celtic crafts. This deprives the disk of its celebrated status as evidence of Bronze Age science, and scholars will continue to study and debate the characteristics of the artifact and theories of its origin.

Rescuing the Nebra sky disk from the hands of smugglers was an extraordinary coup. But even though the curious treasure is safely in expert hands, critical information on the context of the discovery has been lost. Archaeologists rely on contextual clues to interpret prehistoric artifacts, and this case is a harsh example of the high cost of looting. A skilled craftsperson was once moved to render copper and gold into a shimmering scene inspired by the sky. If only we knew when and why.

45

WARRIORS FROM A WATERY GRAVE

450–400 B.C. ◆ Ionian Sea ◆ Hellenic

Submerged for centuries off the coast of Italy near the village of Riace, two bronze statues illustrate the highest attainments of Greek sculpture.

———◆———

Stefano Mariottini was on vacation, spearfishing in the Ionian Sea off the southern coast of Italy in August 1972, when he made one of the most spectacular discoveries ever in the world of classical art.

On his last morning, the young research chemist from Rome decided to go out one more time to explore the water near a village called Riace. When he spotted something dark outlined against the bottom, just 25 feet underwater and 650 feet from shore, he swam down to investigate. To his horror, a human shoulder seemed to be protruding from the sand. "For a moment I thought it was a corpse," he recalled.

Mariottini surfaced at once, then dove a second time and touched it gingerly. It was metal. A little digging revealed that the shoulder belonged to a large statue of a male figure. Looking around, he discovered that the motion of his fins had shifted sand from a knee and the tip of a toe—evidence of a second statue lying a few feet from the first. He left a buoy to mark the site and went to get help.

As soon as he left the beach, Mariottini called Giuseppe Foti, the archaeological superintendent of that region of Italy. Foti put a guard

Years of conservation revealed the perfection of a bronze statue—an elder warrior—rescued from the Ionian Sea along with a similarly stunning younger figure.

on the bronzes and then arranged for divers from the Italian national police to raise the two figures using balloons inflated with air.

Mariottini's accidental discovery proved to be two nude warriors of bronze. One was 6.7 feet tall, the other 6.5—heights that were larger than life-size in antiquity. The statues were encrusted with minerals and corroded, so it was hard to tell anything beyond that. But they were clearly unusual.

Centuries in the sea had left the bronzes in dire need of cleaning and restoration. Experts in Reggio Calabria, a small city about 80 miles away, did their best for a couple of years, but eventually the statues were sent to the Italian government's archaeological restoration center in Florence. There, a team went to work with specialized instruments and techniques: scalpels and pneumatic hammers to remove some of the concretions, ultrasonic tools and micro-sanders for the more delicate areas, and baths of ammonia and alcohol for cleaning. Six more years passed before the results were unveiled to great acclaim.

The statues are now installed in Reggio Calabria's National Archaeological Museum. Known as the Riace bronzes, in honor of where they were found, they stand as stunning, beautifully detailed masterpieces of ancient art.

The warriors' nudity was the traditional way of portraying heroes in Greek statuary. In these idealized versions of masculinity, the muscles are perfectly defined, and the skin is as smooth and glistening in bronze as it would have been in real life. One warrior appears to be about 20, formidable in his athletic pride and power. The other is a battle-weary veteran, more gracefully built but still splendidly athletic.

The warriors' nipples and open lips are highlighted in pinkish copper; the whites of their eyes are calcite. The front teeth of the younger statue are gleaming silver. Their weapons and protective gear have been lost. But judging from the position of their arms and hands, each seems to have once held a shield, probably highly ornate. The younger man may have wielded a sword; the older one could have worn a crested helmet and held a long spear.

Who made the statues? What monument did they grace? How did they end up in the sea? No one knows for sure. But even while they were in the conservation labs, experts were weighing in—with widely varying opinions.

The two bronzes, similar but with differences both obvious and subtle, were probably made by two different artists in the Greek city of Argos around the mid-fifth century B.C. They were likely being shipped to the Italian Peninsula during the first or second century B.C., a time when Roman troops were invading Greece and making off with many Greek treasures. Perhaps the ship transporting the bronzes got into trouble during a storm, the captain made a quick decision to lighten the load, and the two heavy warriors—some 350 pounds each—were heaved overboard.

Such finds are exceedingly rare, because bronze was valuable and often melted down for reuse in the ancient world. Only a couple dozen large-scale, mostly complete bronzes like these have survived from ancient Greece.

The Italian government rewarded Mariottini with the equivalent of $145,000—a token for a find well spotted and promptly reported, but nowhere near what the bronzes might be worth, if a price could even be estimated.

The discovery was big news in Italy, and for Reggio Calabria, the permanent display of the statues has put the once sleepy city on the map. Deemed "the art find of the century," the warriors have become poster boys for the extraordinary artistry of ancient sculpture. They have appeared on banners, stamps, book covers, and T-shirts. They have been re-created in miniature as souvenirs. They have also inspired modern artists, including a former student of Andy Warhol who photographed them using a white veil, a shocking pink boa, and a leopard-print thong as props.

Though much about the warriors is mysterious, they are doubtlessly magnificent ambassadors from their time. They are so fine, and so perfect, that we can only gaze at them in wonder and lament the loss of countless other pieces to the sea—or to ancient recycling.

46

THE CROWN JEWEL OF ATHENS

447 B.C. ◆ Athens, Greece ◆ Classical Greek

*Of all the monumental complexes of ancient Greece,
the Athenian acropolis has survived most intact,
with the Parthenon a potent symbol of the city's golden age.*

———◆———

Its grandeur undimmed by the wars, fires, explosions, earthquakes, excavations, renovations, and other traumas of nearly 25 centuries, the Parthenon—named for a long-lost gold-and-ivory statue called Athena Parthenos, or "maiden"—gleams atop the acropolis, the rocky heart of ancient Athens. Here the smoke of sacrificial fires rose in honor of the patron goddess of the city. Commissioned in 447 B.C. by the Athenian politician Pericles, the Parthenon celebrated the Greek victory over Persia early in the heady classical age, when Athens reached its peak, when Socrates and the playwrights Sophocles, Euripides, and Aristophanes produced some of their finest works. With brash foresight, Pericles proclaimed, "The admiration of the present and succeeding ages will be ours."

By the dawn of the fifth century B.C., Persia, one of the mightiest empires in the world, had slowly been expanding westward across the Aegean Sea. In 499 B.C., Greek settlements along the Ionian coast

---

> **"The admiration of the present and succeeding ages will be ours."**
>
> —*Pericles, fifth-century Athenian statesman*

(now part of western Turkey) revolted, and Persia quickly brought them back to heel. Athens supported the rebellion, and soon the wrath of Persia's ambitious king, Darius, was directed toward them and their neighbors. Some city-states united to stand fast in battles that have come to symbolize heroism and resolute liberty—Marathon, Thermopylae, Salamis. But amid the conflict, Athens was sacked and the acropolis razed in 480 B.C.

Decades later, as older monuments of the acropolis stood in ruins, Pericles was emerging as Athens's foremost politician. He ushered in what is considered "radical democracy," in which the state paid ordinary Athenian citizens to participate in public affairs. Lower-class Athenians could now take part as fully as citizens with property. Pericles also elevated Athens's role within the Delian League, a naval alliance of Greek city-states unified to fight the Persians. He maneuvered Athens to primacy over other league members, first by transferring the league's treasury to Athens in 454 B.C. and then by imposing Athenian weights and measures on all league members three years later.

The Delian League effectively became an Athenian empire. Around 449 B.C., the Delian League signed the Peace of Callias, which brought peace after nearly 50 years of fighting with the Persians. To honor the gods for the victory and to glorify Athens, Pericles proposed using the league's treasury to mount an unprecedented building campaign. Work began in 447 B.C. to turn the acropolis into a breathtaking temple complex, producing the iconic Parthenon, the temple of Athena Nike, the Erechtheion, and the imposing colonnade of the Propylaea, the entrance gateway.

Early Greek temples resembled houses with steep pitched roofs and had columns only at the entrance or the rear. The Parthenon's design was pulled together by a kind of dream team of genius: The

Once a richly adorned temple dedicated to the Greek goddess Athena, the ruins of the Parthenon glow atop the acropolis, the rocky hill in the heart of Athens.

project was overseen by Phidias, the great sculptor of the classical era, at the instigation of Pericles, Athens's most brilliant statesman. Its architects were the well-known Iktinos and Kallikrates. The Parthenon had another advantage over other temples, many of which had been built of stucco-covered limestone. The monumental construction on the acropolis was built of marble, more than 20,000 tons of it.

The acropolis would hardly see such a flurry of activity again until Greece became independent in the 19th century and quickly began archaeological work to study and restore the site. Generations of occupiers, invaders, and tourists had significantly damaged and looted the structures. Postclassical alterations included an apse that Christians added to the Parthenon when transforming it into a church in the Byzantine era and a minaret installed when an Ottoman sultan turned the Parthenon into a mosque. During a large-scale excavation from 1885 to 1890, overseen by Panagiotis Kavvadias with help from German partners (including Wilhelm Dörpfeld, who had previously worked at Troy with Heinrich Schliemann), nearly every inch of dirt over the bedrock of the acropolis was dug up.

The systematic (though not always well-recorded) digging revealed the foundations and other architectural elements of lost buildings such as the Brauroneion, which was a sanctuary dedicated to Artemis, and an older version of the Parthenon that was under construction when the Persians attacked. Excavations in the 19th century also uncovered the buried freestanding statues of young women and men known as *korai* and *kouroi*, which were left as offerings to the gods and became icons of Greek art. Among the most recognizable statues are what experts now call the Peplos Kore, the Kritios Boy, and the Calf-Bearer.

Greek temples were often galleries for sculpture, both freestanding statues that perched on the pediments and relief panels carved in stone, forming friezes that ran around the buildings. Sculpture in the classical age portrayed people and gods alike as idealized humans, thus elevating humanity to Olympian heights. For centuries, museumgoers and historians have sung the rapturous praises of the purity of these sculptural forms. Alas, although some of their admired characteristics are genuine, some are an illusion created by an almost comical accident of time.

"People forget that Greek sculpture was often painted," Chris Faraone, a professor of classics at the University of Chicago, told *National Geographic* in 2000. "The eyes were painted, the skin and clothing were painted in bright primary colors that were fixed with a translucent wax covering, probably looking very much like the brightly colored plastic Madonna on my grandmother's dresser." Weathered by time to clean marble, the statues acquired a wholly different character. The sculptures adorning the Parthenon portrayed scenes from myth, such as battles between the Olympian gods and the Giants, the sack of Troy, the birth of Athena. But the warm, graceful stone they were carved on once sparkled with robust Mediterranean color, entirely in keeping with the noisy energetic city below.

The Greek temple is one of the most influential of all architectural creations, its style echoed in official or state buildings today. It would be difficult to imagine the capital city of the United States without its many Greek features, including the Capitol itself, with its columns and pediments. There are echoes of the Parthenon across countless institutions in the Western world, and yet, as archaeologist Joan Connelly writes in her 2014 book *The Parthenon Enigma,* "Ironically, these unequivocally secular civic structures have appropriated what is, fundamentally, a religious architectural form."

Classical Greece is rightly regarded as a high-water mark of civilization, yet the living, breathing people who produced this culture were not—as it sometimes seems to reluctant students of the humanities—busily intent on turning out masterpieces to adorn museums and libraries of the future Western world. Many, like Pericles, leveraged public art and monument to further their own agenda and prestige. More than 2,000 years later, another statesman recognized the political potential in the Parthenon's masterpieces and set in motion a centuries-long controversy. Beginning in 1801, British diplomat Lord Elgin cut nearly half of the surviving sculptures from the Parthenon, boxed them up, and shipped them out of Athens, which was then under Ottoman rule. In London, Elgin sold the marbles to Parliament for £35,000 in 1816, and they have been housed in the British Museum for more than 150 years.

Greece has long petitioned for the repatriation of the artworks. Actress Melina Mercouri reenergized the campaign when she was minister of culture in the 1980s, once telling a UNESCO conference, "I think that the time has come for these marbles to come back to the blue sky of Attica, to their natural space, to the place where they will be a structural and functional part of a unique whole." The acropolis has been undergoing a massive restoration effort that began in 1975, and in 2009, the new Acropolis Museum opened with specially designed, conspicuously empty spaces to display the missing sculptures—someday. As the U.K.'s exit from the European Union loomed, rumors swirled in 2020 that Greece might try to use the Elgin Marbles as a bargaining chip in negotiating trade deals. Political savvy abetted the creation of the Parthenon; it might help reunite its disjointed pieces, too.

47

THRACIAN GOLD

ca 400 B.C. ◆ Bulgaria ◆ Thracian

*Lacking a written language, the Thracians instead left
a legacy of glittering goldwork, revealed to the world with
the accidental discovery of the "Panagyurishte hoard."*

———◆———

On the frosty morning of Thursday, December 8, 1949, three workers at a ceramics factory near Panagyurishte, Bulgaria, grabbed their shovels and headed to the factory yard to extract more clay for tiles. While the trio—brothers Pavel, Petko, and Mihail Deykovi—turned over the dull earth, something glittering caught their eye. They reached down and, to their astonishment, uncovered one gold object after another. There were strange drinking vessels and an unusual bowl—nothing the brothers had ever seen before.

In keeping with the strict laws under Bulgaria's Communist regime, the brothers dutifully turned over their nine finds to local authorities. Petar Gorbanov, curator at a local museum, closely examined the fully cleaned vessels. He marveled not only at the large scale of the find—roughly 13.5 pounds of gold—but also at the finely wrought figures covering these objects fit for a king's feast. There were rhyta (drinking horns) in the shape of women's heads featuring elegant hairstyles and jewelry, with one wearing a helmet. Others were shaped so that their lower ends resembled the heads of animals: stags, a ram, and a goat. Those artifacts referenced such legends as the Judgement of Paris, Heracles slaying the deer of Artemis, Theseus with the Marathon bull, and other classical scenes. Five concentric circles of decorations adorned a large phiale (libation bowl). And an elaborate amphora (storage jar) had centaurs as its handles and warriors on its bowl.

Such mastery of gold metallurgy was a hallmark of the Thracians, a fractious conglomeration of tribes across the lower Balkans who reached the height of their power in the fifth century B.C., contemporaneous with classical Greece, the expanding Persian Empire, and the birth of Buddhism. Gorbanov wired colleagues in Sofia, the capital, to announce the spectacular discovery: This find from around the turn of the fourth to the third century B.C. was perhaps the richest of all Thracian treasures, and one of the greatest gold hoards ever discovered.

Unlike their Greek neighbors to the south, the Thracians had no written language and left no epic poems or historic chronicles to memorialize their culture. So the Greeks did it for them. In his

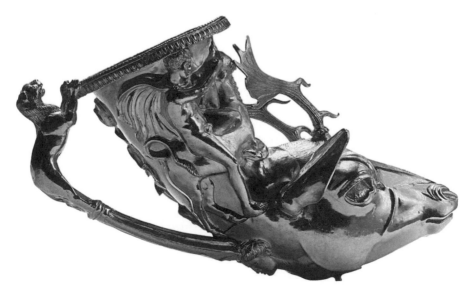

Taking the shape of a young ram's head, an ornate drinking vessel known as a rhyton is one of the Thracian treasures of 24-karat gold found at Panagyurishte.

History, Greek historian Herodotus (ca 484–424 B.C.) described the Thracians as "the most powerful people in the world, except, of course, the Indians; and if they had one head, or were agreed among themselves, it is my belief that their match could not be found anywhere, and that they would very far surpass all other nations."

Where the Thracians did surpass all others was in their goldsmithing, a legacy composed of carats rather than couplets and borne from rich mineral deposits. As a result, Bulgaria is considered an El Dorado, a vast trove of buried treasure where the distinctive beehive-shaped tombs of Thracian royalty and other sites have harbored gold for millennia.

The oldest gold hoard from the Thracians—and in the world— was unearthed in the Bulgarian town of Varna in the autumn of 1972. A tractor operator named Raicho Marinov was excavating a five-foot trench for an electrical cable to a nearby factory. He noticed pieces of shiny yellow sheet metal more than four inches square, and what looked like bracelets of the same material. Subsequent excavations at the site—a Thracian necropolis—uncovered around 2,000 gold objects, from graves dating between 4600 and 4200 B.C. British archaeologist Colin Renfrew described his visit to the Varna excavation in 1980: "My eyes popped as I beheld golden necklaces, bracelets, breastplates," he said. "As [another archaeologist] handed me a necklace of gold beads, I was piercingly aware that I held in my hands an object from the world's earliest golden treasure trove."

In the decades since the fall of communism, archaeologists have been in a race against time and looters to discover and protect other Thracian gold treasures from not only Bulgaria's "valley of the kings," where there is a concentration of royal tombs, but elsewhere across the country as well. They've found stunning necklaces and earrings, gold masks and wreaths, and even elaborate gold appliqués for horse harnesses (a find in keeping with the Thracians' noted equestrian prowess). Modern historians echo the awe expressed by Herodotus as each remarkable discovery further highlights the Thracians' timeless metallurgical mastery and artistry.

48

THE NOK TERRA-COTTAS

500 B.C.–A.D. 200 ✦ Nigeria ✦ Nok

Ornate sculpted figures hint at the sophistication of an undocumented ancient culture in sub-Saharan Africa.

———✦———

What does a scarecrow have to do with archaeology? Not much—except when the object being used to spook marauding birds is a priceless relic of a once unknown culture. In 1943, a British officer ended up changing the world's understanding of African, and human, history. And it all started with a gift from a local farmer.

Bernard Fagg had come to Nigeria in the 1930s after joining the Colonial Service, the British corps that oversaw the empire's colonies. Nigeria's colonial governor charged Fagg with managing tin extraction in the region during World War II. In his free time, Fagg, who had an archaeology degree from Cambridge, worked on his own extracurricular expeditions.

In 1943, a mining engineer gave Fagg an object that had been unearthed at a tin mine site and used by a neighbor as the head of a scarecrow in his yam field. The nearly life-size terra-cotta head, with its carefully crafted face and ornate hairstyle, fascinated Fagg. "Its survival is a tribute to the strength of the material . . . The most striking feature . . . is the expression of life and vigor," he wrote later.

"The most striking feature ... is the expression of life and vigor."

—*Bernard Fagg, archaeologist*

The head's aesthetics rang a bell for Fagg. It reminded him of other artifacts that had turned up in the nearby village of Nok during similar mining operations in the 1920s. The mystery spurred on an archaeological treasure hunt that would change Africa's view of its own history. Fagg started traveling Nigeria in search of similar artifacts. Along the way, he realized that people had been uncovering terra-cotta figures in tin fields for years.

A typical sculpture in the Nok style is a seated human figure with elongated body parts, an ornate hairstyle, and triangular or oval-shaped eyes. Fagg purchased as many of them as he could and conducted his own excavations, too. He was later given an archaeological post under the British government and devoted himself to saving the plentiful artifacts threatened by the British exploitation of Nigeria's natural resources.

The more terra-cotta figures he saw, the more he believed he was looking at remnants of a completely unique civilization. But because so many of the figurines were pulled out of mining sites, it was difficult to establish a time line. Technology was a barrier, too: He could test the surrounding soil for dating but could only infer the age of the terra-cottas themselves. The soil analysis indicated the objects were from 500 B.C., which seemed impossible to experts who had found no evidence of complex societies in West Africa in that era. It would take years for radiocarbon dating to confirm Fagg's conclusions. The ancient timeline was confirmed when Fagg used the then new technique to date a bit of plant matter extracted from one figure. He also eventually dated the scarecrow head to about 500 B.C. by using thermoluminescence, which determines how much time has passed since the artifact was fired.

About 21 inches tall, this Nok terra-cotta depicts scenes from daily life that include processing bundles of grain, transporting water, and preparing food.

Additional analyses have shown that Nok culture—Fagg's name for the mysterious "new" group—existed from about 500 B.C. to around A.D. 200. The Nok people are among the first known people in sub-Saharan Africa to participate in iron smelting, a fact corroborated by 13 iron furnaces Fagg discovered and dated to about 280 B.C. Terra-cotta figures were found near and even inside those ancient furnaces—proof, Fagg thought, that the Nok people used the figurines as totems to assist blacksmiths and iron smelters. They are one of the few cultures in the world that transitioned from stone to iron tools without working with copper or bronze in between.

Further research suggests that the Nok had a society that involved farming, art, and possibly organized religion. However, little is known about what kind of state, if any, the Nok people were governed by, and if it should be considered a centralized society or an affiliation of communities. Analysis of sculptures found over a vast area of 30,000 square miles indicates that the clay most likely all came from the same source, which suggests that a centralized authority controlled the supply.

The discovery of the Nok civilization added complexity, and age, to the world's view of sub-Saharan Africa. But time to find out more is running out. Between the 1970s and 2005, archaeology in Nigeria lagged, in part due to a lack of resources and funding for research within Nigeria. Looting also decimated Nok sites, fueled by a market for smuggled African art. Despite attempts to quell the trade, thousands of figurines flooded out of Nigeria and into the hands of antiquities dealers and even museums like the Louvre and the Musée du quai Branly-Jacques Chirac in France.

More than 90 percent of Nok sites are thought to have been looted—proof of the distinctive figurines' allure, but a tragically missed opportunity to learn more about the mysterious culture that produced them.

49

MACEDONIAN TOMBS OF VERGINA

336 B.C. ✦ Northern Greece ✦ Macedonian

A sensational discovery of royal graves sparked
an enduring debate about the final resting place of
Philip II, Alexander the Great's father.

———◆———

As dirt and dust trickled into the little black hole, Manolis Andronikos told himself to be calm. It was three in the afternoon on November 8, 1977, in Vergina, a northern Greek village west of Thessaloniki. Andronikos and his colleagues had painstakingly uncovered a large Macedonian grave that was likely dug in the fourth century B.C. An unplundered tomb of that period was unheard of. Andronikos was about to climb down to see its interior.

The last shovelful of reddish earth had been peeled back from the roof of the barrel-vaulted structure, which had been buried 23 feet underground. Following the practice of ancient grave robbers, the archaeologists lifted out a keystone from the roof at the very back of the tomb.

Moving the beam of his flashlight about, Andronikos saw a square chamber with a marble door and a marble sarcophagus. He glimpsed bronze vessels and weapons in one corner, silver vessels near another. Scattered on the floor lay decomposed remnants of wood and other materials, among which shone leaves of gold. "Everything is intact!" he yelled.

Already a prominent archaeologist, Andronikos had been digging trenches into a large artificial mound, or tumulus, which he thought seemed a likely burial place of Macedonia's kings, who once reigned in ancient Greece. Then, just as his 1977 dig season seemed to be ending in disappointment, he noticed a small, older mound under the southwestern slope of the "great tumulus." On a hunch, he dug into it and, to his joy, discovered two tombs.

The smaller one had been opened and looted, but it was decorated with rare wall paintings, including a scene of Pluto, the god of the underworld, abducting Persephone. The looters, amazingly, did not make it beyond this tomb to a larger two-chambered burial vault.

Inside a marble sarcophagus in one chamber, the archaeologists found a solid gold casket that weighed almost 24 pounds and was embossed with a sunburst, or star with rays. Within, burned bones were covered with a golden wreath of leaves and acorns. The second chamber contained yet another gold casket, slightly smaller and simpler than the first, but with the same sunburst on the lid. Wrapped in a purple fabric interlaced with gold threads, the burned bones inside lay beside a diadem of intertwined golden branches and flowers.

To Andronikos, these were clearly burials of cremated Macedonian royalty. With artifacts in the tomb dating from about 350 B.C. to 325 B.C., he was convinced he had found the grave of the great Philip II, a powerful Macedonian ruler eclipsed only by the son who fulfilled his vision of conquest, Alexander the Great.

Philip was a deft politician and military strategist who also had a strong appetite for banquets, art, wine, and women. (He had seven

"Everything is intact!"

—*Manolis Andronikos,*
archaeologist

Found in one of the vaulted tombs at Vergina, this gold box held the bones of an adult male. Some experts believe they belonged to Philip II; others disagree.

wives.) Philip conquered warring factions of the Greek mainland until he controlled almost the whole region, then turned his attention to Asia Minor. In the spring of 336 B.C., Philip sent out an advance army 10,000 strong, postponing his own departure until the summer marriage of his daughter. At the wedding, he was stabbed through the heart and killed.

Three years before his assassination, Philip suffered a leg injury that left him permanently crippled. Andronikos argued that the pair of greaves (shin armor) found in the main chamber must belong to Philip because one is shorter than the other, as if customized for someone with legs of different lengths. The second chamber, Andronikos thought, belonged to a woman, perhaps Philip's last wife, Cleopatra. According to one ancient source, Alexander's mother, Olympias, arranged for Cleopatra and her infant child to be killed. Some suspect Olympias may even have induced a disaffected bodyguard to murder the king.

Andronikos, who died in 1992, hardly had the last word on the burials. Without any clinching pieces of evidence like inscriptions identifying the dead, the tombs have been the subjects of endless debate. Some argued that the vaults must have been built later than Philip's death. In that case, the main chamber could not contain Philip, but perhaps a successor, such as the far less gloriously remembered Philip III Arrhidaeus and his young wife, Eurydice. As Andronikos remarked in the 1970s, "It's like a detective story." It's a case that still hasn't been closed, more than 40 years after that November afternoon when he first caught the glint of treasures in the beam of his flashlight.

50

SUNKEN CITIES OF THE PHARAOHS

800 B.C.–A.D. 800 ◆ Egypt ◆ Greco-Roman/Egyptian

Archaeologists are uncovering the ruins of wealthy coastal trading centers that were sent to the bottom of the sea by powerful forces of nature.

———◆———

Founded by Alexander the Great on the shore of the Mediterranean in 331 B.C., the Egyptian city of Alexandria became the world's most magnificent center of trade, culture, and learning under the rulers known as the Ptolemies. The dynasty's greatest legacy, in fact, was the city itself, with its hundred-foot-wide main avenue, its gleaming limestone colonnades, and its harborside palaces and temples overseen by a towering lighthouse—one of the seven wonders of the ancient world, perhaps standing more than 300 feet tall.

Alexandria soon became the largest, most sophisticated city on the planet. It was a teeming cosmopolitan mix of Egyptians, Greeks, Jews, Romans, Nubians, and other peoples. The best and brightest of the Mediterranean world came to study at the Mouseion, the world's first academy, and at the great Alexandria library. There, 18 centuries before the Copernican Revolution, Aristarchus posited a heliocentric solar system and Eratosthenes calculated the circumference of Earth. Alexandria was where the Hebrew Bible was first translated into Greek, and where the poet Sotades the Obscene discovered the limits of artistic freedom when he unwisely scribbled some scurrilous verse about Ptolemy II's incestuous marriage to his sister. He was deep-sixed in a lead-lined chest.

The most famous resident by far was the legendary Cleopatra—Cleopatra VII Philopator, formally—the last queen of the last dynasty before Egypt fell under the rule of Rome in 31 B.C. Cleopatra was born in Egypt, but she was descended from a lineage of Greek kings and queens who had ruled Egypt for nearly 300 years.

The Ptolemies of Macedonia are one of history's most flamboyant dynasties, famous not only for wealth and wisdom but also for bloody rivalries. They came to power after the conquest of Egypt by Alexander the Great, who in a burst of activity beginning in 332 B.C. swept through Lower Egypt, displaced the hated Persian occupiers, and was hailed by the Egyptians as a divine liberator. He was recognized as pharaoh in the capital, Memphis. Along a strip of land between the Mediterranean and Lake Mareotis, he laid out a blueprint for Alexandria, which would serve as Egypt's capital for nearly a thousand years.

By the time Cleopatra ascended the throne in 51 B.C. at age 18, the Ptolemaic Empire was crumbling. The lands of Cyprus, Cyrene (eastern Libya), and parts of Syria had been lost; Roman troops were soon to be garrisoned in Alexandria itself. Still, despite drought, famine, and the eventual outbreak of civil war, Alexandria was a glittering city—with an estimated 325,000 residents—compared to provincial Rome. Cleopatra was intent on reviving her empire, not by thwarting the growing power of the Romans but by making herself useful to them, supplying them with ships and grain, sealing her alliance with the Roman general Julius Caesar with a son, Caesarion, and later taking up with doomed General Mark Anthony.

The wealth of attention paid to Cleopatra today seems inversely proportional to the poverty of material archaeologists have generated about her. Alexandria and its environs attracted less attention than the more ancient sites along the Nile, such as the Pyramids at Giza or the monuments at Luxor. And no wonder: Unstable geology, pounding weather, and the unsentimental recycling of building stones have destroyed the neighborhood where Cleopatra and her ancestors lived.

Much of the glory that was ancient Alexandria, in fact, now lies in the city's harbor under about 20 feet of water. Archaeologists are now finally investigating those sunken remains of Cleopatra's world off the north coast of Egypt. "My dream is to find a statue of Cleopatra—with a cartouche," said French explorer Franck Goddio, who began his underwater investigations here in 1992. Goddio's excavations have allowed researchers to map out the drowned portions of the ancient city, its piers and esplanades, the sunken ground once occupied by temples, royal palaces, and grand gardens.

> **"My dream is to find a statue of Cleopatra—with a cartouche."**
>
> —*Franck Goddio,*
> *archaeologist*

The barnacled discoveries brought to the sea's surface—massive stone sphinxes, giant limestone paving blocks, granite columns and capitals—have allowed experts to reconstruct the topography of the once great harbor using information about the royal, religious, and maritime structures that was surprisingly different from what ancient texts describe.

Goddio has also been working off the coast northeast of Alexandria, in Aboukir Bay, where he and his team have discovered the long-lost ruins of Thonis-Heracleion. Probably founded around the eighth century B.C., the city controlled the trade flowing into Egypt from around the Mediterranean until Alexandria took over that role. More than 70 shipwrecks and 700 anchors attest to the port's busy traffic. One ship, a common Egyptian cargo vessel called a *baris,* fits a description fifth-century Greek historian Herodotus penned. "It's a very rare case when a written source and archaeological

A red-granite statue of Hapy, god of abundance and the annual flooding of the Nile, is hoisted from the ruins of Heracleion beneath the waters of Aboukir Bay.

material make such a perfect match," says marine archaeologist Alexander Belov of the Russian Academy of Sciences.

The city itself, whose submerged ruins lie four miles off the present shoreline, was a prosperous place of islands, canals, and lagoons much like modern Venice. Discoveries include a grand temple of Amun and his son Khonsu (identified with Heracles by the Greeks), colossal statues of red granite, ritual objects, oil lamps, gold jewelry and coins, residences and sanctuaries, and a hiero-glyphic inscription that solved a long-standing mystery.

The names Thonis and Heracleion had turned up separately on texts found on land, implying they were two separate towns. But the text inscribed on a four-foot-tall stela of black stone that was recovered from the sea proved there was a single city with two names—Thonis in Egyptian and Heracleion in Greek.

Aboukir Bay was also the graveyard of another city: the resort and religious center of Canopus, which was once connected to Heracleion by a network of waterways. Each year, during a celebration known as the Mysteries of Osiris, a figure of the god made of sprouted barley was transported from Heracleion to Canopus on a papyrus barge. In the city's submerged ruins, Goddio has found traces of a temple dedicated to Serapis (a Ptolemaic version of the Egyptian god Osiris), parts of statues that depict deities and pharaohs, votive models of papyrus boats made of lead, and coins bearing the profile of Cleopatra. Gold pendants, beads, clasps, and other adornments, also recovered, conjure up legends of Cleopatra's lavish lifestyle. Such wealth helped motivate Rome's conquest of Egypt, which brought access to the gold mines in Nubia and the caravans that delivered other luxuries from the heart of Africa.

But all that power and wealth was no protection against the disruptions of land and sea. Parts of the three cities had been built on soft, wet, coastal ground. Over time, a likely combination of earthquakes, floods, tidal surges, and a rising sea level caused the earth to liquefy, sending temples, houses, and all their fixtures tumbling into the sea. Thonis-Heracleion may have started to go as early as the first century A.D. The low-lying eastern part of Canopus was in trouble but held on until sometime in the eighth century. About that time, Alexandria lost land around its harbor, including buildings in the royal quarter.

But Alexandria was a big city, and some parts survived to be built over. Traces of its bygone splendor still lie beneath the bustling streets and sidewalks of the modern, seaside metropolis in a palimpsest of human endeavor, past and present.

51

CHINA'S TERRA-COTTA WARRIORS

210 B.C. ◆ Xian, Shaanxi Province, China ◆ Qin dynasty

When Chinese farmers accidentally discovered an emperor's vast tomb, the world was awed by the vast treasures he spirited away to the afterlife.

———◆———

In Shaanxi Province, outside the city of Xian, China's earliest emperors lived and died. One of the most celebrated was Qin Shi Huang Di. After defeating six warring states in 221 B.C., he unified China, inaugurated construction on the Great Wall and an extensive road network, established a currency and bureaucratic administration, and declared himself China's first sovereign emperor. But as large as he loomed in life, he was already preparing for death.

It took 36 years to construct the underground paradise where Qin would spend his eternity. The emperor was obsessed with immortality, consulting with magicians for special elixirs and seeking the fabled fountain of youth. But die he did, in 210 B.C., and his body was laid to rest in a magnificent tomb. It would be another 2,200 years before the emperor's funerary complex was rediscovered, revealing a vast, long-hidden world.

The first traces of the complex were found in 1974, when farmers came upon a clay head while digging a well. Archaeologist Yuan Zhongyi of the State Bureau of Cultural Relics came to investigate the tip, assuming the work would take only a week or so. He met a local grandmother who had several shards of curious terra-cotta heads displayed on her mantle. "I collected all the pieces, and then we began to dig," he remembered. "We could not believe what we found."

Journalist Audrey Ronning Topping was in China on assignment for *National Geographic* when she heard rumors of the evolving excavation. Her father, a Canadian diplomat, had a close connection to Chinese premier Zhou Enlai, and the family was able to swing an early visit to the site. Their caravan of black limousines stopped at a nondescript millet field where a layer of earth had been peeled away to reveal the first artifacts. Standing in the pouring rain, Topping marveled at hundreds of battered but beautiful terra-cotta statues semi-buried in the reddish soil. "Some of the astonishingly realistic figures were upright, intact, and poised, as if waiting for a command to attack," she recalled. "Others lay pathetically smashed and scattered . . . here and there a hand stretched out of the soil, and a booted foot struck out from its cold turf-prison. Helmeted heads fallen from proud, broken bodies looked up from their ancient grave with fierce eyes brought glisteningly alive by the rain." Topping was the first Western journalist to report the discovery that soon splashed across headlines around the world.

In time, more and more of what came to be known as Pit 1 was uncovered, filled with more than 6,000 life-size warriors and horses, which drew war chariots. These pottery legions all stood about six feet tall, in uniform formation, each with distinct physical features and faces probably modeled on living warriors. Legs and feet formed a solid base; the rest of each figure was hollow. Torsos, arms, hands, and heads were molded separately, then attached and covered with a fine layer of clay. The warriors were interred in standing position and battle formation, 15 to 20 feet underground: art imitating life.

A few years later, *National Geographic*'s O. Louis Mazzatenta became the first photographer to capture these artifacts as they were being excavated. "Archaeology is ancient history, but it's made new with the discovery of these things coming out of the earth," he said. "This is truly one of the wonders of the world. When you stand on the edge looking down at thousands of terra-cotta soldiers, it's like standing on the edge of the Grand Canyon. It's almost too much to behold."

After unearthing Pit 1, archaeologists began hunting for others nearby. A tip from an elderly farmer led them to a wide field; in 1976, extensive test drilling uncovered Pit 2. Although 15 sections were opened during a trial excavation that year, it was refilled until the official excavation began in March 1994. Brushing away damp earth, archaeologists discovered the remains of a 7,000-square-yard roof of pine logs that sheltered more members of the terra-cotta army. In the end, it took decades to raise the life-size soldiers—and to reveal a 19-square-mile area designed to mirror the plan of Qin Shi Huang Di's capital, Xianyang.

In addition to conducting excavations, scientists have used remote sensing, ground-penetrating radar, and core sampling to uncover more secrets of the emperor's final resting place. One of those is that the complex is even larger than once believed—almost 38 square miles. At its heart stands a tall earthen mound that covers the ruler's tomb, which remains sealed, partly out of respect and partly to keep it intact.

Qin Shi Huang Di spent most of his reign creating this underground wonder. In around 100 B.C., early Chinese historian Sima Qian wrote: "As soon as the First Emperor became king of Ch'in, excavations and building had been started at Mount Li, while after he won the empire, more than 700,000 conscripts from all parts of the country worked there. They dug through three subterranean streams and poured molten copper for the outer coffin, and the tomb was filled with models of palaces, pavilions, and offices, as well as fine vessels, precious stones, and rarities." Artisans fixed up crossbows, Qian continues, so that grave robbers would be shot upon entry; they also created artificial versions of China's rivers with quicksilver, made to flow by some mechanical means. Although we cannot be certain that his description is accurate, it's clear the tomb is meant to inspire admiration. "All of this was a manifestation of the first emperor's quest for immortality and eternal glory and power," says historian Li Yu-ning of St. John's University in New York.

But amid the wonders of Qin's elaborate funerary arrangements are also some macabre mysteries. Archaeologists have discovered mass graves that appear to hold the remains of the

In the funerary complex of China's first emperor, an army of some 7,000 terra-cotta soldiers stands ready to provide eternal protection from attack.

craftsmen and laborers—including convicted criminals in chains—who died during the three decades it took to create the royal mausoleum. It is unknown how many enslaved laborers and conscripted men lost their lives executing the emperor's megalomaniac vision.

Other mass burials appear to tell grisly tales of a brutal struggle to capture the emperor's throne. In an area close to the ruler's burial site, archaeologists have identified a group of about a hundred tombs—but after excavating several, they're still unsure of what they've found. The chambers are empty, and body parts lie strewn in the doorways along with a scattering of pearls and pieces of gold. Were these the royal concubines, buried near the deceased emperor to serve him in the next world as they had in life? Or do these graves represent something sinister?

Over the years, much work has been done to reconstruct China's celebrated terra-cotta troops. "If we find one piece that fits in a day, that's a lucky day," said archaeologist Song Yun, who mended broken soldiers at the tomb site for decades. If a perfect fit couldn't be achieved, the piece went back into the inventory.

But technology has helped. With each soldier's image, description, and conservation history recorded in a database, it has become far easier to restore the statues to their former glory. Such a prospect would have seemed unthinkable to archaeologist Yuan Zhongyi when he first set up his tent and collapsible bed in the middle of an open field—unwittingly pitching camp just meters above one of the largest tombs in the world.

With less than one percent of the vast tomb complex excavated so far, it may take centuries to uncover all that remains hidden. In 2011, the museum of the terra-cotta warriors launched two long-term excavation projects on the flanks of the 250-foot-high central burial mound. More extensive excavations will yield "mind-boggling discoveries," predicts Wu Yongqi, the museum's director. Archaeologists and artists, armed with the latest tools and techniques, will continue to bring that ancient vision back to life.

52

PROBING THE ANTIKYTHERA MECHANISM

ca first century B.C. ✦ Mediterranean Sea, Greece ✦ Greek

A star clock recovered from a Roman ship that sank in Greek waters shows a level of mechanical complexity not seen again for more than a millennium.

———✦———

Some 2,000 years ago, a Roman merchant ship was headed for home when something went terribly wrong. In a dangerous stretch of the Mediterranean Sea south of Greece, it suddenly sank, likely foundering in a storm. It was large for its time at roughly 130 feet in length, and was packed with a heavy load of luxury goods probably destined for well-off members of Roman society given to decorating their villas with all manner of Grecian art.

The wreck settled onto the steeply sloped bottom of the sea more than 100 feet below the surface, off the east coast of the Greek island known today as Antikythera. There it lay, undisturbed, until the spring of 1900, when sponge divers spotted the wreckage. Salvage efforts at the time of discovery and in subsequent decades recovered a wealth of artifacts, now in the National Archaeological Museum in Athens, that included coarse ceramic jars used for wine and other comestibles, fine glassware, marble and bronze statues, jewelry, coins, a flute of bone or ivory, a sarcophagus lid of red marble, and a small bronze disk decorated with the image of a bull. The most famous and most puzzling, however, was a geared device of corroded bronze that has stunned and intrigued modern scientists.

Dubbed the Antikythera mechanism, the device appears to have been housed in a now decayed wooden case about the size of a mantel clock. For decades, its purpose was a mystery. The initial finds were three misshapen lumps, which have broken during handling and been taken apart for conservation. Additional pieces were recovered in later dives, bringing the number of known fragments to 82. X-ray images taken in the 1970s and 1990s showed multiple gears, as well as tiny inscriptions in Greek, suggesting that the device had once displayed the movements of heavenly bodies.

The big reveal occurred in 2006, when the results of high-resolution x-ray tomography and surface scanning were published. The images were clear enough to allow scientists to double the number of inscriptions they could decipher, and to figure out the functions of the intricate inner components. "It would be hard to dispute that this is the single most information-rich object that has been uncovered by archaeologists from ancient times," observed science historian Alexander Jones.

> "It would be hard to dispute that this is the single most information-rich object that has been uncovered by archaeologists from ancient times."
>
> —*Alexander Jones, science historian*

The device was an amazingly sophisticated astronomical computer with what experts now believe were at least 37 gears, each bearing minute, triangular teeth. A knob on the side of the device turned a complex interlocking mechanism that drove various features. There were clocklike hands, one representing the motion of the sun, another the moon, and one for each of the planets that ancient people could see—Mercury, Venus, Mars, Jupiter, and Saturn. A pointer with a black and silver ball indicated the phases of the moon.

Corroded while lying for centuries under the Aegean Sea after a shipwreck, these bronze fragments were once part of a sophisticated mechanized star chart.

As experts began to read the inscriptions, they learned of two additional pointers with balls—a golden orb representing the sun and a red one for Mars, neither of which has survived. Months were inscribed on a calendar dial that was adjustable for leap years. Another dial predicted the dates of solar and lunar eclipses, whereas other markings indicated the cycles of the heavenly bodies in the zodiac. The device also calculated the dates for periodic athletic competitions that included the Olympic Games.

Experts are unsure about when this device was made. The wreck probably dates to the first century B.C., but one scholar argues for evidence that could place the device itself as early as 200 B.C. Similarly, the place of origin is still under debate. One theory suggests that the device was connected to Corinth and its colony at Syracuse. Other theories point to the city of Pergamum, or the island of Rhodes.

What is certain, however, is that this astounding device displays a level of technical sophistication that would not be seen again until the intricately geared astronomical clocks of the Middle Ages. To create that level of complexity, its makers must have had practice with other, similar devices—and yet it's difficult to imagine any star clock that rivaled this exceptional example. We can only wonder what kind of person would have commissioned such a marvel, and to what use it was put—as a teaching aid, perhaps, or more likely as a status symbol meant to surprise and awe all who gazed upon it.

200 B.C.–A.D. 75

Rituals & Religion

In archaeology, faith is everywhere. It comes to light in accidental discoveries, and hides in plain view within rough sites and formal excavations. Fragile scrolls from caves near the Dead Sea offer insights into today's religions, while Maya murals and ritual geoglyphs etched into the desert of Peru represent mysterious ancient beliefs. Graves of finely adorned Bactrian royals, along with bodies preserved in the bogs of Europe, offer evidence of belief in an afterlife. More often than not, politics went hand in hand with religion, as we see with King Herod's constructions at Caesarea Maritima and the legendary site of Masada. Even the Rosetta stone, the key to deciphering ancient Egyptian hieroglyphs, combined the sacred and secular in a decree composed by priests in support of a young king.

A mural celebrating earthly renewal and a new heir at Bonampak reveals costumes and fantastic creatures that appear nowhere else in Maya art.

53

CRACKING THE HIEROGLYPHIC CODE

March 27, 196 B.C. ◆ Rosetta, Egypt ◆ Egyptian

The Rosetta stone's discovery kicked off a two-decade-long effort to decipher the meaning of the mysterious ancient writing inscribed on its face.

———◆———

t's easy to miss on a visit to the British Museum. If you don't know what you're looking for, you might walk right by it—a broken chunk of dark gray stone, about 30 inches wide and 44 inches tall, covered in crowded rows of signs from long-dead languages. It's worth seeking out among the statues, reliefs, and sarcophagi in the Egyptian galleries, though. This unprepossessing piece of granodiorite is one of history's most important decoding devices. Called the Rosetta stone, after the place where it was found, it allowed scholars to unlock the secrets of the hieroglyphs that had mystified all who gazed upon them for centuries.

Its discovery was the result of Napoleon Bonaparte's grand plan to extend France's domain into Egypt and disrupt trade routes between England, its archrival, and India. French troops campaigned in northern Egypt between 1798 and 1801, quickly taking Alexandria and settling into Cairo.

About three and a half feet tall, the Rosetta stone displays three ancient scripts—ancient Greek at the bottom, Demotic in the middle, and hieroglyphs at the top.

In the summer of 1799, soldiers began a project to expand Fort de Saint-Julien in the town of El Rashid, also known as Rosetta, in the western delta. While digging up ancient walls to make way for new foundations, they found an intriguing stone with rough edges and a smooth, inscribed face—obviously part of a broken monument that had been reused as a building block.

The officer in charge, Pierre-François Bouchard, thought it might be important and turned it over to the scientists who had accompanied Napoleon to Egypt. Fortunately, they made copies of the inscriptions, because the stone would soon leave their hands. By the end of 1801, Britain had brought France's incursion into Egypt to an end and had taken possession of such antiquities as the Rosetta stone, as arranged by the Treaty of Alexandria.

Almost as soon as the stone was discovered, linguists had begun to puzzle out the secrets encoded in the three different writing systems displayed on it, which together offer a snapshot of the sweeping changes that transformed Egypt over many centuries. In a small, jagged triangle at the top are 14 precious lines of hieroglyphs, a complex script used from about 3200 B.C. to the late fourth century A.D. to record sacred texts on temples, tombs, coffins, monuments, and statues. The middle has 32 lines in Demotic, a cursive script from Egypt's late pharaonic era that vastly simplified hieroglyphic writing for the purposes of administrative and commercial recordkeeping. The bottom section holds 53 lines in ancient Greek, the official language of the final Ptolemaic dynasty, with which 19th-century European scholars had some familiarity.

When the Rosetta stone was created in the second century B.C., all three of those languages were inscribed on it to ensure that everyone got the message. But with time, the ancient languages became unreadable. In the fourth century A.D., after the arrival of Christianity in Egypt, people stopped learning hieroglyphs because of the script's link to a pagan religion. Egyptians then began to speak Coptic, written mostly with Greek letters but with a few Demotic signs thrown in to symbolize unique sounds. After the Arab invasion of the seventh century brought a new language and writing system, knowledge of the pharaohs' texts died out completely.

The discovery of the Rosetta stone gave modern scholars the key to resurrect it. A translation of the Greek, completed quickly, revealed names such as Ptolemy and Alexander, which would prove crucial to deciphering the rest of the stone. French scholar Antoine Isaac Silvestre de Sacy and Swedish diplomat Johan David Åkerblad began to work independently on the Demotic. Searching at first for the previously identified proper names, they then worked out a list of possible Demotic characters. They believed that Demotic used a phonetic alphabet, like Greek, whereas hieroglyphic writing used pictographic symbols. They were on the right track but not entirely correct.

In England, a physician, physicist, and mathematician named Thomas Young made breakthroughs when he realized that Demotic was a derivative hybrid, with "imitations of the hieroglyphs . . . mixed with letters of the alphabet." He also was able to identify some hieroglyphic signs. But there he stopped.

Enter Jean-François Champollion, a French whiz kid and student of de Sacy who took up the challenge. In 1822, the final piece of the puzzle clicked into place for him: "Hieroglyphic writing is a complex system, a script all at once figurative, symbolic, and phonetic, in one and the same text, in one and the same sentence, and, I might even venture, in one and the same word," he explained. In other words, a sign can represent an object or an idea, but it can also represent a sound. So several hieroglyphs can be strung together to create the syllables of a single word.

> "Hieroglyphic writing is a complex system, a script all at once figurative, symbolic, and phonetic, in one and the same text, in one and the same sentence, and, I might even venture, in one and the same word."
>
> —Jean-François Champollion, hieroglyphics decipherer

At last, the meaning of the Rosetta stone's text became clear. It was a decree issued by a council of priests in Memphis on March 27, 196 B.C., the first anniversary of the coronation of Ptolemy V Epiphanes, indicating their support for the teenage ruler. The text was inscribed onto large commemorative stones known as stelae, each of which had a rectangular base, slightly tapering sides, and a curved top. The stelae were placed in temples throughout Egypt. Fortunately, part of one—the Rosetta stone—survived.

Cracking the code stirred up an enduring worldwide interest in learning about bygone kings and queens, gods and priests, officials and commoners. It was a collaborative effort years in the making, of course. But Champollion had the "aha moment," and it's his name that will be forever linked to deciphering the written records of one of the most long-lived and sophisticated civilizations of the ancient world.

54

EUROPE'S EERIE BOG BODIES

Predominantly 800 B.C.–A.D. 200 • Northern Europe • Celtic, Germanic

Suspended in time by their oxygen-poor graves,
the well-preserved bog bodies of northern Europe
offer clues to ancient rites of sacrifice and violence.

———◆———

"There's something strange here."

Grethe Højgaard put down her spade, rolled up her sleeves, and reached into the mud at her feet. She and her family had traveled from their village of Tollund, Denmark, to this nearby bog to cut blocks of peat to use as fuel. As Højgaard stretched her fingers farther into the ground, they brushed against something hard. Her husband, brother-in-law, and son helped turn the peat over with their spades—and uncovered a man's body. The tanned, rubbery body had a gentle expression on its face and was naked, save for a leather belt, a sheepskin cap—and a leather cord wrapped around his neck.

Fearful that they'd discovered a murder victim or the body of a boy who'd gone missing in the area, the family contacted the police in nearby Silkeborg. Two days later, on May 8, 1950, a detective investigated the scene. The body had been found nearly eight feet underground, yet there were no signs of recent digging. The officer realized this was a case not for the police but for an archaeologist. He summoned Peter Vilhelm Glob, a renowned professor of archaeology at the Aarhus University. Upon surveying the scene and the state of the body, Glob concluded that "Tollund Man" was not a recent victim of misfortune but an ancient bog body.

The term "bog body" *(moorleiche)* was coined in 1871 by German scholar Johanna Mestorf, who published the first catalog of such discoveries. Since the 1800s, hundreds of Iron Age bog bodies and skeletons have been discovered across northern Europe. More than 500 have been found in Denmark alone, most dating to between 800 B.C. and A.D. 200. Others have been unearthed mostly in wetlands in Germany, the Netherlands, the United Kingdom, and Ireland. The cadavers are predominantly adult men and women, but a few children and adolescents have been excavated as well. The acidic, oxygen-starved conditions of peat bogs prevent decay, leaving much of the bodies' skin, hair, clothes, and stomach contents remarkably well preserved. Scientists have marveled at the pristine fingernails, pomaded hair, and stubbled chins on some of the most "famous" bog bodies.

"[Tollund Man] has this three-day beard—you feel he will open his eyes and talk to you," said Karin Margarita Frei, a research scientist at the National Museum of Denmark. "It's something that not even Tutankhamun could make you feel."

> **"[Tollund Man] has this three-day beard—you feel he will open his eyes and talk to you. It's something that not even Tutankhamun could make you feel."**
>
> —*Karin Margarita Frei, research scientist*

Although researchers agree on the science behind how bog bodies have survived through the ages, there have been wildly different theories about how they ended up in their waterlogged resting places. Iron Age Europeans left no written records of their beliefs and customs, but it's known that they looked at bogs as portals to the supernatural world. In his work *Germania,* written at the end of the first century A.D., the Roman historian Tacitus drew on secondhand and thirdhand accounts of Germans killing cowards and people accused of homosexuality and staking their bodies down in bogs. As a result, many bog bodies were subsequently interpreted as people in disgrace, supposedly punished with torture, execution, and burial in the bog instead of cremation, the customary Iron Age practice.

That theory has unraveled as archaeologists have used increasingly advanced tools—CT scans, three-dimensional imaging, and radiocarbon dating—to study these unusual mummies. Some of the

A museum display of the Tollund Man shows what he looked like when he was discovered in a bog: a hat on his head and a braided leather thong around his neck.

damage once interpreted as torture or mutilation was actually inflicted after death. For example, Grauballe Man, discovered in a bog northwest of Copenhagen in 1952, is one of the best preserved bog bodies and now one of the most thoroughly examined. Previous x-rays were hard to read because the bones, demineralized by the acidic bog waters, looked like glass. Now CT scans have shown that Grauballe Man's skull was fractured by the pressure of the bog, compounded by a clog-shod boy who accidentally stepped on the body as it was being excavated. Grauballe Man's broken leg could also be the work of the bog and not, as previous scholars had thought, proof of a vicious blow to force him to kneel for execution.

Peter Vilhelm Glob and subsequent archaeologists have theorized that Grauballe Man and other bog bodies died as sacrifices to the fertility goddess Nerthus, whom Celtic and Germanic peoples believed held the power of life and death. Tacitus described Nerthus as a widely worshipped Mother Earth goddess who "they believe . . . takes part in human affairs, riding in a chariot among her people." A valuable silver bowl covered in engravings called the Gundestrup cauldron was fished out of a bog in Denmark near one of the bodies as if it too had been sacrificed. If a community had a bad harvest, perhaps one of its members was sacrificed to Nerthus so the rest could live. By and large, their deaths were not pretty. Grauballe Man's throat was slit from ear to ear. Tollund Man died by hanging, most likely by acquaintances, because somebody then cut him down, put him in a sleeping position, closed his mouth and eyes, and then placed him in the bog.

Similar scenes of sacrifice may have played out in Ireland's ancient kingdoms. Within three months of each other in 2003, two bog bodies were dredged up by excavating equipment in Ireland, both bodies showing signs of not only deliberate violence but also significant wealth. Clonycavan Man had his nose broken and abdomen sliced open. His lofty pompadour was still styled the way he wore it during his last moments alive, his pomade produced from vegetable oil and resin imported from the South of France. Encircling one of his biceps was an armband of braided leather with a bronze amulet incised with Celtic designs, a costly mark of status.

Only the trunk and arms remained of Oldcroghan Man; he suffered defensive wounds on his arms before being fatally stabbed in the heart. He showed few signs of having performed physical labor in his life, and his fingernails were finely manicured. Chemical analysis showed that he regularly ate meat, but that his last meal included cereals and buttermilk, emblems of fertility befitting a sacrifice to the goddess.

Clonycavan Man and Oldcroghan Man share a telling trait with some 40 other Irish bog bodies: All were buried on borders between ancient kingdoms. Eamonn Kelly, keeper of Irish antiquities at the National Museum of Ireland, interprets that as a sign of royal sacrifice. In ancient times, Irish kings symbolically married the fertility goddess; famine meant the goddess had turned against the king and needed to be mollified. Kelly thinks the Irish bog bodies represented the most splendid of offerings: high-ranking hostages taken to force rebellious lords into obedience, pretenders to the throne, or even the failed kings themselves. Both Clonycavan Man and Oldcroghan Man appear to have had their nipples cut off after death. Kelly theorizes this may have been the mark of a rejected ruler, because in ancient Ireland a king's subjects ritually demonstrated their submission by sucking on the ruler's nipples.

With each new discovery, the picture expands. For example, the examination of Cashel Man in Ireland in 2013 revealed that he fit the pattern of bog bodies that incurred a violent death and were buried along ancient regional borders. But unlike the others, Cashel Man lived in the early Bronze Age, around 2000 B.C.—making him the oldest fleshed bog body ever discovered. This surprising result extends the established time frame for bog bodies in Ireland by centuries and opens up new realms of questions and possibilities for why and how this mysterious practice evolved so long ago.

55

MAYA MASTERPIECES REVEALED

100 B.C. ◆ San Bartolo, Guatemala, and Bonampak, Mexico ◆ Maya

Murals at two sites, separated by centuries, have upended ideas about the Maya and the remarkable longevity of their cultural beliefs.

———◆———

Two artists, each with a distinct style, worked by torchlight and morning sunshine. They had trained for their task since youth, copying images and text from the accordion-fold books that held the sacred stories. Now, under their brushstrokes, the gods and their acts of creation burst to life on polished plaster.

Spanning at least two walls of a room at the base of a pyramid, the result was a masterpiece with two purposes: to honor the gods and to illustrate the divine right of a king. The first made it timeless; the second, short-lived. After only a few decades, the room was buried beneath a larger pyramid: a monument to a new ruler in the ancient city known today as San Bartolo. There the murals remained, hidden in the Guatemalan jungle, for more than 2,000 years before those divine faces again met human eyes. Their discovery reveals not only the great antiquity of Maya painting, but also the long endurance of the Maya stories of creation.

A stroke of pure luck brought archaeologist Bill Saturno to the painted room. In March 2001, he ducked into a trench that looters had cut into the pyramid—and found himself face-to-face with the Maya maize god looking over his own shoulder at a beautiful maiden. After some planning to ensure that further excavation would not cause damage, he began to dig a narrow tunnel inside the mural room. When he finally began to chisel away the stones covering the hidden mural, "it was as if an ancient Maya book had been spread open before me, recounting the birth of the Maya cosmos from the gods' loins," he wrote later.

Aspects of the story were familiar from two much later manuscripts: the 13th-century Dresden Codex and the 16th-century Popol Vuh. But these wall paintings, more than a thousand years older, told the same tale—with startling grace and sophistication. Clearly, Maya painting had achieved glory centuries before the great works of the Classic Maya in the seventh century. In Western terms, it was like knowing only modern art and then stumbling on a Michelangelo or a Leonardo.

The far end of the mural held another surprise. Some scholars thought that at this early stage in Maya history, city-states had not yet evolved into full-fledged monarchies, with all the trappings seen later. But here was a king, named and titled, receiving his crown. In short, this one chamber upended much of what we thought we knew about the Maya.

Almost a mile west of the painted room lay an actual king: the earliest known Maya royal burial. Digging beneath a small pyramid, archaeologists discovered a sealed tomb. Inside were the bones of a man, with offerings that included a delicate frog-shaped bowl and a vase bearing an effigy of Chac, the rain god. On the man's chest rested a concave jade plaque—a symbol of Maya royalty.

After 2,000 years, the power of the ancient gods and kings seemed intact: Just as the team removed the dead king's Chac effigy, the clouds opened and the region's worst dry season in a decade came to an end.

Gourd-rattle players parade along the base of one of the three painted chambers at Bonampak that display scenes of celebration, battle, and sacrifice.

The mural artistry of the Maya that is known today was mostly blank to scholars of the early 20th century. Archaeologists had located many scraps of paintings among rubble of ancient Maya cities that hinted at a sophisticated art form, but no complete murals had been uncovered. Tantalizing rumors of a "temple of paintings" intrigued American explorer-photographer Giles Healey during a 1946 trip to the Chiapas region of Mexico. Healey hired two Lacandón Maya guides, Acasio Chan and José Pepe Chambor, to explore a site they knew to include some paintings. Pushing through a plain doorway, they found three rooms of stunning floor-to-ceiling murals.

These scenes of pomp, warfare, and intimacy profoundly altered Maya scholarship. Mayanists had long believed that Classic Maya civilization, spanning A.D. 250 to 900, was a peaceful Eden ruled by benevolent astronomer-priests. Yet Bonampak's graphic depiction of combat, cruelty, vanity, music, and humor—displayed by a cast of more than 200 characters—demonstrates that the Maya exhibited all the flaws and grace of humanity.

The site was subsequently named Bonampak, from the Maya words for "painted wall." The murals there, found in a building atop an acropolis, depict a dynasty that flourished 1,200 years ago. "I see each room as a chapter in an epic tale," art historian Mary Miller observed. Room One depicts a young heir being presented to prestigious lords, who then hold a lavish celebration. In Room Two, a chaotic battle provides captives for human sacrifice to appease the gods and honor the new heir. In Room Three, Bonampak's elite seal the heir's right to the throne with a dramatic bloodletting ritual.

Scholars had also once held that Maya glyphs merely described arcane celestial events. As epigraphers began to debunk that theory, Bonampak bolstered their case: Its long glyphic text includes elaborate details of political affiliations, dates, and deeds in the life of the city's last known ruler, Chaan Muan, or Sky Hawk.

The murals at Bonampak, like the Maya themselves, still retain many secrets. Classic Maya civilization in the region was near collapse at the time the paintings were made. Perhaps the Maya suffered famine or warfare. We only know that these murals were never finished, and that the young heir they celebrate likely never reached the throne: Bonampak seems to have been abandoned soon after the murals were painted.

The paintings that Healey saw decades ago were murky shadows of what was once there; the building they were in had been constructed in such a way that rainwater leaked through its limestone walls, depositing a brittle crust of calcium over the once brilliant colors. So in 1984 the Mexican government began a program to clean the murals. "Details I had never seen leaped from the walls. Pearls

"Details I had never seen leaped from the walls. Pearls gleamed. Dancers paused for the next drumbeat. Ghostly bodies of defeated foes floated to the surface like drowned men rising from the depths."

—*Mary Miller, art historian*

gleamed. Dancers paused for the next drumbeat. Ghostly bodies of defeated foes floated to the surface like drowned men rising from the depths," Miller wrote.

Before the cleaning, only four hand-drawn copies of these exquisite images had been made—all incomplete and lacking detail. A new kind of copy was needed before time could damage the paintings further. To remedy that, a team from *National Geographic* took color photographs of the cleansed murals and scanned those images into a computer. They then added details gathered by close inspection and infrared photographs. The resulting computer reconstructions—showing about one-fifth of the murals—are as close to the originals as anyone could come without actually having been there as the paint dried.

That any paintings have survived at all at San Bartolo and Bonampak is something of a miracle; the region's heat and humidity have surely destroyed untold numbers of similar murals. And yet, every once in a while, archaeologists find another example. Beginning in 2004, painted walls uncovered at Calakmul, Mexico, showed people performing everyday tasks such as preparing food—themes never before seen in Maya art. In 2010, at Xultún, Guatemala, archaeologists began to reveal the ancient workroom of a Maya scribe. On the walls were hieroglyphic calculations that helped ancient recordkeepers oversee vast amounts of time—and most likely a portrait of the scribe himself.

As new technologies such as lidar reveal more and more sites once hidden under the canopy of the rainforest, who knows how many more stunning works of Maya art may come to light?

56

DEAD SEA
SCROLLS

300 B.C.–A.D. 100 ✦ Israel, Palestine ✦ Judaean

*A 2,000-year-old secret library hidden in
desert caves became the 20th century's most important
discovery in biblical archaeology.*

———◆———

For cloak-and-dagger drama, the Dead Sea Scrolls trump all other biblical discoveries, but their story starts with the sheerest of accidents. In 1947, a Bedouin boy named Muhammad Adh-Dhib from the Ta'amireh tribe was searching for a stray goat in the arid expanse of the Judaean wilderness. Clambering among the stark cliffs bordering the northwest coast of the Dead Sea, he idly cast a stone into a small opening and heard the shattering of pottery. Frightened away, he later returned with a companion, entered, and found several large earthen jars. In one or more of them, he also found some aged scrolls wrapped in foul-smelling linen.

The goatherders didn't know it then, but the scrolls were just a small portion of an impressive library that belonged to a breakaway Jewish sect that took refuge in a religious center at nearby Qumran overlooking the Dead Sea some 2,000 years earlier. As Roman troops closed in to crush the First Jewish Revolt around A.D. 70, these separatists stashed their collection of texts, including biblical scrolls covered in ancient Hebrew script, in the desert caves.

According to one version of the story, the Bedouin herders sold the seven parchments they'd found to two antiquities dealers in Bethlehem. A scholar from Jerusalem acquired three of the scrolls following a clandestine meeting through a barbed-wire fence. A dealer named Khalil Iskander Shahin, also known as Kando, sold the four remaining scrolls to a Syrian archbishop in Jerusalem, who reportedly paid the equivalent of $250. In 1949, spooked by the Arab-Israeli War, the bishop smuggled the scrolls to the United States in hopes of selling them to a museum or university. After getting no takers, he placed a classified ad in the *Wall Street Journal* on June 1, 1954. Working through an American intermediary, Israeli archaeologist Yigael Yadin (who would later go on to excavate Masada) arranged to purchase the scrolls for the Israeli government for $250,000.

When word of the scrolls' discovery spread, a team led by archaeologist and Dominican priest Roland de Vaux descended on Qumran in 1949. By 1956, de Vaux and local Bedouin had found 10 more "scroll caves" containing scores of manuscripts, many of them disintegrated into thousands of fragments. He also reexamined a ruin less than a mile south of the first cave where scrolls were discovered. Known as Khirbat (Ruins of) Qumran, the ruin stood alone on a terrace overlooking the Dead Sea, a barren landscape that evoked biblical stories like David fleeing King Saul and Jesus rejecting the devil's temptations. "When I first visited the excavation with Père de Vaux, I was immediately impressed by the bleak grandeur of the setting," A. Douglas Tushingham wrote for *National Geographic* in 1958. "From the scorched plain that skirts the sea we approached the monastery by a road which twists its way up a steep slope. While readily navigable by pedestrians—or donkeys—the road's turns are terrifyingly abrupt for a motorcar."

At Khirbat Qumran, de Vaux was convinced he was looking at the source of the scrolls: the ruins of a religious complex of the

This fragment of parchment bearing text written some 2,000 years ago was among the first seven Dead Sea Scrolls found in a cave near Qumran in 1947.

Essenes, a Jewish sect that lived a communal and ascetic life marked by daily cleansing rituals, according to the Roman-era Jewish historian Josephus. Among the ruins, the archaeologists indeed uncovered numerous remains of pools that de Vaux believed to be Jewish ritual baths. De Vaux's theory also appeared to be supported by the Dead Sea Scrolls themselves, some of which contained guidelines for communal living that matched ancient descriptions of Essene customs. The archaeologists also found jars at the ruins just like the ones that held the scrolls in the caves.

While archaeologists excavated, other Bedouin did their own digging and sold what they found to Kando, the antiquities dealer. His greatest purchase was the nearly 30-foot-long Temple Scroll, the longest of the Dead Sea Scrolls. In 1967, during the Arab-Israeli Six-Day War, Israeli intelligence officers seized the Temple Scroll from Kando's home, claiming it as government property. After the incident, Kando reportedly started furtively moving his remaining scroll fragments to relatives in Lebanon and later to a bank vault in Switzerland.

It took decades for scholars, working in seclusion and secrecy, to reassemble and translate most of the tattered parchments collected in Qumran. The long delay in publication spawned conspiracy theories that the powers that be—the pope? Zionists?—were deliberately suppressing the scrolls' contents. Finally, by the mid-2000s, the translators finished publishing the bulk of their findings. The scrolls included legal texts, apocalyptic and ritual treatises, and accounts of life in a separatist Jewish sect. Scholars were thrilled to learn that among them was a nearly complete copy of the Book of Isaiah from the Hebrew Bible. Its content was virtually identical to another copy of Isaiah dated almost a thousand years later. The Great Isaiah Scroll would become Exhibit A for scholars who defend the Bible against claims that scribes over centuries of copying by hand had corrupted its text by introducing a multitude of mistakes and intentional changes.

All seven of the original scrolls now reside in their own wing of Israel's national museum in Jerusalem, but in total the vast Dead Sea Scroll collection is made up of around 100,000 fragments of texts, many of them still undeciphered, from more than 900 manuscripts. To ensure their preservation, the Israel Antiquities Authority has established the Dead Sea Scrolls conservation laboratory in Jerusalem, where the delicate bits of parchment and papyrus are meticulously reunited, digitized in partnership with Google, and made public.

Naturally, the precious nature of the manuscripts has inspired forgeries, leading to high-profile scandals. In March 2020, an independent team of art fraud investigators announced that all 16 of the purported Dead Sea Scrolls in the Museum of the Bible, which opened in 2017 in Washington, D.C., were modern fakes. The museum's founder, American businessman and evangelical Christian Steve Green, had acquired the pieces when a new cache of scrolls with unknown provenance suddenly entered the antiquities market in the 2000s. "The fact is, most antiquities are looted, and most buyers don't ask where they came from," says Eitan Klein, deputy director of the Israel Antiquities Authority's anti-looting division. "Because in my view, if you are dealing with antiquities, you must get your hands dirty somehow." The discovery of genuine new scroll fragments in archaeological investigations has dried up since the 1950s, and laws restrict the sale of looted scrolls. However, many hold out hope of recovering scraps penned by the prolific Essene scribes and still hidden in the Qumran caves that are now a part of the Israeli-occupied West Bank.

> "The fact is, most antiquities are looted, and most buyers don't ask where they came from."
> —*Eitan Klein,*
> *Israel Antiquities*
> *Authority*

Advanced imaging technologies also raise the possibility that new texts could be discovered on already known scraps of the scrolls that are locked away in academic storerooms or museums. A group of scholars recently analyzed a collection of Qumran fragments that had been donated to a British scientist in the 1950s to help determine the age of the manuscripts. The scraps were thought to be blank, but after noticing faint traces of a lamed, the Hebrew letter "'L," on one scrap, the researchers photographed the collection using a method known as multispectral imaging. In May 2020, the team announced that once invisible text was now readable on four of these small scraps. Some words like "Shabbat" are easily recognizable, but the fragments have yet to be fully interpreted.

57

TREASURE LOST AND FOUND

First century A.D. ◆ Northern Afghanistan ◆ Kushan

The 2,000-year-old treasures from a group of royal graves along the Silk Road were lost and recovered more than once.

———◆———

In November 1978, archaeologists were digging an unassuming mound called Tillya Tepe on the northern edge of Afghanistan. The country was inching toward civil war, but the methodical pace of excavation continued against this tense backdrop. On a cold, wet day, several rusted fragments of iron bands with nails sticking from them emerged from the ground. One was bent at a right angle and looked a lot like a bracket from a wooden coffin. The team took a break, and when they started digging again after the weather cleared, a workman turned up a disk that gleamed among the clods of damp earth. It was gold.

"We called a military guard and waded in with pounding hearts," archaeologist Viktor Ivanovich Sarianidi recalled. "And soon a grave emerged from beneath our picks and scoops. Staring at us were the hollow eye sockets of a skull, a young woman between 25 and 30, perhaps a princess. Surrounding her were layers of gold jewelry and ornamentation that had collapsed together from her disintegrating clothing."

The land of Bactria on Afghanistan's northern plains was once an important crossroads on the Silk Road that ran from the varied lands of the Roman Empire in the west to the Chinese cities protected by the Great Wall in the east. Bactria was autonomous 4,000 years ago, but through the centuries it was dominated by succeeding expansionist empires: the Persians of the Achaemenid period, the Greek colonizers in the path of Alexander the Great, and the wave of nomadic Kushan and eastern Scythians who ushered in the dark period, a shadowy time during the first two centuries A.D.

In the rainy fall of 1978, that darkness lifted. The archaeologists found the graves of eight people who lived in that little-understood period some 2,000 years ago. And with their bones was the wealth they were to carry to the afterlife—more than 20,000 artifacts, including crowns, pendants, bracelets, and weapons mostly crafted of gold and semiprecious stones such as turquoise, carnelian, and lapis lazuli.

The team worked into the winter with numb fingers as bitter winds leaked into their flimsy plywood huts and meals were reduced to tinned meat carted in from Moscow. The brilliance of the necropolis gradually revealed itself in the thousands of spangles that appeared like so much golden confetti. Each platelet weighed next to nothing, but a single pocketful would have bought a new car in Kabul in 1978. Officials soon sent a two-man team—one Soviet and one Afghan—to guard each grave and tally the findings each day. The potent word "gold" spread across the plains, and a pilgrimage began of village people, tourists, and authorities from Kabul. Some came on donkeys, others walked. The cotton farmer whose fields edged the dig was a constant visitor. After a lifetime of laboring in those pastures, he could hardly believe that gold was lying just underfoot.

Sarianidi, of Moscow's Institute of Archaeology, had carried out several excavations in Central Asia before coming to Afghanistan in 1969 as part of a joint Soviet-Afghan expedition to examine the antiquities that lay beneath the fabled Bactrian Plain. On and off for nine years, the team dug into mounds near Sheberghan, a large village between the foothills of the Hindu Kush and the desert valley of the Amu Darya (Oxus River). At first they focused on a site called Yemshi Tepe, the ruins of a monumental city from the first century A.D. Inside the walls they found a citadel, perhaps the palace of the local ruler who controlled a cluster of villages that over time were consumed by swells of sunbaked earth.

When the team moved on to nearby Tillya Tepe, they first found a village from the third century B.C., and below that, a Bronze Age temple built 3,200 years ago for the worship of fire. Then they uncovered the gold-filled graves. Sarianidi theorized that the graves were deliberately camouflaged, dug in secret for the local rulers, who perhaps lived at Yemshi Tepe and were part of the Kushan Empire.

The Kushan nomads originated on the frontiers of China before traveling southwest across the Central Asian steppes around 130 B.C. Along with the Scythians, they plundered oasis cities on the trade routes, and when they crossed the Oxus River, they laid waste to the cities of the Greco-Bactrian kingdom. At first resistant to city life and Greek culture, the nomads gradually rebuilt the cities they had sacked and created the great Kushan Empire on their own debris. In the time between the Greco-Bactrian period and the well-documented flowering of the Kushan, ancient records fail us. The period was obscure until the discovery of the Tillya Tepe treasures.

The artifacts gave archaeologists a chance to glimpse the extensive trade between the East and West during that time. Nowhere in antiquity had so many different objects from so many different cultures—Chinese mirrors, Roman coins, daggers from Siberia—been found together in situ. Bactrian art in the dark period was seldom pure because patrons of the local goldsmiths combined various traditions. Found among hundreds of gold spangles on a young woman in one grave was a pendant in the form of the goddess Aphrodite with a figure like a Greco-Roman sculpture, Bactrian wings, and a forehead mark imported from India.

But before archaeologists had a chance to make plaster copies of the pieces, or study or display them, war and confusion closed in on Afghanistan. The Soviets invaded the country shortly after the excavation team brought the gold treasures to Kabul's National Museum. Sarianidi and his collaborators were only able to see the artifacts again to take photos in 1982. Many Afghans assumed the treasure was looted along with much of the National Museum's collection after a missile strike in 1993. By August 2003, with the Taliban ousted and President Hamid Karzai's interim government in place, officials found six locked safes in a vault in Kabul suspected to hold the Bactrian gold.

After months of legalities, a team assembled in April 2004 for an old-fashioned safecracking to solve the mystery. Because the keys had disappeared, a workman applied a hammer, a crowbar, then a power saw to the first safe. Sparks flew amid an anxious crowd that included Sarianidi. At last the door opened, and one by one the safes revealed the entire trove—thousands of glittering objects restored to the world.

A young nomadic woman buried at Tillya Tepe wore this gold crown. The five "trees" could be detached, allowing the headdress to be easily transported.

58

CAESAREA MARITIMA'S AMBITIOUS HARBOR

ca 30 B.C. ◆ Caesarea, Israel ◆ Roman

Roman vassal Herod the Great spared no expense in building an ambitious harbor, signaling Judaea's allegiance to Rome's first emperor, Caesar Augustus.

———◆———

Two decades before the birth of Christ, Herod the Great, king of Judaea from 37 to 4 B.C., set out to create an international metropolis on the coast, where no major city had ever stood before. In a career marked by grandiose building projects—the Temple in Jerusalem, the winter palace in Jericho, the lofty Dead Sea citadel of Masada—this was to be his crowning achievement: a city to rival Egypt's Alexandria in terms of trade and opulence. On this sandy strip of land, he vowed to build a hub majestic enough to impress his patron, Caesar Augustus, the almighty emperor of Rome.

Caesarea Maritima was monumental in scale and scope, all the more impressive because it was constructed on an unstable, storm-battered shore at a site lacking a protective cape or bay.

Although the physical site was daunting, work proceeded on the city and harbor at a feverish pace. Thousands of conscripted laborers, speaking a babble of different tongues, toiled in summer's oppressive heat and winter's biting winds. "The King . . . overcame nature," wrote the Jewish historian Josephus. "Although the location was generally unfavorable, [Herod] contended with the difficulties so well that the solidity of the construction could not be overcome by the sea, and its beauty seemed finished off without impediment."

Herod had once been allied with Augustus's rival, Mark Anthony, but had switched sides and was now invested in proving himself a good client king. For this reason he built his great city in the Roman style, softening regional differences in Rome's many provinces by skillfully mixing Roman cultural ideals with local practices. Caesarea Maritima was laid out on a Roman grid plan: a forum, baths, government offices, and temples, with tenements inside the walls and villas outside. Because the city had no rivers or springs, drinking water was brought in by way of a high-level aqueduct—another Roman innovation—from the Shuni springs some five miles away.

Of all the city's innovations, its harbor was perhaps the most impressive. Finished in less than a decade, it encompassed a total area of 200,000 square yards, making Caesarea one of the four largest Mediterranean ports of its time.

To lay the foundations, underwater divers called *urinatores* took turns descending to the ocean floor a dozen feet below, smoothing the bottom where the breakwater would go before ascending again. Rocks too large to move by hand were lashed with ropes and hauled out of the way by cranes.

The engineering technology employed here was remarkably innovative; the use of hydraulic concrete, which hardens underwater, was used on a scale that archaeologists have found nowhere else. Builders also employed unique wave-breaking structures and ingenious sluice systems to reduce siltation. The largest anchorage constructed at that time, Caesarea was arguably home to the world's first modern harbor.

A seaside theater for 4,000 anchored Caesarea, the port city King Herod built to showcase his grandeur. It once hosted classic plays as well as pantomimes.

Freighters sailed up to, but not into, the port, where they were met and towed between two towers topped by six colossal statues. An inner harbor enabled ships to anchor at the base of a giant temple dedicated to Augustus. Perpetuating the "cult of the emperor" in far-flung Roman provinces was a key part of Augustus's ruling strategy; it gave him divine authority while living and inspired loyalty through worship, even when the man himself was rarely seen.

To add to his growing complex, Herod erected a huge theater and a hippodrome, where in 9 B.C. he staged elaborate games to dedicate his city. By 6 B.C., the city had become the headquarters of the Roman government in Palestine.

Over time, Caesarea would become as rich in history as it was in monuments. It served as a base for Roman legions who quelled the Great Jewish Revolt in 66 B.C. It was also the site where General Vespasian was declared Caesar, Pontius Pilate ruled Roman Judaea, and the Apostles Peter and Paul preached.

Herod hoped Caesarea would supplant Alexandria as the region's premier port. But despite its clever construction, it began to sink soon after completion; the concrete used to assemble it was no match for the active geologic fault line on which it was built. Following Herod's death in 4 B.C., the Romans decided to let the troublesome harbor deteriorate, although the city itself would go on to prosper. Toward the end of the sixth century the Byzantines revived the city, adding a perimeter wall and making Caesarea the country's largest fortified metropolis. It was refortified again in later centuries by Arab and crusader armies.

The site lay mostly untouched until the 19th century, when new explorations began. Extensive surveys by Israeli archaeologists in the 1960s revealed many wonders: a theater, ancient shops, mills, fountains, fortifications, and an aqueduct. "The size of the site amazed me," wrote explorer and history professor Robert Hohlfelder, who dove there in 1987. "Although 2,000 years had passed, I could conjure an image of Caesarea's construction."

> **"The size of the site amazed me . . . Although 2,000 years had passed, I could conjure an image of Caesarea's construction."**
>
> —*Robert Hohlfelder, professor of history*

The University of Haifa's Avner Raban and Elisha Linder had studied the site for years, though with limited results; it seemed that a new approach was needed to uncover the marvels of Caesarea's past. As Hohlfelder explained, "only underwater exploration on an unprecedented scale could unravel the harbor's secrets and produce significant scientific results." In 1980, Raban, Linder, and a consortium of universities formed the Caesarea Ancient Harbor Excavation Project (CAHEP), which uncovered many of the city's building innovations, including the use of concrete in the harbor's construction.

Over the years, divers have unearthed tons of ancient pottery, as well as shipwrecks, at the site. In 2016, a late-Roman period wreck yielded bronze statues, coins, and iron anchors preserved in the sands. In 2018 and 2019, researchers from Vanderbilt University excavated a 900-square-meter section of land at Caesarea, revealing the base of the Temple of Augustus and some surprisingly sophisticated plumbing systems. "It's perfectly preserved," said Vanderbilt historian Philip Lieberman. "It looks like it could have been built yesterday."

And there is still more to discover at this monumental city. "The story of Caesarea on the sea is not yet complete," Hohlfelder says. "More surprises lie ahead."

59

SPIRITS IN THE SAND

500 B.C.–A.D. 700 ✦ Southern Peru ✦ Paracas, Nasca

Known as the Nasca lines, more than a thousand designs etched into a desert may have been sacred paths used in rituals to implore the gods for rain.

———◆———

Ruler straight and tack sharp, a curious marking more than a mile long etches the desert in southern Peru. Modern paths that wander across it only emphasize the precision of its design. Throughout hundreds of square miles of arid plateau, other markings abound, most of them concentrated between the towns of Nasca and Palpa. Known as the Nasca lines, they form a geometrical mélange of quadrangles, triangles, and trapezoids; spirals and flowers; narrow lines that extend more than five miles; and a desert zoo of giant creatures—birds, reptiles, and whales, a monkey and a spider.

Because some of the figures resemble those decorating the distinctive Nasca pottery, archaeologists attribute many of the lines to the Nascans, a coastal people whose culture rose, flourished, and declined between about 100 B.C. and A.D. 700.

Since the mysterious desert drawings became widely known in the late 1920s, when commercial air travel was introduced between Lima and the southern Peruvian city of Arequipa, they have puzzled archaeologists, anthropologists, and anyone fascinated by ancient cultures in the Americas.

After World War II, a German-born teacher named Maria Reiche made the first formal surveys of the lines and figures called geoglyphs. For half a century, until her death in 1998, Reiche played a critically important role in conserving them. But her own preferred theory—that the lines represented settings on an astronomical calendar—has been largely discredited.

Since 1997, a large-scale Peruvian-German research collaboration has been under way. The Nasca-Palpa Project has mounted a systematic, multidisciplinary study of the ancient people of the region, starting with where and how the Nasca lived, why they disappeared, and the meaning of the strange designs they left behind in the desert sand. In recent years, the use of drones and satellite images has offered fresh perspectives on the known Nasca lines and allowed dozens of new ones to be discovered.

In the desert of southern Peru, figures etched on the land—including this spider— have inspired wonder in air travelers since first spotted in the 1920s.

The coastal region of southern Peru and northern Chile is one of the driest places on Earth. In the small, protected basin where the Nasca culture arose, 10 rivers descend from the Andes to the east, most of them dry at least part of the year. These fragile ribbons of green, surrounded by a thousand shades of brown, offered a fertile hot spot for the emergence of an early civilization. It was a high-risk environment, though, because the microclimate has oscillated dramatically over the past 5,000 years. When a high-pressure system over central South America called the Bolivian High moves to the north, more rain falls on the western slopes of the Andes. When the high shifts southward, precipitation decreases and the rivers in the Nasca valleys run dry.

Despite the risky conditions, the Nasca civilization flourished for eight centuries. Around 100 B.C., its people emerged out of previous cultures known as Paracas and Topará, settling along the river valleys and cultivating such crops as cotton, beans, tubers, a local fruit called lucuma, and a short-eared form of corn. A famous ceramic tableau known as the Tello plaque—showing several Nasca strolling while blowing their panpipes, surrounded by dancing dogs—has been viewed as an iconic snapshot of a peaceful people whose rituals embraced music, dance, and sacred walks.

The Nasca people moved east or west along the river valleys as rainfall patterns shifted. The Peru-German project has explored the region from the Pacific coast to altitudes of nearly 15,000 feet in the Andean Highlands. Almost everywhere they have looked, they have found evidence of Nasca villages—"like pearls in the valley margins," says archaeologist Markus Reindel. "And near every settlement we find geoglyphs." The parched desert and hillsides made an inviting canvas: By simply removing a layer of dark stones cluttering the ground, exposing the lighter sand beneath, the Nasca created markings that have endured for centuries in the dry climate—undisturbed by the gully washers that would have erased them in wetter places. "The geoglyphs surely provided a kinetic, ritualistic reminder to the Nasca people that their fate

"The geoglyphs surely provided a kinetic, ritualistic
reminder to the Nasca people that their fate was tied
to their environment—its
natural beauty, its ephemeral abundance, and its
life-threatening austerity."

—*Stephen S. Hall,*
journalist

was tied to their environment —its natural beauty, its ephemeral abundance, and its life-threatening austerity," explained journalist Stephen S. Hall.

Though the Nasca were certainly the most prolific makers of geoglyphs, they were not the first. On a hillside abutting a plateau south of Palpa are three stylized human figures with buggy eyes and bizarre rays of hair dating to at least 2,400 years ago—earlier than almost any textbook date for the start of the Nasca civilization. Reindel's team has attributed no fewer than 75 groups of geoglyphs in the Palpa area to the earlier Paracas culture. These renderings, which often depict stylized humanlike figures, in turn share distinct visual motifs with even earlier images carved in stone, known as petroglyphs. During a foot survey of a suspected Paracas site high in the Palpa River Valley, Peruvian archaeologist Johny Isla, the Nasca lines' chief restorer and protector at the Peruvian Ministry of Culture, came across a petroglyph of a monkey—a surprising, earlier incarnation of a famous Nasca geoglyph.

These findings make an important point about the Nasca lines: They were not made at one time, in one place, for one purpose. Many have been superimposed on older ones, with erasures and overwritings, complicating their interpretation.

The early Paracas-era geoglyphs were placed on hillsides where they could be seen from the desert plain. By early Nasca times, the images—less anthropomorphic, more naturalistic—had migrated to the flat desert floor. Almost all of these iconic animal figures, such as the spider and the hummingbird, were single-line drawings; a person could step into them at one point and exit at another without ever crossing a line, suggesting to archaeologists that at some point in early Nasca times the lines evolved from mere images to pathways for ceremonial processions. Later, possibly in response to explosive population growth, more people may have participated in these rituals; the resulting geoglyphs took on open, geometrical patterns, with some trapezoids stretching more than 2,000 feet. "Our idea," Reindel says, "is that they weren't meant as images to be seen anymore, but stages to be walked upon, to be used for religious ceremonies." National Geographic Explorer Johan Reinhard proposes that one of the main purposes of the Nasca lines was related to the worship of mountain deities, due to their traditional connection to water.

Journalist Hall followed the ancient Nasca footsteps around a spiral path while touring the site with Isla. A visitor can read the ancient people's reverence for nature "in times of plenty and in times of desperate want, in every line and curve they scratched onto the desert floor," he observed. "When your feet inhabit their sacred space, even for a brief and humbling moment, you can feel it."

There is little question that water—or more precisely, its absence—had assumed paramount importance by the end of the Nasca culture, roughly between the years A.D. 500 and 600. In the Palpa area, geophysicists have traced the creep of the eastern margin of the desert about 12 miles up the valleys between 200 B.C. and A.D. 600, reaching an altitude of some 6,500 feet. Similarly, the population centers in the river oases around Palpa moved farther up the valleys, as if they were trying to outrun the arid conditions. At the end of the sixth century A.D., the aridity culminated and the Nasca society collapsed, leaving only the sacred paths as testaments to the ancient pleas to the heavens.

60

STANDOFF
AT MASADA

37–31 B.C. ◆ Israel ◆ Judaean

*A supposedly cursed desert fortress was the site of
a tragic standoff between Jewish rebels
and Roman soldiers in the first century A.D.*

———◆———

As ruler of Judaea from about 37 to 4 B.C., Herod the Great
had the difficult job of reconciling the demands of Roman
overlords with his Jewish subjects, but his reign guided the
kingdom to new prosperity and power. Won by a mix of savvy diplomacy and ruthless conquest, Herod's territory stretched from
modern Lebanon and Syria in the north, to Israel's Negev desert in
the south, with a line of fortresses that guarded its eastern flank.
Many of these fortresses were originally built by the Hasmonaeans,
Jewish kings who ruled the region from 141 to 63 B.C. But Herod—
one of the most imaginative and energetic builders of the ancient
world—made the strongholds bigger and grander.

Nowhere is this more apparent than at Masada, an isolated
complex built on the plateau of a narrow, 1,300-foot-high mountain
overlooking the Dead Sea. Herod's northern palace cascades
breathtakingly down a cliff face on three terraces, creating an airy
and luminous residence that was also a virtually impregnable fortress. Roman-Jewish historian Flavius Josephus wrote that Masada

Herod the Great's three-tiered palace cascades down the north face of Masada. The king, long reviled as a villain, is recognized today as a master architect.

could house 10,000 soldiers. Perhaps more impressively, this complex had such a good water management system that it had all the features of a seaside Roman villa—lush gardens, a swimming pool, and baths—in a hostile desert environment.

Herod's vision didn't long survive him. After his death, Judaea's prosperity declined. His descendants frittered away the enormous fortune he had left them and squandered the religious and political harmony he had so carefully fostered. After 10 years of ineffectual rule by Herod's son, the impatient Romans assigned a procurator to govern Judaea directly (in the early 30s A.D., the office was held by Pontius Pilate). To many Jews, the Romans now seemed oppressors and infidels. In the First Jewish Revolt (A.D. 66–70), a faction of rebels held out tenaciously against the Roman legions at both of Herod's hilltop fortresses, Herodium, south of Jerusalem, and Masada. At Herodium, they vandalized Herod's tomb and reshaped the hilltop: changing his triclinium, a lavish dining room, into a synagogue, and digging two Jewish ritual baths, or mikvahs, into the courtyard. The fighters there eventually surrendered. But at Masada, a group of Jewish rebels known as the Sicarii fought to the end. The Romans constructed a massive siege system around the fortress, and the rebels, facing inevitable defeat, reportedly committed suicide rather than become Roman prisoners and slaves. Claiming that 960 people died, Josephus recounted that the men killed their own wives and children before executing each other.

During the Second Jewish Revolt, in the 130s, Masada again became a rebel stronghold. The complex then housed a settlement of Christian monks who abandoned the site around the sixth century. Edward Robinson and Eli Smith, two American Christian pilgrims and explorers, correctly identified the site in 1838 with the help of local Bedouin. Serious archaeological research at Masada wasn't initiated until the mid-20th century, when researchers set about separating fact from fiction. In the early 1960s, Yigael Yadin, the former Israeli military chief of staff turned archaeologist, put out a call for international volunteers to dig at the site. He was flooded with thousands of applications. "One of the greatest surprises—and delights—of the enterprise, long before we had put scoop to rubble, was the response," Yadin later recalled.

> "One of the greatest surprises—and delights—of the enterprise, long before we had put scoop to rubble, was the response."
>
> —*Yigael Yadin, archaeologist*

Lasting from 1963 to 1965, Yadin's excavations were a massive operation, with a few hundred volunteers on-site at any given time. Among the varied remains they uncovered were architectural elements from Herod's royal court, such as column drums and capitals, fragments of wall decorations, and mosaics. Excavators found cooking vessels, eating utensils, baskets, leather waterskins, sandals, and colorful textiles and other artifacts related to the daily life and survival of the Jewish rebels who converted Herod's palaces into command centers. Archaeologists also identified the weapons, armor, and garments of Roman soldiers.

The diggers, however, only uncovered the remains of 28 individuals—inconsistent with the mythology of the site as a mass grave—which has led some scholars to further question the accuracy of Josephus's description of the tragedy. In more recent excavations, started in 2017, archaeologists began reexamining evidence that Masada had a greater diversity of people hiding out during the revolt, including perhaps the Essenes, another Jewish sect responsible for the Dead Sea Scrolls. They've also uncovered the first evidence of vineyards at the complex, yet more proof of Masada's impressive water management system.

Masada remains a prominent landmark for modern-day Israelis, thanks to its strong association with defiant warriors who symbolize religious idealism and courage in the face of oppression. At the complex, Israelis hold candlelight vigils and celebrate bar mitzvahs, and officers used to be inducted into the Israeli army at the site, repeating the fateful phrase, "Masada shall never fall again!" And yet, a growing number of Israelis view the suicidal courage of Masada's defenders as senseless fanaticism. "Many people say they should have negotiated with the Romans, not fought blindly to the death," says Israeli archaeologist Ehud Netzer. Perhaps Herod's entente with the Romans, long considered betrayal, is beginning to seem more like statecraft.

A.D. 75-600

Tombs & Temples

Archaeology reopens places unseen for centuries, revealing them to the world and illuminating the cultures, cosmologies, and religions of the early societies they represent. Treasure-laden burials and the shrouded sacred spaces of different religions offer keys to understanding the past; clues lie hidden in the layout of soaring pyramids, the enigmatic mosaic images assembled on a synagogue's floor, and the secret code of Maya hieroglyphs. They also reside in ruined monasteries, shadowy caves that once served as prayer halls, and a hidden space in one of the world's most holy sites. But not everyone had the privilege of choosing their own grave site. Pioneering archaeologists digging up the buried remains of Pompeii and Herculaneum found the city residents entombed in volcanic ash at the exact moment of their death.

One of many rock-cut chambers at Ajanta, India, this ornate ancient temple displays extraordinary examples of Buddhist art.

61

PETRA, ANCIENT CITY OF STONE

300 B.C.–A.D. 700 ◆ Jordan ◆ Nabataean

*Etched into a desert landscape, the Nabataean capital
built a water conservation system that allowed it
to prosper as a crossroads of caravans.*

———◆———

To the camel driver of two millennia ago, the city of Petra
beckoned like a distant star. It took 12 weeks to get there from
the frankincense groves of Oman, once the camels were
loaded and the campfires stamped out. Then the caravan would set
out through the morning mist, guarding its precious cargo from
bandits, and pass uneasily through the treachery of Yemen.

Later, if things were going well, the caravan would pause to
trade at Medina, drinking from its wells and gathering strength for
the journey ahead. Then it would strike out north across the hellish,
flint-strewn sands of western Arabia, living from one water hole to
the next all the way to the capital of the Nabataeans, who ruled the
lands east of the Jordan River.

What a relief it must have been to see the guards on the red
sandstone ledges, to be waved in after paying the toll, and to breathe

Located at the end of the rocky chasm that leads to Petra, the Treasury is as dazzling to visitors today as it was to Swiss scholar Johann Burckhardt in 1812.

the cool air inside the Siq, the 250-foot-high crack in the rock that was, and still is, the main road into Petra.

For the thirsty, there was water flowing down sinuous stone channels along the roadway; for the grateful and devout, there were carved altars to Dushara, the chief Nabataean god, on the chasm's sandstone walls. Boys on donkeys would dash by, shouting news of the arrival; the smell of cardamom, campfires, and searing meat promised hospitality just ahead. Finally, the caravan would swing wide around a bend to face what is now called the Treasury, a towering edifice carved from rose-colored rock, and plunge into the crowded marketplace beyond.

Centuries have passed, but traces of ancient Petra still endure in the desert of southern Jordan. The facades of its buildings peer out from the banks of drifting sand. Delicate bits of Nabataean pottery lie scattered across the surface. And if you're out early, you just might hear echoes of the ancient city in the local Bedouin drifting by on camels, or in the murmur of voices over pots of steeping tea.

Like other nomadic peoples who wandered through the spotlight of history, the Nabataeans left little behind to explain themselves. They probably moved into Palestine from Arabia several centuries before Christ. By the first century B.C., their capital was a rich city shaped by the sophistication and wealth that Petra—a natural fortress on a pass through rugged mountains—acquired as a crossroads for trade.

Filling a power vacuum left by Greece's decline, the Nabataeans dominated this part of the Middle East for more than four centuries before being subjugated by the Romans, then eclipsed by the Byzantines, and finally dispersed onto the back lot of history. From potsherds we know they were artists; ancient manuscripts describe them as shrewd traders and merchants. Both qualities are reflected in Petra's public architecture, a dizzying array of temples, tombs, theaters, and other buildings chiseled out of russet sandstone. Scattered over 400 square miles and connected by trails and caravan roads, these buildings are monumental and dramatic even when judged against the Greek masterpieces of the day.

But their breakthrough achievement—the one that made all the others possible—came when the Nabataeans mastered their water supply, enabling them to build a metropolis of 30,000 in a desert canyon that gets only six inches of rain each year. Harvesting water like precious grain, the Nabataeans collected it, piped it, stored it, conserved it, prayed over it, managed it—all by devising elaborate systems of hydraulics that make up, even now, the unseen musculature of Petra. Hundreds of cisterns kept Petra from dying of thirst in times of drought, while masonry dams in the surrounding hills protected the city from flash floods after bursts of rain.

In 1812 Johann Burckhardt, a Swiss scholar, traveled there disguised as a Muslim pilgrim. Meeting forebears of today's Bedouin, Burckhardt recognized the ruined city as the Petra of ancient lore, which vanished from most maps in the seventh century. Sandstorms and floods had covered the ruined city in drifts and debris, leaving most of the urban center hidden from view. But the Treasury and other towering stone facades dazzled him and the early European explorers who followed in his footsteps.

Today, a sense of imminent discovery hangs in the air over Petra as archaeologists labor to uncover the capital's history. Practically every stab of a shovel yields something worth talking about, and there's still much more digging to do. "We have uncovered just 15 percent of the city," estimates archaeologist Zeidoun Al-Muheisen of Jordan's Yarmouk University. "The vast majority—85 percent—is still underground and untouched."

> **"We have uncovered just 15 percent of the city. The vast majority—85 percent—is still underground and untouched."**
>
> —*Zeidoun Al-Muheisen, archaeologist*

The most striking modern finds involve water management, though—the channels, terraces, dams, and cisterns that captured and controlled the scant rain and still represent the fundamental brilliance of the site. "Hydrology is the unseen beauty of Petra," says an engineer familiar with Nabataean techniques. "Those guys were absolute geniuses."

62

LAST MOMENTS OF POMPEII AND HERCULANEUM

A.D. 79 ♦ Italy ♦ Roman

*Two wealthy Roman towns were entombed
by a swift disaster, but the discoveries they produced
span the history of archaeology.*

———◆———

The Bay of Naples is a crucible where the African continental plate is crunching into Europe, creating a hot spot for earthquakes and volcanoes. Two thousand years ago, the people living on the fertile slopes of Mount Vesuvius probably did not suspect that their mountain, peaceful for at least 300 years, was a slumbering monster. To the south of the peak, Pompeii was an affluent community of Roman citizens, naturalized foreigners, and freedmen among its population of around 15,000 who had become makers and shakers in imperial trade. Farther up the coast toward Naples, Herculaneum was a quieter seaside resort town. The story of these places forever changed one afternoon in late A.D. 79, when Vesuvius roared like a cannon.

The volcano hurtled a column of ash and pumice into the stratosphere. "Darkness fell, not the dark of a moonless or cloudy night, but as if the lamp had been put out in a closed room," wrote Pliny the Younger, who witnessed the cataclysm from across the bay. The worst was yet to come: Over the next few days, ground-hugging avalanches of superhot gas, ash, and rocks known as pyroclastic flows sped down the flanks of the mountain at high speed. The debris entombed Pompeii and Herculaneum, along with their buildings, art, artifacts, and the thousands of panicked residents who didn't flee in time.

All traces of the cities were lost for centuries. Workers digging an irrigation tunnel penetrated Pompeii's ruins in 1594, but failed to recognize their discovery. Then, in 1709, a well digger accidentally struck a stage buried under hardened soil at Herculaneum. Tunnels were dug, and soon the ruling nobility of Naples began to loot an ancient theater. They stripped away its multicolor marble facings for their villas and carted off the bronze and marble statues. These royal treasure hunters used hundreds of laborers, including some prisoners, to dig numerous additional tunnels out from the theater to plunder the rest of buried Herculaneum.

Haphazard digging continued there and at Pompeii for the next 150 years, growing more systematic over time. In 1863, Italian archaeologist Giuseppe Fiorelli became chief excavator of Pompeii. Already much of the western part of the ancient city had been uncovered, but Fiorelli instituted a new system of digging Pompeii from the top down, instead of digging out the streets to excavate the houses from the ground up, to better preserve their contents. He also developed an enduring technique of injecting plaster into hollows that his diggers came across in the volcanic earth. These hollows were, in effect, the space created when bodies of victims decayed. Thus the plaster preserved the forms and postures of people as they fell, down to their hairstyles and facial expressions in death. Amedeo Maiuri, who was in charge of Pompeii's excavations from 1924 to 1961, once described the startling experience of cracking away the surrounding ash from a newly made plaster cast of victims: "Suddenly we are faced with human beings out of the dim past at their very moment of death. Some show an attitude of fierce struggle against their fate; others recline peacefully as though in sleep."

Many died at Pompeii because they waited too long inside their houses, where they felt safest. Some were killed when their roofs collapsed. Others found themselves trapped inside by the falling pumice and then sealed in and asphyxiated by the scorching avalanche. Until the 1980s, few traces of people had been found at Herculaneum, suggesting most had escaped that town. But then archaeologists uncovered dozens of skeletons of people in flight who made it only as far as the beachfront or the public baths before they met a swift end.

The very pall of rock and ash that eradicated all life in Pompeii and Herculaneum preserved the cities more beautifully than the most skilled museum curator could have done. Pompeii's streets are lined with workshops of tanners and textile makers, and even a laundry. There are fast-food joints and bakeries and production houses for making garum, a fermented fish sauce that was a key part of Pompeii's economy. There are monumental public spaces—temples, theaters, bathhouses—as well as more intimate ones, such as the brothels full of erotic art. Pompeii's floor mosaics are astonishingly intact, and the kind of frescoes painted on interior walls there rarely survive elsewhere in the archaeological record of the Roman world.

At the time of the eruption, Pompeii was gearing up for local elections, as evidenced by the scrawled graffiti and painted political posters in the town center. The candidates make promises such as, "Make Bruttius Balbus duumvir [magistrate]. . . He will preserve

> "Suddenly we are faced with human beings out of the dim past at their very moment of death. Some show an attitude of fierce struggle against their fate; others recline peacefully as though in sleep."
>
> —Amedeo Maiuri, archaeologist

The mosaic-covered walls of a courtyard garden in the house of a wealthy Herculaneum family include a panel depicting the god Neptune and his wife (right).

the treasury," and receive endorsements like, "The fruit vendors and Helvius Vestalis unanimously propose Marcus Holconius Priscus as duumvir with judicial power." Women backed various candidates even though they were not allowed to vote. One plaintive piece of graffiti reads, "I beg you to make Lucium Popidium Secundum aedile [another kind of magistrate]. His anxious grandmother Taedia Secunda asks it." It is a fascinating view of political campaigns not too different from our own.

Released from the protective sealant of ash and earth, the ancient towns began to erode. By the end of 2010, Pompeii was badly in need of repair. The famous school used for gladiator training suddenly toppled. Only 13 percent of the site's 110 visible acres remained accessible to visitors. (Another 54 acres have never been uncovered.) The number of buildings open to the public had been reduced to 10, down from 64 in 1956. The Great Pompeii Project launched in 2012 with a plan for a state-of-the-art restoration involving more than 200 experts. Amid this recent wave of emergency maintenance, archaeologists have also made new discoveries. They've uncovered more victims of the eruption, more homes, more frescoes, and one of the best preserved examples of a lararium, or household shrine. They also discovered a new inscription challenging the August 24 date of the eruption recorded by Pliny. Just before the disaster, a local worker scrawled a joke (translated as "He ate too much") along with a date corresponding to October 17 on a wall in temporary charcoal. Other evidence, such as remnants of autumn fruit and people wearing warm clothing, already suggested a fall date for the eruption. It could be that translation and transcription errors created the confusion.

These fleeting inscriptions and other rarely preserved snapshots of everyday Roman life make Pompeii feel like a living city, even with its copious reminders of death. Maiuri's 1961 description of this impression rings true today: "When one strolls through the streets past the excavated shops and the houses whose murals shine so brilliantly with the images of life, one half expects to hear a sudden roar from the crowd in the distant amphitheater or the rumble of chariot wheels echoing down a side street."

63

AN UNTOUCHED ROYAL TOMB

A.D. 100–700 ✦ Peru ✦ Moche

*The New World's richest unlooted burial yielded
a warrior-priest surrounded by men and women—
and his faithful dog—who had served him well.*

———◆———

Like many a drama, this one began violently, with the death of a tomb robber in the first act.

Near midnight, the chief of police in Lambayeque, Peru, telephoned Walter Alva, director of the local archaeological museum. The chief's voice was urgent: "We have something you must see—right now." Alva couldn't help but wonder which of the many ancient sites that dot the country's arid north coast had been sacked of its contents.

This time, it was an imposing adobe platform at the base of a flat-topped pyramid near the village of Sipán. These structures were built by a people known as the Moche. From about A.D. 100 to the close of the seventh century, their culture flourished in the desert margin between the Andes and the Pacific. Although never empire builders like the later Inca, the Moche extended their domain across a 220-mile-long swath of coast. By diverting rivers into networks of canals and channels, they transformed a barren hinterland into a fertile territory of enviable abundance. They traded far and wide for luxury goods, mastered clever metalwork, and raised huge monuments of sunbaked mud, within which they laid their noblest dead.

They also buried fine gold and pottery so alluring that in decades of excavation archaeologists have rarely found a major Moche tomb unplundered. The artifacts, and the priceless knowledge they represent, almost always disappear in an insatiable international black market for stolen pre-Columbian treasures.

The ruins near Sipán presented an easy target. Weatherworn to the shape of a mound, the platform in front of the pyramid rose a mere 33 feet—within handy reach of nocturnal diggers. Police were tipped off by a looter who felt he hadn't gotten his fair share of the treasures. During a nighttime raid, one of the accomplices was fatally wounded.

The village was in shock. But the artifacts plundered from the platform would lead to a magnificent discovery—one of the richest and most significant tombs ever found in the Americas, and the clearest mirror of the little-known Moche culture.

The passage of time—and looters' shovels—has eroded the massive mud-brick pyramid known as Huaca Rajada, where an intact royal Moche tomb was uncovered.

Alva and his team soon launched a rescue operation, hoping to salvage whatever artifacts had escaped the looters' pillage. Where the treasure hunters had struck the bonanza, there gaped a hole 23 feet deep that branched into a honeycomb of caverns and tunnels. Using ropes and buckets, the archaeologists spent days simply clearing the pit of broken brick.

Digging deeper, they discovered the imprint of wooden beams—traces of the 10-foot timbers that had enclosed a chamber now filled with sand. Wielding paintbrushes and dustpans, they carefully uncovered a male skeleton with a copper mask and headdress, in addition to more than a thousand pots, bowls, beakers, and jars: perhaps the greatest cache of pre-Columbian ceramics ever excavated.

Was this man a sacrificial offering, buried to honor someone of far higher rank who might be entombed deeper in the crypt? "A grand, undisturbed funeral chamber was our dream, although realistically we couldn't discount the chance that we might merely be rooting in debris dumped by the platform builders," Alva said.

Pressing on, the team finally uncovered bright green sheaves of copper strapping that marked the edges of a sealed chamber: the tomb and untouched burial they had speculated about. "For long seconds breath and words would not come," said Alva. "When we finally spoke, it was to babble: 'A coffin! It's sealed . . . Never opened!'" From this extraordinary burial, they recorded treasure after treasure. The central occupant was laid to rest with a solid gold headdress two feet across, a gold face mask, a gold knife, multiple strands of large gold and silver beads, a beautifully crafted rattle hammered from sheet gold and hafted with a solid copper

> **"For long seconds breath and words would not come. When we finally spoke, it was to babble: 'A coffin! It's sealed . . . Never opened!'"**
>
> —*Walter Alva, archaeologist*

blade, gold bells showing a deity engaged in severing human heads, a pure gold warrior's back-flap shield weighing nearly two pounds, and exquisite gold-and-turquoise ear ornaments.

Additional skeletons were also found in the burial chamber—two women, three men, and a dog—along with sumptuous grave goods. These elite retainers must have served the great lord in life and were sacrificed at his death. Experts believe the lord was a warrior-priest—the Lord of Sipán, he was dubbed. "Accepting homage and tribute, performing priestly duties himself, and standing confidently at the apex of the social pyramid with absolute power of life and death over his subjects, he must have seemed like a demigod," wrote Alva.

In the years since this discovery, the clues that archaeologists have continued to reveal about the Moche culture have offered a fuller view of just who held the reins of power.

The burial of a prominent Moche woman discovered in 2013 at the site of San José de Moro in the Jequetepeque River Valley is one of several that have revolutionized ideas about the roles that women played in society. In about A.D. 750 this revered woman was interred in a large chamber some 20 feet beneath the ground. Two adults, presumably sacrificed female attendants, were buried with her, along with five children.

Beside the main skeleton lay an important clue to the woman's identity—the kind of tall silver goblet that appears in Moche art in scenes of human sacrifice and blood consumption. Such vessels have only been found in the tombs of powerful priestess-queens, likely the status of this woman.

She was laid to rest in an elaborate coffin, probably made of wood or cane—long since decayed—and covered with copper plaques tracing out a typical Moche design of waves and steps. A copper funerary mask sat atop the coffin, and at the foot lay two copper sandals.

This regalia must have been displayed in a grand public funeral; the deceased probably ruled one of the Moche communities nearby.

The lavish burial of a Moche warrior-priest known as the Lord of Sipán, surrounded by retainers, has been re-created at a museum in Lambayeque, Peru.

During her funeral, her coffin—with a face and feet that represented the person inside—was likely carried to its final resting place in a grand procession that included an honor guard of warriors, and musicians who played rattles, drums, whistles, and trumpets.

This was the eighth elite female burial found since excavations began at San José de Moro in 1991. The accumulating evidence has convinced archaeologists that the priestess-queens buried there played a large role in governing the political and spiritual affairs of the region, representing a huge shift in thinking about the structure of Moche society.

Other finds made in recent years have placed women at the top of the Moche power structure as well. A tattooed female mummy, unearthed at the site of El Brujo in 2005, was buried with such traditional symbols of power as massive ceremonial war clubs and nose rings with fierce designs: men carrying war clubs, and heads pecked by condors. The mummy also wore tokens of great wealth, including 15 necklaces made of lapis lazuli, quartz crystal, silver, and a gold-copper alloy. The archaeologists who uncovered her believe she was likely a warrior-queen.

Influenced by discoveries like the Lord of Sipán, experts once thought that male warrior-priests monopolized power in the Moche society. But the elite burials of both genders that have since been uncovered suggest that men and women alike filled positions of power—and were assumed to maintain those identities in the great beyond.

64

CITY OF KINGS AND COMMONERS

1000 B.C.–A.D. 900 ◆ Honduras ◆ Maya

The last few decades have brought a giant step forward in our knowledge of the Maya. The site of Copán has played a primary role in that process.

———◆———

I n a tunnel 50 feet below the grassy plazas of Copán, National Geographic staff archaeologist George Stuart crouched as low as he could, clenching a flashlight in his teeth, to peer through an opening in a wall of dirt and stone. There, in a hot, stuffy, earthquake-prone space, he saw a skeleton on a large stone slab, along with artifacts that included ceramic vessels likely meant to hold food and drink for the next life. Stuart's archaeological colleagues had discovered a royal burial—most likely that of K'inich Yax K'uk' Mo', or Sun-Eyed Green Quetzal Macaw. The revered god-king, whose name appears in many of the site's hieroglyphic texts, was the founder of a dynasty that maintained the power of this Maya valley for some 400 years.

Maya scholars have long recognized the enormous significance of Copán. From more than a century of research, they know that the ruined buildings beside the Copán River served as the political and religious capital of an important kingdom before its collapse more than a thousand years ago. Early on, investigators came to realize that the section now known as the Acropolis—a roughly rectangular area that rises high above the river—served not only as the locus of some of the city's most spectacular architecture and sculpture, but also as the seat of governing power during the height of the Maya Classic period, between about A.D. 250 and 900.

The Classic-period rulers of Copán claimed descent from the sun and ruled by that right. They waged war, traded, commissioned monuments to themselves and their lineages, and presided over a kingdom of some 20,000 subjects. These ranged from farmers who lived in pole-and-thatch houses to the elite occupying the monumental palaces near the Acropolis.

When explorer John Lloyd Stephens bought Copán from a local farmer for $50 in 1839, it was completely overgrown. Much of the site is now cleared and restored.

When John Lloyd Stephens, pioneer explorer of the Maya region, and his artist companion Frederick Catherwood approached Copán in the autumn of 1839, the first thing they saw was the great heap of the ruined buildings of the Acropolis. "Soon we came to the bank of a river," Stephens later wrote, "and saw directly opposite a stone wall, perhaps a hundred feet high, with furze growing out of the top."

What Stephens and Catherwood glimpsed that morning was not a wall—as they would realize later—but a sheer cliff eroded by river action. The cliff made it clear that the Acropolis was not a natural hill, but the accumulated mass of centuries of construction. "Each king literally built upon the works of his predecessors," explained Harvard archaeologist William L. Fash. Fash, who still works at the site, headed the Copán Acropolis Archaeological Project at the time.

Since 1885, when Englishman Alfred P. Maudslay began to document and excavate Copán in earnest, generations of scientists have uncovered new arenas of life there: from the traces of the earliest farmers and traders around 1000 B.C. to the humblest valley households of the Classic period and the magnificent building of the Acropolis. The only completely preserved building at Copán is nicknamed Rosalila. "Before we found this, putting together the thousands of fragments of sculpture from the site was like doing a puzzle without the box top," said Honduran archaeologist Ricardo Agurcia Fasquelle, now the executive director of the Copán Association. "This is the box top."

The discovery of Rosalila, probably the best preserved building ever found in the Maya area, confirmed the investigators' belief in the special nature of the Acropolis. They had been drawn there by two monuments, both from the eighth century: a massive hieroglyphic stairway chronicling Copán's dynastic history, which was deciphered in large measure by George Stuart's son David, and a large carved stone known as Altar Q, which lay where Stephens and Catherwood had seen it, at the base of the tallest structure on the

Acropolis. Stephens had immediately guessed the true nature of the altar's imagery as depictions of noble personages. We now know these men as the 16 kings of the Copán dynasty founded by K'inich Yax K'uk' Mo' in 426. Altar Q was dedicated by Copán's last dynastic ruler, Yax Pasah, or First Dawn, in a ceremony of animal sacrifice that included 15 jaguars: the ultimate symbol of Maya royalty.

Of all Copán's known rulers, none ever really overshadowed the revered memory of the founder. On Altar Q, he is shown handing the baton of office to Yax Pasah in 763—a metaphoric transfer of power, because more than 300 years separated their two reigns.

As archaeologists tunneled into the Acropolis, they came to a vaulted chamber in a building they nicknamed Margarita. There, they found what soon became known as the "dazzler" pot: a brilliantly painted tripod vessel on slab feet, left as an offering. Below the offering chamber lay the most elaborately constructed and furnished tomb yet uncovered at the site. The remains of a noble lady rested upon a thick rectangle of stone. She had been richly attired and was wearing one of the most extraordinary arrays of Maya jade ever found. Her bones appeared uncannily bright and red, for after death she had been coated with cinnabar, or mercuric sulfide, a substance sacred to the Maya. She was probably the wife of the founder, archaeologists believe: the queen mother of the next 15 rulers of the Copán dynasty.

With the discovery of the queen's tomb, and with the huge entwined bird emblem signifying the name of the founder on the facade of the Margarita building, it soon became evident that this particular part of the Acropolis constituted a sort of axis mundi—in effect, a sacred stack of burials and buildings hallowed by the presence of one of almost unimaginable power in the eyes of the Copán inhabitants. Given all the clues pointing to K'inich Yax K'uk' Mo', it seemed that his final resting place could not be far away. The eager archaeologists dug deeper into the complex.

Finally, behind a facade of red sun-god masks on a platform, they discovered a skeleton that they believe is that of the founder himself.

"What I saw remains one of the most exhilarating experiences in many years of trying to know the ancient Maya," remarked George Stuart. "On the slab lay the remains and grave goods of a royal personage."

The king was at least 50 years old, had jade inlays in two of his teeth, and passed into the afterlife with a broken lower right arm. There are signs of other wounds, perhaps reflecting injuries or blows suffered in battle, or from the rigors of the Maya's ritual ball game. And on his chest lay a jade pectoral, like the one worn by the founder as depicted on Altar Q.

Continuing investigations suggest that the power derived from the founder began to falter after the capture and sacrifice of Copán's 13th ruler by the king of a rival city-state in 738. By Yax Pasah's time, a quarter century later, the power of Copán's rulership had failed to rebound.

After the Maya abandoned this site to the forest and river, probably by the year 900, its stone buildings gradually crumbled. Lintels collapsed and vaults crashed, bringing down walls and entire structures; many slid into oblivion as the path of the river gradually undercut the eastern edge of the Acropolis. And yet, even in ruin, the site's remaining ornate buildings and sculptures make it one of the greatest treasuries of art and architecture in all the Americas.

"What I saw remains one of the most exhilarating experiences in many years of trying to know the ancient Maya. On the slab lay the remains and grave goods of a royal personage."

—*George Stuart,
archaeologist*

65

TEOTIHUACAN'S COSMIC VISION

A.D. 1–650 ◆ Mexico ◆ Teotihuacan

*The city never deviated from the grand and
sacred scheme that put it in harmony with the landscape,
the heavens, and the cadence of time itself.*

———◆———

The stranger arrived as the dry season began to harden the jungle paths, allowing armies to pass. Flanked by his warriors, he marched into the Maya city of Waka, in present-day Guatemala, past temples and markets and across broad plazas. Its citizens must have gaped—impressed not just by the show of force but also by the men's extravagant feathered headdresses, javelins, and mirrored shields: the regalia of a distant imperial city.

Ancient inscriptions give the date of the encounter as January 8, 378, and the stranger's name as Siyaj K'ak', or "Fire Is Born." Dispatched from Teotihuacan, the mighty city to the west, the foreign warlord founded new dynasties that brought unparalleled splendor to the Maya world. In the coming decades, his name would appear on monuments all across its territories. And in his wake, the Maya reached an apogee that lasted five centuries. Scholars disagree about the nature of his legacy, but there is no question that his arrival marked a turning point.

What kind of a place would send out an armed expeditionary force headed by such an important and influential man? Simply the greatest metropolis in the Americas before the Aztec Empire.

Teotihuacan rose around the beginning of the Christian era, witnessed some seven centuries, then passed into legend. At the height of its prosperity, about A.D. 500, it is estimated to have held between 125,000 and 200,000 people—rivaling Shakespeare's London a millennium later. The city thrived longer than imperial Rome, its contemporary, and in the more extreme setting of a high arid plateau slaked by a brief rainy season. Planned on a grand scale, it covers nearly eight square miles—much still unexcavated. And much remains a mystery. "We still don't know what language the Teotihuacanos spoke, where they came from, or what happened to them," explained University of California archaeologist Karl Taube.

The city was founded on what its builders must have regarded as an almost indescribably sacred spot about 30 miles northwest of what is now Mexico City. Today, much of it is buried under several towns, a large military base, numerous farms, commercial centers, and a string of highways. The site also spreads into lonely backcountry, where dust devils stir the gray, talcum-like soil and foothill slopes with impenetrable clusters of prickly pears challenge the archaeologists who are trying to uncover the city's secrets.

Teotihuacan was planned according to a set of alignments that ties it intimately to the movements of the stars and to the mountains on the horizon. In every direction the city was laid out in harmony with the universe as the Teotihuacanos understood it. The Street of the Dead, the main axis, angles east from true north to point toward the sacred peak of Cerro Gordo. The main east-west

> "We still don't know what language the Teotihuacanos spoke, where they came from, or what happened to them."
>
> —*Karl Taube, archaeologist*

axis lined up with a point on the western horizon where the Pleiades, a star cluster linked to the Mesoamerican calendar, set at the time Teotihuacan was founded. To all who knew it as a place of order and power, whose monumentality rivaled nature itself, the city must have seemed a true wonder of the world. The later Aztec knew Teotihuacan as the Place of the Gods. Today's Mexicans just call it "the pyramids."

The city's builders also gave it sacred hidden dimensions, as it turns out. When Saburo Sugiyama began excavating along the southern edge of the Temple of the Feathered Serpent in the summer of 1983, nothing could have prepared him for the macabre discovery at the bottom of a four-foot-deep trench. Seated, arms crossed in back, was the skeleton of a man. Around his neck was a broad collar made of more than 200 shell beads. Suspended from this had once been a tier of upper human jaws carved from now deteriorated wood and decorated with shell teeth.

Sugiyama and his colleagues would uncover 17 other male skeletons in the grave. Their arms, too, were crossed, and they wore almost identical collars, although two had real human jaws with teeth intact; these men were probably soldiers. On their lower backs were slate disks, once shiny with pyrite, a standard decoration on ancient Mexican military costumes. Weapons had been buried with them, too—the grave yielded 169 spearpoints—which revealed a commanding military presence. Radiocarbon dating on some of the organic material indicated that the burial took place around A.D. 200.

Sugiyama believes the men were sacrificed because the bodies had been carefully positioned in the tomb with their arms tied behind their backs. "It strongly suggests that their killing was part of a ritual that marked the dedication of the structure," he said.

Archaeologists would go on to find 133 skeletons in 21 separate graves in other parts of the pyramid. The corpses—females as well as males—were arranged in segregated groups of 4, 8, 9, 18, or 20: key numbers in the Mesoamerican calendar and cosmology.

Still bearing its original colors, a 14.5-inch-tall ceramic mask from an incense burner depicts Huehuetéotl, the Teotihuacan culture's aged fire god.

Years later, Sugiyama would find similar dedicatory sacrifices inside the Pyramid of the Moon. Tunneling deep into the 140-foot-tall stone structure, he located five burial sites with scenes of carnage: disembodied heads and the remains of foreign warriors and dignitaries, carnivorous mammals, birds of prey, and deadly reptiles. All appear to have been ritually killed to consecrate successive stages of the pyramid's construction.

These grim sacrifices are examples of recent gains in our understanding of Teotihuacan. Modern investigation of the site began in 1918, when Mexican archaeologist Manuel Gamio conducted the first systematic excavations around the Temple of the Feathered Serpent. The archaeologists who followed concentrated initially on the pyramids, palaces, and plazas that give the city its public image. But archaeologists are now beginning to learn about the lives of the Teotihuacanos: what kind of food they ate, how they used the rooms in their houses, and what kind of work they did. They have found out that the metropolis attracted immigrants from far afield, and that it was the center of a vast trading network. They may even have found the first tantalizing evidence of a writing system, still undeciphered.

Yet despite these scholarly advances, Teotihuacan remains a paradox more than 1,200 years after its fall. We speak of it in awe, as we do the pyramids of Egypt. But there is still so much we don't know about it.

One enduring mystery is how such a large and complex community governed itself. Probes into both the Temple of the

Feathered Serpent and the Pyramid of the Sun (the largest Meso-american pyramid of its day at 20 stories tall) have turned up intriguing artifacts—objects of jade, shell, slate, wood, and flaked obsidian, as well as a large quantity of liquid mercury—but no ruler's tomb.

Inexplicably, sometime after the year A.D. 500—and half a millennium after its first flowering as a sacred and secular power—Teotihuacan went into a terminal decline. By 750, the city had suffered a sudden and violent collapse, and much of the population had fled. Though it's still an enigma in many ways, the continuing archaeological work there has begun to populate its cosmic landscape with the householders, nobles, farmers, merchants, priests, and others who took part in this grand urban experiment of the New World.

66

JERUSALEM'S HOLY SEPULCHRE

ca A.D. 345 ◆ Jerusalem ◆ Roman Christian

Jesus' purported tomb, considered the holiest site in Christianity, was opened in 2016 for the first time in centuries.

———◆———

The Church of the Holy Sepulchre is one of the most visited holy pilgrimage sites in the world. But one day in October 2016, the doors to the church were shut early—hours before normal closing time—leaving a bewildered crowd of pilgrims and tourists standing in front of the towering wooden doors. Inside, a scrum of conservators in yellow hard hats, Franciscans in simple brown robes, Greek Orthodox priests in tall black hats, and Copts in embroidered hoods surrounded the entrance to the Edicule, peering into its reaches. Rising above all of them was the facade of that early 19th-century shrine, which marks the tomb of Jesus.

Scholars who study Jesus divide into two opposing camps separated by a very bright line: those who believe the wonder-working Jesus of the Gospels is the real Jesus, and those who think the real Jesus—the man who inspired the stories—hides below the surface of the Gospels and must be revealed by historical research and literary analysis. Both camps claim archaeology as their ally, leading to some fractious debates as researchers scour an ancient landscape for shards of a single life.

Worshippers in Jerusalem's Church of the Holy Sepulchre surround the restored Edicule, a shrine that tradition says was built over the burial place of Jesus.

In the New Testament, Jerusalem is the setting for many of Jesus' miracles and most dramatic moments: his triumphal entry, his cleansing of the Temple, his healing miracles at the Pools of Bethesda and Siloam—both of which archaeologists have uncovered—his clashes with the religious authorities, his last Passover meal, his agonized prayer in the Garden of Gethsemane, his trial and execution, his burial and resurrection.

Although the Gospels offer diverging stories of Jesus' birth, the books reach much closer agreement in their account of his death. Following his arrival in Jerusalem for Passover, Jesus is brought before the high priest Caiaphas and charged with blasphemy and threats against the Temple. Condemned to death by the Roman governor Pontius Pilate, he is crucified on a hill outside the city walls and buried in a rock-cut tomb nearby. The traditional location of that tomb, in what is now the Church of the Holy Sepulchre, is considered the holiest site in Christianity.

The tomb today consists of a limestone shelf or burial bed hewn from the wall of a cave. Since at least 1555, and most likely centuries earlier, the burial bed has been covered in marble cladding, allegedly to prevent eager pilgrims from removing bits of the original rock as souvenirs.

Just yards from the supposed tomb of Christ are other rock-hewn tombs of the period, affirming that this church was indeed constructed atop a Jewish burial ground. But over the centuries, the Church of the Holy Sepulchre has suffered violent attacks, fires, and earthquakes. It was totally destroyed in 1009 and subsequently rebuilt, leading modern scholars to question whether it could possibly be the site identified as the burial place of Christ by a delegation sent from Rome some 17 centuries ago.

In October 2016, researchers seized a rare opportunity to probe that mystery; the tomb was opened for the first time in centuries when the shrine that encloses the tomb, known as the Edicule, underwent a significant restoration by a team from the National Technical University of Athens. Tension between the various Christian religious sects that worship at the church had delayed the badly needed conservation. But when the day finally arrived, the Greek Patriarch of Jerusalem, Theophilos III, acknowledged the many stakeholders who made it possible. "I'm glad that the atmosphere is special, there is a hidden joy," said the patriarch. "Here we have Franciscans, Armenians, Greeks, Muslim guards, and Jewish police officers. We hope and we pray that this will be a real message that the impossible can become the possible. We all need peace and mutual respect."

As the marble cladding was first removed, an initial inspection by the conservation team showed only a layer of fill material underneath. However, as researchers continued their nonstop work over the course of 60 hours, another marble slab with a cross carved into its surface was exposed. Just hours before the tomb was to be resealed, the original limestone burial bed was revealed intact.

"I'm absolutely amazed. My knees are shaking a little bit because I wasn't expecting this," Fredrik Hiebert, National Geographic's archaeologist-in-residence, said at the time. "We can't say 100 percent, but it appears to be visible proof that the location of the tomb has not shifted through time, something that scientists and historians have wondered for decades."

> "I'm absolutely amazed. My knees are shaking a little bit because I wasn't expecting this."
>
> —*Fredrik Hiebert, archaeologist*

In addition, researchers confirmed the existence of the original limestone cave walls within the Edicule. A window was cut into the southern interior wall of the shrine to expose one of the cave walls.

Until recently, the earliest architectural evidence found in and around the tomb complex dated to the crusader period, making it no older than 1,000 years. It is archaeologically impossible to say that the tomb is the burial site of an individual Jew known as Jesus of Nazareth, who according to New Testament accounts was crucified in the year 30 or 33. However, several samples of mortar from different locations within the Edicule were taken at that time for dating, and the results put the original construction of today's tomb complex securely in the time of Constantine, Rome's first Christian emperor.

When Constantine's representatives arrived in Jerusalem to locate the tomb around A.D. 325, they were allegedly pointed to a Roman temple built some 200 years earlier. The Roman temple was razed and excavations beneath it revealed a tomb hewn from a limestone cave. The top of the cave was sheared off to expose the interior of the tomb, and the Edicule was built around it.

During their yearlong restoration of the Edicule, the scientists were also able to determine that a significant amount of the burial cave remains enclosed within the walls of the shrine. The mortar samples were independently dated at two separate labs using optically stimulated luminescence, a technique that determines when quartz sediment was most recently exposed to light. The test results revealed that the lower slab was most likely mortared in place in the mid-fourth century. That 2017 announcement came as a welcome surprise to those who study the history of the sacred monument.

"Obviously that date is spot-on for whatever Constantine did," said archaeologist Martin Biddle, who published a seminal study on the history of the tomb in 1999. "That's very remarkable."

After the surfaces of the tomb were extensively documented and treated for preservation, the burial bed was resealed in its original marble cladding. It may not be exposed again for centuries or even millennia. But the research does not end here. Every millimeter of the tomb, the Edicule, and the surrounding church was photographed to be digitally reconstructed for scholars, and National Geographic stitched the images into a virtual reality experience that allowed people to virtually enter the church and "walk" the floors. The doors of this sanctified monument were thus opened to more visitors than ever before.

67

RESCUING
MES AYNAK

A.D. 200–800 ✦ Afghanistan ✦ International

*Archaeologists are hurrying to excavate
a spectacular Buddhist complex before it's
obliterated by a huge mining operation.*

———◆———

About an hour's drive along the Gardez highway south of
Kabul, beyond the bustling shops, trucks spewing diesel
exhaust, and the clatter of donkey carts, is a sharp left turn
onto an unpaved road. In a district of Logar Province friendly to the
Taliban, the path continues along a dry riverbed, past small villages, paramilitary roadblocks, and sentry towers. A little farther
on, the view opens onto a treeless valley creased with trenches and
exposed ancient walls.

Over the past decade, a team of Afghan and international
archaeologists, and local laborers, has uncovered thousands of
Buddhist statues, manuscripts, coins, and holy monuments at
this epic site. Entire monasteries and fortifications have come to
light, dating back as far as the third century A.D. The excavation
is by far the most ambitious in Afghanistan's history. "My forefa-
thers were Muslim. But we know a lot of generations passed
through this ground" said an Afghan Army veteran and excavation worker named Javed. "When I am working, I am thinking

In 2011, archaeologists uncovered this cache of coins and jewelry on a hillside at Mes Aynak, a stop on the fabled Silk Road trading network of antiquity.

that here was a civilization, a factory, a city, kings here. Yes, this is Afghanistan also."

A fluke of geology has put these cultural treasures in jeopardy, though. Mes Aynak may mean "little copper well" in the local Dari dialect—but nothing about it is little. The lode of copper ore buried below the ancient ruins extends two and a half miles across and runs a mile or more into the Baba Wali, a mountain that dominates the site. It ranks as one of the world's largest untapped deposits, containing an estimated 12.5 million tons of copper.

In antiquity, copper made the Buddhist monks here wealthy. Colossal deposits of purple, blue, and green slag, the solidified residue from their smelting, spill down the slopes of Baba Wali, attesting to production on a nearly industrial scale. Today, the Afghan government hopes copper will help make the country wealthy again (or at least self-sufficient). In 2007, a Chinese consortium won rights to extract the ore under a 30-year lease. The company made a bid worth more than three billion dollars and promised to provide infrastructure for this isolated, underdeveloped district, including roads, a railway, and a 400-megawatt electricity plant. Afghan officials estimated that the mine would provide a $1.2 billion infusion into the country's fragile economy.

Mes Aynak's archaeological potential first came to light in 1963, during the explorations of French geologist Albert de Lapparent, and was confirmed by subsequent surveys. Artifacts were already in danger of being plucked out piecemeal by looters and lost to science when the Chinese deal became public. Afghan cultural heritage advocates demanded that the place's ancient treasures be excavated and recorded properly before open-pit mining began; archaeologists commenced work in 2009.

Originally projected to begin in 2012, the mining project is still stalled. Contractual disputes, sagging copper prices, and Afghanistan's ongoing conflict with the fundamentalist Taliban have all contributed to the delay; this has given archaeologists considerably more time to excavate than they had expected.

The past they're revealing presents a stark contrast to the violence and disorder of their own time.

From the third to the eighth centuries A.D., Mes Aynak was a spiritual hub that flourished in relative peace. At least seven multistory Buddhist monastery complexes, containing chapels, monks' quarters, and other rooms, form an arc around the site, each protected by ancient watchtowers and high walls. Within these fortified complexes and residences, the archaeologists have uncovered nearly a hundred schist and clay stupas, Buddhist reliquaries that were central to worship. The stupas range in size from monumental to easily portable.

Mes Aynak was also a key economic center in Gandhara, a region spanning what's now eastern Afghanistan and northwestern Pakistan. Lying along the fabled Silk Road, the ancient trade network that linked East and West, this was a place where the great religions of Hinduism, Buddhism, and Zoroastrianism met, and where ancient Greek, Persian, Central Asian, and Indian cultures melded.

Within the first few centuries A.D., the Gandharan Buddhists revolutionized the region's art, refining an aesthetic sensibility that had synthesized the vestiges of earlier centuries of conquest. They were among the first artists in the world to depict the Buddha in realistic, human form. At Mes Aynak many chapels have been uncovered, replete with double-life-size Buddha statues still bearing paint—traces of their red, blue, yellow, and orange robes— caches of gold jewelry, and walls adorned with frescoes.

Though much is known about ancient Buddhism's links to trade and commerce, little is known about its relationship to industrial production. This is where Mes Aynak may be able to fill in important blanks, hinting at a more complex Buddhist economic system than has been previously understood. Unlike the far better known Bamian—an ancient Buddhist pilgrimage site and Silk Road caravan center 125 miles to the northwest, formerly home to two colossal, sixth-century Buddha statues blasted to rubble by the Taliban in 2001—Mes Aynak seems to have thrived primarily because it was a copper extraction and production hub: a Pittsburgh to Bamian's New York.

Puzzling out the full meaning of Mes Aynak will require decades of research. Not only is there much more to excavate, but what has already been rescued has created a problem of overabundance. More than a thousand of the most important pieces have gone straight to the National Museum of Afghanistan in Kabul—but thousands of additional objects sit in temporary storage at or near the site. Most have not been analyzed or studied, which makes it impossible to even guess at the scope of the site's importance. Archaeologists can only hope that time is on their side—and that they get the chance to reveal more of this little-known chapter from Afghanistan's glory days.

68

THE MOSAICS OF HUQOQ

Early fifth century A.D. ✦ Israel ✦ Judaean

Surprising and unprecedented mosaic scenes stretch across the floor of a Roman-era synagogue in Galilee.

———✦———

At the end of June 2015, amid the murmured chatter of archaeologists and the scraping of picks and trowels on rocks, a shout suddenly rang out: "Get Jodi! More mosaics!"

The diggers were calling for Jodi Magness, director of excavations at the ancient Jewish village of Huqoq in Israel. Working on a hill high above the Sea of Galilee, the team has uncovered one amazing floor mosaic after another in the buried ruins of a synagogue.

Since the first patch of tiny, naturally colored stones came to light in 2012, Magness, an American professor, and assistant director Shua Kisilevitz, an archaeologist with the Israel Antiquities Authority, kept returning to explore what lies beneath the layers of dirt and rubble that have accumulated through the centuries.

Mentioned in the Old Testament, Huqoq was an ancient Galilean village that attracted settlement over a long period of time, though not necessarily continuously, thanks to its natural spring and fertile land. The remains of the synagogue are buried under the ruins of a more modern Palestinian Arab village, Yakuk, which was abandoned in 1948 after the Arab-Israeli War.

Based on artifacts such as potsherds and coins from the synagogue's foundations, Magness believes the building dates to the early fifth century, a time when Rome ruled this part of the world, and after Christianity had become the official religion of the Roman Empire. Displaying stunning workmanship and artistry, the mosaic panels show the freedom and status that some Jewish communities would have enjoyed under the Late Roman Empire.

"The mosaics were a complete surprise," said Magness. Along with images from biblical stories such as Noah's ark, Moses' spies, and the parting of the Red Sea—which are rare or even unattested in other synagogues of the period—the mosaic artwork has details borrowed from the Greek and Roman world, including cupids and theater masks.

"The mosaics were a complete surprise."

—*Jodi Magness, archaeologist*

In the east aisle of the synagogue, an enigmatic panel depicts a meeting between two male figures, one of whom appears to be a general leading his troops. The scene, which is the first nonbiblical scene ever found in a synagogue, also shows elephants outfitted for battle, a detail that immediately suggests the story of the Maccabees, Judaean leaders who mounted a revolt against the Seleucid Empire in the mid-second century B.C. The Seleucids, descendants of Alexander the Great's generals, are famed for including elephants in their armies. There are no identifying inscriptions, but Magness believes the leader of the army is none other than Alexander the Great himself. His meeting with the high priest of Jerusalem never happened, but it was a piece of historical legend that would have been very familiar to residents of ancient Huqoq.

Regardless of the identification, the scenes would have delivered an affirming message of resilience to the Jews who lived at

On the mosaic floor at Huqoq, an army of battle elephants and soldiers is part of the first nonbiblical story ever discovered decorating an ancient synagogue.

Huqoq under the boot of the Roman Empire. Invasions were nothing new in this part of the world.

"The Jews were frequently conquered by other people," says the expedition's mosaic expert Karen Britt. "The message here is that not only could they hold their own in battle, but they could also reach an honorable and mutually agreeable treaty with their overseers." Under earlier Roman regimes, the Jewish people faced brutal persecution, from Pompey's siege of Jerusalem in 63 B.C. to Vespasian's violent suppression of the Jewish Revolt of A.D. 66–70 that ended in the destruction of the sacred temple. The Huqoq synagogue is a testament to the survival of Jewish culture despite centuries of Roman occupation, while the high quality of the mosaics shows they were prospering by the later period of the empire.

The 1,600-year-old scenes at Huqoq are so remarkably detailed that in a panel featuring the biblical prophet Jonah being swallowed by a fish, archaeologists were able to identify about a dozen different species of sea creatures. In the scene showing the construction of the Tower of Babel, a complicated pulley contraption provides unique insight into ancient Roman building techniques.

The finds at Huqoq contradict the idea that Jewish settlements in Galilee suffered as the influence of Christianity grew in the region, said Magness. What's particularly surprising is that the monumental, elaborately decorated synagogue appears to have been the religious center of a small, albeit wealthy Jewish village. "I have no explanation" for such a grand building in a small settlement, said Magness. "It definitely wasn't on anyone's radar before we started excavating there."

69

THE CAVES OF AJANTA

A.D. 400–650 ♦ Maharashtra, India ♦ Gupta Empire

*Thirty long-lost caverns reveal the spiritual
and artistic brilliance of India's golden age.*

———◆———

In central India in 1819, a cadre of British soldiers set out in a hunting party, hoping to bag a tiger. Traipsing along a horseshoe-shaped cliff above the Waghora River, they stumbled upon something surprising: a network of man-made caves ingeniously and dramatically cut into the rock.

The interiors of the caves, known to bats and local tribes but otherwise forgotten by the outside world for roughly 14 centuries, revealed a singularly astonishing collection of religious art. The immense murals, rock-cut sculptures, shrines (stupas), monasteries, prayer halls, and inscriptions created over centuries exemplify masterpieces of early Buddhist art and the creative achievements of classical India under the influential Gupta dynasty. And yet, surprisingly, only a few local residents knew of their majestic splendor.

About 66 million years ago, a hundred thousand or more years before the so-called "Chicxulub impact" (the arrival of the asteroid credited with killing the dinosaurs), one of the largest volcanic eruptions in history began flooding India's Deccan Plateau with roughly 135,000 cubic miles of lava. The entire region was covered in igneous basalt. Many of the major dynasties of India arose on the plateau, and their rock carvings and inscriptions offer some of the best records of these early societies.

Near the ancient town of Ajanta, roughly 30 caves carved by humans perforate the sweep of a dark basaltic rock face. Their facades are unexpectedly grand, with paintings, pillars, and statuary reminiscent of the sculpted temples in the ancient city of Petra in Jordan and the frescoes of Pompeii.

The lavishness of the Ajanta complex reflects its royal patronage. Although some of the cave temples date from the second and first centuries B.C., most of them were carved during the reign of a Vakataka emperor named Harishena, who ruled a large swath of central India in the mid-fifth century A.D. At one time, several hundred monks lived in the Ajanta caves.

Inside most of the caves, designed as prayer halls *(chaityas)* and living quarters *(viharas),* a central chamber lined with columns opens into a shrine where a statue of the Buddha still waits. Along the outer corridors, doorways open to monks' cells, bare except for stone beds. The architectural mood is solemn, reverential—until you look at the walls.

With a glance, you step into an otherworldly vision. The most elaborate of Ajanta's caves were designed for enlightenment, and many of their walls were covered with inspirational paintings. One of the most enchanting depicts the beatific figure of Bodhisattva Padmapani (or Avalokiteśvara, holding a lotus), a Buddhist deity who represents infinite compassion. Appearing near the entrance of one of the shrines, Padmapani stands as guardian, offering a vision of peace to all who enter. The Indian photographer and filmmaker Benoy Behl, who has been documenting the caves for decades, is still moved by the ancient composition. "The painting is a mirror," he explains. "It shows us the divine part of ourselves." Statues of Bodhisattva Avalokiteśvara greet Behl's many visits to the caves, just as they must have welcomed the pilgrims, monks, and merchants who passed through Ajanta during its heyday.

"The painting is a mirror. It shows us the divine part of ourselves."

—*Benoy Behl, photographer and preservationist*

Only fragments of a majority of the once elaborate murals have survived the centuries. But enough remain to summon the sensual and spiritual atmosphere that infused these temples. All of known creation appears to have paraded across their walls. There are images of the Buddha and of bodhisatt-vas—other enlightened beings. There are princes and princesses, merchants, beggars, musicians, servants, lovers, soldiers, and holy men. Elephants, monkeys, buffalo, geese, horses, and even ants join the human throng. Trees bloom, lotus blossoms open, vines curl and reach.

Most of the figures inhabit crowded, intricately composed murals that tell stories, called *jatakas*, from the many past lives of the Buddha. Others depict incidents from the life of the historical Buddha, an Indian prince who lived a thousand years earlier. The paintings serve as illustrated classics, fifth century style, meant to awaken devotion and heighten spiritual awareness through the act of seeing. For most visitors today, the tales are arcane—and yet the sensation of watching the images emerge from the dark in all their grace and beauty links then and now. A vision of paradise never grows old.

The period of Ajanta as a thriving religious and artistic center appears to coincide with the reign of King Harishena, who died in 478. By the seventh century, the monastery began to empty, the caves were abandoned, and Ajanta's beautiful paintings fell into obscurity. Buddhism gradually disappeared from India, the country of its birth; by the end of the 13th century, its holy places were either destroyed or abandoned in the wake of invasions from Muslim armies.

A painting in Cave 1 at Ajanta depicts a Bodhisattva—a developing Buddha— who holds a *padma*, or lotus flower, possibly a symbol of his spiritual awakening.

In modern times, the world has slowly rediscovered the sublime power of the paintings. *National Geographic* photographer Volkmar Wentzel visited Ajanta and neighboring Ellora on his 1946–47 journey across India. He wanted to photograph the frescoes with the new Ektachrome color film, but the heat was so intense the emulsion melted. Wentzel eventually shipped in ice from 100 miles away and used the shadowy recesses of the cave as a darkroom.

The complex was named a UNESCO World Heritage site in 1983, but an ill-advised attempt at preservation by two Italian conservationists covered many murals in varnish and then shellac, which distorted the colors. Rajdeo Singh, the Archaeological Survey of India's (ASI) chief of conservation, launched an intensive preservation campaign in 1999. Through his photographs and films, Benoy Behl has also done his part to completely document the caves' artwork and reveal how their style fits into broader Hellenic, Hindu, and Buddhist art traditions. "I swooned over the emotions in those faces," remembered Behl. "I saw in them a world of gentleness."

Despite the Ajanta paintings' ethereal beauty, they were once viewed as a "flash in a pan," an isolated, extraordinary achievement. Recent studies—made possible largely by Behl's illuminating photography—have made it clear that the splendors of Ajanta emerged from earlier trends, and their influence spread far and wide. Because of his photographs, said Joan Cummins, curator of Asian art in the Brooklyn Museum, "we no longer see the art of Ajanta as a solitary island; now we see it as part of a long archipelago."

Developments in sacred imagery fed the artistic blossoming at Ajanta. This was the era when the figure of the Buddha achieved an idealized, perfected human form. At first, artists had relied on symbols—footprints, a tree, an empty throne—to represent the historical Buddha. But followers wanted a more personal focus for their devotion. The likeness invented on the Indian subcontinent in the first centuries A.D., with lowered eyes and serene expression, became the prototype for Buddhist images across Asia. It remains the indelible face of the Buddha today.

70

GHOST SHIP OF SUTTON HOO

Early A.D. 600s ◆ Near Woodbridge, U.K. ◆ Anglo-Saxon

A monumental ship burial loaded with treasure reflects an Anglo-Saxon society of wealth, artistry, power, and trade ties.

———◆———

When 16th-century grave robbers dug a shaft into one of the mysterious mounds near the Suffolk coast of southeast England, they had visions of gold, silver, and gemstones. When their search proved fruitless and they moved on, they left behind a broken jug, animal bones, and the ashes of their fire. It would take nearly four more centuries, and digging just 10 feet farther down than the thieves, to uncover the unparalleled treasures of an Anglo-Saxon royal tomb.

The famous burial mound is located on a property known as Sutton Hoo. The owner in the early 20th century, Edith Pretty, inherited an interest in archaeology from her father, who had excavated a Cistercian abbey next to their home. In her youth, she visited the ruins of Pompeii and the pyramids of Egypt. Yet it took 11 years of living at Sutton Hoo before she decided it was time to satisfy her curiosity about the 18 shadowy barrows in her own backyard.

Sailors pay a visit to the excavation of the Anglo-Saxon ship burial at Sutton Hoo, discovered in 1939 just a few miles from the North Sea coast in Suffolk.

Pretty commissioned a local self-taught archaeologist named Basil Brown to investigate. Brown suspected that looters had already absconded with any artifacts of value from the mounds. Indeed, his first excavation of three mounds in the summer of 1938 revealed only a few objects and evidence of human remains.

In the summer of 1939, Brown breached the largest barrow, known as Tumulus One, with a long trench. Within a few days, he spotted iron clinch nails, the type used to secure planks of ancient ships. As the crew painstakingly widened the trench, they uncovered the imprint of a massive mastless rowboat 88 feet long. Although the oak timbers had rotted away in the acidic soil, the ship's outline remained, along with a rich cache of grave goods.

A brain trust of archaeologists, led by Charles Phillips from the University of Cambridge, scrambled to catalog the 263 objects unearthed over 10 days. They found a jeweled sword, gold buckles and coins, and a striking full-face helmet adorned with warrior motifs and fierce creatures. "Tales of buried treasure have a powerful fascination but are seldom true," wrote the stunned Phillips in *National Geographic* in 1941. "Its discovery will compel a reconsideration of the whole background against which the founders of the English people lived and died." The team concluded that this was not a Viking burial site as suspected, but something even older. They had unveiled the largest Anglo-Saxon ship burial discovered up to that time.

> "Tales of buried treasure have a powerful fascination but are seldom true. [This] discovery will compel a reconsideration of the whole background against which the founders of the English people lived and died."
>
> —*Charles Phillips, archaeologist*

The Anglo-Saxon era began with the Roman withdrawal from Britain around A.D. 410 and lasted until the Norman Conquest in A.D. 1066. Those Germanic invaders came from across the North Sea and established kingdoms that are now part of Wales and England. They would build a network of shires and towns, nationalize Christianity, popularize the English language, contribute great works of poetry, and establish England's first code of law. Their identity as a race of "Angles" became the name for all inhabitants of "England."

The discovery at Sutton Hoo came at a particularly unstable time for the English people: Britain declared war on Nazi Germany mere weeks after the excavations ended. The remarkable evidence of Anglo-Saxon power and seafaring prowess was celebrated as a symbol of British might. In a stunning act of patriotism and generosity, Pretty donated the entire contents of what became known as the "million-pound grave" to the British Museum. To safeguard the precious artifacts from German attack, they were stowed away in a bombproof location in the London Underground for the duration of World War II.

In the decades since, further excavations and scholarly research have uncovered greater content and context at Sutton Hoo. The burial's splendor and complexity dispel the notion that post-Roman Britain was a civilization in decline. Its treasures have deepened researchers' understanding of the trade networks between East Anglia, the ruling Anglo-Saxon kingdom of the area at the time of the burial, and the European mainland. They also have provided intriguing clues to whom might have been laid to rest in such a majestic and monumental manner, for ship burials were an honor accorded to only the most important members of society in Anglo-Saxon England. The vessel itself likely exemplifies the type of oar-drawn warship the Anglo-Saxons used to invade the island.

Although the body, like the ship itself, decayed in the soil, there was a human-shaped gap amid the grave goods in the burial chamber, found in the lowest part of the mound. To the right of the gap lay a large leather pouch, its gold-framed lid featuring an elaborate garnet cloisonné design depicting birds, beasts, and man. The pouch held 37 gold coins from Francia, across the English Channel. These coins helped archaeologists date the burial to the early 600s A.D.

Near the feet rested a large silver platter with marks indicating it was from Constantinople (modern-day Istanbul), the capital of the Byzantine Empire. A brass bowl had ornate handles copied from a type imported from the Eastern Mediterra-

The Sutton Hoo helmet, now displayed at the British Museum, has been reconstructed from fragments of iron, copper alloys, cloisonné work, gilt, and silver.

nean, likely Coptic Egypt, and two silver bowls were inscribed with Greek letters.

A sword with a gold-and-garnet cloisonné pommel rested to the body's right, and there was also a whetstone to sharpen the blade, a chain mail shirt, and an iron ax. The iconic Sutton Hoo helmet, now considered one of the most important Anglo-Saxon finds of all time, lay near the left side of the head.

The wealth of these goods, along with the tremendous effort required to drag the ship uphill from the River Deben and then bury it, leads scholars to think Sutton Hoo must be the resting place of an Anglo-Saxon king. A leading candidate is Rædwald, king of East Anglia, who died in A.D. 624, and whose reign coincides with the dates of the Sutton Hoo burial. Even though Rædwald had converted to Christianity, the transplanted faith coexisted at that time with pagan traditions. The boat was believed to carry the man into the afterlife along with his most valuable belongings.

Other scholars prize the "ghost ship" as an invaluable window into the seafaring skills of the Anglo-Saxons, about which little was known. A team of shipwrights, archaeologists, and other enthusiasts is endeavoring to build a full-size replica of the Sutton Hoo ship, with plans to eventually launch it for sea trials. It will be assembled in Woodbridge, on the River Deben, near where the Sutton Hoo ship left the water en route to its final, celebrated resting place.

A.D. 600–1000

──── Surprises & Mysteries ────

Part of the lure of archaeology is the unknown, the feeling that anything's possible. But while archaeologists seek to answer questions scientifically, they're not immune to the wonder of big discoveries. They might hypothesize that a field dotted with monoliths may hold the graves of warrior-chiefs, but are nevertheless awestruck when shovels and trowels suddenly reveal skeletons covered in gold accessories. The ruins of cities and settlements, rich in artifacts, can be just as stunning as the luxury-filled graves of elites—especially when new evidence overturns earlier notions of what we held true. But no matter how much evidence is unearthed, puzzles still cry out to the curious, enticing them to continue excavating, sifting through the clues, and searching for a meaning.

Silent survivors of a lost culture stare across a volcanic landscape on Easter Island, intriguing and mystifying scientists and visitors alike.

71

CEMETERY OF THE GOLDEN CHIEFS

A.D. 700–1000 ◆ Panama ◆ Unknown

*Tombs of powerful, richly adorned warriors
who were laid to rest more than a thousand years ago
are shining new light on a little-known culture.*

———◆———

In a grassy, sun-parched field in central Panama, gold was coming out of the ground so fast that archaeologist Julia Mayo was tempted to yell, "Stop, stop!" For years she had been working for this moment, waiting for it. But now she was overwhelmed.

Determined to uncover new evidence of the ancient society she had been studying since graduate school, Mayo and her team began geophysical surveys in 2005 at a site known as El Caño, named for a waterfall on one of the area's many rivers. The results identified a circle of long-forgotten graves. By 2010 Mayo and her team had dug a pit 16 feet deep and discovered the remains of a warrior-chieftain bedecked in gold—two embossed breastplates, four arm cuffs, a bracelet of bells, a belt of hollow gold beads as plump as olives, more than 2,000 tiny spheres arranged as if once sewn to a sash, and hundreds of tubular beads tracing a zigzag pattern on a

Archaeologist Julia Mayo (left) and members of her team carefully remove an embossed gold breastplate from the richly adorned remains of a supreme chief.

lower leg. That alone would have been the find of a lifetime. But it was just the beginning.

The archaeologists returned the following year during the January-to-April dry season and unearthed a second burial every bit as rich as the first. Bearing two gold breastplates in front, two in back, four arm cuffs, and a luminous emerald, the deceased was surely another supreme chief. Beneath him stretched a layer of tangled human skeletons—possibly sacrificed war captives. Radiocarbon tests would date the burial to about A.D. 900.

Mayo barely had time to catalog the new finds before her team uncovered more gold. Glinting from the walls of the pit, the artifacts marked the edges of four more tombs. As she surveyed the scene, she couldn't help but feel stunned. "I was just speechless—fascinated, but also worried," she remembered. The rains had already begun, and she was now in a race to retrieve all the treasure before the neighboring river flooded the site. She also knew that looters were sure to arrive if news of the discoveries got out. She swore her team to silence and prayed for clear skies.

> "I was just speechless—fascinated, but also worried."
>
> —*Julia Mayo, archaeologist*

This wasn't the first time that an archaeological gold mine had been found in Panama. Less than two miles from where Mayo was working, excavations at Sitio Conte—named for the owners of the land—had unearthed one of the Western Hemisphere's most spectacular collections of artifacts. That trove first came to light in the early 1900s, when a rain-swollen river sliced into a cattle pasture. Golden breastplates, pendants, and other finery began tumbling out of tombs and cascading down the riverbank.

Lured by news of the ancient cemetery, Harvard and then the University of Pennsylvania sent teams to excavate there. Digging in temperatures that often topped a hundred degrees, the archaeologists opened more than 90 tombs, many holding multiple bodies adorned in gold as well as works by highly skilled artisans: intricately painted ceramics, carved whalebones accented with gold, necklaces of shark teeth, ornaments of polished serpentine and agate.

A few others also probed beneath Panama's green pastures in this area, but failed to make remarkable discoveries. At El Caño, an American adventurer named A. Hyatt Verrill uncovered three skel-

Slightly less than an inch tall, a solid gold pendant takes the form of a double-headed, tooth-baring bat with outspread wings—but with crocodile claws.

etons of commoners in 1925, and excavations in the 1970s and '80s produced several more modest graves. Despite those unpromising results, Julia Mayo had a good feeling about this site. She believed she would find burials similar to those at Sitio Conte; it was just a question of figuring out where.

Mayo's instincts were spot on. In field seasons through the spring of 2017, she and her team uncovered the rich burials of great chiefs that belonged to a still unnamed culture and that date from about the eighth to the 10th centuries. Living in small, belligerent communities vying for control of the savannas, forests, rivers, and coastal waters, the chiefs covered themselves in gold to proclaim their rank. Tantalizing hints that fathers bequeathed wealth and power to their sons continued to turn up until finally, in 2013, Mayo found proof: the remains of a 12-year-old male wearing gold arm cuffs inscribed with images of the culture's crocodile god. Close by lay the remains of a chief who wore gold breastplates, beads, bells, mysterious figurines in fantastical shapes, and arm cuffs also inscribed with images of the crocodile god.

Mayo is convinced that the pair attests to inherited power. This theory has great implications for El Caño. "One of the characteristics of complex chiefdoms is that social status is passed down from father to son," she explained. That means this cemetery represents a society that was much more sophisticated than previously believed.

It also means that this site helps build the case for the existence of complex pre-Hispanic cultures in the forests of Central America and northern South America. Unlike the Maya to the north and the Inca to the south, these cultures left no monumental stone architecture. Most of their material culture has rotted away in the heat and humidity—houses of wood and wattle, roofs of thatch, baskets, mats, animal skins, feathers—leaving mainly broken pottery and stone tools. But in this place, at least, people worked gold and other luxury materials with great skill—and the shimmer of the surviving treasures endures as a testament to the culture's centuries of prosperity and accomplishment.

72

THE OSEBERG SHIP

A.D. 834 ◆ Oseberg, Norway ◆ Viking

*The rich and remarkably preserved grave goods
interred with two elite women showcase the culture
and exquisite craftsmanship of the Vikings.*

———◆———

When Oskar Rom bought his neighbor's farm in Oseberg, Norway, in 1903, he had hopes the land would yield more than just crops. The previous owner, Johannes Hansen, had excavated part of a massive, mysterious mound on the farm, spurred on—legend had it—by a fortune-teller's vision of great treasure on the property. But Hansen had quit digging, worried that the mound was a burial for victims of the Black Death.

Rom was undaunted. Twenty-four years earlier, teens in a nearby town had discovered the burial site of a ninth-century Viking prince. Surely something exciting and valuable might be found on his land, too. When Rom pulled out of the mound an eight-inch piece of intricately carved wood, inlaid with silver, it was a tantalizing clue to what else might be inside.

Rom traveled 60 miles to the capital to show his find to Gabriel Gustafson, a professor at the University Museum of National Antiquities. The busy archaeologist was about to brush off the farmer—but he stopped in his tracks when he recognized that the rich, complex carving on the fragment was of Viking origin.

Two days later, on August 10, Gustafson visited Rom's farm. He unearthed several parts of a ship, all featuring Viking-era ornamentation. Gustafson had to wait until the following summer to begin a full excavation of the 19-foot-tall turf-covered mound, but his patience paid off. He discovered a Viking ship burial, holding the remains of two women and some of the finest Viking artifacts ever discovered.

Although grave robbers had long ago plundered any jewels and metals, the rich array of remaining artifacts in the 70-foot-long Oseberg ship, as it is now called, provides an invaluable glimpse into Viking culture and craftsmanship. "On many of the objects there is lavished such artistic and careful work that they can rightly be called treasures of beauty, though the material is only mere wood," Gustafson reported in *The Saga Book of the Viking Society for Northern Research* in 1907.

The ship's remarkably preserved grave goods reflect the prestigious position that its occupants held in Viking society at the time of their burial, which scientists have dated to A.D. 834, based on the wood used in the burial chamber in the ship's stern. High-status Vikings were traditionally buried in ships that were dragged onto land and filled with valuables, or even sacrificed companions. The dead were not set in flaming boats and cast out to sea, as is popular in myth.

The two women of Oseberg were laid to rest on a bed covered in linens and surrounded by a lavish variety of textiles. Ribbons of patterned silk, imported from Central Asia and the Eastern Mediterranean, may have accented the women's clothing. Elaborate multicolored embroideries, thought to have originated in the

> **"On many of the objects there is lavished such artistic and careful work that they can rightly be called treasures of beauty, though the material is only mere wood."**
>
> —*Gabriel Gustafson, archaeologist*

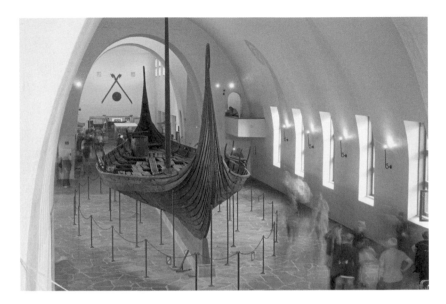

Reconstructed after being crushed by the weight of overlying earth, the intricately carved Oseberg ship has a mast for a sail and spaces for 30 oarsmen.

British Isles, also perhaps served as clothing trim. Ornamental tapestries depict geometric patterns, animals, and people. One tapestry portrays what might be a religious ceremony, with a procession of people, horses, and carts.

One such cart was buried with the women. Its elaborate carvings feature symbols significant to the Vikings. The cart's back is decorated with cats, which in Viking mythology pulled the cart of the fertility goddess Freyja. The cart's front shows a man being attacked by serpents, a scene that echoes the Viking tale of the hero Gunnar being thrown into a snake pit. In addition to the cart, the burial chamber also held three intricately carved and painted sleighs, which would have been used for pageantry.

Beyond the ornamental, the women were well provisioned for their everyday needs in the afterlife. The ship contained farming and spinning implements, pots and pans for cooking, and flints and oil lamps for lighting their way. The women were even accompanied by a menagerie of horses, dogs, and cows.

The ship itself had been crushed into thousands of fragments under the weight of the burial mound. But as archaeologists painstakingly reassembled the elegant oak vessel, they found fine artistry and attention to detail from bow to stern. Animal carvings adorn the ship far below the waterline and up to the very tip of the prow, which spirals into a serpent's head.

Who were the women who commanded such a regal burial? Scientists have teased out some the physiological traits of the pair, who both stood around five feet tall. The older woman, in her 70s, had been seriously injured in childhood, hobbled by osteoporosis and a knee injury in adulthood, and suffered from advanced cancer at the time of her death. The younger woman, in her 50s, had healthy teeth, reflecting that she'd had a good diet in life.

Their biographical details, however, remain a mystery. Some researchers have theorized the ship was the resting place of Queen Asa, grandmother of Harald I, who was the first king of a united Norway. Others have suggested that one of the women could have been a high priestess. Still others, including Gustafson himself, have wondered if one woman was sacrificed to accompany the higher-ranking other on their opulent journey into the afterlife and archaeological history.

73

ANDEAN TREASURES, UNTOUCHED

A.D. 800–1000 ◆ Peru ◆ Wari

Grave robbers had plundered the site of El Castillo de Huarmey for decades. But they missed a royal tomb, hidden for more than 1,000 years.

———◆———

Something important had happened at the site of El Castillo de Huarmey 1,200 years ago. University of Warsaw archaeologist Miłosz Giersz was sure of it. Bits of textiles and broken pottery from Peru's little-known Wari civilization, whose heartland lay far to the south, dotted the slopes. So Giersz and a small research team began imaging what lay underground with a magnetometer and taking aerial photos with a camera on a kite. The results revealed something that generations of grave robbers had missed: the faint outlines of buried walls running along a rocky southern spur.

Plenty of people had warned Giersz that excavating in the site's rubble would be difficult, and almost certainly a waste of time and money. Looters had tunneled into the slopes of the massive hill, searching for tombs containing ancient skeletons decked out in gold and wrapped in some of the finest woven tapestries ever made. The serpent-shaped hill, located on the coast a four-hour drive north of Lima, looked like a cross between the surface of the moon and a landfill site—pitted with holes, littered with ancient human bones, and strewn with modern trash.

Giersz was determined to dig there anyway. And his efforts were rewarded: The faint outline turned out to be a massive maze of towers and high walls spread over the entire southern end of the site. Once painted crimson, the sprawling complex seemed to be a Wari temple dedicated to ancestor worship.

In the fall of 2012, as the team dug down beneath a layer of heavy trapezoidal bricks, they discovered something few Andean archaeologists ever expected to find: an unlooted royal tomb. Inside were interred four Wari queens or princesses, at least 54 other highborn individuals, six human sacrifices, and more than a thousand grave goods, all of the finest workmanship—from huge gold ear ornaments to silver bowls and copper-alloy axes.

The massive tomb at El Castillo de Huarmey was a sacred structure that could be seen for miles around: a constant reminder of the Wari's imperial power.

The tomb at El Castillo has yielded more than a thousand objects made for Wari nobles, including gold and silver ear ornaments— some as big as doorknobs.

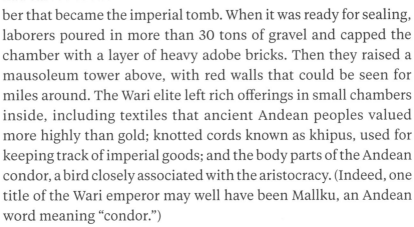

Along the summit of the site, Wari builders had carved out a subterranean chamber that became the imperial tomb. When it was ready for sealing, laborers poured in more than 30 tons of gravel and capped the chamber with a layer of heavy adobe bricks. Then they raised a mausoleum tower above, with red walls that could be seen for miles around. The Wari elite left rich offerings in small chambers inside, including textiles that ancient Andean peoples valued more highly than gold; knotted cords known as khipus, used for keeping track of imperial goods; and the body parts of the Andean condor, a bird closely associated with the aristocracy. (Indeed, one title of the Wari emperor may well have been Mallku, an Andean word meaning "condor.")

By the seventh century, the Wari had emerged from obscurity in Peru's Ayacucho Valley, rising to glory long before the Inca in a time of repeated drought and environmental crisis. They became master engineers, constructing aqueducts and canal systems to irrigate their terraced fields. Near the modern city of Ayacucho, they founded a sprawling capital, known today as Huari. At its zenith, Huari boasted a population of as many as 40,000 people— twice the population of Paris at the time. From this stronghold the Wari lords extended their domain hundreds of miles along the Andes and into the coastal deserts, forging what many archaeologists call the first empire in Andean South America.

Just how the Wari launched their offensive at El Castillo is unclear. But a ceramic flask in the shape of a Wari lord sitting on a balsa raft offers a clue, perhaps, that they had invaded this territory by sea. Also, a ceremonial drinking cup depicts poleax-wielding Wari warriors battling coastal defenders who brandish spear-throwers.

When the fog of war lifted, the Wari were in firm control. The new lord constructed a palace at the foot of El Castillo, and over time he and his successors began transforming the steep hill above into a towering temple devoted to ancestor worship.

To rub shoulders in death with members of the royal dynasty, nobles staked out places on the summit for mausoleums of their own. When they had exhausted the available space there, they engineered more, building stepped terraces all the way down the slopes of El Castillo and filling them with funerary towers and graves. So important was El Castillo to the Wari nobles, Giersz explained, that they "used every possible local worker." Dried mortar in many of the newly excavated walls bears human handprints, some left by children as young as 11 or 12 years old.

When the construction ended, likely sometime between A.D. 900 and 1000, an immense crimson necropolis loomed over the valley. Though inhabited by the dead, El Castillo conveyed a powerful political message to the living: The Wari invaders were now the rightful rulers. "If you want to take possession of the land," archaeologist Krzysztof Makowski said, "you have to show that your ancestors are inscribed on the landscape. That's part of Andean logic."

Today, researchers remain uncertain about why the Wari Empire collapsed. Whatever the cause, it happened suddenly. At one site dedicated to making ceramics, potters seem to have dropped their tools one day and left, perhaps driven out by some as yet unidentified invader.

The Wari left a history-changing legacy, though. They had created something in the Andes that never completely vanished: the idea of an empire. Four hundred years later, building on their foundations, the Inca emerged to revive it.

74

THE PEOPLE OF PETROGLYPH CANYON

ca A.D. 300–1300 ◆ Utah, U.S.A. ◆ Native American

A distinctive culture that flourished in the Utah desert and northerly areas of the American Southwest left wondrous pictographs and an archaeological enigma.

———◆———

Bighorn sheep herd into a tight group, all marching in the same direction. A human figure draws back his bow and arrow. A more mysterious figure with a trapezoidal body and curving horns looms taller than the animals. The "Great Hunt Panel" plays out on the reddish stone of Nine Mile Canyon in Utah. It is one of the most evocative murals among the roughly 10,000 petroglyphs and pictographs that ancient Americans painted or chiseled into the rock. The canyon, which actually stretches for 46 miles, is said to be the longest art gallery in the world.

This rugged region of the United States has long captivated imaginations and raised questions about the communities who dwelled there for centuries. Archaeologists learned that the cliff dwellings of Mesa Verde in Colorado and the extraordinary buildings of Chaco Canyon in New Mexico were constructed by the ancestral Pueblo people. But were they alone?

This was one of the questions archaeology student Noel Morss wanted to answer when he headed into Utah's canyonlands in the mid-1920s. While his fellow students flocked to the traditional regions of New Mexico and Arizona, Morss headed north, across the Colorado River. He found beautifully painted figurines and artifacts of a culture similar to their Pueblo neighbors, but diverging from the standard pattern with some distinctive cultural traits. In 1931, Morss published the defining report on a "new" culture centered near what is today the Fremont River. The name stuck.

The little-known Fremont survived for a thousand years, from approximately A.D. 300 to 1300—and then, mysteriously, abandoned their homeland. Experts characterize the Fremont by their sophisticated, distinctive rock art, a specific style of basketry, and a particular kind of thin-walled gray pottery. Unlike the ancestral Puebloan peoples, they did not wear yucca sandals or rely entirely on farming. Instead, they wore leather moccasins and took a more flexible approach to food.

Their artistic motifs include spiral and abstract designs, animals, and portrayals of broad-shouldered human figures who wear headgear, beads, and other ceremonial items. Morss was captivated by clay figurines crafted with advanced technical skill. "It is remarkable that such delicate objects should have remained, undisturbed and largely undamaged by humans, animals or the elements, in such a location for the several centuries which have undoubtedly elapsed since their manufacture," he wrote.

Like other hunter-gatherers, the Fremont ate native plants, including berries and piñon nuts,

> **"It is remarkable that such delicate objects should have remained, undisturbed and largely undamaged by humans, animals or the elements, in such a location for . . . several centuries."**
>
> —*Noel Morss, archaeologist*

Covering 200 square feet of sandstone, hundreds of symbols at Newspaper Rock, Utah, represent 2,000 years of Native cultures, including the Fremont.

and hunted for wild game such as deer and birds. But they farmed, too, cultivating squash, corn, and beans during settled periods.

Because they dwelled in areas on the edge of the reliable growing season, where late spring or early fall frosts all too often ruined a whole year's crops, the Fremont never fully committed to a farming way of life. Many kept hunting and gathering as a fallback option, and were always ready to pack up and move on depending on the availability of water and food.

The Fremont dwelled in natural shelters like rock overhangs, which archaeologists think served as seasonal homes, or in open areas during good weather. When times were settled, they created elaborate rock art. During hard times they took refuge in defensible villages and hauled their harvests up canyon walls to almost-impossible-to-raid granaries on the edges of cliffs.

These granaries can be found in places like Range Creek Canyon in Utah, which is home to hundreds of Fremont sites. For decades, cattle rancher Waldo Wilcox owned the sites, and preserved them himself, before selling the land to Utah's Trust for Public Land in 2001. Because of Wilcox's stewardship, nearly every artifact in the canyon was undisturbed—a rarity in a region where looting is rampant. Capitol Reef National Park, also in Utah, has many sites as well.

Mountaineer David Roberts has explored the most rarely seen Fremont outposts, often accessible only to rock climbers. In an interview with National Geographic, Roberts described rappelling down a cliff face to reach a granary tucked into an overhang 90 feet off the ground. "The Fremont didn't have that kind of gear and didn't get to it that way. So we tried to figure out how they had done it and why they had done it. I think these are two questions archaeology hasn't fully answered yet. You're risking your life every time you go fill a basket of corn." It is only one of the Fremont mysteries.

Despite their apparent flourishing, by 1350 the Fremont had largely abandoned their homeland. No one knows what became of them. Perhaps some migrated east to the Great Plains and assimilated with nomads who hunted bison. Others may have been wiped out by the Ute, Shoshone, and Paiute who might have surged into the Fremont heartland from the west as early as the 13th century. Perhaps many Fremont simply starved to death.

The Fremont remain eclipsed in scholarly research by other prominent southwestern cultures, but their artistry speaks across generations. Naturalist and author Terry Tempest Williams recalls a singular Fremont bracelet made of falcon talons and rawhide. "There was an aura I cannot explain," she writes. "I wondered about the individual who had worn it, for what occasion it had been made. For a brief moment, I entered sacred time."

75

THE SHINING CITY OF MOORISH SPAIN

ca A.D. 936 ✦ Andalusia, Spain

After lying dormant in Andalusia for centuries, the remains of the palace-city Medina Azahara speak volumes about medieval Muslim Spain.

———◆———

After the doctrine of Islam was revealed to the seventh-century prophet-statesman Muhammad in Arabia, its tenets spread swiftly, stretching across the entire desert peninsula by the time of his death in 632. Six years later, Syria and Palestine were converted. Muslim Arabs then surged out of the Middle East into North Africa from their new capital in Damascus, and crossed the Strait of Gibraltar into the Iberian Peninsula.

A century after its birth, Islam was practiced across a swath of land larger than Rome's empire at its zenith. History named these Muslim conquerors of Spain "Moors," probably because they entered the region by way of Morocco. Most married into Spanish and Visigoth families, creating what would become the culture of the Moorish civilization. They ruled in Spain for almost 800 years—until 1492, when King Ferdinand and Queen Isabella ousted them. And they changed the face of the country forever.

Under the Moors, Spain enjoyed a high degree of cultural achievement relative to the rest of Europe. Its architecture was unsurpassed. Unfortunately, few examples survive in Cordoba, where many Muslims lived.

Cordoba's most celebrated architectural feat of the time was Medina Azahara, or "the Shining City." This great palace-city was constructed at the foot of the Sierra Morena on the order of Abd al-Rahman III, an Umayyad emir (prince) of Cordoba from A.D. 912 and a self-proclaimed caliph from 929. Legends say the complex was built in honor of al-Rahman's favorite wife or concubine. Though few buildings remain, it's clear that it was a place of great complexity, sophistication, and splendor. After lying forgotten for a millennium, it is one of the best preserved remaining vestiges of Muslim Spain.

Abd al-Rahman III inherited a fractured caliphate. His ancestor, Abd al-Rahman I, had taken pains to unify Muslim Spain at the end of the eighth century A.D., but his death undid much of his progress. Al-Rahman III did his best to continue the work of building a cohesive nation, but he had much to contend with. Besides the rebel groups that created their own de facto states inside the Caliphate of Cordoba, there were also the small Christian kingdoms of northern Spain. Although al-Rahman fought against the Fatimid (Muslim) dynasty and the Christian rulers of Leon and Navarre, he nevertheless promoted tolerance of diversity.

After al-Rahman had consolidated his power in the Iberian Peninsula, he needed a city that would serve as a stronghold for Muslim Spain and intimidate any potential rivals. He also wanted to build a brilliant court where art and science could flourish. So he brought craftsmen from Baghdad and Constantinople to build him a mighty palace, and he sent for materials from North Africa and far to the east.

Labor commenced at a feverish pace, but construction still took decades. Historians estimate anywhere from 10 to 40 years. Whereas most cities of the day grew piece by piece, al-Rahman's reared up swiftly from a single, unified plan. Until work was completed around A.D. 961, he lavished a third of the royal budget on his new urban complex, making it the magnificent seat of his power—and the seat of government for all of Muslim Spain. He filled it with scholars, thinkers, and artists, transforming it into the beating cultural heart of the Al Andalus: the Arabic name the Moors gave to the Iberian Peninsula.

Under his son and successor, al-Hakam II, Medina Azahara grew even further. Its double walls, each as thick as 15 feet, enclosed half a square mile. Its many splendors filled those who visited it with wonder. According to 19th-century historian Stanley Lane-Poole, "Travellers from distant lands, men of all ranks and professions in life, following various religions—princes, ambassadors, merchants, pilgrims, theologians, and poets—all agreed that they had never seen in the course of their travels anything that could be compared to it."

> "Travellers from distant lands, men of all ranks and professions in life . . . all agreed that they had never seen in the course of their travels anything that could be compared to it."
>
> —*Stanley Lane-Poole, 19th-century historian*

Not only did Cordoba mark the confluence of cultures, it was rightly viewed as a world capital. No other 10th-century European city offered amenities such as lighted streets and running water or the centers of scholarship where mathematicians practiced algebra and great libraries translated Greek classics into Latin.

Visiting envoys were welcomed into the reception halls of Medina Azahara, where they could gather under marble arches, lounge beside sunken reflecting pools, and enjoy the scent of orange trees. The complex also featured mosques, pavilions, barracks, baths, and workshops, all laid out in a rectangular design covering more than 275 acres. Taking advantage of the uneven terrain, it was divided into three separate terraces: The top level was for the caliph, gardens dominated the middle level, and the lower level housed a market and workers' dwellings. According to one contemporary account, al-Hakam's family, along with his generals and viziers, scribes and translators, workmen and shopkeepers, gave the complex a population of 20,000; the royal bodyguard added 12,000, and the harem 6,000 more. Those who lived there could find anything their hearts desired within its walls.

Barely 50 years after its completion, though, the great palace was sacked and leveled by Berbers as the caliphate dissolved into a score of bickering city-states. Amid the chaos that followed, many Muslim rulers became clients of northern Christian princes, and religious boundaries often became obscured. As wars raged across Spain, the palace lay in ruins. There it remained for nearly a thousand years, until archaeologists rediscovered Medina Azahara in the early 20th century.

Moorish archways open into a basilica at the site of Medina Azahara. Also preserved are a portico, stables, a house, and quarters for servants and guards.

"There was nothing visible when archaeologists arrived in 1910," explained Antonio Vallejo, the current director of excavations. "Foundations outline the caliph's mansion, the mosque, 400 houses, the ancient market, aqueducts, formal gardens, pools— even a zoo." In the ensuing years archaeologists have found the remains of roads, bridges, water systems, and decorative elements that testify to the artistic splendor of the site.

By 2001, only about 10 percent of the site had been fully explored. In 2017, researchers from Boston University, Universidad de Córdoba, and Newcastle University used x-ray technology to analyze the site's soil composition in hopes of determining how ceramics were made there. The palace gate was destroyed in the fire that consumed the city in 1010, but its traces were discovered in 2020.

As it turns out, Medina's hidden nature has been a blessing, because it helped preserve the site in its entirety. This stunning urban complex offers a telling glimpse into the Western Islamic civilization at the height of its power—and as an exciting source of future discovery, will go a long way toward illuminating a long-overlooked chapter in history.

76

THE NEW WORLD'S FIRST EUROPEANS

ca 1100 ◆ L'Anse aux Meadows, Newfoundland, Canada ◆ Viking

*Ruins in coastal Newfoundland definitively proved
the Vikings found and colonized the New World,
making them the first Europeans to do so.*

———◆———

In 1964, Norwegian adventurer Helge Ingstad wrapped his fingers around the worn surface of the stone anvil, his feet pressed to the earthen floor where a Viking blacksmith once forged knives and nails. Three years before, on the northernmost tip of the island of Newfoundland, Ingstad's team had discovered the first proven remains of a Norse settlement in the Americas. "What I touched and held and saw . . . declared beyond doubt that here an unknown sailor-warrior led ashore a brawny crew of Vikings nearly five centuries before Columbus," he wrote in 1964.

For years, scientists and scholars had argued that ancient Icelandic sagas, although somewhat conflicting, must have had some basis in history. For that reason, they believed that "Vinland"—the name Leif Eriksson gave to the place he found on his great voyage west—was a specific place in North America. But where? And for that matter, where did the Norse settle—if, indeed, they settled on the continent at all?

Near the site of the Viking settlement at windswept coastal L'Anse aux Meadows, a living museum re-creates life in the typical Norse timber-and-sod buildings.

The Vikings were the explorers par excellence of medieval Europe, setting sail from their Scandinavian homeland to scavenge for land and treasure. By the eighth century some had voyaged west to what is now Scotland, England, and Ireland, bringing death by the sword in raids immortalized in medieval manuscripts. But they also partook in peaceful activities, pioneering globalization with trade routes and markets for foreign commerce.

As early as the ninth century, Viking merchants had nudged eastward along the shores of the White and Black Seas and navigated the shoals of eastern European rivers. They founded cities on major Eurasian trade routes and bartered for the finest wares from the Old World. The most adventurous among them set their courses far west, into the treacherous, fogbound waters of the North Atlantic.

In the Norse sagas, "Leif the Lucky" plotted a course for a far north land—probably Canada's Baffin Island—which he called Helluland, "land of flat stones." From there he traveled south until he found a spot tempting enough to settle in. Although he returned to Greenland a year later, his brother, Thorvald, soon ventured over to set up a permanent settlement.

These tales make Thorvald the first European to meet with Native Americans. He called them *skraelings,* or "wretched people." Who they were remains unclear, but the Beothuk culture is the likely candidate. But such a derogatory epithet hints at tense relations. "These Norsemen in the New World were in a much more dangerous situation than Columbus and his companions," Ingstad reflected. "Columbus had firearms. The Norse had to fight with hand weapons against an enemy superior in numbers." Records that the Vikings kept suggest volatile encounters between native residents and the newcomers.

Though the Norse won that particular battle, they ultimately lost the war. The native population proved too numerous and warlike, the story went, and so the Norse eventually returned to Greenland. Other theories posit that there were too few residents to sustain a settlement, or perhaps a changing, cooling climate became too much for even the frost-toughened Norse to bear. Whatever the cause, after about a decade of habitation, the Vikings packed up and left North America. But if the sagas held even a grain of truth, these short-term settlers must have left something behind.

Guided by those sagas, Ingstad and his wife, Anne, spent years meticulously combing thousands of miles of Atlantic coastline seeking Leif Eriksson's 1,000-year-old trail. They started in Rhode Island, making their way north into Newfoundland. But it wasn't until 1961, when they arrived at the remote Newfoundland fishing village of L'Anse aux Meadows, or "bay of the meadow," that their luck changed. A local man described ruins that no one ever visited, and the search was on. "It struck me how much of this scene dovetailed with the account of Leif [Eriksson]'s arrival in the New World," Ingstad says, ". . . but a coincidence of landmarks and a few hints of ancient structures were not enough. Only excavation would give firm proof of an ancient Norse settlement."

Not long after they started digging at the site, Anne Ingstad unearthed the first big find: a fireplace lined with slate, a cooking pit, and finally, traces of a hearth. Although they couldn't be certain the artifacts they had found were Norse, the remains did not suggest an Indigenous settlement. No colonial artifacts were ever unearthed.

"Could the site [have been] European [dating] from centuries long after the Norse?" Ingstad wondered. "Was this a shore station of whalers or fishermen . . . or seafarers who arrived after John Cabot voyaged to these shores in 1497?" The answer, it turned out, was no, proven by radiocarbon dating that traced 10 charcoal samples from fire hearths, pits, and a smithy found at L'Anse aux Meadows to around A.D. 900.

Eventually, the Ingstads would discover eight timber-framed turf structures built in the same style as those found in Norse Greenland and Iceland: one forge, four workshops, and three dwellings overlooking a peat bog. There was evidence for iron production, woodworking, and—a little farther afield—weaving.

Was L'Anse aux Meadows the sole Norse settlement in North America? Decades later, in 1999, researcher Patricia Sutherland found fibers on Baffin Island that later turned out to be Norse-style yarn and spindles. The find is controversial—many archaeologists still believe that L'Anse aux Meadows is the only confirmed Norse site in North America—but it's a provocative piece of history.

Today, there is mounting evidence that the Norse traded with Indigenous populations and brought North American goods home with them. In 2010, after analyzing a type of DNA passed only from mother to child, scientists found more than 80 living Icelanders with a genetic variation similar to one found mostly in Native Americans, suggesting that goods weren't the only thing that passed between these different cultures. We can now say with confidence that L'Anse aux Meadows represents a turning point in our understanding of North American history. It proved that the Vikings reached America, serving as a beacon to help historians document their further wanderings in the New World.

77

MUD-BRICK MAZE OF JENNE-JENO

Peak ca A.D. 800–1000 ◆ Mali ◆ Djenné

*The plentiful remains of a metropolis of
brick roundhouses offer proof of urban complexity
and trade much earlier than experts believed.*

———◆———

I n plain sight of the bustling town of Djenné in Mali loomed a
massive teardrop-shaped mound 23 feet tall. Inside was 16 centuries' worth of debris of human occupation—a maze of eroded
house walls, as well as potsherds, glass beads, and corroded metal.
The concealed Iron Age city of Jenne-jeno (also known as Old
Djenné) was silent for centuries—but once it was excavated, its
remnants spoke of a thriving metropolis that changed the way
historians think about West Africa's past.

When archaeologists Susan and Roderick McIntosh began
excavating there in 1977, they had no idea how deep they would end
up digging—or how many mysteries they would uncover. "We
gazed awestruck at what we saw," Susan McIntosh described. "The
dense brown clay was strewn with artifacts. We counted scores of
mud-brick house foundations and spotted the truncated remains
of a massive city wall. Clearly, thousands of people once lived here,
but how long ago?"

"It's a bewildering site," her husband, Roderick, told her at the time.

Excavations there uncovered evidence of roundhouses, iron spears, and even children's toys. Radiocarbon dating from hearth charcoal proved the city had been occupied for 1,600 years, and it predated the powerful Mali and Songhai Empires. Dating of pottery showed that the entire mound was in existence by 1,500 years ago—proving the city was a major settlement several centuries before the Arabs first established trading posts in the Sahara.

Historians once thought that Arabs brought long-distance trade with them when they settled in East Africa in the eighth century. But the discovery of Jenne-jeno turned that assumption on its head. By A.D. 450, the city had both urban complexity and mighty trade networks—both attributed not to incoming migrants, but to Indigenous Africans. The city's strategic location at the junction of both the Niger River and north-south trade routes made it an attractive stopping point for traders.

The early settlers of Jenne-jeno, in the third century B.C., lived in circular straw huts coated with mud, but the city slowly became more and more substantial as it grew. Over time, residents built houses and a city wall of mud brick. Within the city, researchers discovered terra-cotta sculptures, all in household contexts. Some of the figures may have sat in shrines set into the walls of houses, possibly part of the region's tradition of ancestor worship.

At its height, between A.D. 800 and 1000, Jenne-jeno spread across 82 acres and had 10,000 residents or more. It's possible that plentiful food from the fertile agriculture was enough to tempt desert dwellers to the city, and the Niger Delta's floodplain would have made an idyllic setting with rich rice paddies. Sections of the city were designated for specific craftspeople who used iron furnaces to make tools, jewelry, and other objects. There is no iron ore in the floodplain, so it must have been acquired through trade along with gold, stone, copper, and salt. However, it is unclear what local people offered in exchange for those commodities.

It is also unclear why city dwellers abandoned the city in favor of nearby Djenné after the year 1200. One possibility is religion: Djenné was founded by Muslim traders, and they may have encouraged people to leave a city with pre-Islamic architecture and pagan rituals. Or perhaps the new city was increasingly attractive because of the advanced infrastructure and business opportunities.

Though there is more to learn about Jenne-jeno, political upheaval in Mali has long threatened the site. The city suffers from looting and smuggling fueled by social instability. In response, the McIntoshes urged a freeze on the sale and purchase of any Malian antiquities, and the World Monuments Fund helped Mali's culture ministry build a belt of foliage to prevent erosion at the site and fill a nearby ravine to prevent further damage there. The black market is unfortunately deeply embedded in our modern era of globalization, and the exchange of goods—including antiquities—has expanded farther than Djenné traders could ever have imagined.

This intriguing terra-cotta figure was created in the 13th century in complex, sophisticated Jenne-jeno, sub-Saharan Africa's oldest identified urban center.

78

THE ENIGMA OF EASTER ISLAND

A.D. 900–1600 ◆ Rapa Nui (Easter Island), Pacific Islands ◆ Rapa Nui

For centuries, the alluring moai *(sculptures) on Rapa Nui, or Easter Island, have vexed and fascinated all who encounter them.*

———◆———

Rapa Nui, or Easter Island, covers just 63 square miles. Lying 2,150 miles west of South America and 1,300 miles east of the Pitcairn Islands, its nearest inhabited neighbors, it is one of the most isolated places on Earth. That isolation contributed to the unique character of its most mysterious inhabitants: the colossal human statues known as *moai,* which have made the island famous.

When Dutch explorer Jacob Roggeveen first landed there on Easter Sunday in 1722—the island's first brush with Europeans—he found a barren, treeless landscape and a Stone Age culture; its inhabitants had lived and worked there for roughly a thousand years without the benefit of draft horses or wheels. Yet the island was home to some truly impressive artistry: almost 1,000 giant statues, standing up to 30 feet tall and weighing up to 80 tons. Known as moai, they loomed against the sky, huge and haunting, at once godlike and savage. "These idols were all hewn out of stone," wrote Roggeveen in his ship's log, "and in the form of a man, with long ears, adorned on the head with a crown, yet all made with skill, whereat we wondered not a little."

It seemed unlikely to the Dutch that Easter Island's residents could have shaped its signature creations. As explorer James Cook wrote some 50 years later, "We could hardly conceive how these islanders, wholly unacquainted with any mechanical power, could raise such stupendous figures." Surely these locals were too primitive, their island too isolated, for such feats of artistry and engineering.

So who constructed the moai? How were they carried across the rock-stubbed landscape, away from the quarry where they were made, to their current positions along the island's perimeter? These mysteries have captivated explorers and sparked scholarly debate for centuries.

Thor Heyerdahl, the Norwegian ethnographer and adventurer, helped ignite the world's curiosity. He explored Easter Island in 1955 and '56, and believed the statues had been created by pre-Inca from Peru, given the similarities between the Rapa Nui and Inca stonework. But modern science in the form of linguistic, archaeological, and DNA evidence signals that the island's inhabitants— and thus its statue carvers—came from Polynesia (and more specifically, the Marquesas Islands).

These statue builders did leave a written record in the form of glyphs, called *kohau rongorongo,* found on a scattering of wooden tablets discovered in the 19th century. So far, though, no one has cracked the code; instead, the island's history has been passed down through the oral tradition of the Rapa Nui people (the island, language, and people all share the name). But by studying bones, buried weapons, fossilized vegetation, and the changing style of the statues, archaeologists have begun to paint a new portrait of a mysterious culture.

Even now, there is debate about when the original Polynesian inhabitants arrived on the island: Estimates range from A.D. 800 to 1200. Although the time frame and motivation are still uncertain,

For some unknown reason, Easter Island's artists left some 400 moai unfinished, lying in the volcanic quarry known as Rano Raraku.

it is clear that approach by canoe would have been quite a navigational feat—and that the now rocky island was covered in trees when the settlers arrived. In the 1970s and '80s, biogeographer John Flenley of New Zealand's Massey University found evidence—pollen preserved in lake sediments—that the island had featured lush forests for thousands of years, which its new inhabitants used to craft canoes for fishing. People had brought animals with them, too—dogs, pigs, chickens, rats—though over time, the dogs and pigs languished.

Despite a lack of draft animals to assist in heavy labor, Rapa Nui culture and artistry developed, untouched by outside influence, for more than a thousand years. Tribal groups created the unique and impressive sculptures that, according to modern-day islanders, represent the spirits of their ancestors. But at some point, the island's resources were overtaxed; too many trees had been cut down. With food increasingly scarce and the means of getting it more difficult, the locals stopped carving their idols; some researchers believe they started killing one another. When the first Europeans arrived in 1722, only a few thousand inhabitants were left; by 1877, thanks to the European slave trade, there were just over 100.

Over the centuries, the call of the moai has beckoned. Archaeological surveys were carried out in 1886, 1914, and 1934, and excavations began in 1955, to determine how the figures were made. Those forays, in conjunction with later scientific analyses and collaborations with Indigenous islanders, have helped shine a light on their origin.

Researchers have been able to establish that the statues were carved with basalt chisels, mostly using stone from a quarry on the slopes of the Rano Raraku crater. A statue was created in one solid piece, carved on three sides out of sloping bedrock until only a slender "keel" held it in place. The carvers drilled holes through the keel to free it, then lowered it downhill with ropes into a trench, where its back was carved. The statue was somehow transported down dirt roads, each built with gentle slopes to ease the journey, to an *ahu,* or podium. Once erected, the statue's eye sockets were carved out, left vacant except during ceremonies, when white coral and obsidian eyes would be inserted. Since 2010, the Easter Island Statue Project has excavated several of the heads that had been left on the island's grassy slopes to reveal an underlying torso and body, showing that those figures were even bigger than they had first appeared.

Why move the moai? Research conducted between 2015 and 2018 suggested that the placement of the statues around the island's perimeter had less to do with ritual significance than with marking the site of freshwater, a scarce and precious resource on

Rapa Nui. How they were transported to their massive stone platforms, however, has remained a stubborn mystery.

But that hasn't stopped generations of seekers from trying to solve it. In 1955, Heyerdahl's team of 180 strapped a 13-foot, 10-ton moai onto a tree trunk, then dragged it to ascertain the complexities of moving such a behemoth without modern technology. ("You are totally wrong, sir," a Rapa Nui onlooker observed—but Heyerdahl wouldn't be deterred.) In 1986, Czech engineer Pavel Pavel returned with Heyerdahl and a team of 17 helpers to propel another moai forward with twisting motions, keeping the statue fully upright; they damaged the base and had to stop.

A year later, anthropologist Charles Love took another stab at the transportation mystery, moving a 13-foot, nine-ton moai—a replica, this time—onto a wooden sledge and hauling it over rollers; within two minutes, his team of 25 had moved it 148 feet. Some 10 years later, archaeologist Jo Anne Van Tilburg tried a wooden "ladder" instead of rollers—a Polynesian method of moving giant canoes.

The general assumption underlying all these attempts has been that the original inhabitants of Easter Island dragged the statues to their ultimate destination, using ropes and wood. But in the Rapa Nui oral tradition, the moai "walked," animated by *mana,* a spiritual force transmitted by powerful ancestors.

In 2011, archaeologists Terry Hunt of the University of Hawaii and Carl Lipo of California State University, Long Beach proposed another idea. Perhaps, they argued, the statues were "engineered to move" upright in a rocking motion, using only human power and rope. Hunt and Lipo noted that the statues' fat bellies allowed them to be tilted forward easily; their heavy, D-shaped bases could have permitted two groups to coax it forward by rocking it side to side, while a third could have stabilized it from the back. Hunt and Lipo demonstrated that with three strong ropes and a bit of practice, as few as 18 people could easily and relatively quickly maneuver a 10-foot, five-ton moai replica a few hundred yards without using logs.

No one knows for sure when the last statue was carved, because the construction of the moai cannot be dated directly; many were still standing when the Dutch arrived in the 18th century. But by the 19th century, all of them had been toppled—by whom and for what purpose, no one knows.

And yet the moai survived, were set upright, and once again became an everyday sight on the island—a symbol of a culture both past and present. For many of Easter Island's 2,000 or so Indigenous Rapa Nui, descended from the original Polynesian settlers, the answer to the mystery of how they moved is simple. "We know the truth," resident Suri Tuki told *National Geographic* in 2012. "The statues walked."

"We know the truth. The statues walked."

—*Suri Tuki, island resident*

The masterfully engineered sandstone keep of Mesa Verde's Cliff Palace is one of thousands of sites holding clues to ancestral Puebloan culture.

A.D. 1000–1200

Great Builders

According to one origin myth, humankind strives to reach the heavens by building the Tower of Babel, resulting in the development of multiple languages. While that infamous spire may not be real, ancient societies around the world left us monumental structures that serve as testaments to their faith, concerns, and lifestyles. Although countless buildings made of such biodegradables as wood and thatch have been lost, heaped earthen mounds and crumbling constructions of stone endure. The great builders of the past left temples covered in carvings, stepped pyramids oriented to the cycles of the sun, and cliffside refuges designed as escapes from a still unknown danger. Visitors to the ruins of former capitals can walk cobbled streets rutted by centuries of passing wagons and flagstones softened by the footsteps of pilgrims.

79

THE MAGNIFICENT ANGKOR WAT

ca A.D. 802–1400 ◆ Siem Reap, Cambodia ◆ Khmer Empire

A Cambodian jungle long shielded one of the largest cities ever built, boasting some of the period's finest architecture and religious structures.

———◆———

Twice the size of Manhattan and filled with stone temples covered in engravings, a network of canals, and wide boulevards for promenading elephants, Angkor Wat is an archaeological wonder. In its heyday this Hindu-Buddhist temple complex and royal capital, built over centuries by Khmer kings who ruled an empire that stretched from Myanmar to Vietnam, rivaled the physical and spiritual grandeur of the Inca's temples and Egypt's pyramids. And yet, somehow, one of the largest cities of the preindustrial world was eventually abandoned, swallowed by jungle and largely forgotten—for a time.

The empire's capital moved to the area of Phnom Penh in the early 15th century, likely due to several factors, including increased trade with China, droughts and climate variability, food shortages, and invasions. The city was dramatically depopulated, though never entirely abandoned. Buddhist monks continued to care for the temples as nature encroached, and the site drew pilgrims and travelers from around the region—even from Japan and China.

When Westerners first arrived in the 16th century, they found a largely vacant Angkor Wat and believed they had discovered a lost city. Portuguese traders and missionaries were awed when they came across this vast, sacred place half-choked by vines. A Portuguese Capuchin friar named António da Madalena, who explored Angkor in 1586, wrote that it "is of such extraordinary construction that it is not possible to describe it with a pen, particularly since it is like no other building in the world. It has . . . all the refinements which the human genius can conceive of."

Detailed information about Angkor did not reach the Western world for a few more centuries. French explorer and naturalist Henri Mouhot came with an 1860 expedition and drew detailed pictures of the temples, which did much to spark interest in Europe. He mused that the site was "grander than anything left to us by Greece or Rome," and one temple must have been "erected by some ancient Michel Angelo [sic]." The pioneering female journalist

Angkor Wat is the largest and artistically most accomplished temple in the more than 155-square-mile area where a dozen Khmer kings built their capitals.

Strangler figs and kapok trees have taken over parts of Ta Prohm, a traditional Khmer temple built in the 12th century less than five miles from Angkor Wat.

Helen Churchill Candee wrote a full book on Angkor Wat based on her visit in the early 1920s. "We think we have exposed and investigated the secret places of the whole round globe, when there comes word of a new one," wrote Candee. "And not only a secret place, but a place full of secrets." Not until after World War II, when the monument was rediscovered, was the extent of it truly revealed. This was thanks to the aerial surveys by French archaeologist Bernard-Philippe Groslier.

Angkor boasts more than a thousand temples, which reveal remarkable artistry and a high social order that dominated Indochina for more than six centuries. Including forested areas and its newly discovered "suburbs," the complex covers more than 155 square miles. The creations within embody an integrated concept of the universe rooted in myth and deep religious belief. The Khmer were able to adapt aspects of Hinduism introduced to Southeast Asia by Indian traders as early as the first century A.D. and mold them into artistic, religious, and political expressions that became uniquely theirs.

In the language of the ancient Khmer, Angkor means "the city" or "the capital" and Wat is the word for "temple." In fact, the site is made up of several walled cities, stitched together to form the heart of the Khmer kingdom. The Angkor period is said to have begun in 802 when, from a location in the Kulen Range overlooking the future city plain, Jayavarman II proclaimed himself *chakravartin,* or "god king," of the Khmer. Over the next few centuries, a vast urban complex emerged. Kings built temples made of brick or stone to glorify their lives and assure their apotheoses. The largest temple, built by reformer Suryavarman II, arose in the 12th century and represents Mount Meru, the mythical home of all the Hindu gods. Called Angkor Wat, it has soaring towers, a large moat, and 13,000 square feet of bas-reliefs depicting Cambodian history and legend, which include a Hindu story of the creation of the universe and the triumph of good over evil called Churning of the Ocean of Milk.

The celebrated stone bas-reliefs, located on many temple facades, also depict everyday scenes—two men hunched over a board game, and a woman giving birth under a shaded pavilion, for example. Interspersed with visions of earthly harmony and sublime enlightenment are scenes of war; in one, spear-bearing warriors from the neighboring kingdom of Champa are packed stem to stern in a boat crossing the Tonle Sap. Thousands of reliefs show dancing *apsaras,* young women of the 12th-century court, while *devata* women stand guard at temple entrances. Helen Churchill Candee was quite taken by these women. "I am made shy in their presence, while they remain unperturbed," she wrote. "They are so many to know all at once, and their character is to me unfathomable. Coming into the court where they abound is like being shown into a room of living strangers."

The heart of the complex was its advanced irrigation system, which mastered the vagaries of monsoon rains and drought to grow enough rice for a million inhabitants. Channels and reservoirs were constructed to collect and store water coming down from the hills; overflows and bypasses carried surplus water to Tonle Sap Lake south of the city.

As the ancient stone monuments have been gradually over-taken by nature and worn down by the enthusiasm of millions of tourists, preservation and rehabilitation have become crucial to archaeologists' work at Angkor. And although time has eroded some carvings and erased the murals that once decorated the walls, technology has helped unveil some of its long-lost beauty. In 2010, a Singaporean researcher spotted patches of red pigment on one of the Angkor Wat walls. They looked similar to the prehistoric mark-ings in Asian caves he was studying as part of his Ph.D., so he took some pictures and ran them through a program that enhances color differences. The process revealed more than a hundred paintings—stories that had been obscured by the ravages of time.

There is only one written account of Angkor Wat in its heyday. It does not come from the Cambodians but from a foreign envoy, Zhou Daguan of China who visited in 1296 to 1297. He observed households with more than 100 slaves, pious monks, vendors at market day, and the miraculous water conservation during the six-month dry spells. He recorded with admiration the processions of ruler Indravarman III:

> Each time he came out all his soldiers were gathered in front of him, with people bearing banners, musicians and drum-mers following behind. One contingent was made up of three to five hundred women of the palace. They wore clothes with a floral design and flowers in their coiled-up hair . . . All the ministers, officials and relatives of the king were in front riding elephants. Their red parasols, too many to number, were visible in the distance . . . Last came the king, standing on an elephant, the gold sword in his hand and the tusks of his elephant encased in gold.

Perhaps this is the vision of Angkor Wat to hold in mind as we wait for the city to reveal more of its secrets.

80

A SACRED MAYA LANDSCAPE

A.D. 800–1200 ◆ Mexico ◆ Maya, Toltec

*The city of Chichén Itzá was laid out with links
to the Maya cosmos through the cycles of the sun
and the underworld portals of sinkholes and caves.*

———◆———

I n the early 1900s, a journey to Chichén Itzá from the city of Mérida in Mexico's Yucatán Peninsula involved a slow train and a tedious ride on mules, culminating in a hammock slung among the ruins. Half a century later, visitors could drive to the ancient city in less than two hours; luxury hotels competed for their patronage, helping to make it one of the country's most popular archaeological attractions.

Chichén Itzá in its heyday was the powerful, cosmopolitan capital of what was likely the largest Maya state ever. Built in about the ninth century, it spread over an area of at least four square miles, aligned with sacred sinkholes, or cenotes, and with the sun's seasonal movements.

An ancient destination for pilgrimages and place of religious celebrations, the legendary site encompasses architecture from both the Maya and the Toltecs—a warlike people who ruled here after the Maya collapse in about A.D. 900. Its profusion of buildings includes temples, colonnades, ornate platforms, ball courts, a grand pyramid with four staircases known as El Castillo, and a wall of stone skulls that served as a rack for displaying the severed heads of defeated enemies. An astronomical observatory has windows that align with positions of celestial bodies. From there, the sky-watchers of antiquity charted the heavens; with the data they gathered, priests selected auspicious days for planting and harvest, warned of eclipses, and directed sacrifices.

Today, the ruins possess a power of their own, an immortality compounded of stone, silence, and solitude. By afternoon, a sunny tranquility enfolds a cenote called the Well of Sacrifice. Swallows and butterflies dart and flutter above the opening. Small, blind fish from the underground streams that feed the cenote wriggle just below the surface. A majestic egret suns himself on a clump of floating twigs. Halfway up the side, two gorgeous birds—blue-green motmots—engage in territorial battle for a limestone ledge.

Seventy feet below the edge of the cenote lies murky jade water. This is one of the places where the Maya believed the rain god Chac resided. In fact, the Maya thought everything from fertility to rain and lightning originated in cenotes, caves, and tunnels, which were considered openings to the underworld. "The clues they left behind make it clear that they went to great lengths to appease and appeal to the dwellers of this spirit world," says National Geographic Explorer Guillermo de Anda.

In 1904, Edward H. Thompson, the U.S. consul in Mérida, began to dredge the cenote using a derrick, a hand windlass, and a steel scoop. Over the course of several years, he brought up thousands of artifacts of pottery, jade, copper, and gold, as well as a jumble of skeletons—the remains of men and women with grievous head wounds.

From 16th-century Spanish records, we know that the Maya sacrificed people in this sacred cenote. Victims were to intercede with the gods, and the priests instructed them concerning the requests. They were to ask for rain, good crops, knowledge of the future, and, on occasion, relief from hurricanes.

In Yucatán, the absence of rain could cause untold disaster—tragedies properly understood only when standing on its endless shelf of karstic rock, or limestone. Water seeps straight through the karst to groundwater levels; as a result, no river or brook runs here. The Maya depended on seasonal rains to water their crops—mainly corn, beans, and squash. At any point in the yearly cycle, irregular rains meant a smaller ration of food.

The great unsolved archaeological question in this part of the world is why Yucatán city-states such as Chichén Itzá collapsed one after another. But the miracle is that they survived at all, nourished by crops grown in such a harsh environment.

At Chichén Itzá, El Castillo pyramid is oriented to celestial cycles. The setting sun casts serpentlike shadows along its northern stairs on the equinoxes.

While working at Chichén Itzá, de Anda arrived at what he thinks is the city's overarching design—a complex plan that relies on astronomy and a knowledge of the area's water resources. The monumental structure of El Castillo was planned with precision to be aligned to the March and September equinoxes, when the sun's passage makes a serpentlike shadow slither down its side. De Anda found that the structure also stands in the middle of four cenotes within the ancient city's urban limits, probably symbolizing the sacred mountain at the center of the Maya universe. It was also oriented to the moments when the sun reaches its highest point in the sky, further connecting it to the cycles of the heavens.

As de Anda explored the cenote directly northwest of El Castillo's main stairway, he realized that it had probably functioned as a sacred sundial and timekeeper for the ancient Maya twice a year, on May 23 and July 19. On those days, the sun reaches its zenith, a moment when it is vertically overhead and no shadow is cast.

Beneath the cenote's narrow mouth, the walls open up to form a giant dome. Before and after the sun's zenith, and on many other days, the rays slant into the cenote, hit the water, and are reflected onto the domed ceiling. But at the two zeniths, a pillar of sunlight plunges straight into the water, focused by the cenote's small opening, which was shaped into a rectangle, likely to mirror the four-cornered Maya cosmos.

To calibrate their calendar, the Maya had to determine the days of the year when the sun shone exactly overhead, not one fraction of a degree lower or higher. De Anda now believes that Maya astronomers may have been waiting inside the cenote for those two annual zenith moments when sunlight pierces the water.

During a search for the water table beneath Chichén Itzá, de Anda and his team explored a series of underground chambers about three miles east of El Castillo. There, they discovered a trove of more than 150 ritual objects, untouched for more than a thousand years. The cave system is known locally as Balamkú, or "Jaguar God."

De Anda recalls pulling himself on his stomach through the tight tunnels of Balamkú for hours before his headlamp illuminated something entirely unexpected: a cascade of offerings left by the ancient residents of Chichén Itzá, so perfectly pristine that stalagmites had formed around the incense burners, vases, decorated plates, and other objects. Some containers, it turned out, even held traces of food, seeds, and bones—valuable clues to Maya life and beliefs. "I couldn't speak, I started to cry," says de Anda. "Nothing compares to the sensation I had entering, alone, for the first time in that cave. You almost feel the presence of the Maya who deposited these things in there."

> "I couldn't speak, I started to cry. Nothing compares to the sensation I had entering, alone, for the first time in that cave. You almost feel the presence of the Maya."
>
> —*Guillermo de Anda, archaeologist*

The information gathered by specialists in fields such as 3D mapping and paleobotany will offer a much more detailed idea of what actually occurred in Maya cave rituals, as well as the history of Chichén Itzá, which declined for unknown reasons in the 13th century.

"Balamkú can tell us not only the moment of collapse of Chichén Itzá," says de Anda. "It can also probably tell us the moment of its beginning."

81

LOST CITY OF THE MONKEY GOD

1000–1400 • Honduras • Unknown culture

In pursuit of a legendary metropolis built of white stone,
explorers discover the untouched ruins of a vanished culture.

———◆———

On February 18, 2015, a military helicopter lifted off from an airstrip near the town of Catacamas, Honduras, and headed toward the mountains of La Mosquitia on the northeast horizon. Below, farms gradually gave way to steep sunlit slopes—some covered with unbroken rainforest, others partially stripped for cattle ranching.

Picking his way through the summits, the pilot headed for a V-shaped notch in a distant ridge. Beyond it lay a valley surrounded by serrated peaks: an unblemished landscape of emerald and gold, dappled with the drifting shadows of clouds. Flocks of egrets flew below, and the treetops thrashed with the movement of unseen monkeys. There were no signs of human life—not a road, trail, or wisp of smoke. The pilot banked and descended, aiming for a clearing along a riverbank.

Among those stepping from the helicopter was archaeologist Chris Fisher, a Mesoamerica specialist at Colorado State University. The valley was located in a region long rumored to harbor a mythic metropolis built of white stone, a White City, also known as the Lost City of the Monkey God.

Fisher did not believe in such legends. But he did believe that the valley contained the ruins of a real lost city, abandoned for at least half a millennium. In fact, he was certain of it.

The Mosquitia region of Honduras and Nicaragua holds the largest rainforest in Central America, covering some 20,000 square miles of dense vegetation, swamps, and rivers. Anyone venturing into it faces a host of dangers: deadly snakes, hungry jaguars, and noxious insects, some carrying potentially lethal diseases. The persistence of the myth of a hidden White City owes a great deal to the forbidding nature of this wilderness.

But the origin of the legend is obscure. Explorers, prospectors, and early aviators spoke of glimpsing the white ramparts of a ruined city rising above the jungle; others repeated tales, first recorded by Hernán Cortés in 1526, of fabulously rich towns hidden in the Honduran interior. Anthropologists who spent time with the Indigenous residents of Mosquitia heard stories of a "white house," a refuge where people retreated from the Spanish conquest, never to be seen again.

Since the 1920s, several expeditions had searched for the White City, but archaeology in Mosquitia was impeded not only by tough conditions, but also by a generally accepted belief that the rainforest soils of Central and South America were too poor to support more than scattered hunter-gatherers. This was true despite the fact that when archaeologists first began to explore Mosquitia in the 1930s, they uncovered settlements, suggesting that the area was once occupied by a widespread, sophisticated culture.

The people who had lived there constructed their public edifices out of river cobbles, earth, wood, and wattle and daub. Once abandoned, the structures dissolved in the rain and rotted away, leaving unimpressive mounds of dirt and rubble that were quickly swallowed by vegetation. The disappearance of this splendid architecture could explain why this culture remains so marginalized. The culture is still so understudied that it has not been given a formal name. "There is much we don't know about this great culture," Honduran archaeologist Oscar Neil Cruz explained. "What we don't know, in fact, is almost everything."

> **"There is much we don't know about this great culture. What we don't know, in fact, is almost everything."**
>
> —*Oscar Neil Cruz, archaeologist*

When so little is known, anything is possible. In the mid-1990s, a documentary filmmaker named Steve Elkins became captivated by the legend of the White City and embarked on an effort to find it. He spent years poring through reports from explorers, archaeologists, gold prospectors, drug smugglers, and geologists. He also hired scientists at NASA's Jet Propulsion Laboratory (JPL) in Pasadena, California, to analyze data from Landsat and radar images of Mosquitia, looking for signs of ancient settlements. The JPL report showed what looked like "rectilinear and curvilinear" features in three valleys, which Elkins labeled T1, T2, and T3—the T standing for "target."

Then Elkins read about lidar (short for light detection and ranging), a technique that works by bouncing hundreds of thousands of pulses of infrared laser beams off the rainforest below. The resulting three-dimensional "point cloud" can be manipulated with software to remove the pulses that hit trees and undergrowth, leaving an image composed only of pulses reaching the underlying terrain—including the outlines of archaeological features.

A lidar survey of the target area in Honduras revealed ruins strung along several miles of the T1 valley; a site twice the size was evident in T3. Although the larger structures were readily apparent, a finer analysis of the images would require the eye of an

Ruins deep in the Honduran rainforest hold a cache of stone objects, possibly left as offerings, that includes jars decorated with vultures and snakes.

archaeologist—which is how Fisher entered the picture. From the moment he saw the lidar images, he was hooked. He had no doubt that both T1 and T3 fit the archaeological definition of a city.

With the help of the Honduran government, Elkins and a financial backer, Bill Benenson, gathered a team capable of penetrating the jungle to "ground-truth" what the lidar images had identified. The logistics were daunting—aside from having to contend with snakes, insects, mud, and incessant rain, they would risk contracting malaria, dengue fever, and a smorgasbord of other tropical diseases. In the end, at least eight team members contracted leishmaniasis, a potentially lethal parasitic disease transmitted by a tiny sand fly.

While exploring in the almost impenetrable forest one day, the team found—at the summit of a steep prominence—a subtle but unmistakable rectangular depression, likely the outline of a building. Evidence of deliberate construction supported the interpretation of it as an earthen pyramid. Fisher was elated. "It's just as I thought," he said. "All this terrain has been modified by human hands."

In what was probably one of the city's 10 plazas, the team found a stretch of rainforest as artificially level as a soccer field. Linear mounds surrounded it on three sides: the remains of walls and buildings. On another foray, the team mapped three more large public spaces and many mounds. The vegetation, however, blocked any sense of the layout or scale of the ancient city.

Then, while returning to camp one day, cameraman Lucian Read called out. "Hey, there are some weird stones over here."

At the base of a pyramid, just poking out of the ground, were the tops of dozens of beautifully carved stone sculptures. The objects, glimpsed among leaves and vines and covered with moss, took shape in the jungle twilight: the snarling head of a jaguar, a stone vessel decorated with a vulture's head, large jars carved with snakes, and a cluster of grinding tools that looked like decorated thrones or tables, which archaeologists call metates. All the artifacts were in perfect condition, likely untouched since they'd been left centuries before. "This is a powerful ritual display," said Fisher—perhaps an offering.

To protect the region from looting, and from the deforestation of cattle ranching, Honduras has established the Mosquitia Patrimonial Heritage Preserve, an area of about 785 square miles surrounding the valleys surveyed by lidar. If that works, and the discoveries in T1 do indeed tip the scale toward preservation, then it doesn't matter whether the White City is real or myth. The search for it has led to a trove of natural riches.

82

CAHOKIA, AN AMERICAN CAPITAL

1050–1200 ◆ Southern Illinois ◆ Mississippian

Abandoned hundreds of years before Columbus, the awe-inspiring Cahokia Mounds reveal that a sophisticated society thrived in ancient North America.

———◆———

The Cahokia Mounds in southern Illinois stand at the center of what was once the greatest civilization between the deserts of Mexico and the North American Arctic. The site of one of North America's first cities and arguably American Indians' finest achievement, it is the most visible example left today of the Mississippian culture, an agricultural civilization that spread across the U.S. Midwest and Southeast starting before A.D. 1000 and peaking around the 13th century. Nevertheless, until recently relatively few people outside the St. Louis area had heard of it.

That ignorance has deep roots. The first person to write a detailed account of Cahokia's mounds was Henry M. Brackenridge, a lawyer and amateur historian who came upon the site and its massive central mound while exploring the surrounding prairie in 1811. "I was struck with a degree of astonishment, not unlike that

> "I was struck with a degree of astonishment, not unlike that which is experienced in contemplating the Egyptian pyramids ... What a stupendous pile of earth!"
>
> —*Henry M. Brackenridge, lawyer and writer*

which is experienced in contemplating the Egyptian pyramids," he wrote about the hundred-plus mounds he counted. "What a stupendous pile of earth! To heap up such a mass must have required years, and the labors of thousands."

But newspaper accounts of his discovery were widely ignored. Brackenridge complained about this in a letter to a friend, former President Thomas Jefferson; with friends in such high places, word of Cahokia did eventually get around. Unfortunately, it was not news that most Americans, including subsequent presidents, were particularly interested in hearing. Andrew Jackson's Indian Removal Act of 1830, which ordered the relocation of eastern Native Americans to land west of the Mississippi, was premised on the notion that those people were nomadic savages who couldn't make good use of land anyway. Evidence of a prehistoric city—one even larger than Washington, D.C., at the time—would have threatened the narrative. Historians theorized that the mounds were built by an almost comic array of alternate peoples—Phoenicians, Vikings, or even perhaps a lost tribe of Israel—rather than acknowledging Native Americans.

Even U.S. universities took scant notice of Cahokia and other homegrown sites before the second half of the 20th century. They preferred sending their archaeologists to Greece, Mexico, and Egypt, where the stories of ancient civilizations were comfortably distant and romantic. Not until the 1880s did years of fieldwork by the Smithsonian Institution's Cyrus Thomas, originally a skeptic himself, definitively prove the mounds were of Native American origin. But relatively few people championed Cahokia and its neighboring mound centers in East St. Louis and St. Louis (once nicknamed "Mound City"), which fought a mostly losing battle against development, neglect, and treasure hunters for the better part of a century. Though Monks Mound, named for French monks who once lived in its shadow, became a tiny state park in 1925, it was used for sledding and campgrounds. The rest of Cahokia was largely ignored—built on and only sporadically studied—until the 1960s.

Ironically, the biggest construction project to tear into Cahokia would also put it on the map. President Dwight Eisenhower's interstate highway program contained provisions for the study of archaeological sites in its path. This meant more money for excavations than had ever been available, as well as a clear agenda for where to dig, when, and how fast. With two highways slated to skewer the ancient city—I-55/70 now bisects Cahokia's north

Monks Mound marks the site of a pre-Columbian city that had more than a hundred such structures, some 15,000 inhabitants, and far-reaching influence.

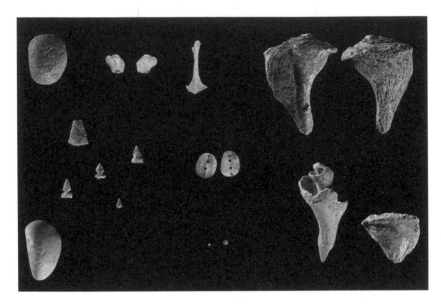

One excavation pit at Cahokia yielded hammer stones, projectile points, bird bones, two copper beads, and whelk shells that likely had a ritual significance.

plaza, creating a road sandwich with Collinsville Road, a quarter mile to the south—archaeologists began to study the site systematically. What they found was nothing less than revelatory.

It became apparent that Cahokia was more than just a stupendous pile of earth or a ceremonial site where scattered tribes congregated once in a while. Nearly everywhere they dug, archaeologists found homes—indicating that thousands of people had once lived in the community—and many of those homes had been built within a very brief span of time. In fact, research revealed that the whole city seemed to have sprung to life almost overnight around 1050. (The regional capital flourished around the same period that medieval Europe and the Near East were embroiled in the Crusades.) People streamed in from surrounding areas, building houses and the infrastructure of a new city—including several mounds with buildings on top and a grand plaza the size of 45 football fields, used for everything from sporting events and communal feasts to religious celebrations.

From the flat top of the colossal Monks Mound—with a footprint of 14 acres, the mound is larger at its base than the Great Pyramid of Khufu—the view encompasses the vast floodplain known as the American Bottom. After directing the construction of what would have been the highest geographic feature in 175 square miles, a chief or high priest would have had a bird's-eye view of the land under his sway.

That scenario presumes that Cahokia had such a single leader, which is not universally agreed upon. It is not even known what the site was called—the name Cahokia is borrowed from a tribe that lived nearby in the 1600s—or what the people who lived here called themselves. With no written language, they left behind the same scattering of meager clues ripe for dispute. "You know what they say," noted Bill Iseminger, an archaeologist who has worked at Cahokia for 40 years and is the area's preeminent expert. "Put three archaeologists in a room and you get five opinions."

Despite the many points of contention among Cahokia scholars, there are still points of general consensus. Experts largely agree that the city quickly developed a couple centuries after corn became an important part of the local diet; that it drew together people from the American Bottom; and that it dwarfed other Mississippian communities in size and scope. The battle lines tend to form along the questions of how populous it was, how centralized its political authority and economic organization were, and the nature and extent of its reach and influence.

At one extreme you have descriptions of Cahokia as a "theater of power," a hegemonic empire sustained by force that reached deep into the Mississippian world and perhaps connected to Mesoamerican civilizations such as the Maya or Toltec. At the other extreme are characterizations of Cahokia as little more than an especially large Mississippian town whose residents had a talent for making big piles of dirt. But with less than one percent of Cahokia excavated, speculation by every camp remains in higher supply than evidence.

Cahokia's demise is perhaps an even greater mystery than its emergence. It was a ghost town by the time Columbus landed in the New World. The American Bottom and substantial parts of the Mississippi and Ohio River Valleys had become so depopulated they are referred to as the Vacant Quarter. Historians note that the city grew to prominence during an especially favorable climate phase and began shrinking around the time the climate became cooler, drier, and less predictable. For an agricultural community dependent on regular crop yields, the changing conditions could have been anything from stressful to catastrophic.

The fact that between 1175 and 1275 Cahokia's inhabitants built (and rebuilt, several times) a stockade encircling the main part of the city suggests that conflict or the threat of conflict had become a standard feature of life in the region—perhaps because there were fewer and fewer resources. Furthermore, dense populations create environmental problems as a matter of course—deforestation, erosion, pollution, disease—that can be difficult to counter and that have been the downfall of many a society.

That Cahokia endured for some 300 years, and was at the peak of its power for half that at most, should not come as a surprise. "If you look broadly at human history, failure is the norm," said archaeologist Tom Emerson of the University of Illinois. "What's amazing is when things last."

83

THE OLD ONES
OF THE
SOUTHWEST

1200–1300 • Colorado • Ancestral Pueblo

*Ancestors of the Hopi, Zuni, and other Pueblo peoples
built the spectacular cliff dwellings now protected in
Mesa Verde National Park.*

———◆———

In the 13th century, in the southwestern United States, the ancestors of the modern Pueblo people decided to change the way they lived. They retreated from the desert valleys into the region's steep sandstone cliffs, where they built clusters of defensive dwellings under the shelter of alcoves. Mountaineer Frederick Chapin, one of the first modern visitors to see these structures, explored the area in 1889 and 1890, and described what is known today as Cliff Palace.

"[It appears] like a ruined fortress, with ramparts, bastions, and dismantled towers," he wrote. With 150 rooms set in dark recesses, this sprawling site is North America's largest cliff dwelling.

For more than 2,000 years the ancestral Pueblo people flourished across an expanse of the desert Southwest the size of New England—from the Grand Canyon east to the headwaters of the Pecos River, from the junction of the Green and Colorado Rivers south to present-day Flagstaff. We do not know what they called

themselves, but for a time, modern historians referred to them as Anasazi—an unfortunate name, because the word, meaning "ancient enemies," is Navajo rather than Pueblo.

Some of the descendants of these ancients still live in houses of sandstone, wood, and mud. About 75,000 in number, they belong to 20 tribes that inhabit the three Hopi mesas in northeastern Arizona, the Zuni pueblo in western New Mexico, and 18 pueblos along the Rio Grande. Among Native Americans, the Pueblo peoples have been especially successful at retaining their ties to the past, maintaining their ancestral religion, and keeping their communities intact.

Long before the time of Christ, the Old Ones (as some Pueblo call their ancestors) had become skilled hunter-gatherers. They chased antelope, deer, and bighorn sheep with flint-bladed spears and darts flung from powerful propelling devices. They collected pine nuts, cactus fruit, and berries by the basketful.

By A.D. 500 the Old Ones had grown more sedentary, making pottery and coaxing squash, beans, corn, and cotton from the inhospitable land. As their culture flourished, they cultivated far-flung contacts with Mexico and the Pacific and Gulf coasts, elevated crafts to fine art, and built distinctive houses and monumental ceremonial structures across the Four Corners region at urban centers such as Chaco Canyon (located in modern-day New Mexico). By the year 1200, the ancient Pueblo numbered well into the tens of thousands; their villages, which had become elaborate grids of square rooms often stacked several stories high, spread across their heartland.

But something happened in the 13th century that forced most of the ancient Pueblo from mesa tops and valley bottoms into defensible villages and dizzying cliff dwellings such as those at Mesa Verde. The cause of the move was likely a cascade of events—a shift in climate leading to the Great Drought, which held North America in its grip for three decades; the resulting food shortages;

The Wetherill family explored many crumbling ruins near their ranch in the 1880s, including Mesa Verde's Cliff Palace, now partly restored.

and internecine conflict, one desperate Pueblo community pitted against another.

Then, just before 1300, the ancient Pueblo suddenly abandoned their laboriously constructed cliffside communities and retreated from half their ancestral domain—every site northwest of a diagonal line drawn between Flagstaff, Arizona, and Pagosa Springs, Colorado, a distance of 300 miles.

Their leave-taking remains the crucial puzzle in the archaeology of the Southwest, despite more than a century of research. For decades, scholars sought an environmental explanation: drought, deforestation, famine, or disease. Or they invoked attacks by hostile nomadic tribes. But in recent years some experts have turned to a cultural theory: By 1300, a new religion may have arisen to the southeast, so compelling that it helped draw tens of thousands of ancestral Pueblo away from the homeland they had inhabited for millennia.

The Pueblo never returned to their cliffside dwellings, which were eerie ghost towns when scientists and settlers came upon them in the late 1800s. A geologist exploring on behalf of the U.S. government in 1875 visited various sites and collected pottery, stone implements, and other artifacts from Mesa Verde that ended up in the Smithsonian Institution in Washington, D.C.

It was a ranching family, however, who really put Mesa Verde on the map as a cultural treasure. Benjamin Kite Wetherill (known as B. K.) and his wife, Marion, established a 160-acre ranch nearby in 1880. While tending their grazing cattle, son Al Wetherill spotted dwellings tucked into the 2,000-foot cliffs under the rim of Mesa Verde. A local Ute, Acowitz, told the family about hidden villages in the hills and accompanied Richard, another son, and his brother-in-law, Charlie Mason, on an exploration in 1888. They brought back artifacts and spread tales of what they had found.

The railroad had arrived about 30 miles from Mesa Verde in 1881, bringing in travelers eager to see the Wild West. The Wetherills realized they could cash in by conducting tours and offering lodging—to Frederick Chapin, among others. They charged two dollars a day for room and board, and five dollars for a guided trip to the ruins. They also collected admission of 25 cents to an exhibit of artifacts that they brought to several Colorado cities. But they were also concerned about the fate of what they were discovering. B. K. Wetherill even reached out to the Smithsonian several times for guidance about the family's explorations and ongoing collecting. In 1890, he sent this prescient plea: "We are particular to preserve the buildings, but fear, unless the Gov't sees proper to make a national park of the Cañons, including Mesa Verde, that the tourists will destroy them." He received no reply.

> "We are particular to preserve the buildings, but fear, unless the Gov't sees proper to make a national park of the Cañons, including Mesa Verde, that the tourists will destroy them."
>
> —B. K. Wetherill, *rancher*

In 1891, the Wetherills hosted Swedish scholar Gustaf Nordenskiöld, who conducted the first scientific exploration of Mesa Verde—digging, sketching, and labeling finds and photographing, measuring, and drawing the ruins. His book, *The Cliff Dwellers of the Mesa Verde*, publicized the site widely and remained the go-to reference for decades.

But as more tourists arrived and more artifacts were pried out of the fragile ruins to be taken home as souvenirs, pressure built to protect the cliff dwellings. Two women in particular took up the cause: Virginia Donaghe, a newspaper correspondent in Colorado Springs, and Lucy Peabody, a political activist in Denver. Although they adopted different strategies and became bitter rivals, the attention they generated finally achieved the desired result: In 1906, the U.S. Congress created Mesa Verde National Park. Encompassing 4,700 archaeological sites, 600 cliff dwellings, and traces of farms and pueblos on top of the mesa, this unique property is a testament to the importance of human history among the special places set aside for the benefit and enjoyment of all.

84

THE CITY OF GREAT ZIMBABWE

ca 1100–1450 • Zimbabwe • Shona

The stone ruins that gave Zimbabwe its name were subject to one of the longest running archaeological fabrications in history.

———◆———

Between the 11th and 15th centuries, the Shona of the Zimbabwe Plateau built a hilltop citadel of towering granite that was once home to perhaps 18,000 residents. Known to locals for centuries as the Great Zimbabwe (Zimbabwe means "stone houses" in modern Shona), the massive ruins were abandoned for hundreds of years. Then, they became the focus of intense attention from European colonialists who insisted they couldn't possibly be the work of Africans.

Though outsiders encountered the site as early as 1531, it took a German explorer to bring it to the Western world's attention—and to spark an infamous denial of the site's true history.

In 1871, antiquarian Karl Mauch was led to the site by another German who lived with the nearby Karanga people who still used the site for ceremonies. In exploring the area, Mauch encountered burned remnants of a wooden support in one of the buildings and wrote in his field journal, "A comparison of it with the wood of my pencil shows great similarity and therefore I suppose . . . that it must be cedarwood." Then he made a massive leap: "It can be taken as a fact that the wood which we obtained actually is cedarwood and from this that it cannot come from anywhere else but from the Lebanon." Drawing on popular myths of the time, Mauch believed that the supposed cedar must have arrived with the seafaring Phoenicians, and that the city was built by none other than King Solomon and the Queen of Sheba.

The site's supposed biblical provenance intrigued other white explorers. Cecil Rhodes, head of the British South Africa Company designed to take over and develop African lands on behalf of white settlers, commissioned an expedition to the ruins and used them to drive interest in Zimbabwe. The theory of ancient settlers arriving on Zimbabwe's shores to bring "civilization" served the British colonists' political narrative as they prepared to take over governance of the land—naming the colonial territory "Rhodesia."

During these expeditions, white explorers took valuable artifacts from the site, threw others away, and destroyed important markers needed for establishing a time line and cultural origin. Richard Hall, appointed curator of the Great Zimbabwe by the British South Africa Company, even claimed he was wiping away the "filth and decadence of the [African] occupation," which, in his eyes, had sullied the ancient Phoenician site.

Despite the mythmaking, naysayers like the Oxford-trained David Randall-MacIver insisted on applying proper techniques of stratigraphy and observed facts to draw a scientific conclusion. His survey in 1905 quickly found overwhelming evidence that the site was African due to the similar style of pottery with that of the surrounding population. Subsequent archaeologists concurred, notably Gertrude Caton-Thompson and her team of "trowelblazing" women archaeologists who mapped Great Zimbabwe in 1929. She skeptically dismissed her predecessors' fantasies, vowing that her research would be free of wild speculation as to "who sacrificed to the morning star, and who worshipped the new moon . . . subjects which have no place at all in the earlier chapters of archaeological research and which lead, unless firmly tethered by chronological data, to wildernesses of deductive error." Caton-Thompson's data faced hostile pushback by the academics in Britain, but she stuck to her guns and the evidence was irrefutable. It is now widely known that the site's occupants were ancestors of the Shona, a Bantu-speaking people who are still the most populous ethnic group in Zimbabwe.

Great Zimbabwe's walls resemble a hilltop fortress, but archaeologists have never uncovered evidence that the walls were used defensively. Instead, they are thought to have projected the power and authority of the elite families—perhaps 200 to 300 at the city's height—who lived in homes studded with sculptures. More of the city extends at the bottom of the hill, likely having expanded organically as the population grew. Residents lived in *dagas,* mud huts, that have since eroded, but the remarkable masonry of the granite walls was built to last. The bricks are layered without mortar, yet the unsupported walls often rise twice as tall as they are wide, and arc gracefully to create concentric passageways and a sophisticated drainage system. One of the best preserved structures, called the Great Enclosure, was built from an estimated one million bricks and may have been used for ceremonies. Caton-Thompson also located what she believed to be a funerary enclosure filled with bodies of evidently high-status people, all women, buried with bangles and beaded necklaces.

The size and prosperity of Great Zimbabwe relative to ruins discovered nearby suggest the city was a regional hub. Coins from Arabia, Chinese pottery dating to the Ming dynasty, and Syrian glass indicate that the inland kingdoms exchanged commodities at the bazaars of the Swahili coast in a vast trade route that extended across the Indian Ocean and on to China. What did they trade? One idea comes from the extensive nearby mines—up to 500 copper mines and more than 4,000 gold mines. But trade alone would not

Within the kingly quarters of Great Zimbabwe, a 30-foot tower, stone brick walls, and graceful archways exemplify the community's skillful engineering.

have supported a large urban population, so the residents likely farmed the plateau and raised cattle as well.

The monument remained a political hot spot. In the 1960s and '70s, archaeologists could even be deported by the apartheid-era government for speaking on the true origins of Great Zimbabwe, and Africans were not allowed to enter for ceremonies. Though the city is now hailed as a UNESCO World Heritage site and its reputation is restored, only a small percentage of the land has been excavated.

For Indigenous Africans, the city is a symbol of unity and self-governance. When nationalists sought to rename Rhodesia as it broke free from its colonial past, the monument provided the answer—Zimbabwe.

85

EAST AFRICA'S CROSSROADS

A.D. 800–1500 ◆ East Africa ◆ Swahili

City-states on the shore of the Indian Ocean enjoyed centuries of wealth, thanks to trade linking them to Arabia, India, and beyond.

———◆———

On June 13, 1325, a 21-year-old Moroccan named Ibn Battuta left his home in Tangier and set off for Mecca on a hajj, the pilgrimage that Muslims are supposed to make at least once in their lifetime. After he reached Mecca, though, he kept on going, returning home three decades later as one of history's great travelers. Driven by curiosity and sustained by the Koran, he journeyed to the far corners of the Islamic world, crossing two continents and logging some 75,000 miles through 44 countries in today's atlas. His memoirs brim with the flavor of his time, documenting a journey of hazard and hardship, opulence and adventure.

Setting out on his first long sea voyage, this pilgrim-jurist-courtier-mystic-politician-diplomat-explorer sailed down Africa's east coast as far as the great trading center of Kilwa, now in Tanzania, 600 miles below the Equator. During its golden age, Kilwa was one of some three dozen prosperous ports that dotted what is known as the Swahili coast. Those ports, which stretched from Mogadishu to present-day Mozambique, had evolved into powerful city-states as they grew rich from Indian Ocean trade.

Ibn Battuta stayed in Kilwa for about two weeks in 1331, until the winds shifted and he could continue his voyage. He probably prayed at the Great Mosque, whose ruins survive at the site today, and must certainly have been impressed with a place that minted its own coins, that had houses with indoor plumbing, and where prosperous residents wore clothing of imported silk. "The city of Kilwa is amongst the most beautiful of cities and elegantly built," he wrote in his memoirs—the only eyewitness account of the Swahili coast that has survived from that era.

The Swahili city-states flourished between the ninth and 16th centuries, when ships from Arabia, India, and even China called at their ports to carry away goods that made the Swahili wealthy—gold, ivory, incense, perfumes, leopard skins, timber, and enslaved people from the African interior. In return, they received exotic luxury items such as spices, Chinese porcelain, fine fabrics, and glassware.

For centuries, boats sailed in and out of these ports on the monsoon winds, which blew southwest between November and March and northeast between April and September. Arabian sailors arriving in Africa found good harbors, a sea full of fish, fertile land, and opportunities for trade. Many stayed to marry local women, bringing with them the Islamic faith. Indeed, the interplay of African and Arabian languages and customs—the mingling of blood and ideas that permeated every aspect of life—created an urban and mercantile culture unique to this coast. Even its name, Swahili, is an adaptation of *sahil,* the Arabic word for "coast."

At its core, though, the culture was African—a fact that early archaeologists failed to recognize. Neville Chittick, first director of the British Institute in Eastern Africa, excavated ancient Kilwa—on Kilwa Kisiwani Island—in the 1960s. He believed that the soaring domes and graceful arches of the Grand Mosque, the 100-room residence of the sultan, and the remains of whitewashed stone houses that once gleamed in the sunlight could only have been created by foreigners. Persians, he reckoned—a theory backed by a legend circulated in a 16th-century Portuguese text.

Subsequent excavations at sites along the coast have shown how wrong that idea was. One of them on Songo Mnara Island was a town that people from nearby Kilwa established in the 14th century. It lasted only about 150 years, so archaeologists have been able to uncover its details without digging through a long, layered history. Songo Mnara, they have found, was a planned community with as many as 1,000 residents. It had a palace of rooms hung with tapestries, several dozen blocks of houses, six mosques lit by oil lamps, and four cemeteries, all inside a wall. The more modest houses were one story, built of mud bricks, and roofed with man-

Built from coral blocks between the 10th and 14th centuries, the Grand Mosque of Kilwa is the oldest structure of its kind still standing in East Africa.

grove beams and palm leaves. Other structures, with two or more stories, were made of mortared coral blocks and plastered white. Fancy details for doorways, window frames, and niches were sculpted from fresh, easily carved *Porites* coral.

A stepped court at the entrance to many houses served as a place to receive guests—especially the merchants who had sailed in from far away—and to negotiate trade deals. Small chambers with attached bathrooms surrounded each court, likely accommodations for visitors who needed a place to stay until the trade winds turned in their favor. The rooms that the family used were located close to the court. Unlike what might be expected in a conservative Muslim community, however, there were no rooms hidden at the back for women. This suggests women played a significant role in entertaining guests—perhaps a reflection of the Swahili matrilocal tradition.

The Swahili trade network fell apart as the Portuguese muscled in and redirected goods toward the Mediterranean and Europe. The newcomers built a fort at Kilwa in 1505, while towns such as Songo Mnara were abandoned. Even as the wealth disappeared and trade hubs became backwaters, though, the rich Swahili culture endured through centuries of colonial occupation. "Swahili history is about adaptation and incorporation," explained Abdul Sheriff, a professor emeritus at the University of Dar es Salaam. "We will survive. Oh, Swahili culture may not be quite the same tomorrow as today, but then nothing living is."

"Swahili history is about adaptation and incorporation . . . We will survive. Oh, Swahili culture may not be quite the same tomorrow as today, but then nothing living is."

—*Abdul Sheriff, professor*

1200–1600

Sovereigns & Citizens

The nature of most cultures—historic and modern—is to have leaders and followers, rulers and subjects. And indeed, discoveries from a time of sweeping empires reveal the spiritual underpinnings of societies, the territorial aspirations of rulers, and traces of ordinary lives. Offerings to the gods, such as a jewel-laden dog and children specially groomed for sacrifice, mark two of the most iconic civilizations of the Americas. Shipwrecks testify to the foundering ambitions of emperors in Asia and Europe who launched conquests by sea. Birch-bark scrolls and parchment manuscripts from the golden age of two cities preserve the ideas of long-gone scholars. And simple mortal remains speak of humble lives pursued in the shadow of royal palaces, serving as reminders that the end awaiting us all, titled or proletarian, can be a boon to science.

Great books and mysterious letters are among the written treasures now preserved in Timbuktu, once a great crossroads of caravan trade.

86

LONDON'S BONES

ca 1200–1600 ◆ London, England ◆ British

A construction boom in London peeled back the modern city's
streets and revealed ghosts of the city's storied past.

———◆———

Beneath the pavement of a grand old city like London, you can find just about anything: a first-century Roman fresco, a pair of medieval ice skates—even an elephant's tooth. As one of Europe's oldest capitals, London has been continuously lived in and built over by a succession of Britons, Romans, Saxons, Normans, Tudors, Georgians, Regency rakes, and Victorians, each of whom added to the pile. As a result, the modern city sits atop a rich archaeological layer cake as much as 30 feet deep.

For many researchers, that variety can be part of the appeal. "The joy of London archaeology for me has always been that the finds reflect the immensely eclectic nature of the city itself," says John Maloney, onetime principal archaeology officer at the Museum of London. "You never know what you'll uncover in a place that has been a nexus of several worldwide empires over the millennia."

The challenge for archaeologists is that London is also a bustling metropolis of nine million inhabitants, chock-full of busy streets and skyscrapers and monumental architecture. Opportunities to lift the concrete veil and poke around in the artifact-rich soil tend to be few and brief. But a perfect storm of landmark engineering projects and a building boom in the archaeological heart of the city has provided an unprecedented chance to peek beneath the surface and explore its deep past.

The resulting haul of archaeological treasures has been almost overwhelming. The discoveries also include the bones of thousands of rank-and-file Londoners who died and were buried in graveyards built over and forgotten centuries ago. "These excavations have provided us with fascinating snapshots into the lives of Londoners through the ages," says Don Walker, a human osteologist, or bone specialist, for Museum of London Archaeology. "It makes you realize that we all are just small, passing players in a very long-running story."

> "It makes you realize that we all are just small, passing players in a very long-running story."
> —*Don Walker, osteologist*

One of the earliest chapters of that story came to light after excavation began in 2010 at the three-acre building site for Bloomberg London, the soon-to-open European headquarters of the financial empire located in the ancient ward of Cordwainer, where leatherworkers had plied their trade since Roman times (when the city was known as Londinium). As the soil was removed, entire street scenes were revealed, complete with timber-framed shops, homes, fences, and yards. Dating from the early 60s A.D. onward, the site was in an astonishing state of preservation. More than 14,000 artifacts were found over the course of the excavation, including coins, amulets, pewter plates, ceramic lamps, 250 leather boots and sandals, and more than 900 boxes of pottery.

The Romans valued their British holdings but Londinium was always an outpost in their far-flung empire. Following the Norman invasion of 1066, William the Conqueror consolidated the city's power and expanded its rule into Wales and Scotland. By the 14th century, London was the wealthiest and most populous city in England.

Isotope and bone analysis from a collection of 14th- and 15th-century skeletons unearthed during an excavation at Charterhouse Square paint a harrowing picture of life during the reigns of the later Plantagenet kings through the Houses of Lancaster and York (including Richard III and Henrys IV through VIII). Many skeletons recovered from that period of civil unrest showed signs of malnutrition, and one in six suffered from rickets. A high rate of back injuries, muscle strains, and osteoporosis even among men in their 30s indicates lives of heavy labor. People of the 1400s had disturbingly high rates of upper-body injuries, possibly consistent with violent altercations that resulted from a breakdown in law and order in the wake of the plague.

And yet London still seemed to be a powerful draw for country folk seeking a better life. Isotope analysis reveals that nearly half

Half of London's population died during the Black Death pandemic of 1348–1350, including these individuals, whose bones were found near Charterhouse Square.

the skeletons tested were those of individuals who had grown up outside the city, some having migrated from as far away as northern Scotland. "It would seem that 14th-century London was already drawing people from all around Britain, just as it does today," Walker said.

By far the biggest boon to London archaeology has been the $23 billion Crossrail project, the new east-west underground commuter rail link that is both Europe's largest engineering project and its biggest archaeological dig. Since work began in 2009, Crossrail's 26 miles of tunnels and more than 40 construction sites have turned up artifacts and fossils spanning the past 70,000 years.

The largest and most spectacular excavation was launched in 2015, in front of the busy Liverpool Street station. Plans to build an underground ticketing hall meant cutting through the old Bedlam burial ground, the city's first municipal cemetery. The job entailed exhuming skeletons of more than 3,300 Londoners; most died in the 16th and 17th centuries, when plague often stalked the city's streets. After study, the bodies were reinterred in a field in Essex.

"The Bedlam burial ground is the most diverse graveyard in the city," said Jay Carver, Crossrail's chief archaeologist, whose team spent months researching the site before starting the excavation. "The whole spectrum of society is represented here, from madmen and criminals to the wife of a former Lord Mayor of London."

87

THE BIRCH-
BARK SCROLLS

ca 1000–1400 ◆ Novgorod, Russia ◆ Rus

*Wet soil has preserved letters and other rare artifacts of the
medieval era in Novgorod, one of Russia's oldest cities.*

———◆———

As the lights dimmed during Europe's Dark Ages, eighth-century Scandinavians penetrated most of the known world during their forays of conquest and trade. Their exploits in western Europe are the most renowned, along with their expeditions to far-flung Greenland and America. But some Vikings took the road less traveled, toward the eastern Baltic, where they thrust deep into the lands of the Slavs.

Viking warriors and voyagers known as the Rus traded with the strong and plundered the weak. In about A.D. 862, they established the city of Veliky Novgorod, an important trading hub that flourished in the medieval period. A local proverbial expression referred to the power of the city at its zenith: "Who can stand against God and the Great Novgorod?" Its sovereignty ultimately dissolved, but the old town, now buried beneath the modern-day capital, has remained remarkably well preserved through the ages. Excavations here have offered up some incomparable treasures, including one of the greatest archaeological finds of the 20th century: birch-bark scrolls that offer a startlingly detailed record of medieval life.

More than a thousand birch-bark documents about everyday life, preserved in the mud of Veliky Novgorod, include this note by a boy in the 13th century.

According to legend, Novgorod ("new town") was first settled by Rurik, a Varangian chieftain, making it one of Russia's oldest cities. The year it was founded, it was already a trading post on the river route between the Varangian and Greek cultures, the beating heart of a land settled by a diverse array of Slavs, Krivichi, and Finno-Ugrian. As the ninth century drew to a close, the city merged with Kiev under the authority of a single prince. But by the 11th century Novgorod was fighting for its independence. It was, some say, where Russia was born.

The city was unique for its government (an aristocratic republic run by nobles instead of princes) as well as its religious tolerance. Connected to the medieval Hanseatic League with a direct line to the European trade hubs of Lübeck, Bruges, Ghent, and London, it boasted vast holdings and by the 1400s became so influential that it was nicknamed "Lord Novgorod the Great." After a series of battles, the city surrendered to Moscow in 1478, and from there declined. But fortunately, its treasures are almost perfectly intact, preserved in Novgorod's mud.

How did this come to pass? The town was built on compacted clay, which doesn't drain well; the moisture did not allow for deep foundations, which safeguarded whatever came to be buried within them. A peatlike deposit called the "cultural layer" has a unique chemical makeup that, over time, has conserved both hard metal and softer materials like leather. Additionally, the wet soil on which the town was built prompted citizens to pave their streets with wooden planks every two or three decades, further boosting preservation. That left archaeologists with multitiered street layers, neatly separated and stretching back some 10 centuries.

Buried within Novgorod's complex layers were the remains of houses, their wooden beams perfectly preserved by the mud—a rare and precious circumstance, because wood, a major building material in medieval times, is generally not long lasting. It conveniently allows researchers to estimate accurately the date of their finds using the dendrochronological method—in other words, by counting tree rings. Some of the household items found within Novgorod's layers can be accurately dated to within 15 to 25 years.

Excavations at the site began in 1932, led by Artemiy Vladimirovich Artsikhovsky. His team found an astounding number of artifacts: some 130,000, from locks and leather items to shoes and jewelry. (These finds refuted the notion that Russian cities imported most artisan items because they didn't have the craftsmen to produce such goods themselves.) Artsikhovsky's team also uncovered 140 artisan workshops specializing in brewing, weaving, dyeing, and more, revealing a level of skill that rivaled any medieval cultural center.

As Valentin L. Yanin, a Russian professor of history who directed excavations at Novgorod in the 1960s, observed: "Given the perfect state of preservation of Novgorod's wooden streets, houses, manors and artifacts, it is almost possible to imagine rich merchants concluding contracts ... peasants selling wares at the market, innumerable sailing ships coming in along the Volkhov laden with expensive foreign wine, the smell of fish, shoemakers stitching sandals ..." The only thing missing in those early excavations were the voices of the city's inhabitants.

In 1951, those voices bubbled to the surface in the form of birch-bark scrolls dating from the 1000s through the 1400s. Known as *beresty,* the scrolls have been found in other Russian cities, but never in such profusion. Approximately 1,000 have been uncovered at Novgorod, revealing aspects of daily life, politics, and trade in the medieval city.

The pull of the past is alluring. Some scrolls hold instructions to craftsmen: "Greetings from the priest to Grechin. Paint me two six-winged seraphim on two icons for the top of the iconoclasts. I kiss you. God will reward you or we'll make a deal."

There are also messages regarding practical matters: "From Boris to Nastasya. As soon as you receive this letter send me a man on horseback, since I have a lot to do here. Oh yes, send a shirt. I forgot one."

> **"Given the perfect state of preservation of Novgorod's wooden streets, houses, manors and artifacts, it is almost possible to imagine rich merchants concluding contracts . . . peasants selling wares at the market, innumerable sailing ships coming in along the Volkhov laden with expensive foreign wine . . . "**
>
> —*Valentin L. Yanin, professor of history*

There are even love letters. "Marry me," says a birch-bark note from a man named Mikita to a woman named Anna. "I want you, and you me."

Several scrolls were clearly written by children, as they include educational writing exercises, dispelling another widely accepted idea: that most medieval Rus were illiterate.

As these and other remarkable artifacts continue to emerge at Novgorod, it's exciting to imagine what else these voices might reveal. But the lost city, preserved for the ages, has already offered startling insight into the medieval world.

88

THE DROWNED FLEET OF KUBLAI KHAN

1281 ◆ Takashima, Japan ◆ Medieval Japan, Kamakura period

Legend has long claimed that a kamikaze ("divine wind")
twice destroyed Mongol invasion fleets threatening Japan.
An underwater archaeologist and a geologist both uncovered
evidence that the legend could have been true.

———◆———

In 1980, Torao Mozai, the "father of underwater archaeology" in Japan, received a three-year grant from the Japanese Ministry of Education. The purpose of the grant was broad: to develop experimental techniques in underwater archaeology, a field in which Japan had lagged behind many other countries. But when Mozai and his colleagues selected the waters around Takashima as ideal for testing new methods, they had a specific target in mind: finding the remains of the massive Mongol armada that seven centuries earlier tried and failed to conquer Japan.

By the late 13th century, the legendary Mongol ruler Kublai Khan had taken control of the lands that his grandfather Genghis Khan had consolidated through ruthless conquest into one of history's greatest empires. After claiming the throne from his own brother, Kublai Khan continued accumulating land, eventually ruling a dominion that stretched from the Danube River through Russia, Siberia, Persia, Tibet, and Mongolia—history's largest contiguous empire. His storied court, in what is now Beijing, included the famous traveler Marco Polo, who traveled the Silk Road and beyond as an emissary of the khan.

Having conquered northern China and Korea, Kublai Khan demanded submission from Japan. The Japanese ignored the command, and the khagan's invasion fleet arrived at their island stronghold in 1274. After a day's successful fighting, a racing storm overtook the armada at night, sinking 200 ships and bringing the total cost in lives to 13,500. Despite the toll, Kublai Khan prepared another attack.

By the spring of 1281, a vast armada that would consist of 4,400 ships and 142,000 Mongol, Chinese, and Korean troops began assembling in ports of China and Korea for a second assault on Japan. (By contrast, the famed Spanish Armada three centuries later numbered only 130 ships and 27,500 men.) This time the Japanese were well prepared. During the seven-year interval, they had built a wall around Hakata Bay, a massive structure over eight feet high and 12.5 miles long.

Having apparently had no knowledge of the wall, the Mongols landed their army's advance troops directly before it. The close quarters robbed them of their most successful tactic: the lightning cavalry charge that had routed the finest armies of Asia and eastern Europe. At length, the invaders got back on their ships. Sailing westward, they joined the main body of their army, which had finally arrived after a two-month delay in China. At last all of the ships and most of the troops were assembled. Toward the end of July, the combined force attacked Takashima.

Meanwhile, the emperor of Japan and other high-ranking officials besought the aid of the gods, performing elaborate Shinto ceremonies at shrines throughout the country on behalf of the defending army. As if in answer to their prayers, the kamikaze ("divine wind") struck the Takashima area in August—with devastating effect.

This battle scene appears in an illuminated scroll that tells the story of Minister Yuriwaka, one of the Japanese leaders who repelled the invading Mongols.

Estimates of Mongol losses vary, but most accounts set the ships sunk at 4,000. The troop casualties probably exceeded 100,000, including those drowned at sea and others slaughtered by the Japanese at Takashima. The Mongols never seriously threatened Japan again. (However, half a century later Japan's ruling Hojo clan was driven from power in part due to discontent over the crippling cost of their preparations for defense against the Mongols.)

For seven centuries, the remains of the Mongol fleet lay largely undistributed on the seafloor off Takashima and the tale of the divine winds settled into legend. Fishermen occasionally brought up earthenware jars, stone bowls, and fragments of porcelain. However, no systematic exploration of the artifact-rich site was ever undertaken. One of the major challenges for any such expedition was that nonmetallic objects buried beneath a foot or two of sand or silt were invisible even to the most sensitive underwater detection instruments.

To solve that problem, archaeologist Torao Mozai worked with engineers at Koden Electronics Co., which by late 1980 had produced an experimental model of a seemingly promising device he termed a "color probe" that surveyed the seafloor with sound waves. Objects made of different materials registered on the screen as different colors (harder objects like stone or metal showed as bright red, while softer materials such as sand or silt appeared as yellow or light green). In the summer of 1981, Mozai and a volunteer team of some 30 divers, scientists, and technicians began searching in earnest for the remains of the defeated Mongol fleet.

The divers scoured the ocean floor off Takashima, bringing up a remarkable variety of items, including what appear to be 13th-century Chinese and Korean tools and implements. Their finds included everything from a barnacle-encrusted sword, probably worn by a 13th-century Mongol officer, to a modern *takotsubo*—an earthenware octopus trap. Within less than two weeks, the diving team recovered iron spearheads, iron and copper nails, stone anchors, heavy stone bowls, curiously shaped bricks, iron ingots, and quantities of porcelain and earthenware pots, vases, bowls, and dishes.

Among the most intriguing finds were bricks. Historians believe that the Mongols used them to build small blacksmith forges aboard their ships for making horseshoes and repairing weapons. Others theorize that Chinese troops brought the bricks to build shrines as soon as they landed to pray for victory. In 1281, the Chinese never had time to erect shrines; the bricks went down with the invaders.

Some of the more valuable artifacts retrieved from the wreck were in fact not found by the divers but were donated by various islanders. One contribution, which an islander had found on the beach years earlier and tossed into his toolbox, turned out to be the most valued treasure: a perfectly preserved bronze seal with engraved inscriptions in the first written form of the Mongolian language, which Kublai Khan himself had actually commissioned a monk to create in 1271. From the inscriptions, Mozai and his team deduced that the seal likely dated to 1277 and was owned by a senior Mongol officer commanding over one hundred soldiers, who may have taken part in the first invasion of Japan and who probably died during the second one.

As for what actually sank all those ships, many researchers have long had doubts that the culprit was divine winds. Although the story of the kamikaze has long been part of Japanese popular lore—especially after World War II, when Emperor Hirohito resurrected it for propaganda purposes as Allied forces closed in—powerful typhoons are relatively rare today in that part of western Japan. Historians tend to give more credit to the Japanese troops defending their land. Divers have also unearthed burned timbers, suggesting Japanese tactics may have included sailing flaming boats into their adversary's fleet.

However, more recently, research led by geologist Jon Woodruff may have given some substance to a less man-made reason for victory. Woodruff and his team excavated sediments from beneath lake bottoms near the coast that suggest typhoons were more common in western Japan half a millennium ago than they are today. Two of the sediment layers may even have been laid down by the very typhoons that inspired the kamikaze legend. "We have fairly strong evidence of two intense inundations at the end of the 13th century," said Woodruff.

Leading maritime archaeologist and shipwreck hunter James Delgado agrees it is likely a huge typhoon could have been involved, but that was one of many factors in Japan's victory. "History isn't simple," mused Delgado. "Too much of an emphasis on the storm takes away from the human elements."

89

RUINS OF THE TEMPLO MAYOR

1325–1521 ◆ Mexico ◆ Aztec

The excavation of a buried pyramid is turning up
clues to the most sacred rituals of an empire—
but so far, no sign of its most feared emperor.

———◆———

On the edge of Mexico City's famed Zócalo plaza, next to the ruins of the sacred Aztec pyramid known as the Templo Mayor, the remains of an animal—perhaps a dog or a wolf— were discovered. It had been dead for 500 years and lay in a stone-lined shaft eight feet deep. It is likely the animal had neither a name, nor an owner. Yet the anonymous canine had evidently meant something to someone. It wore a collar made of jade beads and turquoise plugs in its ears. From its ankles dangled bracelets with little bells of pure gold.

An archaeological team led by Leonardo López Luján unearthed the so-called Aristo-Canine in the summer of 2008, two years into an excavation that began when foundation work for a new building revealed an astonishing object. It was a 12-ton rectangular monolith made of pinkish andesite stone, broken into four large pieces, bearing the mesmerizingly horrific likeness of the earth goddess Tlalte-cuhtli (pronounced tlal-TEK-oo-tli), the symbol of the Aztec life-and-death cycle, squatting to give birth while drinking her own blood, devouring her own creation. It was the third flat Aztec monolith to be discovered by accident in the vicinity of the Templo Mayor, along with a 24-ton black basalt Sun Stone (excavated in 1790) and an eight-ton Disk of Coyolxauhqui (pronounced coh-yohl-SHAU-kee), the moon goddess (found in 1978).

After years of painstaking excavation, López Luján and his crew have discovered, in a deep pit beside the monolith, some of the most exotic Aztec offerings ever found. Removing a stucco patch in the plaza floor, the excavators came upon 21 white flint sacrificial knives painted red—the teeth and gums of the Aztec earth monster, her mouth open wide to receive the dead. They dug deeper and found a bundle wrapped in agave leaves. It contained an assortment of sacrificial perforators made of jaguar bone that Aztec priests used to spill their own blood as a gift to the gods. Alongside the perforators were bars of copal—priestly incense, another spiritual purifier. The perforators and incense were carefully arranged inside the bundle, along with feathers and jade beads.

Laser-driven pulses of light produced a 3D image of a 12-ton stone depicting the earth goddess Tlaltecuhtli, the symbol of the Aztec life-and-death cycle.

To López Luján's surprise, several feet beneath this bundle lay a second offering, this one in a stone box. It held the skeletons of two golden eagles—symbols of the sun—with their bodies facing westward. Surrounding the eagles were 27 sacrificial knives, 24 of them dressed up in fur and other costumes, like raggedy puppets, to represent deities associated with the setting sun. By January 2010, the team had uncovered a total of six offerings in the shaft—the last one 24 feet below street level and containing a ceramic jar filled with 310 greenstone beads, earplugs, and figurines. The placement of every excavated object appeared to be governed by an exquisite logic, re-creating the Aztec Empire's entire cosmology. López Luján's crew labors painstakingly because the exactitude of the Aztec requires no less. "Everything has a cosmic significance," he explained. "The challenge for us is to discover the logic and the spatial distribution patterns."

> "Everything has a cosmic significance. The challenge for us is to discover the logic and the spatial distribution patterns."
>
> —*Leonardo López Luján, archaeologist*

At the very bottom of the second offering box, López Luján encountered the elaborately ornamented animal. Covering it were seashells and the remains of clams, crabs, and snails—creatures brought to this spot from the Gulf of Mexico, and the Atlantic and Pacific Oceans. In Aztec cosmology, López Luján knew, this tableau suggested the first level of the underworld, with the canine serving to guide its master's soul across a dangerous river.

But which human soul? Since the Spaniard Hernán Cortés's conquest of Mexico in 1521, no Aztec emperor's remains had been discovered. Yet historical records note that three Aztec rulers were cremated, their ashes buried at the foot of the Templo Mayor. When the Tlaltecuhtli monolith was found, López Luján noticed that the god depicted held a rabbit, with 10 dots above it, in its clawed right foot. In the Aztec writing system, 10-Rabbit is 1502—the year, according to the codices surviving from the era, that the empire's most feared ruler, Ahuitzotl (pronounced ah-WEE-tzohtl), was laid to rest amid great ceremony.

López Luján is convinced that Ahuitzotl's burial place is somewhere near where the monolith was found. If he is right, then the Aristo-Canine may be a subterranean guide into the mystique of a people we know as the Aztec, but who called themselves Mexica (pronounced meh-SHEE-ka), and whose legacy forms the core of the Mexican identity. If López Luján finds Ahuitzotl's tomb, it will be the culmination of a remarkable 32-year inquiry into one of the most mythologized and misunderstood empires in the Western Hemisphere. Alas, little is certain when it comes to the Aztec Empire—a reign simultaneously brutal and complex, brief and literally paved over.

Unlike the Maya, Mesoamerica's other pre-Columbian powerhouse, the Aztec are exclusively identified with Mexico; today, the country spares no opportunity to mythologize them. In the center of the Mexican flag is the Aztec eagle, which is also incorporated into the logos of the nation's two main airlines. There is Banco Azteca and TV Azteca; the national soccer team wears uniforms featuring the iconic eagle and plays its home games in Estadio Azteca. And, of course, Mexico City itself—the nerve center of the nation—is an implicit homage to the city-state of Tenochtitlan, and to Aztec indomitability.

The first Aztec, or Mexica, migrated from the north—from Aztlán, it was said, though this ancestral homeland has never been located and perhaps existed only in legend. The group spoke the Nahuatl tongue of the mighty Toltec, whose dominance across central Mexico had ended in the 12th century.

But language was the Mexica's only connection to greatness. Chased off from one Mexico Basin settlement after another, they at last happened upon an island in Lake Texcoco that no one else wanted; in 1325, they proclaimed it Tenochtitlan. Little more than a swamp, Tenochtitlan lacked drinkable water, and stones and

Bells of pure gold dangled from the hind legs of a canine interred as an offering, carefully placed according to Aztec cosmology at the site of the Templo Mayor.

wood for building. But its new inhab-itants, though "almost totally uncul-tured," as renowned scholar Miguel León-Portilla put it, compensated with what he termed "an indomitable will."

The Mexica subjugated town after town in the Mexico Basin. Under Mocte-zuma I, in the late 1440s, they and their allies marched more than 200 miles to extend their empire south-ward into the present-day states of Morelos and Guerrero. By the 1450s, they had pushed into the northern Gulf coast. And by 1465, the lone holdout in the Mexico Basin was vanquished.

Then, on the eighth of November 1519, 500 Spaniards arrived in Tenochtitlan under the command of Cortés. As awed as the Spaniards were by the spectacle of this gleaming city on a lake— "some of our soldiers even asked whether the things that we saw were not a dream," one eyewitness recalled—they were not daunted by their host's prowess. Thereafter, the facts are unassailable. The streets of Tenochtitlan ran red with blood, and in 1521 an empire was buried.

"We're persuaded that sooner or later we'll find Ahuitzotl's tomb," said López Luján. "We're digging deeper and deeper."

But no matter how deep the archaeologist digs, he will never unearth the core of the Aztec mystique. It will continue to occupy modern Mexico's psyche—there to be felt if not seen, at once prim-itive and majestic, summoning from ordinary mortals the power to turn swamps into kingdoms.

90

THE LOST TOWN OF MACHU PICCHU

1450 ◆ Peru ◆ Inca

A royal retreat in the Andes became a treasured window into Inca history after explorer Hiram Bingham introduced it to the world.

———◆———

On hands and knees, three men crawled up a slick and steep mountain slope in Peru. It was the morning of July 24, 1911. Hiram Bingham III, a 35-year-old assistant professor of Latin American history at Yale University, had set out in a cold drizzle from his expedition camp on the Urubamba River with two Peruvian companions to investigate reported ruins on a towering ridge known as Machu Picchu ("old mountain" in Quechua, the Inca language). The explorers chopped their way through thick jungle, crawled across a "bridge" of slender logs bound together with vines, and crept through underbrush hiding venomous fer-de-lance snakes.

Two hours into the hike, at nearly 2,000 feet above the valley floor, the climbers met two farmers who had moved up the mountain to avoid tax collectors. The men assured an increasingly skeptical Bingham that the rumored ruins lay close at hand, and sent a young boy along to lead the way.

When Bingham finally reached the site, he gaped in astonishment at the scene before him. Rising out of the tangle of undergrowth was a maze of terraces cut from escarpments and walls fashioned without mortar, their stones fitting so tightly together that not even a knife's blade could fit between them. The site would prove to be one of the greatest archaeological treasures of the 20th century: an intact Inca ghost town hidden from the outside world for nearly 400 years. "It seemed like an unbelievable dream," he later wrote. "What could this place be?"

Bingham acknowledged that he was not the first to discover Machu Picchu. Local people knew about it, and a Peruvian tenant farmer, Agustín Lizárraga, had even inscribed his name on one of its walls nearly a decade earlier. But Bingham did bring the mountaintop citadel to the world's attention as the account of his work there and at other sites in the region filled the entire April 1913 issue of *National Geographic* magazine.

Bingham was also the first to study Machu Picchu scientifically. With financial support from Yale and the National Geographic Society, he returned twice to the site. His crews cleared the vegetation that had reclaimed the peak, shipped thousands of artifacts to Yale's Peabody Museum of Natural History—including decorated ceramics, delicate bronze shawl pins, and human bones—and mapped and photographed the ruins. The thousands of photos he shot would change archaeology forever, demonstrating the power of images to legitimize and popularize the science. "Would anyone believe what I had found?" Bingham later said of his first visit to the site. "Fortunately, in this land where accuracy of reporting what one has seen is not a prevailing characteristic of travelers, I had a good camera and the sun was shining."

As news of the "lost city" spread, scholars tried to puzzle out just what kind of place Machu Picchu was. A fortress? A ceremonial site? For many decades, no one really knew. There were no accounts of Machu Picchu in any of the much studied chronicles of the Spanish conquest and occupation. "The Incas knew that Machu Picchu, in the most inaccessible part of the Andes, was so safely hidden in tropical jungles on top of gigantic precipices that the Spaniards would not be able to find it unless they were guided to the spot," explained Bingham. It was clear that European invaders had never discovered it, and there was nothing to document that it even existed at all, let alone to indicate its purpose.

> "The Incas knew that Machu Picchu, in the most inaccessible part of the Andes, was so safely hidden in tropical jungles on top of gigantic precipices that the Spaniards would not be able to find it unless they were guided to the spot."
>
> —*Hiram Bingham,*
> *explorer*

Bingham believed he had found Vilcabamba, the so-called lost city of the Inca where the last of the independent Inca rulers waged a years-long battle against Spanish conquistadors. He argued for and justified his conclusions for almost 50 years after his discovery, and his explanations were widely accepted.

A breakthrough came in the 1980s, when historians found a dusty legal document from 1568, less than 40 years after the Spanish conquest of Peru. Descendants of the ruler Pachacutec Inca Yupanqui, in a petition to the Spanish court, stated that in the mid-15th century their royal ancestor had owned lands at a place called Picchu, very close to the location of Machu Picchu today. Subsequent studies of the site's architecture and artifacts—from simple pots used by servants to bronze mirrors fit for a queen—suggested that Pachacutec lived in comfort at this mountaintop retreat, dining from silver plates, washing in a private stone bath, and relaxing in an orchid-scented pleasure garden. The citadel was, in fact, relatively small by Inca standards and maintained only about 500 to 750 people, some of whom came from different areas of the empire.

The royal retreat of Machu Picchu testifies to the Inca's masterful building skills with its precision-cut stones and perfectly placed cascades of terraces.

Johan Reinhard, a National Geographic Explorer, has spent years studying ceremonial Inca sites at extreme altitudes. He has gathered information from historical, archaeological, and ethnographical sources to demonstrate that Machu Picchu was built in the center of a sacred landscape. The site is nearly surrounded by the Urubamba River, which people in the region still revere today. The mountains that cradle the site also are important sacred landforms. "Taken together, these features have meant that Machu Picchu formed a cosmological, hydrological, and sacred geographical center for a vast region," Reinhard says.

Some of the site's buildings were precisely oriented to play a periodic role in that complex symbolism. Take the Torreón, an unusual curve-walled temple, for example. On June 21, winter solstice in the Southern Hemisphere, its east-facing window directs the first rays of the sun rising over the nearby San Gabriel Mountains to fall parallel to a straight edge carved in a sacred stone.

The names of Inca rulers, including Pachacutec, still resonate with power and ambition long after their empire's demise. Employing a shrewd combination of diplomacy, intermarriage, and military coercion, they conquered a vast realm extending 2,500 miles along the Andes, the mountainous spine of South America. By about 1400, the Inca had been a growing local power for centuries and had already subdued their neighbors. But they had even grander ambitions. After launching their first conquests beyond the region of Cusco, their capital, in about 1470, they pushed on to the coast to defeat the Chimú Empire. Turning south just a few decades later, they captured a vast territory that extended their reach to the edge of Patagonia. In a final thrust, they expanded eastward into the Amazon Basin.

Their extraordinary ability to triumph on the battlefield and to build a civilization, stone by stone, sent a clear message, says Dennis Ogburn, an archaeologist at the University of North Carolina at Charlotte. "I think they were saying, 'We are the most powerful people in the world, so don't even think of messing with us.'" At its height, the Inca Empire ruled as many as 12 million people, who spoke at least 20 languages. This fractious conglomeration fell apart quickly, though, after the Spanish conquest in 1532.

In modern times, the fate of the artifacts Bingham collected during his three expeditions became the source of a bitter dispute between the Peruvian government and Yale University. As the hundredth anniversary of Bingham's first visit to the site drew near, Yale yielded and returned some 5,000 artifacts to Peru. More than 350 museum-quality pieces are now on display in Cusco in a colonial-era mansion built on the foundations of an Inca palace. They serve not only as resources for researchers but also as symbols of an iconic architectural wonder that caused Bingham to exclaim, "It fairly took my breath away."

91

A TREASURE TROVE OF KNOWLEDGE

1100–1600 ◆ Mali, West Africa ◆ International

Experts are trying to find—and protect—long-hidden manuscripts dating to the time when Timbuktu was a wealthy crossroads of trade and learning.

———◆———

A t its peak, the city of Timbuktu boasted 50,000 residents and streets swollen with arriving camel trains that stretched for miles. Today, its population is about the same, but the caravans are all but extinct. Sand blown in from the desert has nearly swallowed the paved road that runs through the heart of the city, reducing the asphalt to a wavy black serpent; goats now browse along the roadside in front of mud-brick buildings. It isn't the prettiest city, an opinion that foreigners who have arrived with grand visions have repeated ever since 1828, when René-Auguste Caillié became the first European to visit Timbuktu and return alive.

The mosaic of Timbuktu that emerges from history depicts an entrepôt made immensely wealthy by its position at the intersection of two critical trade arteries—the Saharan caravan routes and the Niger River. Merchants brought cloth, spices, and salt from places as far afield as Granada, Cairo, and Mecca to trade for gold, ivory, and people to enslave from the African interior.

As its wealth grew, the city erected grand mosques, attracting scholars who in turn formed academies and imported books from throughout the Islamic world. Parchment and vellum manuscripts arrived via the caravan system that connected northern Africa with the Mediterranean and Arabia. Wealthy families, who measured their importance by the books they accumulated, had the documents copied and illuminated by an army of local scribes, building extensive libraries that contained works of religion, art, mathematics, medicine, astronomy, history, geography, and culture. As a result, fragments of the *Arabian Nights,* Moorish love poetry, and Koranic commentaries from Mecca mingled with narratives of court intrigues and military adventures of mighty African kingdoms. Huge libraries were created in this way. Nobody knows how many manuscripts were in the city during its golden age, in the 15th

Scholars in the wealthy city of Timbuktu imported texts like these from around the Islamic world. Books arrived in camel caravans stretching for miles.

and 16th centuries, but they almost certainly numbered in the hundreds of thousands.

Timbuktu's downfall came when one of its conquerors valued knowledge as much as its own residents did. After the Tuareg founded it as a seasonal camp in about 1100, the city passed through the hands of various rulers—the Malians, the Songhai, the Fulani of Massina. Timbuktu's merchants generally bought off their new masters, who were mostly interested in the rich taxes collected from trade.

But when the Moroccan Army arrived in 1591 to take control of the gold trade, its soldiers looted the libraries and rounded up the most accomplished scholars, sending them back to the Moroccan sultan. This event spurred the great dispersal of the Timbuktu libraries; the remaining collections were scattered among the families who owned them. Some were sealed inside the mud-brick walls of homes; some were buried in the desert; many were lost or destroyed in transit.

By the late 19th century, Timbuktu's territory had fallen under the rule of France. Soon after it gained its independence in 1960, the new country of Mali began to seek out and preserve the long-lost manuscripts of Timbuktu.

The Ahmed Baba Institute, founded as part of this effort, was named for Timbuktu's most famous teacher, Ahmed Baba al Massufi, who was held in exile in Marrakesh, Morocco, after the 16th-century takeover and forced to teach in a pasha's court. Beginning in 1973, the institute's staff fanned out across the city, traveled by dugout canoe and camel caravan to villages, and reached out to other countries in West Africa in their quest to recover manuscripts that had been dispersed and hidden centuries ago.

Today, the institute is a repository for rare books and manuscripts, the oldest of which date back to the city's founding in the 12th century. Its current holdings number about 30,000. In addition, Timbuktu is home to more than 60 private libraries, some with collections containing several thousand manuscripts and others with only a precious handful. "The manuscripts are the city's real gold," Timbuktu tour guide Mohammed Aghali told *National Geographic* reporter Peter Gwin. "The manuscripts, our mosques, and our history—these are our treasures. Without them, what is Timbuktu?"

In 2012, a new peril emerged as jihadists—armed with weapons seized in Libya after the fall of Muammar Qaddafi—overran northern Mali. Overnight, Timbuktu was plunged into a nightmare. The police, the army, and all government officials fled, along with thousands of ordinary citizens. Looters filled the streets. Threatened with destruction as a brutal sharia regime was established, many of the city's priceless manuscripts were spirited out of the city to safety.

> **"The manuscripts are the city's real gold."**
> —*Mohammed Aghali,*
> *Timbuktu tour guide*

Night after night, a dedicated team directed by scholar and community leader Abdel Kader Haidara quietly packed the ancient works into metal chests, then transported them away in mule carts and 4x4s. They often worked by flashlight because the jihadists had cut all the power. During nine traumatic months, the group managed to rescue an estimated 350,000 manuscripts from 45 different libraries in and around Timbuktu; they hid them in Bamako, Mali's capital, more than 400 miles from the jihadist-controlled north. Other volumes were secreted away in the city itself.

To preserve these fragile treasures for the future, experts are now conserving and digitizing them. It's a big enough task, complicated by the ongoing fight against jihadists. But it's only part of the rescue effort. The search for ancient texts is tantalizingly unfinished, says Mohamed Gallah Dicko, director of the Ahmed Baba Institute. "There are hundreds of thousands of manuscripts still out there."

92

FROZEN MUMMIES OF THE ANDES

1500 ♦ Peru ♦ Inca

After 500 years in their icy mountain tombs,
sacrificed children have revealed the details of
their last days and untimely deaths.

———◆———

About 14 years old, and four feet 10 inches tall, she had long black hair, a thin, graceful neck, and well-muscled arms. And when she gave her life to the mountain god, the Inca maiden was dressed in colorful garments of the finest alpaca wool.

The teenager died five centuries ago on the summit of Nevado Ampato, a 20,700-foot-tall volcano in the Peruvian Andes, in a ritual ceremony known as *capacocha*. Wrapped in a cocoon of textiles, she was set to rest in an earthen tomb. Priests would have placed offerings around her—miniature statues, coca leaves, and corn—and prayed to the gods of the land, sky, and the underworld.

To the Inca, Ampato was sacred, a god who brought life-giving water and good harvests. And, as a god, it claimed the highest tribute: the sacrifice of one of their own.

National Geographic Explorer Johan Reinhard found the remains of this teenager in September 1995, when he was climbing Ampato with Peruvian colleague Miguel Zárate. Ash from a nearby erupting volcano had darkened the snow; as it absorbed the heat from the sun, the ash melted the snowcap and caused Ampato's summit ridge to disintegrate. Ice and rock slid downslope, taking with them the mummy and the contents of her tomb.

Zárate first spied a tiny fan of reddish feathers protruding from the slope—the headdress of the sort found on Inca ceremonial statuettes. Three such artifacts made of gold, silver, and rare *Spondylus* shell had once been buried facing the highest point of Ampato's summit. They wore colorful textiles that looked as good as new—and their feathers were nearly perfect, so they must have been exposed only briefly to the elements.

Below the ruins of a walled stone structure—likely a collapsed ceremonial platform—Reinhard found the cloth bundle of the mummy on an icy outcrop. "I felt a jolt of excitement," he said. "In 15 years I'd climbed more than a hundred peaks in the Andes and conducted various high-altitude archaeological investigations. But not once [had I] seen a mummy bundle like this on a mountain."

Near the mummy, strewn about on the ice, were pieces of cloth, a miniature female figurine made of *Spondylus* shell, llama bones, shards of pottery, and two cloth bags containing corn kernels and a corncob.

The impact of the mummy's fall had torn off one of her outer wraps, spilling the cloth bags, shell figurine, and other burial artifacts onto the slope above the outcrop where she lay.

The girl's facial features had dried out in the sun, so Reinhard and his partner first thought her body must also be desiccated. But when they had to strain to lift the ice-encrusted bundle—which must have weighed 80 pounds or more—they knew the body was still largely frozen.

They then faced a dilemma of ethics and logistics. If they left the mummy on the mountain, the sun and volcanic ash would

Five centuries after priests sacrificed a teenager to the gods, archaeologist Johan Reinhard found her frozen remains on Argentina's Llullaillaco volcano.

damage her further, and looters could plunder the site. What's more, it was the time of year for the weather to change, and heavy snowfall could soon bury the summit.

There seemed no alternative but to carry the mummy and her artifacts down the mountain. In accordance with local custom, the climbers left an offering of food, incense, and coca leaves, and Reinhard then lifted the precious bundle onto his back. Zárate went ahead, cutting steps into the ice as the two men made a perilous descent to their camp 1,500 feet below. From there, they wrapped the mummy in their foam sleeping pads to insulate her from the warm sun, and loaded her onto the back of a burro. A 13-hour trek then took them to the town of Cabanaconde, and from there bus service linked them to Arequipa. Sixty-four hours after they began their descent, they were able to place the mummy in a freezer at the university that was Reinhard's academic base in Peru.

The study of a similar mummy from a peak in Argentina has revealed what likely happened to this young woman: She may have been selected for sacrifice around the time of puberty, a year or so before her death. She then lived away from her family, under the guidance of priestesses. She ate elite foods like maize and animal protein, perhaps llama meat, and chewed a great quantity of coca leaves. During her final weeks, she may also have drunk large amounts of alcohol in the form of *chicha,* a fermented brew made from maize. On the day of her death, the drugs may have made her more docile, putting her in a stupor or perhaps even rendering her unconscious. Today, that may seem profoundly brutal, but Reinhard put it in perspective with this explanation: "These children didn't die in the sense that we think. They went to live in a paradise with the gods. It was considered a great honor."

> **"These children didn't die in the sense that we think. They went to live in a paradise with the gods. It was considered a great honor."**
>
> —*Johan Reinhard,*
> *high-altitude archaeologist*

The maiden found on Ampato may have come from Cusco—certainly the pottery, statues, and textiles buried with her are classic Inca and of a quality representative of that great city. To reconstruct her final journey takes an act of imagination, informed by historical accounts, Reinhard's discoveries, and examinations of her and the accompanying artifacts.

The teenage girl's long trek to the summit was probably part of a pilgrimage, beginning as a lively procession winding out of the Colca Canyon. Priests and their helpers most likely led the way, along with the llamas and their heavy cargo, which included pottery, food, and ritual offerings. Behind them would have come villagers, young and old, singing and dancing as they walked to a "base camp" at 16,300 feet.

The next day, the priestly entourage likely left with the llamas for a campsite at 19,200 feet. Progress in the thin air would have been slow, and by afternoon the girl may have had to be carried. At sunrise the following morning, the priests probably made some simple offerings of food and drink to the mountain. The group, llamas included, then climbed to the summit, where they spent the night.

In the morning more offerings would have been made, and a ritual last meal of vegetables prepared for the girl. We can only suppose what her last moments were like. Although she may have been frightened, she surely felt special to be selected as a sacrifice, imagining perhaps that she was entering a glorious afterlife in a palace within the mountain. According to a CT scan, she died from a blow to the right side of the head, which caused a massive brain hemorrhage, before then being interred.

Returning to Ampato later with a full-scale archaeological expedition, Reinhard uncovered two more frozen mummies, possibly less important "companions" to the teenager on the summit. These children, a boy and a girl, may have been ritually sacrificed together in a symbolic marriage—the kind of event that Juan de Betanzos, a Spanish soldier, described in 1551.

The system of control that brought these children to a remote mountaintop at extreme altitude may have occurred as part of a military and political expansion of the Inca Empire that took place just prior to the arrival of the Spanish in 1532. At that time, the powerful empire—based in the city of Cusco—extended 2,500 miles from Colombia to central Chile. High elevation sanctuaries dot mountaintops throughout Inca territory, and Reinhard has since discovered even better preserved teenage mummies on the frosty summit of Argentina's Llullaillaco volcano.

"In their early death, I cannot help but think, the Ampato maiden and the two other Inca sacrifices have given new life to the memory of their people," wrote Reinhard. "One of ancient history's greatest civilizations."

93

SHIPWRECK OF THE *MARY ROSE*

1545 ✦ Portsmouth, England ✦ Tudor England

The first well-preserved Tudor war vessel paints a personal portrait of life onboard King Henry VIII's favorite ship.

———◆———

The fishermen in the channel off of Portsmouth, England, weren't exactly sure what they were catching, but something during June 1836 kept snagging their nets. Several divers were brought in to investigate what might lie beneath the surface of the Solent, as the waterway is known.

Professional diver John Deane and his brother Charles had an advantage in their underwater explorations: a diving helmet that Charles had adapted from a breathing apparatus he invented for firefighting. Through the helmet's oval lens, they spotted a cannon and timbers of a sunken ship emerging out of the murky waters. They brought a few boards, along with several guns, up to the surface for closer investigation. It became clear this was no ordinary shipwreck. The divers had found the *Mary Rose,* King Henry VIII's favorite ship, which sank nearly 300 years earlier during the Battle of the Solent.

Henry VIII himself was on hand on July 19, 1545, for the battle against a French fleet of more than 200 vessels—significantly larger than the formidable Spanish Armada invasion four decades later. The king watched onshore from Portsmouth's Southsea Castle as the 700-ton *Mary Rose* fired from its starboard side, and then turned to fire a volley from the port side. But as the ship turned, a shore breeze came up, heeling the ship dangerously on its side. Water began flooding its open lower gunports, sending cannons crashing headlong across the slanting decks. In a matter of minutes, the top-heavy vessel sank to the bottom like a stone, taking all but 30 of the possible 700 passengers with it. The French ships continued to face fierce resistance and poor weather on multiple fronts. Three days after the sinking of the *Mary Rose,* the invaders retreated from the channel.

The English made several attempts to salvage *Mary Rose,* the first one immediately after the sinking. But by 1552, all efforts were called off, and memories of the mighty ship faded over the passing years. After its discovery in 1836, the ensuing salvage was motivated by profit rather than preservation. Many retrieved artifacts were sold off. In 1843, the site was abandoned again. The silt that engulfed the remains of the hull was left undisturbed, and the ship lay entombed in the Solent.

But *Mary Rose* was not forgotten, at least not by one man. In 1965, Alexander McKee, a journalist, scuba diver, and military historian with a lifelong interest in historic ships, launched Project Solent Ships. A team of archaeologists and divers searched the coastal area off Portsmouth for underwater wrecks—in particular, for *Mary Rose*. Like the Deanes and their diving helmet, McKee's team had a technological advantage: magnetometers and sonar to survey wide areas of the seafloor.

The team had its first glimmer of success in the fall of 1970, when a winter storm dredged up a 16th-century cannon near the point where underwater detection instruments indicated *Mary Rose* might be found. The following spring, divers discovered that subsequent storms had laid bare the ends of several massive ship timbers, which resembled a row of great blackened teeth. "In all my years of archaeological exploration, I can recall no more beautiful sight," recalls Margaret Rule, the researcher who supervised the team. "The long search for *Mary Rose* was over."

Mary Rose was the first well-preserved Tudor warship ever discovered. The fine silt that penetrated every corner of the remaining structure sealed everything inside from the corrosive effects of saltwater and oxidation, and the destruction from microorganisms. Virtually everything that had gone down with the ship—weapons, tools, clothes, personal objects, and even normally perishable stores—remained in a remarkable state of preservation. When the preserved 120-foot-long starboard half of the lost ship's hull was lifted out of its watery grave on October 11, 1982, nearly 60 million people worldwide watched the extraordinary event on television. It was later transferred for study and reassembly to a dry dock within a hundred yards of where it had been built nearly five centuries before.

In all, a team of more than 500 volunteer divers recovered more than 19,000 artifacts, which now reside, along with the hull, in Portsmouth's Mary Rose Museum. Those artifacts, large and small, provide an invaluable comprehensive portrait of not only the ship but also its crew members.

Salvaged from the bottom of a branch of the English Channel in 1982, the hull of the *Mary Rose* was kept wet during conservation at a museum in Portsmouth.

A state-of-the-art ship for its time, *Mary Rose* was equipped for battle with, among other weaponry, a cast-iron antipersonnel weapon known as the "square murderer" and 60 to 80 cannons, including the first shipboard cannons found on wheeled carriages.

Longbowmen were also a formidable fighting force aboard *Mary Rose*. More than 130 longbows and thousands of arrows were recovered from the ship. Several skeletons showed telltale signs of os acromiale, a condition that archers suffer in their shoulder blades due to the repeat stress on their arm and shoulder muscles.

The barber-surgeon's large wooden chest was so well preserved that his finger marks were still visible in a small jar of ointment inside. The 64 items catalogued in the chest included a mortar and pestle, drug flasks, razors, and the handle of what was likely an amputation saw.

It appears the cook also left his mark on the tools of his trade. The name Ny Cop or Ny Coep was graffitied on a bowl and tankard found in the galley at the lowest part of the ship. His larder was well preserved, too. Samples of fresh pork, venison bones, beef, and mutton were found, along with the remains of rats that had avoided detection by the ship's dog.

The dog's skeleton was found in the cabin of the ship's carpenter, who brought with him not only the tools of his trade—mallet, planes, rulers, and so on—but several luxury items that only a person of wealth would have owned: silver coins and jewelry, pewter pieces locked in a chest, and a sundial in an embossed leather case.

But even the humbler artifacts recovered on *Mary Rose*—sturdy leather shoes, nit combs, a pomander of spices to offset foul scents—offer poignant, personal glimpses of shipboard lives that came to a sudden, terrible end when the strong shore breeze set physics in motion and sent the top-heavy ship sinking into the Solent's depths.

1600–PRESENT

A Changing World Order

Archaeology has the potential to rewrite even recent history as it uncovers long-lost evidence, upends long-held theories, and fleshes out stories we thought we knew well. The latest work at sites in the United States has revealed stark realities about early colonial life, the slave trade, and the Civil War, adding sobering information to chapters in the American narrative that define national identity to this very day. Underwater investigations have added to legends of swaggering pirates of the Caribbean and the doomed voyage of *Titanic,* a tragic tale that continues to captivate new generations. Finally, from the steamy Amazon to the thawing Arctic, the careful accumulation of clues is putting a spotlight on native cultures that were more sophisticated and complex than previously known.

Archaeologist Rick Knecht scouts a possible new dig site near the Bering Sea, where climate change is exposing fragile Native Alaskan artifacts.

94

SETTLING THE RAINFOREST

1250–1500 ✦ Amazon Basin ✦ Unknown culture

Forget nomadic tribes and pristine jungle.
Before Columbus, the rainforest was likely covered
in a network of large villages and ritual geoglyphs.

———◆———

Before Spanish invaders conquered South America, experts once believed, groups of nomadic peoples clustered along the Amazon River and mostly left the surrounding rainforest in a pristine state. But recent research suggests a very different scene: an Amazon region peppered with fortified villages and ceremonial earthworks.

The new studies challenge a common perception of the pre-Columbian Amazon rainforest as sparsely populated—an idea that has endured despite early European accounts of large, interconnected villages. "Many people have the image that it's an untouched paradise," says University of Exeter archaeologist Jonas Gregorio de Souza, who took part in a recent project to study traces of the human footprint in the Amazon.

In fact, much of Amazonia is unexplored. Covered in dense rainforest, it has been all but inaccessible to archaeologists interested in learning more about life away from the mighty river. But in the areas that have been cleared for agriculture, strange geoglyphs have come to light. Surely signs of organized human endeavor, these enormous ditched enclosures—which can be as wide as 430 yards—appear as circles, squares, and polygons. Some are situated near traces of ancient villages, while others surround village sites completely. About 450 have been identified so far, and scientists suspect that heavily forested areas may hold many more.

De Souza's team first used satellite imagery to try to identify village mounds and geoglyphs in a previously unexplored part of the Brazilian state of Mato Grosso. Then, armed with the coordinates of likely features, they headed to the field. Sure enough, each target they visited—24 of the 81 sites identified—was the real deal. An excavation at one site revealed decorated ceramics as well as charcoal, amounting to evidence of a village from about 1410–1460.

The researchers used their findings to predict where other sites might be located by creating a computer model that took into account everything from elevation to soil pH and precipitation. They showed that people would likely have built geoglyphs in areas of higher elevation with large variations in rainfall and temperature. The model also revealed that people wouldn't necessarily have built close to rivers, suggesting that there were likely 1,000 to 1,500 continuously occupied villages in the southern rim of the Amazon, two-thirds of which have yet to be found.

Some 104 geoglyphs turned up in the research area. They appear to have been created over time, many connected by a network of causeways. And they were likely constructed in the dry season, a time of year when the forest was easier to cut back. What they were used for is still a mystery, but experts believe they may have had a ritual purpose.

The computer model also predicted population densities that were much larger than expected. The team now thinks that between 500,000 and a million people once lived in just 7 percent of the Amazon Basin. That flies in the face of previous estimates that some two million people lived in the entire Amazon Basin. It also alters the traditional vision of a virgin Amazon forest. People—lots of them—lived there, and they must have used and altered that landscape. The forest we're seeing today is what some scientists call a "cultural parkland"—a terrain that was extensively managed.

The distribution of the potential sites suggests an interconnected, advanced series of villages that flourished between 1200 and 1500. Based on this estimate, "we need to re-evaluate the history of the Amazon," says archaeologist José Iriarte, who also worked on the survey project. Recent discoveries, including thousands of paintings of now extinct animals in rock shelters in the Colombian Amazon, and a network of villages revealed by lidar in the Brazilian state of Acre, hint at how much there is yet to find.

> "We need to re-evaluate the history of the Amazon."
>
> —*José Iriarte, archaeologist*

But how was such a large population possible? As every Ecology 101 student knows, Amazonian rainforest soils are fragile and impoverished. If farmers cut down the canopy of trees overhead to clear cropland, they expose the earth to pummeling rain and sun, which quickly wash away its small store of nutrients. The certainty of wrecking the land, environmentalists argue, makes large-scale agriculture impossible in the tropics.

Nevertheless, scientists have discovered big patches of *terra preta do índio* (black Indian earth) in scattered parts of Amazonia. It's found only where people lived, which means that it is an artificial, human-made soil, dating from before the arrival of Europeans. Lush and dark, terra preta formed a rich base for agriculture in a land where it was not supposed to exist—a clue to how villages survived deep in the forest.

The soil is rich in vital minerals such as phosphorus, calcium, zinc, and manganese, which are scarce in most tropical soils. It has vast quantities of charcoal, too, made by burning plants and refuse at low temperatures. Charcoal seems to make a kind of artificial soil within the soil, partly because nutrients bind to the charcoal rather than being washed away. Scientists have also discovered that,

Planned with geometric precision, this geoglyph in a cleared area of the Amazon is one of several hundred such mysterious markings in western Brazil.

unlike ordinary tropical soils, terra preta remains fertile after centuries of exposure to the elements.

Although this agricultural hack allowed people to live in Amazonia for several centuries, the European conquest did them in. Disease and genocide wiped out entire villages, and many survivors abandoned agriculture altogether. But the traces they left behind mean there's still much more to learn about their now vanished civilization. Evidently, those people were able to live in the Amazon rainforest and radically transform parts of it. That successful manipulation of the fragile ecosystem may offer ideas for how to manage that land and use it sustainably in the future.

95

THE COLD TRUTH OF JAMESTOWN

Most of what American schoolchildren are taught about Jamestown has little to do with the dark reality.

———◆———

A merican elementary schools' history curriculum has long included the Jamestown settlement in the colony of Virginia, the first permanent English colony in the Americas and by some accounts the birthplace of the United States. What was taught, though—often focusing on romanticized versions of interactions between settlers like John Smith and Native Americans such as Pocahontas—was almost entirely wrong. There was a reason for this. After only a few decades, the colony's capital moved to Williamsburg in 1699, and Jamestown began to slowly disappear from view. Not much was left for researchers to glean from except for the accounts of a few literate settlers.

That changed in 1994, the year a breakthrough excavation led by archaeologist William Kelso began unearthing a million artifacts that reveal in minute detail the lives and deaths of settlers, both elite and ordinary, as they struggled to establish a colony. The story told by those artifacts—everything from simple glass beads and bits of pottery to crucifixes and cannonballs—was not one of brave exploration and cultures coexisting but a tale of terror, privation, violence, and even cannibalism. Journalist Charles C. Mann, who investigated the discovery for *National Geographic,* declared, "Much of what we learned in grade school about the New World encountered by the colonists at Jamestown is wrong."

> "Much of what we learned in grade school about the New World encountered by the colonists at Jamestown is wrong."
>
> —*Charles C. Mann, journalist*

The idea that the English were "settlers" of an unpopulated land is complete fiction. In fact, when 104 colonists disembarked from three English ships onto Jamestown peninsula on the southern fringe of Chesapeake Bay on May 14, 1607, they found themselves in the middle of a small but rapidly expanding Native American empire. Called Tsenacommacah, the empire had grown under its paramount chief, Powhatan, to where it controlled roughly 8,000 square miles of land and included more than 14,000 people among about 30 tribes. The Jamestown colonists settled near one of the most powerful groups within the Powhatan Confederacy, the Pamunkey.

The new colony at Jamestown was a private enterprise funded by a group of venture capitalists called the Virginia Company. Much like investors in today's start-ups, the backers wanted a quick return. They believed, incorrectly, that the Chesapeake Bay region was laden with vast stores of gold and silver. In the 1580s, both the Spanish and the English attempted to establish colonies but neither survived.

Nevertheless, the Virginia Company directors promoted another experiment, at a safe distance inland to minimize the chance of a sudden assault by Spanish ships. But Spanish rivals would soon be the least of their worries. Marshy, mosquito-ridden, and without freshwater, Jamestown was poorly situated for a colony, to put it mildly. By the end of September, nearly half of the original colonists had died, many from diseases associated with contaminated water. Initially the strangers had hoped to trade with the Native Americans for food while they spent their days hunting for gold. But the region was deep into a seven-year drought, and the Pamunkey did not want to part with what little food they had. By January, only 38 colonists were alive—barely.

The colony continued to struggle even after new convoys arrived. But even though Jamestown was nearly defenseless, Powhatan didn't attack. For the first year or two of the colony's existence, he seems to have decided that the foreigners' trade goods—guns, axes, glass beads, and copper sheets, which the Native Americans prized much the way Europeans prized gold ingots—were worth giving up some not-very-valuable real estate. Historians believe that Powhatan wanted to integrate Jamestown as another subordinate settlement within his wide-ranging chiefdom, even performing an adoption ceremony with Captain John Smith to formalize the alliance, a ceremony that Smith misinterpreted as an assassination attempt narrowly intercepted by Powhatan's daughter Pocahontas. In reality, the act was a scripted element of the ceremony. By some accounts, the English refused to pay the contractual tribute that the surrounding villages gave to Powhatan and viewed uncultivated land as up for grabs, including the Native Americans' territorial hunting grounds.

In 1609–1610, the crisis reached a critical stage known as the "Starving Time." The expected fleet of resupply ships from the Virginia Company was struck by a hurricane and only one ship belatedly arrived at Jamestown. Kelso's team unearthed remains of this desperate winter. Already low food supplies had to be stretched even further after relationships with Powhatan collapsed, leading to a siege of Jamestown. Colony president George Percy wrote that facing extreme hunger, some colonists ate their boots, shoes, and any

A crucifix that may have belonged to one of James-town's few Catholics speaks to the colonists' faith, to which they hoped to convert the Native people.

other leather they could find. Others left the fort to search for roots in the woods, but were killed by Native Americans.

Outside the palisade to the north, in an unmarked, pre-1650 cemetery, lay evidence of hasty burials. Bodies appeared to have been tossed into the burial shafts, some two to a grave, face down, and without ceremonial shrouds.

As the siege continued into the winter, Percy wrote in an eyewitness account: "And now famine beginning to look ghastly and pale in every face that nothing was spared to maintain life and to do those things which seem incredible, as to dig up dead corpses out of graves and to eat them, and some have licked up the blood which hath fallen from their weak fellows." According to several colonists, one man killed his pregnant wife and chopped her into pieces, which he then salted and ate for food. He was executed for murder.

Digging in a trash deposit at the fort in 2012, Kelso's archaeologists uncovered portions of a butchered skull and shinbone from a 14-year-old English girl they dubbed "Jane." A study of Jane's remains by Doug Owsley, one of the foremost forensic anthropologists in the world and head of physical anthropology at the Smithsonian National Museum of Natural History, concluded that the cut marks and splintering on her bones indicated postmortem cannibalization.

This was the first proof of such a practice at Jamestown. It was also the first artifactual evidence of cannibalism by Europeans of Europeans at any Spanish, French, English, or Dutch colony from about 1500 to 1800, according to James Horn, vice president of research for the Colonial Williamsburg Foundation.

Kelso said he hadn't believed previous historical accounts regarding cannibalism. He thought such stories were politically motivated, intended to discredit the Virginia Company. "Now, I know the accounts are true," he said. Jamestown was "a very dark undertaking," according to Kelso. This evidence "almost puts you in the time," he added.

Ultimately, of the 6,000 settlers the Virginia Company sent to Jamestown between 1607 and 1625, 4,800 died. One after another, business schemes failed, and those who had envisioned riches turned to praying for survival. Many colonists, most likely including Jane, perished within months of stepping ashore. Still, in 1619, they persevered to cast votes for the first gathering of a representative governing body in the Americas, a General Assembly elected by all the free white male settlers in the colony. This stands as a historic milestone in America's great experiment with democracy.

The year 1619 also marked the arrival of the colony's first documented African residents, including a Ndonga woman kidnapped into slavery. Her Anglicized name appears in the census roles as Angela, property of the plantation of Captain William Pierce. Archaeologists of the Jamestown Rediscovery Foundation are excavating the plantation and Angela's grave site to find out more about her life. This is one way historians and archaeologists seek to piece together a more inclusive picture of colonial history. Ashley Atkins Spivey, an anthropologist and member of the Pamunkey tribe, is also working to tell her people's experience with Jamestown. "You can't talk about the 'first government' without talking about the American Indian people and a government that were already here," she explains. In 2015, the Pamunkey became the first Virginia tribe recognized by the U.S. federal government, and a grave marker for the famous chief Powhatan now stands on Pamunkey reservation land.

No one knows her name, but today she's called Jane. Jamestown colonists ate the 14-year-old after she died during the hungry winter of 1609–10.

96

WHAT THE THAW REVEALS

1600s ◆ Southwestern Alaska, U.S.A. ◆ Indigenous North America

*The warming Arctic endangers the Yup'iks' future
while revealing artifacts that support their oral history.*

———◆———

The archaeological site of Nunalleq on the southwest coast of Alaska preserves a fateful moment, frozen in time. The muddy square of earth is full of everyday things that the Indigenous Yup'ik people used to survive and to celebrate life here, all left just as they lay when a deadly attack came almost four centuries ago.

Around the perimeter of what was once a large sod structure are traces of the fire that was used to smoke out the residents—some 50 people, probably an alliance of extended families, who lived here when they weren't out hunting, fishing, and gathering plants. No one, it seems, was spared.

As is often the case in archaeology, a tragedy of long ago is a boon to modern science. Archaeologists have recovered 100,000 artifacts at Nunalleq, from typical eating utensils to extraordinary things such as wooden ritual masks, ivory tattoo needles, pieces of finely calibrated sea kayaks, and a belt of caribou teeth. The ground's frigid state even preserved rare organic material such as grass ropes, salmonberry seeds, head lice, and grass strands woven into baskets. "This grass was cut when Shakespeare walked the Earth," marvels lead archaeologist Rick Knecht, who is based at the University of Aberdeen in Scotland. Beyond the sheer quantity and variety, the objects are astonishingly well preserved, having been frozen in place since about 1660.

Knecht sees a link between the destruction at the site and the old tales that modern Yup'iks remember. Oral tradition preserves memories of a time historians call the Bow and Arrow Wars, when Yup'ik communities fought one another in bloody battles sometime before Russian explorers arrived in Alaska in the 1700s. Nunalleq offers the first archaeological evidence, and the first firm date, for this frightful period, which affected several generations of Yup'iks.

Knecht believes the attacks were the result of climate change—a 550-year chilling of the Earth now known as the Little Ice Age—that coincided with Nunalleq's occupation. The coldest years in Alaska, in the 1600s, must have been a desperate time, with raids probably launched to steal food.

"Whenever you get rapid change, there's a lot of disruption in the seasonal cycles of subsistence," says Knecht. "If you get an extreme, like a Little Ice Age—or like now—changes can occur faster than people can adjust."

In Quinhagak, the modern Yup'ik village just four miles from Nunalleq, changes brought by the weird weather are a common topic of conversation. "Twenty years ago the elders began to say the ground was sinking," says Warren Jones, president of Qanirtuuq, the Yup'ik corporation that owns and manages the community's property. "The past 10 years or so it's been so bad everybody's noticed. We're boating in February. That's supposed to be the coldest month of the year." The strangest thing? Three successive winters without snow.

For centuries, Yup'ik people on both sides of the Bering Sea have made the Arctic tundra their home, hunting mammals on land and sea, foraging berries, and fishing salmon. Today's unpredictable

Starting in 2012, excavations at Nunalleq have uncovered artifacts such as a ceremonial wooden mask, arrowheads, and harpoon points of caribou antler.

and increasingly violent weather has not only thrown off the rhythm of subsistence hunting cycles, it has driven Nunalleq to the brink of oblivion. In winter, the Bering Sea hurls vicious storms at the coast. If the waves get big enough, they crash across a narrow gravel beach and rip away at the remains of the site.

The Arctic wasn't always like this, but global climate change is now hammering Earth's polar regions. The result is a disastrous loss of artifacts from little-known prehistoric cultures—like the one at Nunalleq—all along Alaska's shores and beyond. A massive thaw is exposing traces of past peoples and civilizations across the northern regions of the globe—from Neolithic bows and arrows in Switzerland to hiking staffs from the Viking age in Norway and lavishly appointed tombs of Scythian nomads in Siberia. So many sites are in danger that archaeologists are beginning to specialize in the rescue of once-frozen artifacts.

In coastal Alaska, archaeological sites are now threatened by a one-two punch. The first blow: average temperatures that have risen more than three degrees Fahrenheit in the past half century. As one balmy day follows another, the permafrost is thawing almost everywhere. When archaeologists began digging at Nunalleq in 2009, they hit frozen soil about 18 inches below the surface of the tundra. Today the ground is thawed three feet down. That means masterfully carved artifacts of caribou antler, driftwood, bone, and walrus ivory are emerging from the deep freeze that has preserved them in perfect condition. If not rescued, they immediately begin to rot and crumble.

The knockout blow: rising seas. The global level of oceans has risen about eight inches since 1900. That's a direct threat to coastal sites such as Nunalleq, which is doubly vulnerable to wave damage now that the thawing permafrost is making the land sink. "One good winter storm and we could lose this whole site," says Knecht.

"One good winter storm and we could lose this whole site."

—*Rick Knecht, archaeologist*

He speaks from experience. Since the start of the excavation, the relentless action of the sea has torn about 35 feet from the edge of the site. The winter after the 2010 dig was particularly brutal. Residents of Quinhagak remember huge chunks of ice slamming into the coast. By the time Knecht and his crew returned, the entire area they had excavated was gone. Since then, Knecht has pressed on with a renewed sense of urgency.

Archaeology's potential to inspire an appreciation for the past is what motivated Jones to start the dig. When wooden artifacts began washing up on the beach, he invited Knecht to assess the eroding site, then helped convince the village's board of directors that excavating Nunalleq was a good idea. Their meeting grew into a unique collaboration in which the community and the visiting archaeologists work as partners.

Like many of the older villagers, Qanirtuuq chairperson Grace Hill initially opposed the excavation because Yup'ik tradition says ancestors shouldn't be disturbed. But she came to see the dig as a way to preserve their culture and language, which have faded over centuries of government pressure to assimilate. The younger generations wear store-bought clothes rather than beaver-skin parkas and spend more time watching TV than playing traditional music. "I'm hoping this will get the kids interested in their past," she says. A group of Quinhagak children have formed a traditional dance group, with the permission of their elders, and performed at a dance festival where the Nunalleq artifacts were displayed. "That was the first time there had been traditional dancing in Quinhagak in more than a century," Knecht told *Archaeology* magazine. "It's all part of this revival that is growing along with the finds."

Yup'ik from the wider area around Quinhagak now drive ATVs to the site to learn more about their heritage and to touch the artifacts—a carving tool or doll that may look strikingly similar to their own. Workshops at the new culture and archaeology center celebrate Yup'ik culture past and present, as artists demonstrate mask making, hide sewing, drumming, and dance. Jones is proud of the partnership that made this possible. He also looks forward to more discoveries at the site and sees a promising future for the center. "I want our kids who are in college now to run [the center] and be proud that it's ours," he says.

97

THE WICKED CITY OF PORT ROYAL

June 7, 1692 ✦ Jamaica ✦ British Colonial

Centuries after a devastating earthquake, divers uncovered drowned remains of the pirate citadel of the Caribbean.

———✦———

On a calm June morning in 1692, the church rector of Port Royal, Jamaica, was running late for a lunch appointment, but a friend entreated him to delay just a while longer. It was a small choice that saved his life.

The ground began to roll and rumble, but the friend waved off the rector's alarm; earthquakes on the island usually passed quickly. But this quaking only increased in intensity, and the two men soon heard the church tower collapse into rubble. The rector sprinted outside, racing for open ground. By his description, the land split open, swallowing crowds of people and homes in one gulp and then sealing closed. The sky darkened to red, mountains crumbled in the distance, and geysers of water exploded from the seams ripped in the earth. He turned to see a great wall of seawater swelling high above the city. In a letter describing the disaster, the shocked rector wrote, "In the space of three minutes . . . Port Royal, the fairest town of all the English plantations, the best emporium and mart of this part of the world, exceeding in its riches, plentiful of all good things, was shaken and shattered to pieces."

Condemned by the Catholic Church as "the wickedest city in Christendom," Port Royal was indeed among the wealthiest ports in the Caribbean during the 17th century, famous for its state-sanctioned pirates, liquor, and brothels. An earthquake and tsunami tore it apart on June 7, 1692. The quake sent most of the city to the watery depths, killing 2,000 people immediately (many more died soon after) and sinking nearly every ship in the harbor. It remained untouched for nearly three hundred years until marine archaeologists began to bring artifacts to the surface. These discoveries have helped us find out if the dastardly legends are true.

When the English captured Jamaica from the Spanish in 1655, they noticed the port's strategic potential at the entrance to Kingston Harbour and set about strengthening its defenses. Bristling with fortifications, the harbor was expanded to accommodate ships. Traders flocked to the protected haven. But in addition to legitimate trade, the port's prosperity also derived from less salubrious endeavors: piracy. During the mid-17th century, England and Spain fought a primarily naval war that frequently targeted the others' shipping lanes.

The plan was simple: The English crown gave license for pirates to attack Spanish shipments on sea and on land. The pirates became known as buccaneers, or the more dignified-sounding privateers, in a form of state-sanctioned piracy. Port Royal's position at the heart of the Caribbean surrounded by the Spanish Main put it in striking distance of the main shipping routes between

Taking the typical shape of a lion guarding a Chinese Buddhist temple, this imported porcelain incense burner was recovered from Port Royal's sunken ruins.

the New World and Europe, making it the buccaneering capital of the world. The wealth accrued from legitimate trade and pirate booty turned it into one of the richest ports in the Caribbean, with brick houses of two to four stories, piped water—and innumerable brothels, gambling dens, and taverns. During a crackdown on privateering in the 1670s, though, those charged formally with piracy met their end on Gallows Point.

Due to its licentious reputation, Port Royal faced what to many people must have looked like Judgment Day. It certainly felt that way to the church rector, who sought shelter aboard a ship in the harbor as the aftershocks raged. In letters he confessed that he longed to escape the scene of the disaster but his conscience drove him to stay, venturing into the city day after day to pray with survivors in a tent pitched amid their flattened houses, which were looted nightly by "lewd rogues." "I hope by this terrible judgment, God will make them reform their lives, for there was not a more ungodly people on the face of the earth," he wrote.

> "I hope by this terrible judgment, God will make them reform their lives, for there was not a more ungodly people on the face of the earth."
>
> —*Rev. Emmanuel Heath, church rector of Port Royal, 1692*

Much of the bawdy buccaneers' capital—whose remnants are today a sleepy fishing village—lay covered by silt and 20 to 40 feet of murky water. Amateur archaeologist Edwin Link and his wife and research partner, Marion, visited the location in 1956, and pulled up a cannon from the fort but concluded that more specialized equipment would be needed to plumb the muddy bottom. They returned in 1959 with the *Sea Diver,* an innovative vessel that Edwin had designed himself for underwater exploration. Over the course of a 10-week expedition sponsored by the National Geographic Society, the Smithsonian Institution, and the government of Jamaica, the Links' crew, along with elite U.S. Navy divers, recovered hundreds of relics. By applying high-pressure water jets against the bricks, then sucking up debris and silt with an airlift, the salvors uncovered walls of brick and mortar. Once uncovered, breakable objects were brought to the surface by hand.

In the harbor's clouded waters, divers usually could barely see a hand held before the face and resorted to working by touch alone, groping in the ooze. One diver explained his experience of working blind: "I guess you develop a sixth sense once you have been down there awhile . . . You get so engrossed in what you may find there that you forget everything else. You lose sense of time. You even forget to wonder if there are sharks near you." But the dangers were very real. Sea urchins, stingrays, moray eels, and scorpion fish lurked, mostly unseen, on the muddy bottom. There was also constant danger of cave-ins as a dredge sucked at the base of old brick walls.

What the team found in the sunken pirate capital was akin to an underwater Pompeii. Marion Clayton Link described what originally attracted her and her husband to the site. "Unlike cities on land, which change with the years, this one remained exactly as it had been more than two and half centuries before—sealed by the seas in an instant earthquake. Whatever we might find in the ruins would be truly indicative of the time." This was proven when her husband identified the site of a complete kitchen hearth, including a copper pot where a stew was brewing when the earthquake hit. "It would be hard to find another kitchen in the world today with everything just as it was . . ." Edwin explained. "That's the advantage of underwater archaeology." Researchers use the term "catastrophic sites" for such places where a sudden disaster has preserved important artifacts and the context of life around them.

From pewter tableware to Chinese porcelain, there were many signs of personal wealth. There were also numerous domestic objects denoting life in an ordinary household, such as spoons and lanterns, as well as elegant items like a wrought-iron swivel gun that would have been in use when Columbus sailed for America. A truly astonishing number of bottles and pipes were found, which gave the impression that people in old Port Royal spent most of their time drinking and smoking. Edwin even inserted a hypodermic needle into the cork of a bottle and withdrew a sample of yellow fluid for a taste test. "Horrible. Tastes like strongly salted vinegar," he sputtered. "I guess 1692 must have been a bad vintage year."

The most fascinating discovery, however, was probably an elegant brass watch. Manufactured in Amsterdam in 1686, it had stopped at what was considered the exact time of the earthquake: 17 minutes to noon.

The earthquake that devastated Port Royal killed 5,000 people and sent two-thirds of the city—warehouses, homes, shops, and streets—to the bottom of the sea.

98

AMERICA'S LAST SLAVE SHIP

The schooner Clotilda *smuggled African captives into the United States in 1860, more than 50 years after importing enslaved people was outlawed.*

———◆———

I n May 2019, 400 years after shackled Africans first set foot in the English colony of Virginia, a team of underwater archaeologists announced that the charred, sunken remains of *Clotilda,* the last known slave ship to reach U.S. shores, had been discovered near Mobile, Alabama.

In 1860—52 years after the United States had banned the import of enslaved people—a wealthy landowner hired the 86-foot schooner and its captain to smuggle more than a hundred African captives into Alabama, a crime punishable by hanging. Once the nefarious mission was accomplished, the ship was set ablaze to destroy the evidence.

The captives were the last of an estimated 389,000 Africans delivered into bondage in mainland America from the early 1600s to 1860, making *Clotilda* an infamous bookend to what has long been called "America's original sin."

Rare firsthand accounts left by those who enslaved people and their victims offer a one-of-a-kind window into the Atlantic trade in human beings, says Sylviane Diouf, a noted historian of the African diaspora.

"It's the best documented story of a slave voyage in the Western Hemisphere," says Diouf, whose 2007 book, *Dreams of Africa in Alabama,* chronicles *Clotilda*'s saga. "The captives were sketched, interviewed, even filmed," she says, referring to some who lived into the 20th century. "The person who organized the trip talked about it. The captain of the ship wrote about it. So we have the story from several perspectives. I haven't seen anything of that sort anywhere else."

Clotilda's journey began when Timothy Meaher, a Mobile landowner and shipbuilder, allegedly bet several northern businessmen a thousand dollars that he could smuggle a cargo of Africans into Mobile Bay under the nose of federal officials.

Importing enslaved people into the United States had been illegal since 1808, and southern plantation owners had seen prices in the domestic slave trade skyrocket. Many, including Meaher, were advocating for reopening the trade.

Meaher had little trouble getting investors for his illegal scheme. His friend and fellow shipwright William Foster had built a sleek, speedy schooner named *Clotilda* a few years earlier to haul lumber and other cargo around the Gulf of Mexico. Meaher chartered the boat for $35,000 and enlisted Foster as captain.

Foster and his crew set sail for the notorious slave port of Ouidah, in present-day Benin. The 110 young men, women, and children who boarded *Clotilda* in May 1860 came from Bantè, Dahomey, Kebbi, Atakora, and other regions of Benin and Nigeria.

One man, Kupollee, had a small hoop in each ear, which meant he had been initiated in an *ile-orisha*—house of the god—into the

Yoruba religion. Like 19-year-old Kossola (later known as Cudjo Lewis), several were victims of a raid by the kingdom of Dahomey, which traded in enslaved people. Kossola said he came from modest means, but his grandfather was an officer of a Bantè king. At 14, he trained as a soldier and later began initiation into the Yoruba *oro,* the male secret society. A young girl, Kêhounco (Lottie Dennison), was kidnapped, as were many others.

For the first 13 days at sea, every captive remained confined in the hold. Decades later, in 1906, when Abache (Clara Turner) talked to a writer from *Harper's* magazine of the filth, the darkness, the heat, the chains, and the thirst, "her eyes were burning, her soul inexpressibly agitated at the memory." Two people reportedly died during the brutal six-week voyage. Purchased for $9,000 in gold,

Clotilda's cargo hold became a hellish dungeon for 110 African captives. Two died during the six-week Atlantic crossing; others longed for death's release.

the human cargo was worth more than 20 times that amount in 1860 Alabama.

After transferring the captives to a riverboat owned by Meaher's brother, Foster burned the ship to hide their crime. *Clotilda* kept its secrets over the decades, even as some deniers contended that the shameful episode never occurred.

Several attempts to locate *Clotilda*'s remains had been made over the years, but the Mobile-Tensaw Delta is rife with sloughs, oxbows, and bayous, as well as scores of shipwrecks from more than three centuries of maritime activity. In January 2018, Ben Raines, a local journalist, reported that he had discovered the remains of a large wooden ship during an abnormally low tide. The vessel in question turned out to be another ship, but the false alarm focused national attention on the long-lost *Clotilda*. The incident also prompted the Alabama Historical Commission (AHC) to fund further research in partnership with the National Geographic Society and the archaeology firm SEARCH, Inc.

Researchers combed through hundreds of original sources from the period and analyzed records of more than 2,000 ships that were operating in the Gulf of Mexico during the late 1850s. They discovered registration documents that provided detailed descriptions of the schooner, including its construction and dimensions. The oral history of the last ship to carry enslaved humans had been passed down for generations and the descendants were closely watching the search unfold. "If they find evidence of that ship, it's going to be big," said Lorna Woods, a descendant of a *Clotilda* survivor. "All Mama told us would be validated. It would do us a world of good."

"If they find evidence of that ship, it's going to be big. All Mama told us would be validated. It would do us a world of good."

—*Lorna Woods, descendant of a* Clotilda *survivor, in 2019, before the discovery*

When maritime archaeologist James Delgado of SEARCH, Inc. and Alabama state archaeologist Stacye Hathorn deployed divers and an array of devices—including a magnetometer for detecting metal and a side-scan sonar for locating structures on the river bottom—they discovered a veritable graveyard of sunken ships. Most were easily eliminated: wrong size, metal hull, wrong type of wood. But one particular vessel, highlighted in the earlier survey conducted by journalist Ben Raines and researchers from the University of Southern Mississippi, stood out from the rest. Over the next 10 months, Delgado's team analyzed the sunken vessel's design and dimensions, the type of wood and metal used in its construction, and evidence that it had burned. It "matched everything on record about *Clotilda*," he said.

After the Civil War ended in 1865 and enslaving people was abolished, the displaced Africans from *Clotilda* put down roots as free Americans, but they didn't relinquish their African identities. Settling among the woods and marshes upriver from Mobile, they built simple homes, planted gardens, tended livestock, hunted, fished, and farmed. They founded a church and built their own school. And they created a tight-knit, self-reliant community that came to be known as Africatown.

What's left of the burned-out wreck is in poor condition. It's not clear if the ship will be restored or raised to the surface. But a national slave ship memorial—akin to the watery grave of the U.S.S. *Arizona* in Pearl Harbor—may be an option. Many descendants of those who arrived on *Clotilda* still live in Africatown today. The shipwreck now carries the dreams of the community, which has suffered from declining population, poverty, and a host of environmental insults from heavy industries. The story of these extraordinary *Clotilda* survivors—their trials and triumphs, their suffering and resilience—is one the people of Africatown are proud to remember, and a legacy they are fighting to save.

A member of the National Association of Black Scuba Divers, Ken Stewart, co-founded the maritime archaeology organization

Forensic scientist Frankie West examines samples of wood from the ship's hold in hopes of recovering DNA from captives' blood or bodily fluids.

Diving With a Purpose. In Africatown, the group has conducted scuba training to introduce high school and college students to fundamentals of diving and maritime careers. "There were over 12,000 ships making over 40,000 voyages over 250 years of slave trade," noted Kamau Sadiki, a lead instructor for Diving With a Purpose. So why have only a few been documented? Divers and archaeologists are investigating shipwrecks to bring these submerged memories to light. Each ship that once carried human cargo reveals a little more of the history of Africa and the forced African diaspora, essential information we need to reckon with the past.

99

THE DISAPPEARANCE OF THE H. L. HUNLEY

1864 ◆ Near Charleston, South Carolina, U.S.A. ◆ American

The Confederate vessel was the first submarine in history to sink a warship, but it took more than a century to divine its fate.

———◆———

Shortly after sunset on the night of February 17, 1864, eight Confederates squeezed inside a claustrophobic iron vessel at a dock near the entrance to Charleston Harbor in South Carolina. Named the *H. L. Hunley,* this strange and secret new weapon was a "diving torpedo-boat" and the Confederates' best hope for breaking the Union Navy's choke hold on the harbor.

Affixed to the boat's bow was a long spar tipped with a deadly charge of black powder. At the helm was Lt. George Dixon. Behind him, wedged shoulder to shoulder on a wooden bench, sat seven crewmen whose muscles powered the sub's hand-cranked propeller. As the crew began turning the heavy iron crankshaft, Dixon consulted a compass and set course for a daunting target—the steam sloop U.S.S. *Housatonic,* stationed four miles offshore.

At 8:45 p.m., John Crosby, acting master aboard the *Housatonic,* spotted something off the starboard beam that looked at first like a "porpoise, coming to the surface to blow." There had been warnings of a possible attack by a Confederate "infernal machine," and Crosby was swift to sound the alarm. The Union sailors let loose a barrage of small arms fire at the alien object barely breaking the surface, but the attacker was unstoppable. Two minutes later the *Hunley* rammed its spar into the *Housatonic*'s starboard side, well below the waterline. As the sub backed away, a trigger cord detonated the torpedo, blowing off the entire aft quarter of the ship. Five Union sailors were killed.

"This was the first time in history that a submarine succeeded in sinking an enemy warship," said Robert Neyland, head of underwater archaeology for the U.S. Navy and the *Hunley* project director. "The *Hunley* is to submarine warfare what the Wright brothers' airplane is to aviation. It changed the course of naval history."

But though the Wright Flyer would become a famous icon, the *Hunley* was fated to become an obscure footnote. Though it accomplished its historic mission, it never returned to shore. Its fate, and that of its crew, became one of the Civil War's great mysteries.

> "The *Hunley* is to submarine warfare what the Wright brothers' airplane is to aviation. It changed the course of naval history."
>
> —*Robert Neyland,*
> *underwater archaeologist*

Then in May 1995, a group of shipwreck hunters led by adventure novelist Clive Cussler discovered the long-lost sub outside Charleston Harbor, buried under three feet of silt only a thousand feet from the spot where it ambushed the *Housatonic.* It took years for a team of archaeologists and engineers led by Neyland to plan the sub's difficult recovery and preservation.

An assessment of the submarine showed that its iron hull was surprisingly sound, but scrutiny of the rivets holding it together wasn't so reassuring. Neyland feared the 24-ton artifact would break apart as they tried to lift it until a team from Oceaneering International, Inc., came up with a winning solution: Slings could be passed beneath the sub and attached to a supporting truss, cradling the entire vessel like a hammock. Bags on each sling could then be filled with expanding polyurethane foam. The foam-filled bags would conform to the hull's shape, ensuring that every inch was supported during the lift.

The plan took heroic effort—and $2.7 million—to pull off. Nineteen divers toiled for three months in water so turbid they had to work more by touch than sight. Claire Peachey, an underwater archaeologist with the National Park Service and the Navy recalled, "I dove every day, two times a day for two weeks, and did not see the submarine once."

Using handheld suction dredges, divers carefully vacuumed away 25,000 cubic feet of sand and mud—the loads of 115 dump trucks—to expose the submarine and any artifacts nearby. Two

Securely ensconced in a cradle of steel beams and padded slings, the corroded and encrusted *H. L. Hunley* rises from its grave like a Confederate ghost.

giant pilings were then sunk into the seafloor at either end of the sub to provide footings for the truss.

On August 8, 2000, the crane operator finally throttled up the diesel engine and pulled a lever. Minutes later the *Hunley,* snug in the padded sling, broke through a slight swell. It was intact, a time capsule unopened since the night it was lost.

The *Hunley* was placed in a 75,000-gallon steel tank full of water at the Warren Lasch Conservation Center, a state-of-the-art archaeology lab on the old Charleston Naval Base. Through a meticulous excavation of the inside of the submarine, all eight crewmen were found still at or near their posts, their bones remarkably well preserved in the mud that filled their iron coffin. Even their brains, though shrunken, remained. Archaeologists recovered the equipment and personal items of the crew, including a lantern, binoculars, jewelry, a bandana, leather shoes, canteens, an oilcan, and a warped gold coin on Dixon's body—the same one that, legend has it, saved his life in the Battle of Shiloh when it deflected a bullet. Today visitors to the center can see the *Hunley* in the lab's conservation tank as well as artifacts and interactive exhibits in a small museum.

No damage to the submarine's hull could explain its sinking, and the cause of *Hunley*'s demise is still debated. Did it collide with another Union ship that arrived on the scene? Did the men miscalculate their oxygen supply? Were they trapped underwater by the tides?

One popular theory is that the torpedo detonation fatally damaged the submarine. In 2017, researchers who performed experiments on a miniature model of the *Hunley,* nicknamed the C.S.S. *Tiny,* proposed that the crew were instantly killed by a lethal shock wave generated by the torpedo explosion. That theory may be supported by another piece of evidence from the ship. In 2003, researchers who opened Dixon's gold pocket watch found that it had stopped right around the time the attack reportedly occurred.

100

FINDING THE
TITANIC

1912 ◆ Atlantic Ocean ◆ British

*In 1912, the largest, most luxurious cruise ship
of its day sank. Its discovery after decades of searching
revealed stunning details of the tragedy.*

———◆———

At 2:20 a.m. on April 15, 1912, the "unsinkable" R.M.S. *Titanic* disappeared beneath the waves, taking with it some 1,500 souls. Why does this tragedy exert such a magnetic pull on our imagination more than a century later? And why do people still lavish so much brainpower and technological ingenuity upon a graveyard of metal more than two miles beneath the ocean's surface?

For some, the sheer extravagance of *Titanic*'s demise lies at the heart of its attraction. This has always been a story of superlatives: A ship so strong and so grand, sinking in water so cold and so deep. For others, fascination with the *Titanic* begins and ends with the people on board. It took two hours and 40 minutes for the great vessel to sink, its lights blazing; one coward is said to have made for the lifeboats dressed in women's clothing. But most people were honorable, and many heroic. The captain stayed at the bridge, the band played on, the wireless radio operators continued sending their distress signals until the very end. The passengers, for the most part, kept to their Edwardian stations. How they lived their final moments is the stuff of universal interest, a *danse macabre* that never ends.

More than 2,000 passengers and crew were aboard the *Titanic*, but the ship had lifeboats for only 1,178. To make matters worse, not all the lifeboats were filled to capacity during the desperate evacuation. Only 706 people survived. Most of the 1,521 victims died of hypothermia at the surface of the icy water. Hundreds may also have died inside the ship as it sank, most of them immigrant families in steerage class, sailing to a new life in America.

But something else, beyond human lives, went down with the *Titanic:* an illusion of orderliness, a faith in technological progress, a yearning for the future that, as Europe drifted toward full-scale war, was soon replaced by fears and dreads all too familiar to our modern world. "The *Titanic* disaster was the bursting of a bubble," filmmaker James Cameron told *National Geographic* magazine. "There was such a sense of bounty in the first decade of the 20th century. Elevators! Automobiles! Airplanes! Wireless radio! Everything seemed so wondrous, on an endless upward spiral. Then it all came crashing down."

> "The *Titanic* disaster was the bursting of a bubble. There was such a sense of bounty in the first decade of the 20th century. Elevators! Automobiles! Airplanes! Wireless radio! Everything seemed so wondrous, on an endless upward spiral. Then it all came crashing down."
>
> —*James Cameron, filmmaker*

Many historical accounts of the *Titanic*'s sinking describe the 882.5-foot-long passenger ship as "slipping beneath the ocean waves," as though the vessel and its passengers drifted tranquilly off to sleep. Nothing could be farther from the truth. Based on years of analysis of the wreck, using simulations and flooding models from the modern shipping industry, experts are able to paint a tragic portrait of *Titanic*'s death throes.

The ship's fate was sealed on its maiden voyage from Southampton, England, to New York City. At 11:40 p.m. on April 14, 1912, it sideswiped an iceberg in the North Atlantic, buckling portions of the starboard hull along a 300-foot span and exposing the six forward compartments to the ocean's waters.

From this moment onward, sinking was a certainty. The demise may have been hastened when crewmen pushed open a gangway door on the port side in an aborted attempt to load lifeboats from a lower level. Because the ship had begun listing to port, gravity prevented the crew from closing the massive door. By 1:50 a.m., the bow had settled enough to allow seawater to rush in through the gangway.

By 2:18 a.m.—the last lifeboat having departed 13 minutes earlier—the bow had filled with water and the stern had risen high enough into the air to expose the propellers and create catastrophic stresses on the middle of the ship. Then the *Titanic* cracked in half.

Once released from the stern section, the bow fell to the ocean floor at a fairly steep angle. Parts began to shear away as it gained velocity: Funnels snapped. The wheelhouse crumbled. Finally, after five minutes of relentless descent, the bow nosed into the mud with such massive force that it left ejecta patterns on the seafloor.

The stern, lacking a hydrodynamic leading edge like the bow, tumbled and corkscrewed downward. Compartments exploded. Decks pancaked. Heavier pieces such as the boilers dropped straight down, while other pieces were flung into the abyss. For more than two miles, the stern made its tortured descent—rupturing, buckling, warping, compressing, and gradually disintegrating. By the time it hit the ocean floor, it was unrecognizable.

For decades, a number of expeditions sought to find the *Titanic,* without success—a problem compounded by the North Atlantic's unpredictable weather, the enormous depth at which the sunken ship lies, and conflicting accounts of its final moments.

After catastrophic stresses caused the *Titanic* to crack in half, the hydrodynamic bow fell at a steep angle while the stern tumbled and corkscrewed.

At last, 73 years after it sank, the final resting place of the *Titanic* was located by National Geographic Explorer Robert Ballard and French scientist Jean-Louis Michel on September 1, 1985. The *Titanic* lay roughly 380 miles southeast of Newfoundland in international waters.

Recently declassified information has revealed that the discovery stemmed from a secret U.S. Navy investigation of two wrecked nuclear submarines, the U.S.S. *Thresher* and *Scorpion*. The military wanted to know the fate of the nuclear reactors that powered the ships, and to see if any evidence supported the theory that Soviets had sunk the *Scorpion*. (None did.)

Ballard had met with the Navy in 1982 to request funding to develop the robotic submersible technology he needed to find the *Titanic*. The military was interested, but for the purpose of gathering its own intel. Once Ballard had completed the submarine search, he could do what he wanted if he had time. He was finally able to begin to look for the *Titanic* with less than two weeks to spare. And then, suddenly one day at 1:05 a.m., video cameras picked up one of the ship's boilers. "I cannot believe my eyes," he wrote about the moment of discovery.

In the years since Ballard's expedition, organic processes have been relentlessly breaking down the *Titanic:* Mollusks have gobbled up most of the ship's wood, while microbes eat away at exposed metal, forming icicle-like "rusticles." Salt corrosion contributes to the decay. The hull has started to collapse, taking staterooms with it. "The most shocking area of deterioration was the starboard side of the officers' quarters, where the captain's quarters were," said *Titanic* historian Parks Stephenson after a manned submersible dive in 2019. Using state-of-the-art equipment, the dive team captured images of the wreck that can be used to create 3D models, helping researchers further study the past and future of the ship.

How long will *Titanic* remain intact? "Everyone has their own opinion," says Woods Hole Oceanographic Institution research

A submersible's lights give a ghostly glow to the *Titanic*'s increasingly fragile prow, now draped in "rusticles"—stalactites created by iron-eating bacteria.

scientist Bill Lange, who was a member of the discovery team. "Some people think the bow will collapse in a year or two. But others say it's going to be there for hundreds of years."

However long the wreck lasts, the story will surely live on—of a vessel with too much pride in her name, sprinting smartly toward a new world, only to be mortally nicked by something as old and slow as ice.

AFTERWORD

By Fredrik Hiebert

———◆———

The 100 great discoveries featured in this book represent many periods throughout the human journey on Earth—from the origins of our species and the rise of great civilizations to such fabled modern events as the sinking of the luxury ocean liner *Titanic*. But these excavations have only scratched the surface of our epic story.

And that's a good thing, because the 21st century has ushered in a new age of science. Modern archaeologists are equipped with tools that their predecessors could never have dreamed of. Among other advances, computers are now so powerful they can process in seconds what would have taken months or years to accomplish just a decade ago. The opportunities for what we can learn—and the questions we'll finally be able to answer—seem almost limitless.

Also, more than ever before, interactions with local communities are critical to the success of research. Gone are the days when scientists arrived from afar to study an ancient culture and left without contributing to the place where they worked. Archaeologists today engage with and educate the people who live near their excavations. They also tap the expertise of local historians and scientists who provide vital perspectives to the study of the past.

Many frontiers in the realm of archaeology still await exploration around the globe. From the details of legendary places and people to little-understood expanses of land and sea, countless pages of history have yet to be deciphered. Prospects that may hold surprises, large and small, include the following categories.

In art as in life, Alexander the Great faces eternal battle in ancient bronze. The location of his grave, and the riches it may hold, is one of archaeology's greatest mysteries.

WELL-KNOWN SITES

The Great Wall of China: Stunning discoveries are being made almost every day, it seems, at the earliest sites of one of the world's proudest civilizations. Part of the Great Wall, for example, was recently found to be a Bronze Age fortress—revealing it to be as ancient as the cities of Mesopotamia. That's just one tantalizing indication of what is yet to be uncovered there.

The Parthenon: The famed temple that crowns the acropolis in Athens still holds many secrets. We know very little about the way the building was used, for instance, or about the original painted appearance of its marble statues.

Valley of the Kings: You might think that the celebrated royal cemetery of Egypt's New Kingdom was exhausted after more than two centuries of digging—but there's always a chance that archaeologists may unearth another burial like King Tutankhamun's. Since its discovery in 1922, two more rock-cut chambers have come to light. Could another be right around the corner? And if it's an untouched royal grave, could that change our understanding of ancient Egyptian history? The possibilities are exciting—especially because, despite a continuing search, the fabled Queen Nefertiti is still lost.

MISSING TOMBS OF FAMOUS FIGURES

Alexander the Great: The death and burial in 323 B.C. of the celebrated leader of the Greek world are still shrouded in mystery. Legend has it that Alexander's embalmed remains traveled from Mesopotamia to Syria, were hijacked to Greece and then taken to Egypt, where his final resting place was moved at least three times. Today's advanced technologies could reveal where he was finally laid to rest: likely in the ancient royal quarters of Alexandria, under many feet of accumulated debris and saturated with water. In that case, experts will need to figure out how to excavate a site beneath a crowded city.

Genghis Khan: This nomadic, horse-riding conqueror from Mongolia dominated Asia from China to India in the 13th century. But his life is not well documented, and people have been searching for his mortal remains for centuries. Satellite imaging, drones, and ground-penetrating radar may help pinpoint the location of his tomb.

THE VAST UNKNOWN

Central Asia: This mountainous region stretching from the Caspian Sea to China holds clues to the exchanges between East and West that go back thousands of years. Archaeologists have barely begun to fill in many of the blanks about those long-range connections.

The Amazon: New research methods will likely continue to reveal settlements in this immense, unstudied region—maybe even an unknown culture that holds the keys to sustainable existence on our planet.

Deep Oceans: National Geographic Explorer Robert Ballard has pioneered the mapping of the world's seas. While doing so, he has encountered what he calls "the greatest museum of the world"—well-preserved shipwrecks. Such time capsules lie at the bottom of the watery depths waiting for the development of ways to investigate them.

Remains in the Permafrost: As archaeology documents ancient cultures with increasing precision, it can shed light on global climate changes over the course of millennia. In addition, animals and artifacts have already emerged from the thawing permafrost, and human bodies may be uncovered in the future. Imagine the discovery of a long-frozen Neanderthal, allowing scientists to come face-to-face for the first time with one of our most fabled ancestors!

Sure, treasures are indeed made of gold sometimes. But more often, the excitement resides in learning about our shared past. Knowing where we've come from—the challenges our ancestors faced and the heights their cultures achieved—connects us to the grand sweep of human experience. And it also can inspire us to make informed choices now, so that future generations can survive and thrive.

THE FUTURE OF STUDYING THE PAST

———◆———

Archaeology isn't just about digging in the dirt anymore. It's a rapidly evolving, multidisciplinary science relying on a wide range of new technologies. Here are some of the modern methods that have revolutionized the field over the last several decades and promise to continue to move it forward.

aerial imagery: Some 400 miles up in space, satellites collect images of Earth that can be used to identify buried landscapes with astonishing precision. Since the 1980s, those images have helped scientists locate and map long-lost rivers, roads, and cities, as well as discern archaeological features in conflict zones too dangerous to visit. Commercial vendors such as DigitalGlobe provide many of the high-resolution images that archaeologists use today. National Geographic Explorer Sarah Parcak launched a project in 2017 that allowed citizen scientists to examine satellite images for signs of archaeological sites in Peru. Some 80,000 participants from more than a hundred countries discovered at least 700 large features that did not appear in the Peruvian government's database. Other sources of useful aerial imagery include declassified U-2 spy plane photos taken from about 13 miles up in the 1950s and '60s, and the camera-equipped drones that many excavations are now employing.

carbon 14: This form of carbon can be used to date biological artifacts that are up to 50,000 years old. The rare, naturally occurring isotope has an atomic weight of 14 instead of the element's normal 12, and is radioactive (meaning it loses energy at a specific rate). All living things contain carbon, including C12 and C14, and the element is constantly replenished with the ingestion of nutrients. When a living thing dies, however, its store of C14 begins to diminish as the isotope decays. The rate of decay can be used to calculate a date for a wide range of artifacts, including wood, charcoal, bone, antler, shell, peat, dung, grain, linen, parchment—even beeswax. Acacia wood from Egyptian king Djoser's Step Pyramid at Saqqara was the first object tested by Willard F. Libby, who pioneered the C14 technique in the 1940s.

computed tomography (CT): In modern medicine, CT scans are used to provide 3D images of what's inside a human body. In archaeology, they can peer into the mummified remains of someone long dead, such as Egypt's king Tutankhamun. They can also identify the contents of a cloth-wrapped mummy bundle—a human, a crocodile, or a cat, perhaps. During the procedure, narrow x-ray beams slice through the body from various angles, providing a stack of 2D images with a resolution of about one millimeter. A computer then assembles the slices into a 3D view. Some researchers are now using micro-CT, which provides stunningly detailed images with a resolution of one-thousandth of a millimeter.

ground-penetrating radar (GPR): A GPR system can reveal underground ruins without archaeologists ever lifting a shovel. It works on the principle that different materials reflect energy in different ways—a buried mud-brick wall, for instance, will likely reflect differently than the surrounding soil. GPR sends out energy in the form of radio waves and records the speed and strength of what's bounced back. Specialized computer software then interprets the distance the radio waves traveled before they hit something, as well as the time it took them to return to the antenna; it then prepares a 3D map of what lies beneath the surface of a site.

In 2020, archaeologists used GPR to map the entire underground site of Falerii Novi, a third-century Roman city.

light detection and ranging (lidar): Operated from an aircraft, lidar equipment bounces hundreds of thousands of pulses of infrared laser beams off Earth's surface and records the point location of each reflection. The three-dimensional "point cloud" can be manipulated with software to remove the pulses that hit trees and undergrowth, leaving an image composed only of pulses reaching the underlying terrain—including the outlines of archaeological features. In 2018, Maya researchers scanned some 800 square miles of northern Guatemala with lidar, identifying the ruins of more than 60,000 houses, palaces, elevated highways, and other human-made features that had been hidden for centuries under the rainforest—an effort that would have taken decades to achieve if archaeologists were mapping only what they could survey on the ground.

magnetometry: Certain human activities can leave subtle magnetic signatures behind. Burning, for instance, boosts the magnetism of tiny iron particles in the soil, allowing buried features such as hearths, fired bricks, and ceramics to be identified with special equipment. The technique, also called magnetic surveying, can pick up variations where soil has been disturbed in such places as pits, ditches, and graves. This kind of survey helped archaeologists locate pre-Columbian burials deep underground at the site of El Caño in Panama.

metal detecting: A handheld metal detector is one of the tools that archaeologists can use to gain a better understanding of what lies a foot or so beneath the surface of a site. Hobbyists also use the machines, sometimes finding spectacular, newsworthy treasures. Many discoveries made by people who are not archaeologists are never reported and end up on the black market. In the best cases, though, archaeologists are called in and are able to conduct a professional excavation that retrieves the kind of valuable contextual information needed to fully interpret a site. That's what happened with the Staffordshire Hoard, a trove of 1,400-year-old Anglo-Saxon military trappings of gem-studded gold and silver found beneath a farmer's field in 2009. Under the provisions of Britain's Portable Antiquities Scheme, the finder, Terry Herbert, received half the treasure's assessed value of almost $5.3 million.

multispectral imaging (MSI): Artifacts that were found long ago are now revealing new information through the use of multispectral imaging. That technique captures light from as many as 10 electromagnetic wavelengths such as infrared and ultraviolet, most of which are invisible to the human eye. Using MSI, researchers have been able to find hidden texts in the third century-B.C. Dead Sea Scrolls, and read words on scrolls that were charred as the volcanic eruption of Vesuvius hit the ancient Roman town of Herculaneum in A.D. 79.

strontium isotope analysis: The food and water that a person consumes as a child deposit elements such as strontium in still forming adult teeth. Experts studying the movement of ancient populations may extract different isotopes of strontium from tooth enamel and compare the levels to what's found in nature in different locations. Strontium is found in most rocks, but its isotope signatures vary subtly from place to place. That means if you grow up in, say, Buffalo, New York, then spend your adult life in California, tests on the isotopes in your teeth will always reveal your eastern roots.

ACKNOWLEDGMENTS

———◆———

The editors would like to thank the talented writers who contributed to this book: Katharine Armstrong, Chris Barsanti, Erin Blakemore, Megan Gannon, and Kristin Baird Rattini. We are grateful for the expert consultation from Jamie Shreeve and research by Sharon Moore. Thank you to the National Geographic staff behind the book, including Lisa Thomas, Hilary Black, Moriah Petty, Nicole Miller, Susan Blair, Melissa Farris, Jennifer Thornton, Judith Klein, and Meredith Wilcox. The National Geographic Society Archaeologist-in-Residence, Fred Hiebert, also provided invaluable guidance.

We owe a debt of gratitude to the generations of writers, photographers, and explorers who reported on these discoveries for National Geographic, as well as the editorial staff who published their stories in the pages of the magazine. Many, many thanks to the archaeologists, anthropologists, scientists, and researchers who shed light on our ancient past, along with the excavators, laborers, translators, fixers, and guides who work in the field.

Finally, the National Geographic Society has funded archaeological expeditions for more than 130 years. Thanks to its commitment and dedication, today's grantees are at work around the world, striving to illuminate our past. We eagerly await their next big discovery.

ILLUSTRATIONS CREDITS

———◆———

INDEX